CHRISTMAS 2018

F 01

I'm excited to be a part
of your life, and I'm
looking forward to growing
and learning together.

— Johnny

THE MAN WHO CLOSED THE ASYLUMS

THE MAN WHO CLOSED THE ASYLUMS

*Franco Basaglia and the Revolution
in Mental Health Care*

John Foot

VERSO
London • New York

This English-language edition first published by Verso 2015
© John Foot 2015

First published as *La 'Repubblica dei matti':*
Franco Basaglia e la psichiatria radicale in Italia, 1961–1978
© Feltrinelli 2015

1 3 5 7 9 10 8 6 4 2

Verso
UK: 6 Meard Street, London W1F 0EG
US: 20 Jay Street, Suite 1010, Brooklyn, NY 11201
www.versobooks.com

Verso is the imprint of New Left Books

ISBN-13: 978-1-78168-926-4 (HC)
eISBN-13: 978-1-78168-928-8 (US)
eISBN-13: 978-1-78168-927-1 (UK)

British Library Cataloguing in Publication Data
A catalogue record for this book is available from the British Library

Library of Congress Cataloging-in-Publication Data

Foot, John, 1964– , author.
[Repubblica dei matti. English]
The man who closed the asylums : Franco Basaglia and the revolution in mental health care /
John Foot.
p. ; cm.
Includes index.
Translation of La repubblica dei matti: Franco Basaglia e la psichiatria radicale in Italia,
1961-1978 / John Foot. 2015.
ISBN 978-1-78168-926-4 (hc) – ISBN 978-1-78168-928-8 (ebook (US)
– ISBN 978-1-78168-927-1 (ebook (UK)
I. Title.
[DNLM: 1. Basaglia, Franco. 2. Psychiatry–Italy. 3. Hospitals, Psychiatric–history–Italy.
4. Psychiatry–history–Italy. WZ 100]
RC443
362.2,1–dc23

2015011739

Typeset in Adobe Garamond by Hewer Text UK Ltd, Edinburgh, Scotland
Printed in the US by Maple Press

To Corinna and Lorenzo

Contents

PART II
Beyond Gorizia: The Long March

Acknowledgements

In 2008, I found myself in Trieste. I was there to study Italy's divided memory. I had heard of Franco Basaglia, and I knew a little about the story of the 1978 law, but in general my knowledge was pretty basic about the mental health system in Italy and its transformation. By chance, it was the thirtieth anniversary of the law that year, and a series of events were being held to commemorate and discuss those events. My interest was piqued by a film showing at a small cinema in the city – the title was *San Clemente*, directed by the French photographer Raymond Depardon. The audience was small. It was a late screening. Introducing the film was somebody called Peppe dell'Acqua, whom I had never heard of (I later discovered that he was an extremely important person in the story I would tell). The next ninety minutes shocked me to the core. Shot in the late 1970s, the documentary was an account of the last days of one of Venice's island asylums after the Basaglia law had been passed. It showed people with severe problems, and it also showed an institution struggling to change. It was an uncompromising account. I was hooked. I never forgot that evening. I knew, from that moment on, that I had to study that period in history, those institutions and the way they changed.

Since then, I have been on a journey that has ended with this book. This journey was made possible by the Wellcome Trust, which provided me with a small grant to make an exploratory tour of Trieste, Arezzo, Rome, Imola and Venice. In this early phase, I received great assistance from Nils Fietje, who encouraged me to develop the project and gave me extremely useful feedback on the initial draft.

On these first visits I began to understand something about the role of Franco Basaglia, and also about those places called 'manicomi', which had once housed the 'mentally ill'. In 2009 I submitted an application to Wellcome Trust for a much larger research grant, which was eventually successful. Since then, I have immersed myself in stories of patients, nurses, psychiatrists and anti-psychiatrists, electroshock treatment and anti-psychotic drugs, reform, revolution and counter-reform, and the language of mental illness. This journey has taken me across Italy (and beyond – to New York, for example) and brought me into contact with an extraordinary array of people. In 2011, I first met Enrico Basaglia over a perfect lunch in Venice, where I was staying with my partner, Sarah, and my young daughter, Corinna, in the beautiful surroundings of the Fondazione Cini on the island of San Giorgio Maggiore. Since then, we have corresponded regularly over this project, and about many other things besides. He translated this book into Italian – the best translator I have ever had by far. But he has also provided me with a series of comments, opinions and acute judgements about his father and many other aspects of that period and the movement that have been invaluable and highly entertaining. Working with Enrico has been the most rewarding part of this whole project.

What follows will be a list of the many other people who have helped with this research at various points and in different ways. This list is incomplete and the mere ledger of names is insufficient. And, as the saying goes, all responsibility for what is included in this book is mine. So, here goes. Huge thanks (in no particular order) to Alberta Basaglia, Emma Macca, Carlo Slavich, Silvia Spada, Carla Giacomozzi, Domenico Casagrande, Bruno Benigni, Christian De Vito, Silvia Jop, Chiara Strutti, Erica Mezzoli, Franco Basaglia, Albertine Cerrutti, Nereo Battello, Emanuela Piga, Elena Trivelli, David Forgacs, Leopoldo Tesi, Massimiliano Boschi, Piero Brunello, Simon Levis Sullam, Tullio Seppilli, Carlo Corinaldesi, Camillo Brezzi, Filippo Tantillo, Vanessa Roghi, Barbara Taylor, Lesley Caldwell, Duncan Double, Paolo Maggioni, Massimo Cirri, Stefano Graziani, Stefano Boeri, Fiora Gaspari, Luigi Armiato, Silvia Balconi, Walter Barberis, the Einaudi Archive, the Basaglia Foundation, Howard Caygill, David Reggio, Pompeo Martelli, Franco Perazza. I would also like to thank my colleagues and friends in the Italian Department of University College London, where I spent eighteen happy years, and in particular John Dickie, Bob Lumley and Dilwyn Knox. UCL generously awarded me a faculty leave grant which enabled me to spend more time on this project. Thanks also to Eleanor Chiari, Sofia

Serenelli and Stuart Oglethorpe. I have almost certainly left out some names. You know who you are, I hope.

This has been a difficult and complex book, which has, at times, (literally) given me nightmares. I have read about torture, suicide, suffering and terrible illness. But it is also a story of liberation and radical change, against all odds. Much of what is in this book is inspiring, and it certainly inspired me. This story shows that a small group of people can change the world. In the early 1960s, when Franco Basaglia and Antonio Slavich began to dismantle Gorizia's asylum from within, nobody took any notice. Every step was a battle, every patient untied was a struggle. But by the end of the 1960s, people were flocking to Gorizia to see how a 'total institution' had been overturned. This book tells the story of this 'revolution', warts and all – because if a historian doesn't dig around in the dirt, what kind of historian is he?

PART I

GORIZIA, 1961–68

ONE

Gorizia: A Revolution at the Edge of Europe

'It was a revolution. A class revolution. The most important to take place in Italy. It gave people back their souls, their faces, even their clothes – and they had been deprived of everything.'

Enzo Quai[1]

'People asked me: "What do you want to change? It's not possible." But, day by day, things changed. Then they asked me. "Where are you going with this?" and I said, "I don't know." And it was true. I didn't know.'

Franco Basaglia[2]

A photo from Gorizia in 1965 captures the situation inside the psychiatric hospital in the city before journalists and photographers arrived to spread the word. The caption reads 'Self-portrait: 1965. Ward B.' There are forty or so men in shot, some standing, some sitting. They look a bit like a football team or a school class inexplicably comprised entirely of grown-ups. Franco Basaglia can be seen in the middle of the image, in a shirt, jacket and tie. His colleague Antonio

---

1   Michele Sartori, 'L'infermiere della rivoluzione', *L'Unità*, 8 December 1996.

2   Corso di aggiornamento per operatori psichiatrici. *Trascrizione di due lezioni/conversazioni di Franco Basaglia con gli infermieri di Trieste, lezioni intervallate da un dibattito.* 1979. deistituzionalizzazione-trieste.it.

Slavich is nearby. A few nurses also seem to be present, in white coats. The rest are patients. The group is on the steps of one of the hospital's buildings, in the sun. Few people had heard of Gorizia or Franco Basaglia in 1965, but by 1968 this would become a celebrated and exalted place, a hotbed of change, an extraordinary example of 'an overturned institution', somewhere that was soon 'idealized and mythologized'.[3]

Beginnings: In Exile

'I want to say to say this to Slavich: when we started all this activity within the institution, there were just the two of us here. Now there must be at least a hundred of us here . . . We did a series of things and those acts led to certain results.'

Franco Basaglia (1968)[4]

'Gorizia was, like all the other Italian asylums, a concentration camp.'[5]

'As long as we are within the system our situation will remain contradictory: the institution is managed and denied at the same time, illness is "put into brackets" and cured, therapeutic acts are refused and carried out . . . We are destined to inhabit the contradictions of the system, managing an institution which we deny.'

Franco Basaglia[6]

---

3   Michael Donnelly, *The Politics of Mental Health in Italy*, London: Tavistock, 1992, p. 41.

4   Franco Basaglia, ed., *L'istituzione negata. Rapporto da un ospedale psichiatrico* (1998), Milan: Baldini & Castoldi, pp. 253–4. There are various editions of this book, which is discussed in detail in the text. I will also be making reference to the editions from 1968, published by Einaudi in Turin.

5   Alberto Manacorda and Vincenzo Montella, *La nuova psichiatria in Italia. Esperienze e prospettive*, Milan: Feltrinelli, 1977, p. 48.

6   'Il problema della gestione', included in the appendix of the second edition of *L'Istituzione negata* originally published in April 1968, now in Franco Basaglia, *Scritti. I. 1953–1968. Dalla psichiatria fenomenologica all'esperienza di Gorizia*, ed. Franca Ongaro Basaglia, Turin: Einaudi, 1981, p. 521.

It looked like a dead-end job. A vacancy at a grim mental asylum, right on the edge of Italy, miles from anywhere: a new director was needed there. The first time that Franco Basaglia visited the place, it made him feel physically sick. He remembered the smell of 'death, of shit'. Memories of the six months he had spent in a fascist prison in Venice in 1944, as a twenty-year-old, came flooding back. It was 1961, winter, and Gorizia seemed like the end of the earth.[7] In many ways, it was, at least in European terms. This provincial[8] psychiatric hospital (built under Austrian rule, in 1911, and originally named after Franz Joseph I) had the iron curtain – the border separating Italy from Yugoslavia and therefore from a different world, the Communist Bloc itself – running through its very grounds (where it was marked, at times, simply by white signs on the ground). Yugoslav guard posts overlooked the hospital. It was a peripheral place, in a forgotten, ossified city. It was the 'most peripheral, the smallest and the most insignificant of all the Italian asylums'.[9] Edoardo Balduzzi referred to that post as 'an authentic form of exile'.[10]

Inside, behind the classic asylum architecture of high walls, gates, fences, bars and heavy closed doors, Basaglia found over 600 patients.[11] Two thirds of them were of Slovenian origin, and about half did not speak Italian as a first language.[12] Around 150 of these were in the hospital as part of post-war peace agreements. Basaglia referred to this group

---

7   According to Antonio Slavich, Basaglia's first day at work in Gorizia was 2 November 1961. *La scopa meravigliante. Preparativi per la legge 180 a Ferrara e dintorni 1971–1978*, Rome: Riuniti, 2003, p. 257, n. 1.

8   The Province of Gorizia as a whole, which was served by this hospital, contained some 130,000 people at the time (a figure provided by Basaglia in 1965, 'La "Comunità Terapeutica" come base di un servizio psichiatrico', in Basaglia, *Scritti. I*, p. 263). ISTAT gives a figure of 133,550 in 1951 and 137,745 in 1971. The pre-1947 province had been almost double that size, with some 250,000 inhabitants.

9   Antonio Slavich, interviewed in Silvia Balconi, *L'esperienza Goriziana dal '61 al '72. Un percorso paradigmatico di valorizzazione della professionalità in ambito psichiatrico*, Unpublished thesis, Università degli studi di Torino, 1997–98, p. 495.

10   Edoardo Balduzzi, *L'albero della cuccagna. 1964–1978. Gli anni della psichiatria italiana*, Edizioni Stella, Nicolodi Editore, 2006, p. 38.

11   According to Slavich there were 629 patients there in March 1962 (interview in Balconi, *L'esperienza Goriziana dal '61 al '72*, p. 495). Donnelly talks of a 'large (800 bed) local mental hospital', *The Politics of Mental Health in Italy*, p. 40.

12   This issue is rarely if ever dealt with in the existing literature about Basaglia and Gorizia.

as 'patients who could not be removed and for whom an internal solution was necessary . . . they had no prospects beyond the hospital walls'.[13] The Cold War, which had so deeply affected Gorizia, was reproduced in a stark way within the asylum walls. But the history of the asylum had always been caught up in the city's own tragic history. Inaugurated in 1916, the hospital had been completely destroyed during World War One, like most of Gorizia itself, and was subsequently rebuilt under Italian rule.

Gorizia's *manicomio* (madhouse) was a dark and sinister institution, a dumping ground for the poor and the 'deviant', a place of exclusion. As in most Italian asylums at that time, an architecture of containment and control had developed over time, with cages for the most unruly patients and beds with holes in them through which the immobilized could defecate. Some patients were tied to their beds most of the time, and the hospital's beautiful gardens were hardly used. Even when inmates were allowed outside, they would often be bound to trees or benches. All the wards were closed under lock and key, and the vast majority of those inside were contained against their will. They were inside because they were, in the opinion of the judiciary and the medical staff, a 'danger to themselves and to others'. Many had been left to rot for years, inside the asylum, with no prospect of release. 'Therapy' was largely confined to electroshock and insulin shock treatment, and occasional work in the asylum's kitchen gardens. The introduction of anti-psychotic drugs in the late 1950s was just beginning to have an impact by 1961.[14]

It was the last place where you might think about starting a revolution. But Basaglia took the job, and within eight years Gorizia was to become the most famous mental asylum in Italy, if not in Europe. It was here that a spark was lit, leading to a movement that would undermine the very basis of all such 'total institutions'. Nobody expected this outcome in 1961, certainly not the provincial authorities that had employed

---

13   Basaglia, 'La "Comunità Terapeutica"', p. 263. According to Basaglia the funds for these patients came directly from the Ministero degli Esteri as part of a deal over 'war reparations'.

14   Medication was widely used under Basaglia in Gorizia, it seems, and a debate on this issue did not take place until later. See Franco Basaglia, Franca Ongaro Basaglia, Agostino Pirella, Salvatore Taverna, *La nave che affonda*, Milan: Raffaelo Cortina Editore, 2008, p. 85.

him, nor Basaglia himself. Most asylum directors at the time simply managed the situation they inherited. Many were failed academics. Very few tried to implement any kind of change at all. In this, as in so many other things, Franco Basaglia was very different to the rest. The 'revolution' in Gorizia took place almost by chance. If Basaglia had gone somewhere else, the asylum there would probably have remained as it was.[15]

It was, however, a time of change. A 'great transformation' was taking place.[16] Italy, in 1961, was in the middle of an unprecedented boom: the so-called economic miracle. After thousands of years, rural economies and cultures began to disappear almost overnight. Peasants flooded to the cities, and factories sprung up everywhere. This rush to modernity inevitably affected Italy's outdated and static institutions, including the antiquated asylum system. As Basaglia himself put it, 'it wasn't by chance . . . that the experience of Gorizia took place at a moment of deep cultural and economic transformation, which inevitably also affected health organizations'.[17]

Franco Basaglia (born in Venice, 1924) had a comfortable upbringing. His father, Enrico Basaglia, managed a lucrative tax collection company. Franco grew up in the Venetian neighbourhood of San Polo. His family were loyal to the fascist state, but Basaglia soon grew into a rebel. He became involved in the anti-fascist movement in the city as a teenage student. One of his teachers at the Liceo Classico Foscarini was the legendary Agostino Zanon dal Bo, who played a 'fundamental role in the formation of numerous anti-fascists and partisans'.[18] Dal Bo helped to set up the anti-fascist Partito d'Azione (Action Party) in the Veneto

---

15　In many other places, as the 1960s wore on, change was pushed from the outside, by politicians like Mario Tommasini, Ilvano Rasimelli and Michele Zannetti.

16　Paul Ginsborg, *A History of Contemporary Italy. Society and Politics 1943–1988*, London: Penguin, 1990, p. 1, and Karl Polanyi, *The Great Transformation. The Political and Economic Origins of Our Time*, Boston: Beacon Press, 2001.

17　Basaglia et al., *La nave che affonda*, p. 31.

18　Giulia Albanese et al., eds, *Memoria resistente. La lotta partigiana a Venezia e provincia nel ricordo dei protagonisti*, Istituto veneziano per la storia della Resistenza e della società contemporanea, Portogruaro: Nuova Dimensione, 2005, p. 297.

in 1942. Zanon Dal Bo's influence led to a whole group of anti-fascists emerging from the Foscarini school: 'recruiting a large number of his students to the anti-fascist cause, who were able to make a tremendous contribution to the movement thanks to their age and their energy'.[19] But perhaps there was something more to Basaglia's rebellion, something that went beyond the role of one of his teachers. Lucio Rubini, another student of Zanon Dal Bo's, later claimed that Basaglia 'was always anti-fascist . . . he didn't go to the fascist gatherings, he refused to . . . he was in opposition to it all'.[20]

Venice was spared many of the worst excesses of the war. Above all, it was rarely bombed, unlike almost every other city in Italy (although bombs were dropped on the Porto Marghera industrial zone and on Mestre, at times into the lagoon itself and occasionally onto the city).[21] The size and particular form of the city made armed resistance there difficult, with no natural escape route available.[22] Venice was a key part of the Italian Social Republic, and the city played host to a number of cultural ministries from that government. After 8 September 1943, the Nazis were also present in Venice.

Yet despite the structural and geographical constraints in Venice, the city developed a relatively strong resistance movement. Perhaps because of the unique form and history of the city, there were also many unusual and inventive moments of protest, such as the distribution of thousands of leaflets from the Campanile in Piazza San Marco in February 1944. When the fascists climbed the stairs to the top, they found nobody there. The anti-fascists had used timed detonators. On 12 March 1945 the famous Beffa del Goldoni (the Goldoni joke or hoax) took place in the city's Goldoni Theatre. A performance of a Pirandello play was interrupted and an anti-fascist speech was read out (by Communist partisan Cesco Chinello) to the astonished audience while armed partisans looked on.[23]

19   Giulio Bobbo, *Venezia in tempo di guerra. 1943–1945*, Padua: Il Poligrafo, 2005, p. 47.

20   Albanese et al., *Memoria resistente*, p. 1506.

21   Bobbo, *Venezia in tempo di guerra*.

22   Giulio Bobbo, 'La Resistenza a Venezia e nella sua terraferma' in Albanese et al., *Memoria resistente*, p. 780.

23   Bobbo, *Venezia in tempo di guerra*, pp. 417–25, and Chinello's own account, 'La mia

Armed resistance was rare in the city until 1944. In that year a number of actions by the partisans in Venice led to bloody reprisals. On 6 July 1944 a leading fascist, Bartolomeo Astra, was shot dead by partisans. In revenge for this assassination, the fascists arrested and shot six men in the back of the head in the Cannareggio area, although one survived to tell the tale. Then, on 26 July, a resistance bomb smuggled into the building in a trunk destroyed a fascist headquarters, killing over twenty people. This dramatic event prompted the fascists to take thirteen prisoners from the Santa Maria Maggiore prison, who were quickly tried and convicted by a special court. The men were executed on the rubble of the newly bombed building. Their bodies were then taken to the San Michele cemetery island and buried in unmarked graves. The bomb was a spectacular moment but left the tiny partisan groups very exposed to the reprisals and arrests that inevitably followed.[24]

Tensions ran high that summer. In early August 1944, the Nazis shot seven men at dawn after a German soldier had gone missing. They also carried out extensive roundups in the Castello area of the city. It later turned out that the German soldier in question had drowned, probably after one glass too many. These men became known as the 'seven martyrs'. After the liberation, streets would be named after them and monuments dedicated to their sacrifice.[25]

Life in the city was increasingly hard as the war wore on. Food became scarce, restaurants were requisitioned and the population was swollen by numerous refugees, reaching some 200,000. It was pitch dark at night and people were often found dead after simply falling into canals. Towards the end of the war, even the vaporetti (water-buses) stopped running, and it was more and more difficult to move around the city. Venice's morphology led to some spectacular incidents. One prisoner

---

"educazione sentimentale". Autobiografia resistenziale' in Giulia Albanese and Marco Borghi, eds, *Nella Resistenza. Vecchi e giovani a Venezia sessant'anni dopo*, Istituto veneziano per la storia della Resistenza e della società contemporanea, Portogruaro: Nuova Dimensione, Ediclon Editore, 2004, pp. 72–82.

24   Bobbo, *Venezia in tempo di guerra*, pp. 301–22, and 'La Resistenza a Venezia e nella sua terraferma', pp. 781–2; Chinello, 'La mia "educazione sentimentale"', pp. 26–7, 57–9.

25   Bobbo, *Venezia in tempo di guerra*, pp. 327–44. For the public memory of this event, see John Foot, *Fratture d'Italia. Da Caporetto al G8 di Genova. La memoria divisa del paese*, Milan: Rizzoli, pp. 13–14.

escaped by jumping out a window into the Grand Canal and swimming off despite the fact that he was wearing handcuffs.

Venice had an historic Jewish population, many of whom lived in the ghetto area (the word *ghetto* was originally a Venetian term). In 1943–44 Italian fascists arrested all the Jews they could find (some had already left the city). One of the biggest roundups took place during the night of 30 November 1943, and fascists then ransacked the houses of many Jews. The arrested Jews were held in the ghetto area, which was surrounded by barbed wire, and then sent to Venice's prison before moving on to transit centres and camps in Germany and Poland. Some 246 Venetian Jews were deported during the war.[26] Very few returned. Jews were also picked out of the city's psychiatric hospitals, general hospitals and old people's homes and deported, in some cases straight to Auschwitz.[27]

Venice's Santa Maria Maggiore prison was and still is located in a key strategic position in the city, close to railway and road links into the city. Opened in 1926, it was a nerve centre for the history of the war in Venice and in particular the resistance. Throughout the 1943–45 period there was 'continual flow of anti-fascists and partisans (real and presumed) between the security wing of Santa Maria Maggiore and the offices of the political police, where they were "interrogated" in sessions which often ended up in torture'.[28] Prisoners were constantly being deported to Germany and elsewhere directly from the prison. As was the case across Italy, the torture of prisoners was commonplace, almost routine, both by the fascist police and in prison (where one wing was run by the SS).

In the spring (Lucio Rubini remembers it as March or April) of 1944, Franco Basaglia and a colleague (Nenè Mentasti) crept into a classroom in the Liceo Marco Polo at night and covered the walls with anti-fascist slogans and leaflets. They also wrote 'Morte ai Fascisti, Libertà ai Popoli'

---

26   The Fondazione CDEC gives a figure of 230. cdec.it.

27   Angelo Lallo and Lorenzo Toresini, *Psichiatria e nazismo. La deportazione ebraica dagli ospedali psichiatrici di Venezia nell'ottobre del 1944*, Portogruaro: Nuova Dimensione, 2001; Diego Fontanari and Lorenzo Toresini, eds, *Psichiatria e nazismo. Atti del Convegno. San Servolo. 9 Ottobre 1998*, Centro di Documentazione di Pistoia Editrice, Fondazione IRSESC (San Servolo), Collana dei Fogli d'Informazione 27, Pistoia, 2002.

28   Bobbo, *Venezia in tempo di guerra*, p. 39.

(Death to the fascists, freedom for the people) on every blackboard.[29] Angela, one of Franco's sisters, and Rina Nono, sister of the Venetian composer Luigi Nono, distracted the guards while the young men slipped into the classrooms. The discovery of the protest the next day caused near panic, and the school was closed while it was cleaned up. Basaglia was part of the anti-fascist milieu in the city in that period, which included shopkeepers, tailors, lawyers, painters, school and university students, teachers and others. His friend (and future brother-in-law) Alberto Ongaro was one of the first anti-fascists to be arrested in Venice and spent a month in prison there before being released. Ongaro then left the city to become a partisan in the mountains. A kind of book club was formed, linked to the Querini Stampala library in the city where individuals would report back to each other on radical texts that were absent from their school studies.

Basaglia was arrested, probably after a tip-off, on 11 December 1944.[30] After five days (and nights) of police interrogations he was sent to prison in Venice. Dozens of other anti-fascists were arrested at the same time. The authorities had discovered the key anti-fascist base in a tailor's shop (that of Leone Cavallet), and this had given them a link to a whole network of activists. The time in the police station was terrifying, and the young men arrested were subjected to violence and threats. Lucio Rubini later said: 'They questioned us, they hit us and kicked us . . . it was a terrible four to five days.' It is said that Basaglia's wealthy father, Enrico Basaglia, used his influence to prevent his son from being deported, and that Basaglia senior was shocked by what he saw going on in the police station. Basaglia would spend the next six months in a series of large group cells in Venice's forbidding central prison.

---

29   A similar protest took place in the Foscarini school. Basaglia had been *bocciato* (dismissed) at the Foscarini and finished his studies at the Marco Polo, the other classical *liceo* in Venice. For this action, see the accounts of Renzo Biondo, 'I giovani del Partito d'Azione', and Lucio Rubini, 'Prima del Coprifuoco', in Giuseppe Turcato and Agostino Zanon Dal Bo, eds, *1943–1945 Venezia nella Resistenza*, Venice, 1975–76, pp. 516, 531–3. As far as I know Basaglia never wrote about this event, nor did he ever go into any detail about his role in the Resistance.

30   A man called Luzi or Francesco Luzzi is named by both Ongaro and Rubini as the source of this information (Albanese et al., *Memoria resistente*, p. 1276, 1511), although in Giulio Bobbo's study it appears that it was Lucio Rubini, Basaglia's cousin, who may well have named him and others after being arrested and beaten up by the fascist police (Bobbo, *Venezia in tempo di guerra*, pp. 412–14).

The prison during the war was a place of fear, suffering, bedbugs and filth, illness and resistance. For Chinello, who was there before Basaglia, 'life in prison was hard, difficult'.[31] Basaglia shared a cell for a time with Rubini and many others from across the whole range of the anti-fascist movement. Movement between these large collective cells was common. The prisoners passed the time playing cards, singing, reading, chatting, sharing ideas, plotting and sleeping. They were fed once a day, at lunch-time, and they slept on the floor. It was a dark time. Nobody knew how or when the war would end.

On 26 April 1945, the city's prison was the site of the uprising that kicked the Nazis out of Venice. The guards (led by a Communist called Leonardo Cutugno) and political prisoners took control of Santa Maria Maggiore. For a time, there was a serious danger of violent clashes inside the prison between ordinary prisoners and political internees. Then, after a struggle (and with the common criminals closed back in their cells) armed political prisoners and guards defended the prison from Nazis and fascists who were attempting to break in. A long pitched battle followed. Then the fascists withdrew, and the prisoners (including Basaglia) broke out into the city itself. Basaglia presumably played a part in this uprising, although he would never write a word about it in the years to come. An armed insurrection followed across the city.[32] The Nazis finally left Venice on 28 April, and the Allies arrived the very next day. The war was over. Venice was spared the worst of the violence of the post-war 'showdown'. Only one fascist, it seems, was summarily shot in the aftermath of the liberation.

Basaglia's time in prison had a deep impact on him, although he rarely spoke about his experiences there, even with friends or family. He would, however, sometimes sing songs that he had learnt inside the cells. His intense, almost visceral reaction to the asylum system in Gorizia 1961 has often been traced to his memories of time behind bars as a young man. As he later stated, in an oft-cited passage:

---

31   Chinello, 'La mia "educazione sentimentale"', p. 52.

32   See Bobbo, *Venezia in tempo di guerra*, pp. 436–54, and Giuseppe Turcato, ed., *Kim e i suoi compagni. Testimonianze della resistenza Veneziana*, Venice: Marsilio, 1980.

The first time that I went to prison I was a medical student. I was an active anti-fascist and I was imprisoned as a result. I remember the terrible situations which I found myself in. It was the time of slopping out. There was a terrible smell, the smell of death. I remember that it felt like being in an anatomy theatre where the bodies were dissected. Thirteen years after I graduated, I became the director of an asylum and when I entered the building for the first time, it took me straight back to the war and the prison. It didn't smell of shit, but there was the symbolic smell of shit. I was convinced that that institution was completely absurd, that its function was only to pay the psychiatrists who worked there. In the face of this absurd, disgraceful logic of the asylum – we said 'no'.[33]

His anti-institutionalism was intimately connected to his own time as a prisoner and what he had seen around him at that time. He was also deeply affected, later on, by his first reading of the work of Primo Levi, and in particular *If This Is a Man*.[34] All of these autobiographical details form part of the background to Basaglia's moral, political and humanistic rejection of the asylum *as an institution* after he became director in Gorizia in 1961.

The resistance patterned Basaglia's life in other ways. Alberto Ongaro, a school friend of Franco's, was a key participant in the Venetian movement, a semi-mythical figure as one of the first students to openly oppose the regime. Arrested before Basaglia, after his release back to the army he deserted to join the partisans in the mountains. Alberto introduced Franco to his sister Franca Ongaro. The couple would marry in 1953, and they remained together until Basaglia's death in 1980. Though the relationship between Franca Ongaro and Franco Basaglia has rarely been studied, it is central to any understanding not just of their respective biographies, but also of the vast quantity of published writings and

---

33   Franco Basaglia in Franca Ongaro Basaglia and Maria Grazia Giannichedda, eds, *Conferenze brasiliane*, Milan: Raffaello Cortina Editore, 2000, p. 49. The text in this edited volume is different from that originally published in Domenico De Salvia and Adolfo Rolle, eds, 'Franco Basaglia. Conferenze brasiliane', *Fogli d'informazione* 100, March 1984, p. 38.

34   This text turns up continually in Basaglia's later writings. For the relationship between Levi and Basaglia see Massimo Bucciantini, *Esperimento Auschwitz*, Turin: Einaudi, 2011, pp. 69–91.

practical activities carried out by Basaglia, Franca Ongaro and others after 1961.

In 1943 Basaglia had signed up to study medicine and surgery in the prestigious and venerable university in nearby Padua. He would later claim that he had chosen his degree subject completely at random. Nonetheless, he was a brilliant student. He graduated in 1949 (despite the war years and his time in prison) and spent the entire next decade studying philosophy and psychiatry. Although he was working in a psychiatric clinic he was always more interested in ideas, and his knowledge of the practical aspects of mental health care was relatively limited. It seemed that Basaglia was destined to have a dazzling university career, but, as is common in Italy (then as now), that institution used him and then spat him out. He had worked as an assistant to a distinguished professor (Giambattista Belloni) for the entire period from 1949 to 1961, but a real job never materialized. In 1952 Basaglia specialized in the field of *Malattie nervose e mentali,* and in 1958 he qualified as a doctor in that area. But he was eventually told, in no uncertain terms, that he would never be allowed to progress within the university system. He was probably too sharp, too unorthodox, too original, not servile enough, and he was advised to look elsewhere for a career. Then the Gorizia job came up. Belloni told him to take it.

Some, looking back on Basaglia's life, have compared the university itself to an asylum, as another kind of total institution. Basaglia himself made this point in an interview-book published in the 1970s:

> When I went to Gorizia as director of the provincial asylum I had worked for ten years in an institution as a university assistant. I had learnt (in a personal way) about the workings of institutions, and how power can destroy people and how you can become ill with a kind of 'university sickness'. It was as if someone's entire existence came down to one thing only: a university career. I couldn't stand it any more and I applied for a job in an asylum.[35]

Basaglia was certainly frustrated in Padua, and when he went back into the university system in Parma in the early 1970s his promotion

---

35 Basaglia et al., *La nave che affonda,* pp. 94–5.

was again blocked from above, at least twice.[36] During this time as a pure researcher in Padua, he published a number of academic articles and came into contact with psychiatrists and others who were exasperated with the stale, conservative world of Italian psychiatry. He read widely and was particularly influenced by the work of Sartre, Minkowski, Husserl, Heidegger and Merleau-Ponty, among others. It was in the 1950s that Basaglia began to define himself as a phenomenologist.[37] Soon, his professor began to refer to him, a little disapprovingly, as 'the philosopher'.

The time in Padua was important in terms of friendships and acquaintances. Basaglia studied with Antonio Slavich, who would become the second member of the Gorizian équipe in 1962 and would share the whole Gorizian experience, as well as that in Colorno. Links were also forged with psychiatrists such as Agostino Pirella and others through the academic world of conferences and workshops. Moreover, Basaglia developed a close friendship with a powerful academic neurologist of Armenian descent, Hrayr Terzian, who had been born in Addis Ababa in 1925 and educated at the Armenian College in Venice. Terzian would later prove to be an important ally of the movement and turned up on various appointment commissions.[38]

Basaglia was not a complete outsider, and neither was he a loner. He had friends in high places and knew how to build alliances and work with those who had power. He also tended to work *within* institutions, and after Padua he would take up positions of authority for himself. Moreover, the philosophical and political ideas he developed in Padua were crucial to his approach to running an asylum after 1961. His life and career would be marked by both radical breaks *and* strong continuities.

---

36 The source for this information is Basaglia himself (Ongaro and Giannichedda, *Conferenze brasiliane*, pp. 155–6), but is confirmed for Bologna by Fabio Visintini, *Memorie di un cittadino psichiatra (1902–1982)*, Naples: Edizioni Scientifiche Italiane, 1983, p. 189.

37 Much of the existing literature on Basaglia has dedicated a great deal of space to his ideas and philosophical thought. See, for example, Mario Colucci and Pierangelo Di Vittorio, *Franco Basaglia*, Milan: Bruno Mondadori, 2001; and Alvise Sforza Tarabochia, *Psychiatry, Subjectivity, Community. Franco Basaglia and Biopolitics*, Oxford and New York: Peter Lang, 2013.

38 Terzian would later become the first rector of the new university in Verona in 1982. He was also one of the founders of the journal *Sapere*.

Tall, charismatic and good looking, Basaglia was something of a work-aholic. Michele Risso compared him to a 'big cat'. Once he had power, he fought hard to get his way and could be intolerant towards dissent. He loved to talk and argue things out. Occasionally, he could act in an authoritarian manner, and he was stubborn, but he also worked collectively and was aware of the importance of building a team. Basaglia was ambitious and enjoyed fame and authority, but was completely uninterested in money.

He would usually wake early and work until very late, fuelled by chain-smoking, bottles of Coca Cola and occasional glasses of whisky. Almost all of his writing (after Padua, in particular) was carried out largely *by and with* Franca. Risso also left these other memories of his friend, after Basaglia's death:

> He would transfer from one jacket to another pieces of paper folded into four, notes, lists full of telephone numbers (recently he had got himself an enormous diary, which he would forget). He was always on the phone. If the phone rang at your house, he would answer it. He smoked a lot and coughed, and would complain about his coughing. Sometimes he would fall asleep in the middle of a conversation, but he could talk with someone for an entire night.[39]

Basaglia drove fast and badly, until he fell asleep at the wheel once too often and nearly died. After that, he usually preferred to be driven by others and would fall into a deep sleep almost as soon as the car set off (usually to or from Venice) only to wake on arrival. His roots were very much in Venice, and he tried to return to the city every weekend after leaving Gorizia in 1969. Basaglia rarely took holidays, and when he did go away with the family (sometimes to a house they had bought in the Trentino mountains at San Martino di Castrozzo), his time there would often be taken up with discussions over work and future strategy. He was anti-establishment, but his trappings were bourgeois. He rarely went out of the house without a tie, especially in the 1960s. In Gorizia, lunch and dinner would be served by a maid, at set times, with all the family present. He

---

39 Michele Risso, 'Quando Basaglia disse "Apriamo le tombe dei sepolti vivi. . ."', *La Repubblica*, 31 August 1980. 'Franco was a leader', Risso added.

was a strict father.[40] The clash between the generations was also something that took place within the Basaglia family itself.

Many were seduced by his intellect and his personality (including those who had never met him). He was charismatic and charming, and he inspired love and admiration, but also fear, jealousy and sometimes hatred. He became a hero to many, but also a villain for those who were opposed to the movements linked to 1968 (as well as for some who were key figures in '1968' itself). In that year he became a symbol for a whole epoch overnight, a household name. A key law was later named after him, a rare honour in Italy, especially for a non-politician. He was seen as a 'good man' but also criticized for what some considered extreme irresponsibility. He had a strong empathy with his patients but was blamed by some for abandoning them to their fate.[41] He loved to talk and to discuss everything, but he could also be intolerant and at times even a little authoritarian. His life was sometimes chaotic, but he never missed an appointment. Work was at the centre of his life. He dedicated himself totally, for nearly twenty years, to 'the struggle', and he paid a heavy price for this commitment. Various epithets were applied to him over time, some linked to his well-to-do background and Venetian upbringing: 'natural leader', 'aristocrat', 'patrician'. These were labels used, in the main, by those who did not know him.

The Gorizia post was distinctly unpromising, and risky. It implied political and geographical isolation, in a sector of the psychiatric system that was going nowhere. Basaglia's whole family would be uprooted, and he would be in charge of a place that had made him feel physically sick. The only point of taking the job was to try to transform the whole system from the edge, from the extreme periphery. He would not simply manage things in the old way, as did most asylum directors at the time in Italy. But there was no clear plan at the beginning, apart from a desire to change things. On 3 November 1961, he made his first statement of intent: 'On his first day as director in Gorizia, when the head nurse passed him the list of people who had been tied up that night for official approval, he said, "I'm not signing."'[42] One advantage of the fact that he

---

40 See his comments in Ongaro and Giannichedda, *Conferenze brasiliane*, pp. 192–3.

41 There are many stories that testify to his ability to communicate with patients.

42 Slavich, *La scopa meravigliante*, p. 160.

was in a dead-end job, in the middle of nowhere, was that nobody expected anything of him. He had a strange kind of freedom he would not have had elsewhere. It would take years even for most Gorizians to notice what was happening on their doorstep, let alone people from the rest of Italy.

Gorizia had always been contested territory. The city's history in the twentieth century was marked by tragedy, death and destruction. Razed to the ground more than once during World War One, it had been paralysed by the machinations of the drawing of borders during the Cold War, a process which had removed a large part of the previous area covered by the Province of Gorizia. The international frontier, laid out in 1947, cut right through the town, dividing families, separating peasants from their land and even splitting up the dead inside cemeteries. Across the border were the Communists, and a huge red star was placed on the old Austro-Hungarian train station, just over the frontier to the east. On top of the station there was an ominous message for the people of Gorizia (in Italian): 'Here, we are building socialism'.[43] Armed guards patrolled the border. When people tried to escape to the west (usually at night), they were sometimes shot dead, and their bodies would only be found in the morning. Permanent checkpoints were built at all the road crossings, some of which were yards away from the walls of the psychiatric hospital.

A central factor in Gorizia was the divide between 'Slavs' and Italians. Deep political and ethnic animosities had been exacerbated by fascist policies of ethnic cleansing between the wars. Mass deportations of Italians followed the liberation of Gorizia by Tito's partisans in 1945.[44] All this was fresh in the minds of Gorizians in 1961. Gorizia's monuments and shifting borders reflected this history of division, hatred and conflict. This was a city in some ways frozen in time, highly strategic but also largely forgotten. Everyone in Europe knew about Berlin, but very few were interested in Gorizia. The city was a place of conspiracies and plots, of arms dumps and battlefields, of spies and intrigue, of nostalgic fascists and secret anti-communist military groups. Politically, Gorizia was very much on the centre-right axis. A large number of Gorizians voted regularly for the

---

43   Oreste Pivetta, *Franco Basaglia. Il dottore dei matti*, Milan: Dalai Editore, 2012, p. 75.
44   See John Foot, *Fratture d'Italia*, pp. 33, 119–97.

Christian Democrats, although a significant minority backed more extremist and neo-fascist groupings. The left was extremely weak in the city. In the 1948 political elections, 68 per cent of Gorizians chose the *Democrazia Cristiana* (DC), and only 14 per cent the left-wing Popular Front (which grouped together Communists and Socialists). In 1953 the neo-fascist Italian Social Movement (MSI) won 14.3 per cent of the vote, the Italian Communist Party (PCI) 9.6 per cent and the DC 54.4 per cent This was a very unlikely place indeed to start a radical experiment in any field.

The Basaglia family (Franco, Franca and their two young children, Enrico, eight, and Alberta, six) moved to Gorizia in late 1961.[45] They took residence in a spacious flat on the top floor of the imposing provincial government building, right in the centre of Gorizia, ten minutes from the asylum by foot. The kids went to local schools. At that time, most Italian asylums were managed and financed by provincial councils, and this was also the case in Gorizia. The hospital covered the whole province, and not just the city of Gorizia itself. But the role of the psychiatric hospital in the city was what it had always been throughout the twentieth century in Italy as a whole – to incarcerate the 'mad' and thereby 'protect society'. *Custodia* (custody) was what mattered, not *cura* (cure). Italy's asylums were still regulated by laws that dated back to 1904 and 1909. Article 1 of the 1904 law read as follows:

> people affected by any kind of mental illness should be kept and cured in asylums, when they are dangerous to themselves or to others or they cause public scandal, and they can't be conveniently kept or cured outside of asylums.[46]

People often ended up in asylums after a request from their relatives, something that had to be subsequently confirmed by a complicated legal procedure. In the first instance (a month at most) patients were

---

45   Sometimes the beginning of Basaglia's Gorizian experience is dated to 1962. Slavich remembered that he and Basaglia both commuted to Padua for a time (Slavich, *La scopa meravigliante*, p. 257, n. 1).

46   'Legge 14 Febbraio 1904, N. 36', oaser.it. In 1930, the Fascist regime introduced a measure which meant that all inmates in asylums were also given a criminal record.

supposed to be kept on observation wards. The decision on a permanent stay (or not) was taken by the director of the asylum, and later ratified by a magistrate. On other occasions patients were sent to psychiatric hospitals directly by the police or carabinieri. Release, once again, was linked to the director's point of view and then ratified or checked by the judicial authorities. The 1904 law (and subsequent decrees) gave asylum directors a high level of power within the asylum:

> The director has full authority in terms of the internal health policy of the institution . . . for everything which is linked to the treatment of the patients, and is responsible for the running of the asylum and the execution of the current laws there.

As Basaglia later said, 'As director I had the power to manipulate things, to make decisions, to authorize.'[47] The law referred to inmates throughout as *alienati* – the insane.[48]

Once inside asylums, patients effectively became 'non-persons'. They were stripped of their civil rights and deprived (in theory, only temporarily) of their 'worldly goods'. Often, they had their heads shaved and were given uniforms to wear. Little packets of their possessions were catalogued and kept in store. Many were never to be returned. As Michael Donnelly argued, the entire system 'codified the public mandate of psychiatry to defend society against the "dangerousness" of the insane'.[49] Basaglia later called the 1904 legislation 'an ancient law, which veered between assistance and an idea of security, pity and fear'.[50] Inside the asylum walls men and women were kept rigidly apart. Torture and suicide were commonplace, too normal to even cause surprise or comment. For many, the only way out was death itself. For Basaglia, these inmates were already less than human beings. They were merely surviving. Ugo Cerletti, the inventor of electroshock treatment, wrote in 1949 of 'bars on windows, courtyards surrounded by metal

---

47   Ongaro and Giannichedda, *Conferenze brasiliane*, p. 55.

48   More details about these rules and how to apply them were provided by a decree issued 16 August 1909, no. 615, 'Regolamento sui manicomi e sugli alienati', roma.itc.cnr.it.

49   Donnelly, *The Politics of Mental Health in Italy*, p. 26.

50   'La distruzione dell'ospedale psichiatrico come luogo di istituzionalizzazione' in Basaglia, *Scritti. I*, p. 249.

fences and in these cages, the sad swarms of the mentally ill, crowded into these spaces with their differing, bizarre and odd attitudes and behaviour'.[51] Asylums were places of horror, as in Cerletti's description of an institution in the south of Italy,

> A large deserted courtyard covered in stones that jutted out from the ground. In the middle was a large plane tree and, under its meagre shade, a bunch of a hundred or so human bare-footed and dishevelled creatures, dressed in shapeless uniforms . . . crushed together . . . to escape from the unrelenting rays of the sun. From a distance they appeared like a beehive. From within came cries and shouts of all kinds.[52]

In 1967 'Andrea', one of the Gorizian patients, looked back to the period before Basaglia's arrival as director:

> Before, those who were here prayed that they would die. When someone died they used to ring a bell . . . and everyone would say, God, I wish that had been me . . . I am tired of this life. And those who aren't dead could have lived a healthy life – but instead they are dejected . . . there was no way out, so people simply stopped eating. They would be force-fed through their nose, but it wouldn't work because they had no hope.[53]

Inside the hospital, a large number of nurses were employed to 'look after' the patients. These nurses were untrained and often appointed for their physical strength alone. Their work was hard, back-breaking, stressful and badly paid. Given the small numbers of doctors working in asylums (and the tiny amount of time they spent inside these hospitals), the nurses were usually the main faces of the system. They organized the running of the hospital, they restrained, fed, clothed and washed the patients. Psychological and physical violence was used to keep those same patients in check. Any change in the system would need to take the nursing staff into account. The relationships among doctors, nurses and

---

51   Cerletti, 'La fossa dei serpenti', *Il Ponte*, V 11, 1949, p. 1373.
52   Ibid.
53   *L'istituzione negata*, Turin: Einaudi, 1974, pp. 19-20.

patients would turn out to be a key and difficult factor in the transformation of the asylum system. In addition, many of the nurses in Gorizia
were on the right of the political spectrum. One doctor later recalled
that some 70 per cent of the nurses in the asylum were members of the
neo-fascist trade union.[54]

The language of madness was important. '*Manicomio* meant, literally,
place for the care or custody of the mad.'[55] Later the more neutral term
'psychiatric hospital' was used in official discourse, but *manicomio* was
still a common term (and remains so even today). The Basaglians tried
to appropriate the word for their own use, as a way of underlining that
the asylums were not hospitals at all, but total institutions.[56] This was
also occasionally true of words or phrases like 'mad', 'the mad' or 'crazy
people' (*i matti* or *i pazzi*), which were used self-referentially or ironically
by the Basaglian movement.

As director in Gorizia, Basaglia quickly became convinced that the entire
asylum system was morally bankrupt. He saw no medical benefits in the
way that patients were treated inside these institutions. On the contrary,
he became convinced that some of the eccentric or disturbing behaviour
of the patients was created or exacerbated by the institution itself. Although
referred to officially as hospitals, these places were very similar to prisons:
architecturally and functionally. For the most part their objective was what
Foucault described as to 'discipline and punish'.[57]

These convictions were hardened and sharpened by the texts Basaglia
came across in the early 1960s, especially those by Erving Goffman,
Frantz Fanon and Michel Foucault. Goffman's *Asylums. Essays on the
Social Situations of Mental Patients and Other Inmates* unpicked the per-
verse workings of what he dubbed 'total institutions', a phrase which
would soon become a key part of the Basaglian lexicon.[58] Foucault,

---

54   Interview with Slavich in Balconi, *L'esperienza Goriziana dal '61 al '72*, p. 501.

55   David Forgacs, *Italy's Margins. Social Exclusion and Nation Formation since 1861*,
Cambridge: Cambridge University Press, 2014, p. 198. I would like to thank David Forgacs for
having given me the chance to read a chapter of this book in draft form.

56   Ibid., p. 199.

57   Michel Foucault, *Discipline and Punish. The Birth of the Prison*, London: Penguin, 1991.

58   Goffman's work is present in the first collective book to come out of Gorizia, Franca
Ongaro Basaglia, 'Commento a E. Goffman: "La carriera morale del malato mentale"' in Franco

meanwhile, provided a historical and philosophical focus on the workings of asylums and a theoretical and methodological approach to the study of madness (*The History of Madness*) and the containment of deviance.[59] Both of these books first appeared in 1961, the year Basaglia took over in Gorizia.

These texts circulated in English (and French) before being translated into Italian (in the case of Goffman by Franca Ongaro) in the 1960s. A distinct and specific 'Basaglian canon' began to emerge in Gorizia, including philosophical studies and research into the way psychiatric hospitals actually worked. Basaglia also studied the ideas and practices linked to radical psychiatrists working in France, Germany and the UK. He travelled widely. Over time, he also developed a sharp social critique of the asylum system, which analysed psychiatric hospitals as places where the poor and the deviant were locked up. These three strands to Basaglian thought – anti-institutionalism, a social analysis and a biting critique of the medical establishment – were to take shape over the next twenty years. But they were all present, in nascent form, right from the start.

In those early years, Basaglia was isolated, like Gorizia itself. At first, he was forced to move slowly, almost painfully so. His ideas were extreme ones, and at academic conferences colleagues often treated him as something of a pariah, or as an eccentric. Nobody else in Italy was calling for the destruction of the asylum system, although a small minority was

---

Basaglia ed., *Che cos'è la psichiatria?*, Milan: Baldini & Castoldi, 1997, pp. 235–98, and permeates *L'istituzione negata*. Franca Ongaro translated *Asylums* for Einaudi and the book came out in the same Nuovo Politecnico series as *L'istituzione negata* in June 1968, just three months after the Gorizia book, with a preface written by Franco and Franca Basaglia: *Asylums. Le istituzioni totali. La condizione sociale dei internati e i meccanismi dell'esclusione e della violenza*, Turin: Einaudi, 1968. For Goffman and Basaglia see Ruggero d'Alessandro, *Lo specchio rimosso. Individuo, società, follia da Goffman a Basaglia*, Milan: Franco Angeli, 2008.

59   Michel Foucault, *Folie et Déraison. Histoire de la folie à l'âge classique,* Paris: Editions Gallimard, 1961. Parts of this book were read by the Gorizian équipe. Einaudi discussed Foucault but it was Rizzoli who first translated and published the *History of Madness* in 1963: *Storia della follia nell'età classica*, Milan: Collana BUR, 1963. Basaglia had read Foucault's introduction to Ludwig Binswanger's *Traum und Existenz* in the 1950s (*La rêve et l'existence*, Desclée de Brouwer, 1954) according to Agostino Pirella, 'Franco Basaglia, o della critica pratica alla psichiatria istituzionale' in Diego Giachetti, ed., *Per il Sessantotto. Studi e ricerche*, Pistoia: Massari Editore/CDP, 1998, pp. 119–20.

arguing for reform. Most seemed happy with the status quo or with
small-scale reform. There was considerable resistance to radical change
from within the system as a whole (the medical, political and social
structures which supported the asylums). Asylums provided jobs and
attracted resources, and served a purpose that was both popular and seen
as necessary. Families usually had no desire to look after those who were
seen as mad, and the state resolved this problem by incarcerating those
with supposed mental health problems, often for life.

The category of the 'mad' at that time (which was often confused with
'people inside asylums') was a broad one, including, for example, people
with Down's syndrome, alcoholics and epileptics. Moreover, this broad
and heterogeneous group of mad people were widely seen as dangerous,
and society, people believed, needed protection against them. The high
walls, fences, gates and bars of Gorizia's asylum (and of all the other asylums
in Italy) were testimony to this supposed function. Like most Italians,
Gorizians largely ignored their asylum, and were happy for it to continue
doing what it had always done. In 1961, there was little popular support
for psychiatric reform, or even for a relaxation of the regime. There was
no debate, no discussion. The issue did not exist.

In order to change things, Basaglia required blueprints from elsewhere,
models of change. He had little to work with in Italy alone. His philosophical notions, on their own, were not enough. He read widely and
took on ideas from an eclectic mix of sources to add to those he already
had. This process required research and travel. Basaglia visited other
asylums, forged friendships and was always ready to experiment, always
open to new ideas and new practices.

Biographies and studies of Basaglian thought and accounts of the
movement have often, in retrospect, imposed a coherence that was
not necessarily there. Basaglian ideas (and practices) were flexible and
dynamic, and they moved with the times. Things were tried out and
then abandoned. These ideas and practices were also very personal,
sometimes reflecting an emotional response to his own past (those
crucial six months in prison in 1944), his philosophical studies and
his political commitment (which was never revolutionary in an abstract
sense, but radical and critical), his openness to new texts or to fragments of existing texts. Basaglia was never dogmatic – he absorbed

what he read and shaped the fragments into a new form. Sometimes, what emerged was incomprehensible. On other occasions, especially towards the end of the 1960s, he seemed to be entirely in tune with the times.

He usually tried to avoid empty rhetoric (especially in the Gorizia phase) although he did indulge in radicalese, especially in the 1970s, and he flirted with forms of Maoism and sloganeering.[60] But he never lost touch with the importance of engagement with power structures and powerful people, and their ability to carry out reforms. He understood power but had no desire to enter politics, which, for Basaglia, was a means to an end. Hence, he was able to work with Socialists, Christian Democrats, Communists and, at times, those from the far left, as well as intellectuals, artists, actors, publishers, photographers, journalists, film-makers, union leaders and bureaucrats.

He was never a slave to any party line and often managed to bring people of different shades over to his point of view. During his career Basaglia worked largely *within* institutions, usually in order to change them, and often in an attempt to close them down altogether. This combination of pragmatism, radicalism and energy was extremely rare in 1968 and in particular in post-1968 Italy, where hollow phrases and political posturing were omnipresent. Basaglia was ambitious, but he was also willing to put his career on the line. He constantly undermined the basis of his own profession. As a result, people often found him hard to pin down. Who was he? Which side was he on?

Nobody had ever tried to 'overturn' an asylum from the inside before. In Italy, there was nothing to go on, no models with which to work. Basaglia looked towards France, to Scotland, to London, to the USA. Some places had already attempted reform, and with success. Basaglia sought out reformers and went to see what they had done. If he could not go personally, he sent friends or collaborators, or Franca. He commissioned reports and made contact with those interested in change,

---

60   In particular in these books edited by Franco Basaglia and Franca Basaglia Ongaro, *La maggioranza deviante. L'ideologia del controllo sociale totale*, Turin: Einaudi, 1971, and *Crimini di pace. Ricerche sugli intellettuali e sui tecnici come addetti all'oppressione*, Milan: Baldini Castoldi Dalai, 2009 (original edition Einaudi, 1975).

such as Maxwell Jones in Scotland.[61] He devoured texts and commissioned translations where they were required. The time was ripe for new ideas in the world of psychiatry. By the mid-1960s a small group of radicals in the UK, France, the USA and Italy had begun to shake up the conservative world of psychiatry. Soon, these ideas would capture the imagination of a whole generation. Basaglia was no longer alone.

In the UK, two psychiatrists called David Cooper and Ronald Laing were making their ideas known to a wider public. Laing had set up a so-called 'Rumpus Room' for female schizophrenics inside a Scottish asylum in 1954–55.[62] A number of the 'worst' patients were moved from wards to a more normal room where they were allowed to mingle with nurses and doctors. The Rumpus Room 'provided a clean, calm and friendly environment for highly disturbed patients to ride out their tantrums'. A crucial factor in the Rumpus Room experiment was the way that the role of the nurses was supposedly transformed by the experience. Although the real extent of what went on in the Rumpus Room is in some doubt, it was a pioneering attempt to do something different within a total institution. It also underlined the importance of the institutional setting in exacerbating madness, and the possibilities (and limits) of experimentation within total institutions. Moreover, beyond what had actually happened inside that Glasgow asylum, the Rumpus Room was a powerful symbol of change.

Laing's classic study *The Divided Self* came out in 1960, although it took some years for it to become a seminal text. This book was based in part on Laing's experiences with patients during the Rumpus Room period.

---

61   Basaglia visited Scotland and presumably England in the early 1960s, although he calls it England as Italians often do: 'Sono stato in Inghilterra nel 1961–1962'. Ongaro and Giannichedda, *Conferenze brasiliane*, p. 107.

62   Allan Beveridge, *Portrait of the Psychiatrist as a Young Man. The Early Writing and Work of R. D. Laing, 1927–1960*, Oxford: Oxford University Press, 2011, pp. 202–23. Jonathan Andrews, 'R. D. Laing in Scotland: Facts and Fictions of the "Rumpus Room" and Interpersonal Psychiatry' in Marijke Gijswjt-Hofstra and Roy Porter, eds, *Cultures of Psychiatry*, Amsterdam: Atlante, 1998, pp. 121–50. J. L. Cameron, R. D. Laing, A. McGhie, 'Patient and Nurse. Effects of Environmental Changes in the Care of Chronic Schizophrenics', *The Lancet*, 31 December 1955, pp. 1384–6. David Abrahamson, 'R. D. Laing and Long-stay Patients: Discrepant Accounts of the Refractory Ward and "Rumpus Room" at Gartnavel Royal Hospital', *History of Psychiatry* 18: 203, 2007, pp. 203–15.

Among other things, Laing argued strongly that schizophrenia and madness could be understood. The language of madness was intelligible. Laing had left the institutional world of psychiatry by the early 1960s, dedicating himself to his private patients and to his writings. His work soon became a key part of a new radical counter-culture. By the mid- to late 1960s *The Divided Self* was a runaway bestseller, and its success prefigured that of *L'istituzione negata* (The Negated Institution).

Meanwhile David Cooper, a South African–born psychiatrist, ran an open, experimental ward from 1962 to 1966 within an asylum on the outskirts of London, and later described his experiences there in another classic text, *Psychiatry and Anti-psychiatry*.[63]

In all of these cases, total institutions were being (temporarily) overturned and reformed or undermined from within. Other more radical, extra-institutional experiments, such as Kingsley Hall in London (1965–70), looked to set up entirely new places as alternatives to psychiatric hospitals. In France, as well, radical experiments within mental health systems (sectoral reforms and 'institutional psychotherapy') had a strong influence on Basaglia and other reformers.[64]

Before moving on to the story of what happened in Gorizia itself, we need to try and understand the meanings of the various terms and labels which emerged in the 1960s, and which have often been applied to the Gorizian period: 'anti-psychiatry', critical psychiatry, radical psychiatry.

---

63   David Cooper, *Psychiatry and Anti-psychiatry*, London: Tavistock, 1967. Translated as *Psichiatria e anti-psichiatria*, Rome: Armando, 1969.

64   See Giuseppe Micheli, *Il vento in faccia. Storie passate e sfide presenti di una psichiatria senza manicomio*, Milan: Francoangeli, 2013, pp. 16–19.

TWO

Anti-psychiatry, Critical Psychiatry, Movements and Working Utopias

'There has not been only one anti-psychiatry, just as there has not been only one psychiatry.'

Patrizia Guarnieri[1]

'We can transform each institution – family, school, university, mental health, factory – each art form, into a revolutionary centre for a transforming consciousness.'

David Cooper[2]

One of the key problems in studying radical psychiatry in the 1960s and 1970s is the term 'anti-psychiatry'. Words are important, and they often change in meaning; 'anti-psychiatry' is no exception to this rule. It is a strange word, toxic even, packed with power and yet often emptied of real meaning. Today, this term is bandied about, usually in a negative sense. For some it has almost become an insult, and

---

1 Patrizia Guarnieri, 'The History of Psychiatry in Italy. A Century of Studies' in Roy Porter and Mark Micale, *Discovering the History of Psychiatry*, New York and Oxford: Oxford University Press, 1994, p. 252.

2 Archives of the Philadelphia Association, Dialectics of Liberation, transcript of the Seminar discussions (1967) in David Cooper, ed., *The Dialectics of Liberation*, London: Penguin, 1968, p. 197.

its uses differ widely in different national and academic contexts. It is rarely defined or analysed in any depth, often identified simply with a belief in the bland assertion that 'mental illness does not exist'.[3] Giovanni Jervis wrote in the 1970s that anti-psychiatry was 'a sign of dissent, but it isn't clear what it is against or what it denies', which could also be understood as a 'tendency, a cultural orientation, a kind of critical ferment'.[4]

This semantic problem is compounded by the fact that most who are usually described as the 'leaders' of anti-psychiatry have denied, at one time or another, that they were ever anti-psychiatrists. There was a sense that people were already avoiding the term by the mid-1970s. Jervis wrote, 'I don't know anyone who calls themself an anti-psychiatrist'.[5] This is a term that almost everyone (from the time) rejects, yet it continues to be used.[6]

Take R. D. Laing, for example, who wrote this in his autobiography:

I have never called myself an anti-psychiatrist, and have disclaimed the term from when first my friend and colleague, David Cooper, introduced it. However, I agree with the anti-psychiatric thesis that by and large psychiatry functions to exclude and repress those elements society wants excluded and repressed.[7]

---

3   Even leading anti-psychiatrists were reluctant to define what they meant by the term. See David Cooper, for example, who is widely thought to have invented the term in the first place: 'The organizing group consisted of four psychiatrists who were very much concerned with radical innovation in their own field – to the extent of their counter-labelling their discipline as anti-psychiatry' (Cooper, *Dialectics of Liberation*, p. 7). Nor is the term or label defined at any point in *Psychiatry and Anti-psychiatry* (1967). Later on, the term was often used almost as an insult, as a way of simply dismissing an opponent.

4   Giovanni Jervis, 'Il mito dell'antipsichiatria' in *Il buon rieducatore. Scritti sugli usi della psichiatria e della psicanalisi*, Milan: Feltrinelli, 1977, pp. 125 and 136.

5   Ibid., p. 137.

6   Thomas Szasz also rejects the term as applied to his own work, and he has always been very clear concerning his argument that mental illness is a construct and a label, *The Myth of Mental Illness*, New York: Harper & Row, 1961. For the ideas of Szasz, and for his analysis of anti-psychiatry see Thomas Szasz, *Anti-psychiatry. Quackery Squared*, New York: Syracuse University Press, 2009, and Michael Staub, *Madness Is Civilization. When the Diagnosis Was Social, 1948–1980*, Chicago and London: University of Chicago Press, 2011, pp. 89–93, 101–14.

7   R. D. Laing, *Wisdom, Madness and Folly. The Making of a Psychiatrist*, London:

Yet Laing was the most famous anti-psychiatrist of all – 'the father and the Pope of anti-psychiatry'[8] – despite his protestations. Or we could cite Basaglia himself, who said this in response to a question in the late 1970s:

> I would like to say that this child, anti-psychiatry, which is ten years old, does not exist – or rather exists only in the heads of people because this word has had great success from the ideological more than the practical point of view. We have never been anti-psychiatrists – we were simply employees . . . we worked in the real world within psychiatric institutions in order to give people who were suffering an alternative to the violence and repression of the asylum.[9]

Basaglia added later in the same interview that 'I don't understand what anti-psychiatry or non-psychiatry actually means'.[10] Even those who defined themselves as anti-psychiatrists, and really did deny that mental illness existed, are now suffering from the syndrome of denial.[11]

So what are we to do with this 'child' called 'anti-psychiatry', one which causes so much anguish, and which some say does not even exist – a child that has grown up and has been disowned by its parents and

---

Macmillan, pp. 8–9. In a footnote on p. 2, Laing writes: 'The term "anti-psychiatry" was coined by the psychiatrist David Cooper because he felt that psychiatry as the theory and practice of medical psychiatry was and is predominantly repressive, anti-psychiatric in the sense of the science and art of mental healing. Quite a few medical psychiatrists agree with him.' It is also worth noting Laing's criticisms of what he saw as having happened in Italy on pp. 4 and 9. The first observation is that psychiatrists in Italy 'refuse to make these decisions [about what to do with a person suffering from 'mental illness'], they are trying to develop the art of helping 'the group' to resolve 'the crisis within itself', p. 4. Later he says that 'psychiatry' in Italy no longer took part in 'exclusion', p. 9.

8   Jervis, *Il buon rieducatore*, p. 139.

9   'Basaglia e l'antipsichiatria', n.d., but probably around 1978–79, posted 5 September 2010 by forumsalutementale, youtu.be/xFYX144BrV8.

10   See also Franca Ongaro Basaglia and Maria Grazia Giannichedda, eds, *Conferenze brasiliane*, Milan: Raffaello Cortina Editore, 2000, 'I am not an anti-psychiatrist because this is the kind of intellectual that I refuse to accept', pp. 153, 184.

11   See the comments in Libero Bestighi et al., eds, *Specialista in relazioni umane. L'esperienza professionale di Edelweiss Cotti*, Bologna: Pendragon, 2001.

former friends? In order to answer this question we need to go back to the 1960s and begin to trace the history and genealogy of 'anti-psychiatry' from its origins up to the present day.

Anti-psychiatry: Genealogy and History of a Term

'A revolution . . . is going on in relation to sanity and madness, both inside and outside psychiatry. Modern psychiatry came into being when the demonological point of view gave way 300 years ago to a clinical viewpoint. The clinical point of view is now giving way before another point of view that is both existential and social. The shift, I believe, is of no less radical significance.'

R. D. Laing (1964)[12]

'In the 1960s and 1970s a series of tendencies which called into question the dogmas attached to traditional psychiatric "science" were grouped together with the generic term "anti-psychiatry".'

Giovanni Jervis (1975)[13]

GIOVANNI JERVIS: 'In one sense it is very easy today to practice anti-psychiatry.'

FRANCO BASAGLIA: 'No, we are non-psychiatrists.'

L'istituzione negata (1968)[14]

In the heady atmosphere of the late 1960s, the buzzwords of 'anti-psy-chiatry' and 'non-psychiatry' took on a series of meanings, both for those who uttered them and for the followers of the movement. The current of thought and activity which became known as 'anti-psychiatry' (both with and without capitals and quotation marks) covered a wide range of opinions and ideas, and was identified with a number of texts, leaders

---

12 R. D. Laing, 'Schizophrenia and the Family', *New Society*, 16 April 1964, cited in Nick Crossley, 'R. D. Laing and the British Anti-psychiatry Movement', *Social Science and Medicine* 47: 7, 1998, p. 882.

13 Giovanni Jervis, *Manuale critico di psichiatria*, 10th ed.,1980 (1975), p. 59.

14 Franco Basaglia, ed., *L'istituzione negata*, Turin: Einaudi, 1968, p. 269.

and experiences in a series of countries, including those in Gorizia and then Trieste.

As a first step, then, we need to try and define what 'anti-psychiatry' was *then*, and what it means for us, historically, *today*. Put very simply, as a starting-point: *Anti-psychiatry was a critical and radical movement that emerged from within the world of psychiatry itself.*[15] It was a political, cultural and social 'moment'[16] in history, 'a symptom . . . a catalyst, and a point of convergence'.[17] It was flexible and malleable,

> a state of mind, a language, a way of thinking, that is to say a way of life . . . not an ideal closed in upon itself or an easy to copy model but rather a perpetually renewed incitement to look beyond the appearances and prejudices that social conformism wraps us up in – at things themselves.[18]

It can also be fixed in time. We can give anti-psychiatry a set of broad dates, for example: the 1960s and 1970s. Nonetheless, the phrase 'anti-psychiatry' continued and continues to have a history even if the movement itself no longer exists in the same way (or at all).

David Cooper first coined the term in his volume *Psychiatry and Anti-psychiatry*, published in 1967, and it was used again in his introduction to the celebrated publication based on the Dialectics of Liberation Congress in London.[19] Nonetheless, in these two books there is very little on what the term actually means. Moreover, in his final comments in *Dialectics*, Cooper warned his readers about 'false' solutions that might easily emerge from an over-simplistic or illusionary reading of some aspects of anti-psychiatry. He could already see how his words might be misused or create dangerous and false hopes, even as the term was being introduced. Was it simply a new, chic and radical label, or was it

---

15   Crossley, 'R. D. Laing and the British Anti-psychiatry Movement', p. 878.

16   Peter Barham, 'From the Asylum to the Community: The Mental Patient in Postwar Britain' in Gijswjt-Hofstra and Porter, eds, *Cultures of Psychiatry*, p. 236.

17   Jacques Postel and David Allen, 'History and Anti-psychiatry in France' in Roy Porter and Mark Micale, eds, *Discovering the History of Psychiatry*, Oxford: Oxford University Press, 1994, p. 396.

18   Ibid., p. 406.

19   Cooper, *The Dialectics of Liberation*.

something linked to concrete and alternative forms of practice, such as in the new unit run by Cooper known as Villa 21, which he himself described as 'an experiment in anti-psychiatry'?

So what was it that held this nascent movement together (a movement riven right from the start by ideological, practical, political and personal divisions and arguments)? First, there was a *critical* approach towards traditional theories and practices of psychiatry (and the medical world in general). This critique ranged from the workings of the asylum system to bio-organic theories of mental illness to the ways in which the mentally ill were labelled, incarcerated and treated in hospitals and clinics. Often, radical psychiatry in this period called into question traditional definitions and diagnoses of mental illness. This 'calling into question' took in a range of positions, from Basaglia's desire to 'place the diagnosis in brackets', to the denial that whole categories of mental illness really existed. Many radical psychiatrists were inspired by phenomenology and advocated forms of practice that allowed for the construction of relationships with their 'patients' on an equal footing, at least in theory. Often, the whole separation of 'patients' and 'doctors' was undermined or abolished. As Laing and his fellow authors put it way back in 1956, in their description of the Rumpus Room experiment in Glasgow, 'The barrier between patients and staff is not erected solely by the patients but is a mutual construction. The removal of this barrier is a mutual activity.'[20] Sometimes, as in the case of the short-lived patients' movement in Heidelberg, illness was celebrated 'as a weapon'.[21] Therefore, anti-psychiatry was a term associated with a movement that covered an assortment of positions, among which there were indeed some activists and thinkers who denied the 'existence of mental illness'.

---

20   J. L. Cameron, R. D. Laing, A. McGhie, 'Patient and Nurse. Effects of Environmental Changes in the Care of Chronic Schizophrenics', *The Lancet*, 31 December 1955, p. 1386.

21   See Zbigniew Kotowicz, *R. D. Laing and the Paths of Anti-psychiatry*, London: Routledge, 1997, pp. 79–82, 87; Wolfgang Huber, *SPK: Turn Illness into a Weapon for Agitation by the Socialist Patients' Collective at the University of Heidelberg*, KRRIM Verlag für Krankheit, 1993; Dora Garcia, 'Radical Politics, Radical Psychiatry, Radical Art. An Introduction to the "Mad Marginal" Project' in Dora Garcia, *From Basaglia to Brazil*, Trento: Fondazione Galleria Civica, 2010, pp. 10–21, and Dora Garcia, 'An Interview with Carmen Roll' in ibid., pp. 146–59. A wealth of material on the SPK can be found at spkpfh.de.

Radical psychiatrists usually tried to understand mental illness as a social creation. What was known as mental illness, it was argued, was in some way created by social forces, inside and/or outside the family unit. This characteristic has been seen, by some writers, as the essence of anti-psychiatry. For Julian Bourg: 'Anti-psychiatry was an international radical tendency generally inclined towards viewing madness as socially constructed. It brought the spirit of anti-authoritarian revolt to the mentally ill and their caregivers.'[22]

Sometimes, this social analysis was extended to the whole system governing mental health care, which was placed firmly within an analysis of capitalist power structures and the 'repression of deviance'. These strands of radical psychiatry brought together Marxism, forms of Maoism (as in the contestation of power structures, the Western translation of the Cultural Revolution) and new anti-authoritarian ideas coming out of 1968. Thus, anti-psychiatry was critical (and *self*-critical), social, political and cultural, all at the same time. To understand anti-psychiatry, we need to take a wide-ranging approach to the subject. As Peter Barham has argued, it was 'far more significant within a cultural history than a distinctly psychiatric one'.[23]

It is useful to delve a little deeper into this term or label. D. B. Double further divides up the positions taken by the various 'leaders' of anti-psychiatry into a number of different strands:[24]

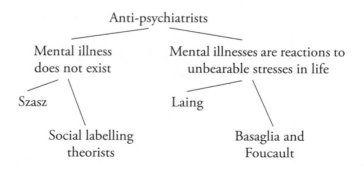

22   Julian Bourg, *From Revolution to Ethics. May 1968 and Contemporary French Thought*, Montreal and Kingston: McGill-Queens University Press, 2007, p. 106.

23   Barham, 'From the Asylum to the Commmunity', p. 236.

24   D. B. Double, 'Historical Perspectives on Anti-psychiatry' in D. B. Double ed., *Critical Psychiatry. The Limits of Madness*, London: Palgrave, 2006, p. 31.

These sub-categories can be further separated in different ways. As Double argues,

> The group who recognize that the use of the term mental illness is metaphorical and, thereby, do not want to minimize the suffering of people with mental health problems can also be subdivided into two. The first would include Laing, who emphasizes that reactions identified as mental illness relate to interpersonal behaviour, particularly within the family. The second subdivision, containing authors like Franco Basaglia . . . and Michel Foucault . . . emphasize that broader societal factors rather than the family are involved in presentations of mental illness.[25]

We can also understand anti-psychiatry by what it was *against*. To cite Double again: 'The essence of anti-psychiatry derives from the sense in which psychiatry itself is regarded as part of the problem.'[26]

Thus, in the late 1960s and early to mid 1970s, anti-psychiatry was a disparate but international political movement that aimed to reposition (in a radical way) psychiatric theory *and* practice. It was also a very broad church. Anti-psychiatry contained within its flexible borders a whole range of positions, which was part of its strength but also a clear weakness. Agreement was almost impossible. Sects and sectarianisms developed, as well as personal conflicts.[27] Debates were interminable. Basaglia's attempts to create an organization (Psichiatria Democratica) out of this mass of activists was commendable and important, but was paralysed at times by ongoing conflicts. The same was even truer of short-lived international umbrella organizations that attempted to bring together anti-psychiatrists.[28]

---

25   Double, 'Historical Perspectives on Anti-psychiatry', p. 32.

26   D. B. Double , 'The History of Anti-psychiatry: An Essay Review', *History of Psychiatry* 13, 2002, p. 235. Colin Jones underlined 'the act of negation and inversion at the heart of the [anti-psychiatry] movement', or, in other words, the '"anti" element in anti-psychiatry', in 'Raising the Anti. Jan Foudraine, Ronald Laing and Anti-psychiatry' in Gijswjt-Hofstra and Porter, *Cultures of Psychiatry*, p. 285.

27   For this see Giuseppe Micheli, *Il vento in faccia. Storie passate e sfide presenti di una psichiatria senza manicomio*, Milan: Francoangeli, 2013, pp. 42–4.

28   Such as the *Réseau di alternativa alla psichiatria* (the Italian name given to this loose

Anti-psychiatry can also be understood as a more general form of methodology. There was, at the time, a general attempt to *overturn*, to *negate* what was already there, the structures of intellectual (and in this case medical) power. This 'anti' element was crucial to the workings of the movement.[29] Institutional power was contested in all its forms – as encapsulated in the protagonists of this power: teachers, doctors, psychiatrists, lecturers, priests and politicians. Those with power often contested *themselves*, by denying their own authority, by stripping themselves of the symbols of power (white coats, for example, as a first step, but also titles), or by attempting to place themselves on the same level as those they were treating, teaching or giving sermons to. Radical psychiatry was part of a larger movement, and to understand it we also need to look more deeply at 1968 and the 1970s. As Fulvio Marone puts it, 'The movement of alternative psychiatry was . . . a subset of a vast movement.'[30]

In the 1960s and 1970s, the use of the term 'anti-psychiatry' was commonplace. This is true with relation to Basaglia, to Jervis and to other parts of the movement in 1968. In 1978 Ernesto Venturini also used the label in an edited book that attempted to survey the whole Italian movement.[31] Far from being rejected by the Basaglians and others in the movement, the anti-psychiatry label was actively embraced by

---

organization) which held regular international meetings through the 1970s and 1980s. For the 1977 congress in Trieste see below and also the proceedings collected in *Il circuito del controllo. Dal manicomio al decentramento psichiatrico. Atti e documenti del Réseau di alternativa alla psichiatria*, Trieste: Cooperativa libraria, Centro culturale, 1980.

29   Jones, 'Raising the Anti', p. 285.

30   Fulvio Marone, 'La psichiatria alternativa italiana', *La psicoanalisi. Rivista del campo Freudiano* 25, January–June 1999, p. 107.

31   Ernesto Venturini, *Il giardino dei gelsi. Dieci anni di antispsichiatria italiana*, Turin: Einaudi, 1979. See also the title of the much-cited interview book published in 1978: Franco Basaglia, Franca Ongaro Basaglia, Agostino Pirella, Salvatore Taverna, *La nave che affonda. Psichiatria e antipsichiatria a dieci anni da 'L'istituzione negata'. Un dibattito*, Rome: Savelli, 1978. The term was also taken up by Einaudi; see *Cinquant'anni di un editore. Le edizioni Einaudi negli anni 1933–1983*, Turin: Einaudi, 1983: 'above all thanks to the work of a combative psychiatrist who defined himself as a "anti-psychiatrist", Franco Basaglia', n.p. Nico Pitrelli claims that 'Basaglia was interested in these movements, he went to see the open communities set up by Laing and Cooper in Great Britain, but he always rejected the anti-psychiatrist label', in Nico Pitrelli, *L'uomo che restituì la parola ai matti. Franco Basaglia, la comunicazione e la fine dei manicomi*, Rome: Riuniti, 2004, p. 64.

them for a time.[32] In January 1968, for example, Basaglia wrote to Giulio Bollati using these words:

> In this moment, for me, I think another period of action is beginning – out of the crisis in which I find myself – in order to escape from the ideology which I myself have encouraged. I am worried about the problem of illness as part of a specific anti-institutional problem – but we are faced with a specific form of anti-institutional struggle – anti-psychiatry.[33]

Some within the movement called for the abolition of the whole category of 'psychiatry', while many others agitated within *and* against psychiatry at the same time. There were those who explored the idea of a scientific revolution inside the discipline, while others called for a revolution *against* science itself. Many anti-psychiatrists worked *as* psychiatrists in one form or another: anti-psychiatry was part of the world of psychiatry.

Moreover, it is important to distinguish between the often-sophisticated (and occasionally incomprehensible) theoretical debates among the leaders and theoreticians of the movement, and wider networks of followers and supporters. It is clear that, while Basaglia's position attempted to place mental illness 'in brackets', or suspend judgement, or avoid labelling patients, the movement as a whole often tended towards a much cruder analysis of these problems, rejecting institutions *tout court*, as well as psychiatry and mental illness. For Edoardo Balduzzi, 'Basaglia never clearly denied that there was something called "mental illness", but the decodification of his message, above all in the years of "contestation", was read in that way.'[34]

Crude positions were often reproduced by journalists and others in their reports on Basaglian institutions and ideas. In this sense, it is

---

32   For example, see this extract from a letter from Basaglia to Bollati in 1967 (they were discussing *The Negated Institution*) where Basaglia said, 'It is important that there is nothing psychiatric on the cover . . . given the "anti-psychiatric" and "anti-scientific" structure of the entire work.'

33   19 January 1968, Basaglia to Bollati. Einaudi Archive. Basaglia Folder.

34   Edoardo Balduzzi, *L'albero della cuccagna. 1964–1978. Gli anni della psichiatria italiana*, Edizioni Stella, Nicolodi Editore, 2006, p. 39.

possible to see how Basaglia could become 'in any case, historically, the father of Italian anti-psychiatry' despite his own frequent denials of this role in a specific sense.[35] Jervis also underlined how extremist positions were taken up by many within the movement after 1968, a period which saw 'an unexpected process of the popularization and vulgarization of so-called "anti-psychiatric" themes'.[36]

Anti-psychiatry (both as an identifier and as something symptomatic of a wider movement and new ideas) was extremely à la mode for a time, and was almost impossible to avoid. It became a kind of brand. Then, very quickly, it slipped out of fashion and was discredited and removed from the history of that period. History was read backwards, as so often happens. Even those who had tolerated the term or accepted it soon began to reject it (such as Basaglia and Laing). Its meaning also changed over time.

Today, the consensus in Italy is that Basaglia himself was *not* an anti-psychiatrist.[37] This oft-repeated statement tends to derive, in turn, from a caricatured and simplistic view of the meaning of 'anti-psychiatry', as a (discredited or extremist) movement or current of thought which denied the very existence of mental illness. But very few anti-psychiatrist practitioners (perhaps surprisingly) actually claimed that mental illness 'did not exist'. R. D. Laing spent much of his career studying and working with people who were generally seen to be mentally ill. His approach

---

35   Anacleto Realdon, 'L'antipsichiatria: un movimento internazionale?' in A. Realdon, V. Cristoferi Realdon, R. De Stefano, B. Spazzapan, *Oltre l'antipsichiatria. Dopo nove anni a Gorizia, riflessioni critiche da un ex ospedale psichiatrico*, Padua: Piccin Editore, 1981, p. 47. Giovanni Jervis was one of the most lucid analysts of the movement of which he had once been a part; see 'L'antipsichiatria fra innovazione e settarismo', *MondOperaio* 5, 1986, p. 125, cited in Patrizia Guarnieri, *La storia della psichiatria. Un secolo di studi in Italia*, Florence: Olschki, 1991, p. 36. Jervis also argued that Basaglia himself was a victim of many of his own followers, who often took up simplistic anti-psychiatric positions. Others warned of the danger that anti-psychiatry itself would become institutionalized and lose its edge. To some extent this seems to have happened. Quite quickly, anti-psychiatry created its own institutions and its own sets of (rigid) ideologies and dichotomies, something Basaglia was concerned about right from the start.

36   Jervis, 'L'antipsichiatria fra innovazione e settarismo', p. 126.

37   Conversely, outside of Italy (especially in the English-speaking world) he is often described as an anti-psychiatrist.

was radically different, however, to that adopted by traditional medical practitioners.

Far from denying the existence of mental illness, anti-psychiatrist practitioners (as opposed to journalists and followers of the movement) usually took mental illness very seriously indeed, and attempted to search for its origins and possible new solutions to it.[38] One of the differences between radical and traditional psychiatry in practice, for example in Gorizia, was that the psychiatrists under Basaglia were present in the hospital all the time, discussing and talking with the patients. Before Basaglia, doctors were notable only by their absence. Slavich later underlined Basaglia's 'continual presence in Gorizia'.[39] It might be argued that radical psychiatrists were much more interested in the mentally ill than the traditional psychiatrists they tried to replace. Some even suggested, for example, that anti-psychiatrists were 'burnt out' by their constant and close contact with those who were considered mentally ill, in particular those defined as schizophrenics.[40]

Unfortunately, the simplistic and ahistorical equation of 'denial of the existence of mental illness = anti-psychiatry' has been taken up by a number of contemporary supporters of Basaglia. This has led to numerous simplifications and misrepresentations, usually along the lines of 'Basaglia

---

38   A different position was taken by Thomas Szasz, whose work was widely read within the movement, despite the fact that he himself rejected it and was trenchant in his criticisms of the ideas behind anti-psychiatry. A piece from Szasz was also included in the anthology edited by Franco and Franca Basaglia in 1975, 'La psichiatria a chi giova?' in *Crimini di pace. Ricerche sugli intellettuali e sui tecnici come addetti all'oppressione*, Milan: Baldini Castoldi Dalai, 2009 (original edition Einaudi, 1975), pp. 385–98.

39   Antonio Slavich, *La scopa meravigliante. Preparativi per la legge 180 a Ferrara e dintorni 1971–1978*, Prefazione di Giovanni Berlinguer, Rome: Riuniti, 2003, p. 175.

40   Clancy Sigal, who was there, later argued: 'My own opinion is that Laing was one of the many doctors and nurses (including Cooper and Atkin) whose too-close proximity to the fierce heat of schizophrenia burned them out via over-identification with their patients. Working with the "loony" you are very tempted to cross the line as an act of solidarity and because you have convinced yourself that therapy-at-a-distance is a betrayal of the tortured and self-torturing patient. There is plenty of room for argument about whether this is a good or harmful thing to do. But, Mary Barnes aside, there are a number of men and women alive and functioning today because a few good doctors, nurses, and their well-meaning if clumsy accomplices had the guts to walk into the furnace and stay there till the job was done.' Letter to the *New York Review of Books*, 19 December 1996. I think this kind of analysis could also be applied to many of those involved in the Italian movement.

never denied the existence of mental illness, and therefore he was not an anti-psychiatrist.' An approach of this kind simplifies and distorts the past. Here we will adopt a much more nuanced and multi-layered approach to the whole question of the definition and understanding of anti-psychiatry.[41] To cite Norman Dain,

> Anti-psychiatry can perhaps best be understood as a variety of groups and individuals who believed that psychiatry was either a vehicle for or an obstacle to attaining certain goals that they valued, goals that often went beyond concern about the plight of mental patients or the faults of psychiatry.[42]

With the demise of the movement that gave rise to anti-psychiatry and provided it with a mass base, traditional psychiatrists have tried (with some success) to take back the reins of power, and have tended to dismiss or ignore anti-psychiatry altogether. Thus, anti-psychiatry is often described today, very simply, as the 'negation of mental illness', or it is not even mentioned. Discourses once used by radical psychiatrists (or their supporters) and *anti*-anti-psychiatrists have converged. An alternative tactic is to blame anti-psychiatry for a whole series of failures within the mental health system as a whole. 'An anti-anti-psychiatry movement' has developed.[43] But both of these are ahistorical and incorrect formulations, straw men that are far too easy to knock down. Since the end of the 1970s, with some notable exceptions, the work of anti-psychiatrists and radical psychiatrists has been systematically misrepresented, ridiculed and/or excised from history.[44] Anti-psychiatry has

---

41   For a discussion of anti-psychiatry in a historical context see Nick Crossley, 'R. D. Laing and the British Anti-psychiatry Movement' and his *Contesting Psychiatry*, London: Routledge, 2006 (1998).

42   'Psychiatry and Anti-psychiatry in the United States' in Porter and Micale, eds, *Discovering the History of Psychiatry*, p. 416. 'Much anti-psychiatry has been primarily interested in the power and influence wielded by the psychiatric profession, not only over the mentally ill but over society as a whole. Opposition to psychiatry has often been part of a larger agenda in which mental patients are of incidental concern.'

43   Crossley, *Contesting Psychiatry*, p. 241.

44   For a sustained unpicking of misrepresentations of Laing see Samantha Bark, *Descandalizing Laing: R. D. Laing as a Social Theorist*, unpublished dissertation, Nottingham Trent University, 2009. This also seems to have happened to Basaglia in the English-speaking

become a term of abuse. The attack on the term 'anti-psychiatry' (from left and right) was so successful in undermining the legitimacy of the movement that those who had used the phrase in 1968 were already distancing themselves from it by the end of the next decade.

Basaglia himself had clearly lost patience with the term by the end of the 1970s. During a series of lectures in Brazil in 1979 he said:

> I am not an anti-psychiatrist because I don't believe in that type of intellectual. I am a psychiatrist who wants to give a different response to the patients from what they have had up to now . . . Those who say that mental illness does not exist . . . are imbeciles who do not have the courage to push to the limit the life that we live.[45]

This rejection has been mirrored by many historians of psychiatry, who have simply excised the anti-psychiatric movement altogether.[46]

Anti-psychiatry is something that is difficult to capture, or study, in today's world. At its peak, it was very much part of a mood, an eclectic movement, a Zeitgeist. It was also slippery, a slogan, a catch-all phrase, a way of pushing the envelope. It was as well, in part, an emotional reaction to a horrific system. The asylum and the way mentally ill patients were treated, and the way that sane people *were* often labelled as mentally ill, were clear examples for many of the most oppressive features of the capitalist system.

Asylums provided an institutional focus for political action. The ideas

---

world. But see also Donnelly, *The Politics of Mental Health in Italy*, and Kotowicz, *R. D. Laing and the Paths of Anti-psychiatry*, for good accounts of Basaglia, albeit largely based on secondary sources. Some of Basaglia's work has been translated into English; see Nancy Scheper-Hughes and Anne Lovell, eds, *Psychiatry Inside Out. Selected Writings of Franco Basaglia*, New York: Columbia University Press, 1987, but also 'Breaking the Circuit of Control' in David Ingleby, ed., *Critical Psychiatry. The Politics of Mental Health*, London: Penguin, 1981, pp. 84–92. There are numerous descriptions of Basaglia as an anti-psychiatrist: John Clay, 'Basaglia was an Italian anti-psychiatrist', from *R. D. Laing. A Divided Self*, London: Hodder and Staughton, 1996, p. 283, but also Ingleby, *Critical Psychiatry*, p. 17.

45   Ongaro and Giannichedda, *Conferenze brasiliane*, pp. 153 and 179.

46   Another way of rubbishing anti-psychiatry has been to expose its protagonists as morally reprehensible and/or 'professionally lax' in their private and professional lives. This is a tactic that has been used time and again with R. D. Laing and David Cooper.

that the mind could be freed, and that the system or the family drove people mad, and even that the sane were the ones who were actually mad, all quickly gained currency within the radical movements of the 1960s. Jervis wrote in 1968, 'The psychiatrists have not been at the service of power, but an integral part of power itself.'[47] Anti-psychiatrists were at the heart of these movements and currents of ideas. In 1967, the celebrated Dialectics of Liberation conference, held in the Roundhouse in Chalk Farm, North London, was organized by a small group of radical psychiatrists. R. D. Laing, Joseph Berke, Gregory Bateson and David Cooper were also key speakers at the event. The proceedings of the conference, edited by Cooper and published by Penguin, were soon to be seen on the shelves of most left-wing activists and were translated across the world. But every country had its own anti-psychiatric movement, with its own charismatic leaders and specific features, and often its own key texts and geographical sites. This was a truly transnational movement, with constant exchanges of ideas and people, collective publications and translations of key texts. Volunteers moved from country to country, and the anti-psychiatric movement also had extra-European links. Its tentacles reached far and wide, and its effects were long lasting. The struggle was not simply one between psychiatry and anti-psychiatry. A battle was going on within psychiatry itself, for the very soul of what the profession was meant to do, and how. As Jervis wrote in 1967, 'Psychiatry is in crisis, and as psychiatrists we no longer know what we are doing.'[48] This was also a clash over the very meaning of the terms that were being used. Anti-psychiatry itself was an umbrella under which bitter debates raged for years.

In Italy, with time, the simplistic and ahistorical 'negation of mental illness = anti-psychiatry' formula has taken root, especially with relation to Basaglia. Meanwhile, in the English-speaking world, Basaglia is often simply lumped in with Laing and Cooper and described as an anti-psychiatrist (usually in a negative sense). These two misinterpretations

---

47   'Giulio De Matteo' (pseud.), 'Una lezione di violenza', *Quaderni Piacentini* 7: 36, Nov. 1968, p. 78. Jervis later claimed that he was forced to adopt a pseudonym by Basaglia for this article, in Gilberto Corbellini and Giovanni Jervis, *La razionalità negata. Psichiatria e antipsichiatria in Italia*, Turin: Bollati Boringhieri, 2008, pp. 113–14.

48   This article followed a report from the Dialectics of Liberation Congress in London, which Jervis attended, 'Gli psichiatrici e la politica', *Quaderni Piacentini* 32, 1967, p. 20.

are two sides of the same coin. Both fail to recognize the original features of the Basaglian experience, and both tend to lose touch with the radical language and excitement of the movement at its height, in the late 1960s and through the 1970s. They are ahistorical formulations, abstracted from a sense of what really went on and how things changed over time.

So, can we rescue the term anti-psychiatry from these misinterpretations and negative uses? Some have tried to do so. Nick Crossley utilizes the term in his important work on the history and post-history of radical psychiatry in Britain for two reasons, first because 'anti-psychiatry was the label that stuck to the activities of Laing et al. in the 1960s and 1970s, whether they liked it or not', and also because it 'demarcates something of significance'.[49] Catherine Fussinger also keeps the term but sidesteps any discussion of its use and avoids providing any definition.[50] Zbigniew Kotowicz notes that 'the term "anti-psychiatry" has been criticized and rejected by almost everyone, including those that the term was meant to denote', yet adds, 'but although rejected, the term stuck'.[51] He claims that the term is still useable today because it is 'accurate', is often mentioned in the literature (a somewhat circular argument) and because 'no other term seems to quite fit . . . it highlights the "anti-" aspect of these thinkers', because 'they were all against establishment psychiatry or against establishment tout court'. So, many writers, especially those working in English, either use the term almost by default (in a positive sense, in the context of historical, sociological or philosophical studies) or in a negative sense, as a way of dismissing figures from that period.

Meanwhile, Double argues for the use of the term *critical psychiatry*, in order to 'avoid' the 'polarization' created by anti-psychiatry. For Double,

---

49   Crossley, *Contesting Psychiatry*, p. 2449.

50   Catherine Fussinger, 'Therapeutic Community. Psychiatry's Reformers and Anti-psychiatrists. Reconsidering Changes in the Field of Psychiatry After World War II', *History of Psychiatry* 22, 2011, pp. 146 and 160, n. 1.

51   Kotowicz, *R. D. Laing and the Paths of Anti-psychiatry*, p. 5.

The word 'anti-psychiatry' is not without meaning, but it does seem difficult to define precisely. Anti-psychiatry tends to be seen as a passing phase in the history of psychiatry . . . in this sense it was an aberration, a discontinuity with the proper course of psychiatry. However, it is difficult to accept there was no value in the approach and what may be more beneficial is to look for the continuities, rather than discontinuities, with orthodox psychiatry.[52]

So, given the relatively toxic nature of the term 'anti-psychiatry' today, especially with regard to the Basaglian experience and in the Italian context, I will use the terms *critical* or *radical* psychiatry in this book. This is not because I accept the equation 'anti-psychiatry = denial of the existence of mental illness'. When I do use the term 'anti-psychiatry', it will be in the sense underlined in this section, in view of its *historical* weight. However, these new terms (critical or radical psychiatry) fall down in one crucial area: they fail to capture the central sense in which the movement was *self-critical*, an attack on psychiatry itself, not merely a movement *within* that discipline for change (although it was *also* the latter). Hence, I will also use the term 'anti-psychiatry' in this book where I feel it is appropriate to the context. And, here, context is everything.

Institutions: The Asylum and the Family

Proponents of critical psychiatry usually took up very clear and radical stances with regard to traditional psychiatric institutions. Many called for the abolition or closure of *all* asylums as a matter of urgency (a position held publicly by Basaglia from the early to mid-1960s onwards), while at the same time working *within* asylums in order to reform or humanize them, or to display them either as examples of living hells or 'working utopias'. Others left the system altogether, such as the group around Laing in the UK. But radical psychiatrists disagreed about what was to replace asylums and about the tactics needed to achieve abolition. Some argued that patients should simply be released. For others it was essential that new institutions and institutional practices be created to

---

52   Double, 'Historical Persepectives on Anti-psychiatry', p. 38.

replace asylums, staffed by psychiatrists or without staff altogether. There were also attempts to deal with mental illness 'at source' – in society, within the family – a strategy which (in theory) would remove any need for asylums.[53] But there were further disputes over the causes of mental illness. French anti-psychiatrists developed a different strategy, known as institutional psychotherapy, which accepted the fact of an asylum-like institution (or clinic) and tried to run them in a radically different way, subverting them from within.[54] Others argued for institutional decentralization, *sectoral* reform, although this also implied that the asylum system itself would be preserved in some way.[55]

Critical psychiatry also linked in well with a set of radical critiques of another institution which came under fire in the late 1960s across the world: the family. The family was seen by many as the place where mental illness was created, or as the only setting within which it could be explained. Laing's research looked into the families of schizophrenics as much as it did into the schizophrenics themselves. In order to comprehend the mad, it was argued, we needed to look at the sane. Gregory Bateson's influential analysis of the 'double-bind' saw the family or family dynamics as the location for the understanding of the origins of schizophrenia.[56] Cooper wrote that

> most people who are called mad and who are socially victimized by virtue of that attribution (by being 'put away', being subjected to electric shocks, tranquillizing drugs, and brain-slicing operations, and

---

53   See Chapters 17 and 19 on the experiences in Perugia and Reggio Emilia. Kingsley Hall also aimed to prevent people either entering or returning to asylums.

54   Parts of this strategy had an influence on Basaglia and others interested in reform in Italy, although in the French case the idea of the asylum as a refuge, which developed during World War Two, was very different from the way many Italian radicals saw psychiatric hospitals. For radical psychiatry in France see Bourg, *From Revolution to Ethics,* pp. 125–37; and Postel and Allen, 'History and Anti-psychiatry in France', pp. 396–414; Germaine Le Guillant and Lucien Bonnafé, 'La condition du malade à l'hôpital psychiatrique', *Ésprit* 197, 1952 (Misère de la psychiatrie); Louis Le Guillant, Hubert Mignot, Lucien Bonnafé, *Problèmes posés par la chronicité sur le plan des institutions psychiatriques*, Masson et C éditeurs, 1964.

55   See for this strategy Balduzzi, *L'albero della cuccagna.*

56   Gregory Bateson et al., 'Towards a Theory of Schizophrenia', *Behavioral Science* 1, 1956, pp. 251–64, collected in Gregory Bateson, *Steps to an Ecology of Mind*, Chicago and London: University of Chicago Press, 2000, pp. 201–27; see also the whole of Part III, pp. 159–339.

so on) come from family situations in which there is a desperate need
to find some scapegoat . . . Most of the people about whom I shall be
writing in this volume . . . have been precipitated into the psychiatric
situation by others, usually their families.[57]

By escaping from the family unit, or creating alternatives to the traditional nuclear family (through leaving home, going 'on the road', gay
relationships and/or communes) people felt they could free themselves
from the possibly toxic effects of their own families.[58] For many young
people in the 1960s and 1970s, this became a necessity. They *had* to get
away, somehow. But the emptying of the asylums advocated by many
radical psychiatrists sometimes had the contradictory effect of pushing
ex-patients back into the family unit. This could make things worse,
possibly even lead to tragedy.

Critical psychiatry allowed for the liberation of the self, something
that again was crucial to the philosophy of 1968. By facing up to those
described as mentally ill, people were also obliged to look into their own
lives and question their own role in society. Distinctions were broken
down, in every sector of society. Relationships were central to the critical
psychiatry movement. These relationships changed everyone's lives,
including those of doctors, nurses and volunteers.

Critical psychiatry was never just about psychiatry. It associated mental
health with society, the family, the state and its institutions, and with
the psychiatric profession itself. As Basaglia made clear in *L'istituzione
negata*, 'Our anti-institutional and anti-psychiatric (that is, anti-spe-
cialist) struggle cannot remain within our own, specific, field of work.'[59]
Social and political change was necessary. On their own, psychiatrists

---

57   Cooper, *Dialectics of Liberation*, p. 7, and *Psychiatry and Anti-psychiatry*, 2001 (1967),
p. x. See also R. D. Laing, and A. Esterson, *Sanity, Madness and the Family. Families of
Schizophrenics*, London: Penguin, 1980 (1964).

58   For a study of the influence of these theories in an Italian provincial town in the 1960s
and 1970s see Sofia Serenelli Messenger, 'Il Sessantotto e la "morte della famiglia"? Storia di una
comune nella provincia anconetana' in Enrica Asquer et al., eds, *Famiglie del Novecento. Conflitti,
culture e relazioni*, Rome: Carocci, pp. 239–62; 'Il Sessantotto e la famiglia. Storia di una comune
nella campagna marchigiana 1976–1987', *Italia Contemporanea* 255, 2009, pp. 173–202; and
'Private 1968 and the Margins: The Vicolo Cassini's Community in Macerata, Italy', *Memory
Studies* 6: 1, 2013, pp. 91–104.

59   Basaglia, *L'istituzione negata* (1968), p. 7.

could do very little. They could expose the workings of the system, but real change would have to come from elsewhere.

Society and Politics

Strands of the movement outlined a strong link between mental illness and capitalism, both in terms of cause and effect and as an explanation for the asylum system. Basaglia himself introduced a social analysis of asylums, arguing that 'the mentally ill person is "ill" above all because he is excluded'.[60] He also drew heavily on Foucault's historical studies of the asylum system and Goffman's sociological account. Non-psychiatric texts were a key part of the anti-psychiatric canon.

Basaglia's social analysis of the asylum population, however, was not based on first-hand research of any kind, but rather on his practical experience in Gorizia (and other asylums).[61] Like Pier Paolo Pasolini's well-known articles about the so-called levelling processes introduced by Italy's consumer society, Basaglia's intuitions about the social nature of mental health were highly influential, but also subject to biting critiques from both within and outside the movement.[62] It *seemed obvious* that asylum inmates were mainly the poor, the dregs of society, the excluded, the deviant. Further texts produced from within the movement, in particular photographs, reinforced this impression. This kind of analysis was a powerful weapon in the struggle, a way of understanding the asylum system as an integral part of capitalism, a fusion of Marxism and critical psychiatry. Social divisions were also reproduced in the treatment reserved for rich and poor patients. It appeared clear that social class dictated the way mad people were diagnosed and cured by the health system.

Take, for example, this quote from the preface by Franco Basaglia and Franca Ongaro to Maxwell Jones's *Ideologia e pratica della psichiatria sociale*, published in 1970:

---

60   Ibid., p. 33.

61   As well as texts such as that by August Hollingshead and Fredrick Redlich, *Classi sociali e malattie mentali*, Turin: Einaudi, 1965 (original edition 1958).

62   See my critique of Pasolini in *Milan since the Miracle. City, Culture, Identity*, Oxford: Berg, 2001, pp. 19–36.

The madhouse in the paleocapitalist phase, the therapeutic community in the neocapitalist phase, mental health centres in the advanced capitalist phase – these institutional functions, which were born as innovatory technical features in a particular sector – limited themselves to cosmetic changes, and left structures intact: that is the economic and social organizations which created and shaped them and determined their very nature.[63]

The same piece claimed that patients inside asylums were part of a reserve army of labour. Basaglia's ideas, it should be noted, have not been subject to any serious critical research. They are often simply accepted as true (as with Pasolini). The slogan-title *Morire di classe* (translated literally as *Dying Because of Your Class*) is taken as read. But was it really true that the asylums were full of poor people? The simple answer is, we do not know. It certainly appeared that way (it also depended on what you were looking for), but the mad were not all poor by any means.[64]

A Movement Against, a Movement For?

What kind of movement was this, and how can we describe it? On the one hand, it was a movement of technicians, of psychiatrists and nurses (plus, with time, patients). In Italy, a key role would be played later on by sympathetic (and occasionally angry) local administrators – a new generation of politicians, most of whom were elected to positions of power in or after 1965. The movement as a whole has often been described as 'Basaglian', but it is more correct to use a term that can also take in other important aspects of experiences within and around Italian asylums from the 1960s onwards. Here it is useful to refer to the analysis of Edoardo Balduzzi, who uses the term 'anti-institutional movement'.[65] This shift allows us to understand the broad scope of the movement that

---

63   Now in Franco Basaglia, *Scritti. II. 1968-1980. Dall'apertura del manicomio alla nuova legge sull'assistenza psichiatrica*, ed. Franca Ongaro Basaglia, Turin: Einaudi, 1982, II, p. 119.

64   In addition, anti-psychiatry was a movement that led to the empowerment of patients, nurses, doctors and administrators. It connected or inspired a series of movements and organizations in the UK, Italy and elsewhere: Crossley, *Contesting Psychiatry*, Chapters 6–9.

65   Balduzzi, *L'albero della cuccagna*, p. 18.

was not linked exclusively to the Gorizia–Parma–Trieste historical axis that followed the personal journey of Franco Basaglia. We cannot understand the movement against asylums, or for asylum reform, without taking into account what happened in Perugia, Colorno and Materdomini, to cite only the most important examples. This was also an international movement, where texts circulated freely among the protagonists, activists and thinkers involved across various countries and in different sectors. Only by shifting the focus away a little from Basaglia himself can we understand the central role he played in the movement.

Was this a social and a political movement? To some extent it was, especially after 1968. Before 1968, the movement was confined to groups of intellectuals, psychiatrists, some administrators and politicians, and some academics, as well as, in a few isolated places, a minority of nurses and patients. After 1968, the movement expanded greatly, taking in students, workers, journalists and a disparate group of people attracted by the ideas and practice of critical psychiatry.

Young graduates and volunteers came to the sector in order to participate in the movement. The psychiatrists were still the leaders of the movement, in the main, but they now had a mass of followers with which to work, and to manage. We might attempt a simple (and simplistic) definition of this movement (in the Italian context) as follows: 'a movement within *and* against psychiatric hospitals which began in the early 1960s and eventually led to legislation in 1978 closing down all asylums'. This movement also benefitted from the spaces opened up by those interested in sectoral reform, decentralization and new forms of therapy.

On the one hand, this was a movement *against*. Its followers were opposed to psychiatric hospitals (sometimes in general, as a matter of principle, and sometimes in terms of the specific way they were run). It was *against* the psychiatric establishment, and often this slipped into a critique of psychiatry *tout court*. There was also opposition to forms of treatment used at the time for patients, especially the more degrading and painful methods, such as lobotomies and insulin therapy. Later on, electroshock therapy became a symbol of what had been wrong with the way psychiatric hospitals worked. Radical psychiatry also criticized prevailing definitions of madness (and sometimes any idea of madness at all), as well as the labelling of patients with certain

characteristics. Often, and increasingly, the critique of asylums was
extended to all total institutions run by the state, to capitalism itself,
and to the bourgeois family.

But this was also a movement *for*, where change could be creative and
positive. Radical psychiatrists argued for new forms of treatment for
those suffering from mental illness, and not just for the removal of old
systems of repression. They called not only for the closure of asylums,
but also for their replacement with new institutions and alternative path-
ways of treatment. The movement, in the meantime, tried to break down
status differences and hierarchies *inside* medical institutions, but also
within society as a whole. Often, this outlook entailed an entirely new
understanding of mental health and the mentally ill. Radical psychiatry
rewrote the rulebook *and* the textbook. It (re)formed a whole generation
of psychiatrists.

We might attempt a chronology of the movement. A key year was
1961, marking the slow beginnings of the Basaglian revolution in
Gorizia as well as the publication of a number of key texts. Discussions
over the future of asylums became mainstream in 1964. By 1965–66,
a number of crucial and linked events pushed the movement further:
the contact between Mario Tommasini in Colorno and Franco Basaglia
in Gorizia, the beginnings of general assemblies in Gorizia, the reforms
carried out by Sergio Piro in a private asylum in the south of Italy and
the election of a new generation of politicians in provincial elections
in a number of cities, some of whom quickly made asylum reform a
priority: Tommasini himself in Parma, Ilvano Rasimelli in Perugia.
This soon led to the beginnings of a more extensive reform movement,
with institutional and political support, in Perugia, which combined
aspects of anti-institutional analysis with a strong push towards decentralization. In 1967 and 1968, the movement reached a new level, with
the publication of *L'istituzione negata* (after connections were formed
between the Einaudi publishing house and Gorizia in 1966–68).
Reforms that year provided more space for asylums to change. After
1968, Basaglians and other reformers took up positions of power across
Italy. The student movements and the anti-institutional/anti-asylum
movements merged, allied and fed off each other. The next ten years
saw a strong push towards deinstitutionalization, decentralization and

political reform in the mental health sector. 1978 was the year of the 180 Law, and it then took twenty years of hard work to actually close down all the psychiatric hospitals in Italy.

Working or Concrete Utopias

In the 1960s and 1970s, the movement created a series of 'working', 'living' or 'concrete' utopias in order to experiment with alternative forms of care and spread the word about radical change. These were places where, it was argued, theory and practice would be welded together and which could inspire others. Nick Crossley has called these places 'physical embodiments of scientific theories'.[66] They were and to some extent still are (in historical terms, or thanks to memories which survive) 'sites for the reformation and reproduction of a movement *habitus*' which 'people visit . . . in order to learn how to practice differently, how to perceive, think and act in different ways'.[67] They also became (and in some cases remain) 'places of mass pilgrimage' which encouraged 'new ideas and practices', where the symbolic and the concrete work in tandem and 'spaces where the aspirations of the movement appear, to some degree, to have been realized'.[68] Gorizia and Kingsley Hall, in very different ways, were places that worked at a number of levels. On the one hand 'they excite and energize activists, symbolizing the feasibility of the hoped for future and lending meaning to struggle by embodying the dream'.[69] They generated networks 'that effective social movements presuppose. They are social capital generators.' And 'for activists they constitute proof of the veracity of critiques and proposed alternatives. Though, of course,

---

66 'R. D. Laing and the British Anti-psychiatry Movement', p. 885.

67 Nick Crossley, 'Working Utopias and Social Movements', *Sociology* 33: 4, 1999, p. 817, cited in Dora Garcia, *From Basaglia to Brazil*, p. 53.

68 Crossley, 'Working Utopias and Social Movements', pp. 811 and 822, *Contesting Psychiatry*, pp. 2852 and 3870. Scheper-Hughes and Lovell use the term 'practical utopia' in their 'Introduction. The Utopia of Reality. Franco Basaglia and the Practice of Democratic Psychiatry', in *Psychiatry Inside Out: Selected Writings of Franco Basaglia*, New York: Columbia University Press, 1987, p. 49. Franco Basaglia, 'L'utopia della realtà' in Basaglia, *Scritti, II*, pp. 339–48. Maria Grazia Giannichedda, *Introduzione*, in Franco Basaglia, *L'utopia della realtà*, ed. Franca Ongaro Basaglia, Turin: Einaudi, 2005, pp. xvi–lv.

69 Crossley, *Contesting Psychiatry*, p. 2855.

critics watch them closely in the hope of them providing refutations';
they are 'experimental' *and* 'pedagogic'.[70]

Working utopias existed before the age of anti-psychiatry. In fact, the
therapeutic communities at Dingleton in Scotland or in other parts of
the UK as well as experiments in France acted in similar ways for future
leaders of the movement. In this context they were 'physical embodiments of scientific theories'.[71]

Critical psychiatry managed to create a movement around a loose set of
ideas and slogans in the 1960s and 1970s. The movement was international but had national characteristics in each country where it took root,
as well as regional and local features. This was a movement that acted
(and began) within the world of psychiatry (psychiatrists, patients and
nurses, as well as medical students and potential psychiatrists) but also
spread out to the wider world. It mobilized students, journalists, film-
makers, artists, political activists and politicians in positions of power,
as well as those already working within institutions, and patients themselves. A 'space for new ideas and relationships to emerge' was often
created thanks to this movement.[72]

Yet the radical phase of the movement was short-lived, and the backlash was – and still is – extremely strong. Critical psychiatry has taken
the blame for a whole series of ills. It was widely acknowledged and is
constantly argued that things went too far. Even the leaders of the movements admitted defeat. Italy was the country where things went furthest,
and where national policy was tied up with the demands of critical
psychiatrists. The history of the movement in Italy is rich and complicated, shot through with controversies, alternating narratives and
long-running disputes. It is a hornet's nest, and all the more interesting
for that.

---

70   Ibid., p. 2861.
71   Crossley, 'R. D. Laing and the British Anti-psychiatry Movement', p. 885.
72   R. Eyerman and A. Jamison, *Social Movements: A Cognitive Approach*, Cambridge:
Polity, 1991, p. 60, cited in Crossley, 'R. D. Laing and the British Anti-psychiatry Movement',
p. 880.

THREE

Reading Gorizia: Sources and Narratives

'The actual history of the anti-institutional movement he led is not to be found in Basaglia's own writings . . . It must be reconstructed from numerous books and articles.'

Lovell and Scheper-Hughes[1]

I n her introduction to the new edition of *L'istituzione negata*, published by Baldini and Castoldi in 1998 after the rights were sold on from Einaudi, Franca Ongaro told a story of a failure – her own personal failure. In the beginning of the 1990s she had decided to look back at the Gorizian period in order to demonstrate that many of the later accusations against the Basaglia law were wrong. In doing so she had come to realize that

the deeper meaning of that 'institutional overturning' had, over the years, disappeared and had been reduced to a sterile if necessary debate between those who were for and those who were against a reform which appeared detached from the services it was designed to produce, and this meant that nothing was done in a practical sense.[2]

---

1 'Introduction. The Utopia of Reality: Franco Basaglia and the Practice of a Democratic Psychiatry' in Scheper-Hughes and Lovell, eds, *Psychiatry Inside Out*, p. 5.

2 Franca Ongaro Basaglia, 'Nota introduttiva alla nuova edizione' in Franco Basaglia, ed., *L'istituzione negata*, Milan: Baldini & Castoldi, 1998, pp. 1–2.

Ongaro had started to re-examine Gorizia. 'I didn't want to tell the story in the first person', she wrote. Instead she collected a series of writings which, 'chronologically, laid out what had happened'. But

> when the work was finished, I found myself faced with something that seemed dead: works, debates, judgements, speeches which were disconnected from the reality of those years, from the tiny things which changed bit by bit and the meaning they had.[3]

Something was missing.

> It was an account of an experience – critical and self-critical – which was lacking in the vitality, the physicality, the effort, the concrete contradictions, the anxiety, the problems, the emotions and the sense of relationships and connections . . . what was missing was the reality of life as it was lived in those years in Gorizia.[4]

For Ongaro, the here and now was what mattered. She wanted to (re) examine the past in order to inform the present, to finish what Franco Basaglia had started (something which became her mission in life after he died). Ongaro argued that there had been a series of mistaken or wilful misinterpretations of that past. It was time to make that past known to the present generations, the daily problems linked to the 'opening up' of that place, and how it had been possible to bring life back to those forgotten places and return so many people who had been cancelled out and 'disappeared' to life 'outside'. So Franca Ongaro gave up her attempt to recreate the past. *She simply waited for the books from that time to come out again.* Those books which, 'born during the time of struggle . . . and which registered, as it happened, discussions, judgements, reflections about those tiny, real things which were a sign of change. These were books', she wrote, 'which were alive'.[5] The history of Gorizia was difficult

---

3   Ibid., p. 2.

4   Ibid. For an account partly based on the 'reality of life as it was lived' in Gorizia see Alberta Basaglia, *Le nuvole di Picasso. Una bambina nella storia del manicomio liberato*, Milan: Feltrinelli, 2014.

5   Ongaro, 'Nota introduttiva alla nuova edizione', p. 3.

to tell, in part because it had already been told (though only partially) at the time.

It was not easy, therefore, to write about Gorizia, even (or perhaps especially) for someone who was there. Let us take another protagonist from the time, Agostino Pirella. In 1982, in a special issue of the periodical *Sapere* dedicated to Franco Basaglia, he wrote: 'It is so difficult to write about Franco Basaglia.'[6] Later in the same piece, he seemed to contradict himself. First he argued that 'the experience of Gorizia is too well known to be described', but then he went on to correct his own statement: 'Perhaps [Gorizia] has not been sufficiently debated.' Pirella concluded that 'this history has not been written, and we are all partly responsible for this state of affairs'.[7]

Most of the accounts we have of Gorizia from 1961 to 1972 are those of the équipe themselves, either thanks to memoirs and accounts written later, or those from the time. The secondary studies written by journalists, historians, sociologists and others are largely based on these internal narratives.[8] Central to all this are the two collective books published by the Gorizian équipe in the late 1960s: *What Is Psychiatry?* (1967) and *The Negated Institution* (1968). In addition, numerous journalists visited and wrote about Gorizia, especially during and after 1968, and their accounts were almost always sympathetic. As Pirella later wrote, 'I remember Michele Tito, Sergio Zavoli, Luciano Doddoli, Fabrizio Dentice, Giorgio Pecorini, Sesa Tatò, Carlo Rognoni.'[9]

This is not an ordinary list of journalists, but a group of extremely powerful professionals and intellectuals, some of whom would rise to positions of great influence (or already had done so in the late 1960s). By 1968, Basaglian ideas were reaching out to a wide readership, across

---

6   Agostino Pirella, 'Il giovane Basaglia e la critica della scienza' in *Sapere* 851, November–December 1982, p. 4.

7   Ibid., p. 8.

8   This is true of Mario Colucci and Pierangelo Di Vittorio's *Franco Basaglia* (Milan: Bruno Mondadori, 2001), for example, and of Oreste Pivetta's *Franco Basaglia. Il dottore dei matti* (Milan: Dalai Editore, 2012), but can be extended to most of the studies that deal with the Gorizia period in some way.

9   Agostino Pirella, 'E a Gorizia? Nascita di un'alternativa alla segregazione manicomiale', *Territorio. Bollettino* 10, November 1984, p. 33.

left-intellectual and the radical chic milieu in the press and even within the RAI television and radio services. Visitors and others quickly became converted to the Basaglian cause, carrying the word out to the wider world. An accepted version of the Basaglia story took hold. It was the version the Basaglians wished to portray, and it has largely held sway in the literature up to the present day.

Finally, we have the films by Pirkko Peltonen (1968), Michele Gandin (1967), Sergio Zavoli (1968) and Marco Turco (2010) (all made for television) and the photos of Gianni Berengo Gardin, Ferdinando Scianna, Mario Dondero and Carla Cerati and others. There are also reflections on the Gorizian experience in the books that have been published about Basaglia's life and work.[10]

Beyond the first-hand accounts and images, much of the research on Basaglia and Gorizia has concentrated on his theories, philosophy and ideas. This has meant that many of the accounts of Gorizia tend to be circular and repetitive.[11] This circularity of internal sources has also meant that there is a standard Gorizia story, which has been told and retold in various formats.

This book is not about the private lives of its protagonists. However, in a study of psychiatry, set in a period when the personal was political, it would be ridiculous and wrong to ignore the personalities, relationships and psychological traits of the people who appear in this story. This becomes even more important when we think about Basaglian

---

10   Above all in Colucci and Di Vittorio, *Franco Basaglia*, especially pp. 75–232, and in many sections of Pivetta, *Franco Basaglia*. Valeria Babini's *Liberi tutti. Manicomi e psichiatri in Italia. Una storia del novecento*, Bologna: Il Mulino, 2009, contains an extended analysis of the Gorizian experience.

11   The classic accounts of the Gorizian experiment were all written largely by the équipe themselves. There are the two collective books on Gorizia, *What Is Psychiatry?* and *The Negated Institution*. Then there are Basaglia's own reflections, both during his time at Gorizia, and in the years that followed. Some of these were published posthumously. In addition, we have the writings of Franca Ongaro Basaglia in various interventions, interviews and written accounts. The same is true of other members of the core équipe or volunteers: Lucio Schittar, Giorgio Antonucci, Domenico Casagrande, Agostino Pirella, Letizia Comba Jervis. Antonio Slavich's account was left unpublished when he died, but there are plans to publish this work, which will be of great importance. Giovanni Jervis often returned to Gorizia in his writings and interviews, and his most complete account of that period was written as part of a long semi-autobiographical introduction to a collection of his essays, published in 1977, *Il buon rieducatore*.

philosophy, which underlined the need to create a close personal relationship between doctors and patients.

In 1977, Giovanni Jervis provided a different account of Gorizia, setting himself up at the same time as an alternative (perhaps *the* alternative) critical historian/narrator of the movement. But this version has usually been excluded from official or Basaglian accounts, and is rarely even cited. The concentration on Basaglia's ideas and writings in order to tell the Basaglia story has also meant that the historical details about Gorizia are rather vague. *Nobody has written a history of what happened there.* The Gorizia narrative is well known, but critical and new approaches towards it have been rare. There are also lots of gaps in this story. In truth, we know very little about Gorizia beyond what the Gorizians told us.

Moreover, most of the accounts we have are Basagliacentric. Generally the story is told in this way: Franco Basaglia had some original ideas, he applied them and then he moved on and applied them somewhere else. (There is also very little material on Gorizia itself after 1969; this story follows Basaglia.) Contemporary accounts play down the collective aspects of the Gorizia story (often excluding Franca Ongaro) and tend to ignore the other members of the équipe, the patients and the nurses. Exceptions to this are two works not translated into Italian: a Brazilian doctoral thesis and a fascinating Belgian study.[12]

Most of the accounts we have from Gorizia are therefore circular, limited, insular and top-down. They rarely tell the story from the point of view of the citizens of Gorizia at the time and afterwards, the patients, the nurses, the non-Basaglian doctors, the local politicians or the administrators. The Basaglians wrote the history of their movement, and this history has been taken forward in a subjective and partial way. It is a

---

12   Michel Legrand, *La psichiatrie alternative italienne*, Toulouse: Editions Private, 1988, and Maria Stella Brandão Goulart, 'De profissionais a militantes: a Luta Antimanicomial dos psiquiatras italianos nos anos 60 e 70', Universidade Federal de Minas Gerais, Tese de Doutorado, Belo Horizonte Maio de 2004. It is interesting that Legrand's research was never translated into Italian. There is also an 'anti-Basaglian' bibliography, both from within psychiatry and on the left/anti/non-psychiatry wing of the movement. Elena Trivelli, *Assembling Memories and Affective Practices around the Psychiatric History of Gorizia: The Study of a Remembering Crisis*, unpublished Ph.D., Department of Media and Communications, Goldsmiths University, 2013.

standard story which has rarely deviated from that laid down in the late 1960s or been subject to serious historical research.

These accounts thus became the main sources for what happened and how to analyse it, and were often simply cited or translated into other media – film, journalism, documentaries. This is not to say that the Basaglian account was acritical on its own terms. One of the main features of Basaglian thought was the sense that everything was fair game, but even this critical approach was quite tightly controlled. What we do not have are the details, a sense of the story that goes beyond the canonical texts, a view from outside the core group. Gorizia has not been subjected to any kind of serious research, so much so that even the key facts (when people arrived, when they left, the numbers of patients, the arrival and departure of nurses) are difficult to ascertain and often contradictory. The *way* the story has been told has also affected the story that has been told.

A further repercussion of this standard way of telling the tale is that other key experiences, from Perugia to Varese to Nocera Inferiore to Naples to Colorno itself (without Basaglia) have often been ignored or simply reduced to a footnote. This is also true to an extent of the fate of the Basaglian diaspora. Antonio Slavich's activities in Ferrara have led to very little research, for example, as has Lucio Schittar's work in Pordenone. There is more available on Pirella's time in Arezzo and Jervis's period in Reggio Emilia, but it is the Gorizia–Trieste–Basaglia story that dominates. Even the terms used are problematic. Originally, this book was to be called 'A History of the Basaglian Movement'. But as the work has moved on, it has become increasingly clear that this is an incorrect way of describing what happened. A more clumsy term has had to be used – the anti-asylum movement, critical or radical psychiatry, anti-institutionalism. Paradoxically, one of the results of this work about Franco Basaglia has been the repositioning of Basaglia's own role in the movement.

FOUR

Basaglia and the British:
A Missing Translation?

The history, biography and practice of Franco Basaglia and the movement he partly led and inspired has, with a few exceptions, been consistently misinterpreted in the English-speaking world (and in particular in the UK).[1] Let us take, for example, the judgements of two of the leading historians of madness and asylums. In 2002 Roy Porter wrote this: 'In Italy, leadership of the movement was assumed by the psychiatrist Franco Basaglia, who helped engineer the rapid closure of institutions (chaos resulted)'.[2] In 1994 Porter referred to Basaglia as 'Enrico Basaglia' and labelled him a 'boisterous anti-psychiatrist'.[3] Andrew Scull's judgement on Basaglia was similarly brief, in 2010: 'In Italy, led by the charismatic Franco Bassaglia [sic.], the political left led the charge'.[4]

The origins of these snap and inaccurate judgements lie in several

---

1   One exception is Shulamit Ramon, ed., *Psychiatry in Transition. The British and Italian Experiences*, London: Pluto, 1988.

2   Roy Porter, *Madness. A Brief History*, Oxford: Oxford University Press, 2002, p. 210.

3   Roy Porter and Mark Micale, 'Introduction. Reflections on Psychiatry and Its Histories',' in Mark Micale and Roy Porter, eds, *Discovering the History of Psychiatry*, New York and Oxford: Oxford University Press, 1994, p. 20.

4   Andrew Scull, *Madness. A Very Short Introduction*, Oxford: Oxford University Press, 2011, p. 113. A more balanced and well-informed account (with some errors) can be found in Tom Burns, *Our Necessary Shadow. The Nature and Meaning of Psychiatry*, London: Allen Lane, 2013, pp. xlvi, 148–9, 183. However, even here, Basaglia is described as a 'Gramscian Marxist'.

areas. First, Basaglia's work was not translated in English, including (and most importantly) *L'istituzione negata*. This book was, however, quickly translated with success into German, French and numerous other languages. There are no convincing explanations of this non-translation, although there are various accounts available.[5] The non-translation of *L'istituzione negata* became something of an issue for the ex-équipe and perhaps, in particular, for Basaglia. They wanted to have an influence in the English-speaking world, a world that had been an inspiration for them and their practice.

Basaglia's writings and those of the équipe were only translated into English in piecemeal fashion and usually in hard-to-find or largely academic publications, and often well after the events described in his work had taken place. The Scheper-Hughes and Lovell collection/study is from 1987, and a short and much-quoted article appeared in David Ingleby's *Critical Psychiatry* in the early 1980s.[6] The lack of a translation of *L'istituzione negata* was especially important. It was the central text of the movement, and it had been influential in Germany and France. English-speaking readers were never given the chance to read it. Second, Basaglia was the subject of a series of extremely hostile but influential studies in English in the 1980s in the wake of the Basaglia law and debates in the UK about the closure of asylums, as well as the backlash against anti-psychiatry.[7] These articles then led directly to critical comments on Basaglia and the Basaglia law in important books about psychiatric reform and the meaning of mental illness, particularly in the light of attempts to regain the ground lost to R. D. Laing and the anti-psychiatry movement.

---

5   Some claim that R. D. Laing himself blocked a translation, but I have found no evidence to back up this claim; see F. A. Jenner, 'On the Legacy of Ronald Laing', janushead.org.

6   Scheper-Hughes and Lovell, eds, *Psychiatry Inside Out*; Franco Basaglia, 'Breaking the Circuit of Control' in David Ingleby, ed., *Critical Psychiatry: The Politics of Mental Health*, Harmondsworth: Penguin, 1981, pp. 184–92. Other bits and pieces of Basaglia's work were translated over the years; see for example 'What Is Psychiatry?', *International Journal of Mental Health* 14: 1–2, 1985, pp. 42–51. See also the short piece in Ramon, *Psychiatry in Transition*, 'Crisis and Identity: Extracts from the Theory of Franco Basaglia. Selected by Maria Grazia Giannichedda', pp. 252–60.

7   Kathleen Jones and Alison Poletti, 'Understanding the Italian Experience', *British Journal of Psychiatry* 146, 1985, pp. 341–7. See also Kathleen Jones and Alison Poletti, 'The Mirage of a Reform', *New Society* 70: 1137, 4 October 1984.

A striking example of this kind of analysis can be found in Martin Roth and Jerome Kroll's *The Reality of Mental Illness* (1986).[8] This book was intended as a rejoinder to anti-psychiatrists and was widely read at the time, and it would appear to be the source for some of the snap and dismissive judgements made by Porter and Scull. Roth and Kroll appeared unaware that Basaglia had died in 1980 when they wrote that 'Basaglia is a Marxist'.[9] They went on to argue that Basaglia's analysis of mental illness was 'ideologically driven and very naïve and, in a sense, very callous'. Basaglia was accused in no uncertain terms of throwing asylum inmates onto the streets for political reasons, and the 180 Law was described as a 'disaster', in social and human terms. The conclusion was that mental patients were 'exploited . . . as pawns in an ideological struggle'.[10] Roth and Kroll ended their comments by giving their support to moves to repeal the 180 Law.

Roth and Kroll's trenchant criticism takes its cue, in turn, from a notorious article published by Jones and Poletti in the *British Journal of Psychiatry* in 1985. This article was six pages long and led to a major debate in the journal, including a flurry of critical letters.[11] In this piece, Jones and Poletti set out to analyse what they called the 'Italian experience'. They defined this as the implementation of the 1978 law and made only perfunctory reference to what had happened before that date. The only Basaglian text examined in any detail was a talk he had given in the UK in 1979. The authors claimed that the passing of the 180 Law had been seen as one of the 'great success stories of psychiatric history' in the UK, and that they wanted to present a more balanced picture. Their study was based upon research into published sources and a study tour of Italy in 1984. On this tour they had visited a series

---

8   Cambridge: Cambridge University Press, 1986.

9   Ibid., p. 17.

10   Ibid., pp. 23–4.

11   Jones and Poletti, 'Understanding the Italian Experience'. The articles were heavily criticized by the Italians. Franco Rotelli called the original article 'comic', in 'Changing Psychiatric Services in Italy' in Ramon, *Psychiatry in Transition*, p. 190, n. 4. Benedetto Saraceno dubbed the series of articles as 'sinister', in 'La "Distorsion Anglaise". Remarques sur la réception de la pensée de Franco Basaglia', *Les Temps Modernes* 67: 668, April–June 2012, p. 56, n. 5. Saraceno explains this process through the resistance of Anglo-Saxon psychiatry to phenomenological and existential thought.

of mental health institutions, 'chosen at random'. They claimed that the 180 Law had lost support and was due to be repealed (as I write, in 2015, this has not happened).

The analysis was blunt, to say the least. Basaglia, once again, was described as an 'anti-psychiatrist'. Jones and Poletti then went on to tell their readers about Basaglia's homeland. 'Italy', they wrote,

> is not like any other country in western Europe: it is a narrow and mountainous peninsula, nearly 800 miles long, stretching from Europe towards Africa, its northern borders guarded by the Alps. European ideas seep slowly into such a country, and Trieste, on the Gulf of Venice, is one of the few cities where they might be expected, for purely geographical reasons, to flourish.

Three somewhat random 'Italian' traits were then examined. The final part of the article considered what the authors called 'the negative effects' of the law.[12]

It is beyond the scope of this book to examine in detail the effects of the 1978 law. However, what is interesting for us, here, is the way in which the Basaglia law was blamed for a whole series of problems on the basis of flimsy evidence, and that part of this blame was transferred back to the ideas and practice of Basaglia himself. But this was at least nuanced to some degree. As Jones and Poletti wrote,

> A third reason [for the failures of the 180 Law] is a possible confusion between the thought of Franco Basaglia, the current aims of Psichiatria Democratica, the intention of Law 180, and the outcome. The politico-social theory, the pressure-group campaign, the legislative provision and the state of the services seven years later are causally and temporally linked, but not identical. Basaglia, who cared about the condition of his patients, might have taken a very different view in 1985 if he had lived.[13]

---

12   This section involved a series of somewhat random quotes from the press, many of which had their titles misspelt.

13   Jones and Poletti, 'Understanding the Italian Experience', p. 347.

Jones and Poletti's 1985 article led to something of an outcry, and they were forced into a clarifying article in 1986. This involved further trips to Italy, and this time they visited Trieste. In this second article, the picture they painted was detailed and positive (about Trieste). But they also argued that the hospital had not really been closed at all and questioned the real content of services in the city.[14]

There was wide-ranging debate among practitioners, activists and researchers in the UK about the Basaglian experience and especially about the impact of the 180 Law, with both positive and negative evaluations of the Italian case, but only one side of this debate appears to have been picked up by many commentators. It is not true that reaction in the UK to the law and its aftermath was universally negative, but it does seem to be the case that the negative aspects and arguments have survived the debate, while the other points and discussions have been forgotten or marginalized. Thus, it becomes possible that Basaglia can be simply dismissed as an anti-psychiatrist and his reforms equally dismissed as simply leading to 'chaos'. While it is clear that many activists and practitioners were inspired by the Basaglian experience, and especially by Trieste, the historical discussions that have followed have not, with very few exceptions, taken this into account.[15] The lack of key texts in English, especially *L'istituzione negata* and *What Is Psychiatry?*, certainly impoverished the debate that took place.

These comments and the focus of the discussion probably led to the

---

14   Kathleen Jones and Alison Poletti, 'The "Italian Experience" Reconsidered', *British Journal of Psychiatry* 148, 1986, pp. 144–50. See also Shulamit Ramon, 'Understanding the Italian Experience', *British Journal of Psychiatry* 14, 1985, pp. 208–9; Michele Tansella, 'Community Psychiatry without Mental Hospitals: The Italian Experience: A Review', *Journal of the Royal Society of Medicine* 79, 1986, pp. 664–9; Shulamit Ramon, 'The Italian Psychiatric Reform' in S. P. Mangen, ed., *Mental Health Care in the European Community*, London: Croom Helm 1985, pp. 170–203; Simon Lovestone, 'Community Care, Italian Style', *British Medical Journal* 297: 6655, 22 October 1988, pp. 1042–3, and 'Misunderstanding the Italian Experience', *British Journal of Psychiatry* 147, 1985, pp. 450–2.

15   One exception is the work of Nick Crossley, who details the impact of many UK activists in particular of Trieste and Basaglia's legacy in *Contesting Psychiatry*, London: Routledge, 2006, pp. 3824–943. Crossley argues that Basaglia and his movement provided an inspiration to a whole series of social movements (in particular those involving patients) that developed in the 1970s and 1980s in the UK. Trieste became a 'working utopia' and was visited by many campaigners and activists.

lapidary and dismissive conclusions by Porter and Scull. This book is, in part, an attempt to correct this interpretation, and provide the Basaglian movement with historical background and content from the period *before* the 1978 law was passed.[16]

Back in Gorizia in the early 1960s, Basaglia needed help to break through the isolation he had imposed upon himself, and his first step was to try and create a group of like-minded allies. Over time, he slowly built up a team – an équipe. The idea of working in a group, collectively, was alien to the traditional and ultra-hierarchical world of Italian psychiatry, but crucial to many of the experiments going on elsewhere, such as those in France (hence the term 'équipe') and the UK. The formation of the équipe was a gradual process, which took years and led to a series of bitter struggles with local doctors, politicians and administrators.

---

16 There is also a consistent strand of anti-Basaglia literature in the academic world (outside of medical academia). For example, Lola Romanucci-Ross and Laurence Tancredi in *When Law and Medicine Meet. A Cultural View*, Springer, 2007, describe the 180 Law and the Basaglia movement as an 'experiment which failed' and a 'great cultural error', p. 11.

FIVE

Building the Team:
The First Équipe in Gorizia, 1961–69

'It all began with a "no".'

Franca Ongaro[1]

'We would meet every day, and often twice a day, and our discussions led to a constant flow of ideas and proposals.'

Giovanni Jervis[2]

'The "Gorizian group" was idealized by its supporters as politically homogeneous (which it never was) and it became linked to "anti-psychiatric" formulas which were rather simplistic.'

Giovanni Jervis[3]

The photo is probably from 1967. It is of a small room in Gorizia, inside the psychiatric hospital. There are seven people sitting in a circle around a small table. Six of them are men, all wearing suits. One is smoking a pipe. To the left is the leader, Franco Basaglia, hands in his pockets. He is laughing. This is a rare shot of the

---

1 Franca Ongaro, 'Nota introduttiva' in Franco Basaglia, ed., *L'istituzione negata* (1998), p. 3.

2 Giovanni Jervis, *Il buon rieducatore*, p. 25.

3 Ibid.

core Gorizian équipe: a group that would become celebrated and famous in 1968.

The 'Gorizians'[4]

Franco Basaglia: 1961–69*
Franca Ongaro: 1961–69
Antonio Slavich: 1962–69
Lucio Schittar: 1965*–69
Agostino Pirella: 1965–71
Domenico Casagrande: 1965–72
Leopoldo Tesi: 1962–68, 1969*[5]
Giorgio Antonucci: 1969–70*
Maria Pia Bombonato: 1962–66
Giovanni Jervis: 1966–69
Letizia Comba Jervis: 1966–69

The idea of working collectively, in a *team*, was central to the Basaglian project in Gorizia right from the start. The équipe took shape in Gorizia over the whole 1961–68 period. People came and went in those years, but the core, historic équipe was in place by 1967 and oversaw the most fertile and exciting phase in the life of the 'overturning' hospital, with the production of Gorizia's two collective books. The équipe was a kind of extended family. In some ways, it was *more* than a family. During the heightened years of the late 1960s, it was not unusual for members of the équipe to spend more time with each other than with their own children. Gorizia was and is a small city, and the whole équipe lived within a short distance of each other.

The équipe was a place of continual discussion inside and outside of meetings. It was marked by agreements and riven at times by disagreements, factions and debate, hierarchies and counter-hierarchies, but also

---

4   I have placed an * where I am unsure about the dates of arrival or departure.

5   Tesi however states that he arrived 'soon after Basaglia' in Libero Bestighi et al., eds, *Specialista in relazioni umane. L'esperienza professionale di Edelweiss Cotti*, Bologna: Pendragon, 2001, p. 189.

by unity, loyalty and a strong collective sense of a radical mission. Gorizia itself, its form, its political set-up, its morphology, helped to create a siege mentality, which reinforced the unity of the équipe, especially in its dealings with the outside world. The équipe moved as a group, from the hospital to Basaglia's flat in the centre of the city. They were like aliens in Gorizia, and seen as such by many locals.

The acknowledged leader of the équipe was, of course, Franco Basaglia. He created the équipe from scratch and formed it in his own image. Nobody could join without his assent, and most (if not all) of its members were directly recruited by him. He also exercised control over the status of his colleagues. Nonetheless, he was never in *total* control, and from late 1966 onwards he had a serious challenger for the intellectual and political leadership of the entire group: Giovanni Jervis.

People joined the équipe in various ways, and with different levels of experience. Some were colleagues or associates of Basaglia from his time as an academic (Slavich); some had family or local connections (Casagrande, Schittar); some were like-minded psychiatrists from other institutions (Pirella). Others arrived as volunteers, or as young graduates (such as, in different ways, Tesi, Bombonato and Antonucci[6] – but these three were not really part of the core équipe and did not contribute to collective publications). Finally, Giovanni Jervis and Letizia Comba came to Gorizia as a couple and on their own initiative, offering a direct link with the Einaudi publishing house. They were thus different to many of the others, and this distinction was to mark their relationship with Basaglia and the rest of the équipe.[7]

The time in Gorizia was a prolific and creative period for the entire équipe. As well as their daily and exhausting work in the hospital, many members were involved in other related activities – writing, translating, collaborative work with publishers, meetings and the collective production of two books about Gorizia, political activism of various kinds. Looking back, it is sometimes difficult to believe that the members of the Gorizian équipe had any time to eat or sleep.

---

6   Clarissa Brigidi, 'Intervista a Giorgio Antonucci su l'antipsichiatria. I Parte', centro-relazioni-umane.antipsichiatria-bologna.net.

7   Jervis and Basaglia were in correspondence with each other from 1965 onwards, and already on good terms (Archivio Basaglia).

The équipe was built up gradually, and it contained a mix of qualified psychiatrists, volunteers, family members and others. It also changed over time. There were at least two specific équipes, one that created the core of the therapeutic community and put together *L'istituzione negata*, and a second équipe that was formed after 1968–69. Before we move onto the therapeutic community itself, we need to introduce the individual members of the équipe. There is only one place to start here: very close to home, with Franco Basaglia's wife, Franca Ongaro.

i. Franca Ongaro (1961–69)

'He is an irrational man with a high level of imagination, and I have become a very logical person. I think that I built myself, in a way, as complementary to him – given that I believed in what he was doing and what he thought because that which he did corresponded with me.'

Franca Ongaro[8]

'At the end of the day I was there all the time.'

Franca Ongaro[9]

'[Franco Basaglia] lived in a splendid house with two children and his beautiful and intelligent wife, Franca Ongaro, who played the role of his secretary and wrote his articles for him.'

Giovanni Jervis[10]

'Now that my long struggle with and against the man who I loved is over, I know that every word written over the years was the result of an endless discussion with him, to understand, and to make myself understood, and sometimes there was a dialogue.'

Franca Ongaro[11]

---

8   Franco Basaglia, Franca Ongaro Basaglia, Agostino Pirella, Salvatore Taverna, *La nave che affonda. Psichiatria e antipsichiatria a dieci anni da 'L'istituzione negata'. Un dibattito*, Rome: Savelli, 1978, p. 98.

9   Ibid., p. 97.

10   Jervis, *Il buon rieducatore*, p. 20.

11   This section is called 'Congedo' (the taking of leave/discharge), in Franca Basaglia

The first and most faithful member of the Basaglian équipe was Franca Ongaro (who was also known, at various times, as Franca Ongaro Basaglia and Franca Basaglia). Franca Ongaro was an elegant, beautiful woman who wore her hair short, and she became something of a feminist icon for many in the 1970s. She was strong, independent and a powerful personality, a relatively equal partner in a marriage with a famous and charismatic husband. Yet, she also lived in his shadow, never receiving full acknowledgement of her role in his success or in the movement as a whole. She is not present in the équipe photo taken (probably) in 1967. They were inseparable throughout their lives together, but their union was not without its tensions. In fact, their differences and those very tensions provided some of the spark for the most powerful and influential work they wrote as a couple.

Franca was there in Gorizia right from the start, and throughout. She gave up her own work as a writer[12] in order to throw herself into the struggle, and this would become her life's mission, despite having two small children to look after in the early years. Yet Franca Ongaro was not an official part of the équipe and was never employed inside the hospital itself (or in fact, in any asylum).[13] She nevertheless became part of the équipe in a clear if unofficial sense, was central to the publications linked to the Gorizian experiment, was often in the hospital and participated in all the discussions about strategy.

Franca and Franco met in Venice when she was just seventeen, in 1945. Franca had been a brilliant school student but family circumstances had prevented her going to university. She was forced to work as a typist for a big electricity company. Franca had literary ambitions and wrote various children's stories for *Il Corriere dei Piccoli* in the 1950s and 1960s. Her proposals for books were turned down by various publishers.[14] She was constantly at her husband's side in the Gorizian period. But this was not just another example of the clichéd idea of

Ongaro, *Una voce. Riflessioni sulla donna*, Milan: Il Saggiatore, 1980, p. 147.

12   She had published various stories, some of which were illustrated by Hugo Pratt, a childhood friend and later a celebrated illustrator.

13   She had not trained as a psychiatrist and did not attend university apart from a brief period in Trento in the late 1960s. Ongaro is occasionally described as a 'sociologist' in some publications but she never graduated.

14   Some of her letters from this period are in the Einaudi Archive.

support from within the family. Franca was always a key part – *the* essential component and instrument – of Franco Basaglia's writing process and his theoretical and political development. In fact, she was as much if not more responsible for their written output as he was. She physically 'wrote' *all* of their articles (and many of their letters) and books from the Gorizian period onwards, although later pieces were sometimes written in a different way.[15] Franca also penned articles that were not jointly attributed. She contributed her own pieces to both *What Is Psychiatry?* and *The Negated Institution*, and translated key texts such as Goffman's *Asylums*. Moreover, she was one of those who signed the famous resignation letter of the équipe in 1972, the moment that officially closed the Basaglian experience in Gorizia.

After 1969, things changed. Franca settled back in Venice with their two children, while Franco moved on to other asylums. She remained a key figure and was a constant presence in Colorno and in Trieste throughout the 1970s, but she was never as central to the movement as she had been in Gorizia.

She was not an active part of the feminist movement, but she played an important symbolic role. For example, in 1977, she wrote the introduction to a text that was a key part of the feminist Zeitgeist in Italy, *Processo per stupro* (Rape Trial).[16] Franca was also part of the key link to Giulio Bollati and Einaudi. As the person who did the actual writing, she was in constant contact with Bollati during the production of a series of books, from *The Negated Institution* onwards. Her strong friendship with Bollati mirrored that between Basaglia himself and the editor.

It is worth spending a little time to try and unpick the process behind the joint authorship of the Basaglias. Franco Basaglia's ideas and thought processes were eclectic and rich, but often confused and sometimes baffling. Franca would bring them shape and narrative, although their work

---

15 It is not clear if this was also true of Basaglia's more academic output from 1953–61.

16 The book told the story of a rape trial in the south of Italy which also became the subject of a documentary that shocked the nation, *Processo per stupro*, transmitted by Italian TV in 1979 (60 minutes, director Loredana Rotondo). The book came out in 1980: Maria Grazia Belmonti et al., *Un processo per stupro. Dal programma della Rete 2 della televisione italiana*, Preface by Franca Ongaro Basaglia, Turin: Einaudi, 1980.

was often obscure in style and fragmentary in form. It is clear that the two usually wrote together. Their individual pieces are different from their joint publications. Franca Ongaro's later work does not have the spark or levels of complexity of their collective publications from the late 1960s and 1970s, and Franco Basaglia's earlier articles are far more academic in style, *before* Gorizia. Franco Basaglia's natural disorder and flurry of ideas were brought into line and put down on the page by Franca. This was never easy or straightforward. There were constant discussions between the two over every word.

This appears to be what happened with the collective writing of the Basaglias, from *What Is Psychiatry?* onwards. First, the two would discuss what they were doing, at some length. Franca would take notes and type up a draft. This version would then be re-discussed, again at length. Finally, a new version would be produced, and typed up once more by Franca. In no way could this procedure be described as simple dictation. If anything, most of the writing was hers, not his. But they each brought different things to the process. Franco never wrote about this process, and Franca left us with just one fascinating quote (cited at the beginning of this section) about her 'long struggle with and against' the man she loved. Their letters, too, were collective, constructed as a dialogue, spontaneous. She was also one of the few people who could actually read Franco's handwriting (which he used when he really did write something alone).

Critical work on Basaglia has usually downplayed Franca Ongaro. Sometimes she has been discounted altogether. On other occasions she is dismissed as a mere typist, or even as a kind of glorified secretary. Michele Zanetti calls her 'his valuable collaborator'.[17] This is despite the fact that most of their work is jointly signed. Critics have tended to

---

17   Francesco Parmigiani and Michele Zanetti, *Basaglia. Una biografia*, Trieste: Lint Editorial, 2007, p. 32: 'the main collaborator with Franco Basaglia'. Other examples include: Saverio Luzzi, *Salute e sanità nell'Italia repubblicana*, Rome: Donzelli, 2004, p. 333, n. 2. Ongaro was not at all religious, although Valeria Babini refers to her as a 'believer' in *Liberi tutti. Manicomi e psichiatri in Italia. Una storia del novecento*, Bologna: Il Mulino, 2009, pp. 267–8. Babini also describes Franca Ongaro as 'his companion in all his institutional battles', p. 267. See also the special issue of *Fogli d'informazione* after the award of an honorary degree to Franca Ongaro Basaglia from the University of Sassari, 29: 188, January–February 2001. However, apart from some sections of the introductory text by Maria Grazia Giannichedda, there is very little on Franca herself in this volume.

ignore this acknowledged joint authorship completely, or confine any mention of it to a condescending footnote. In general, *their* [the Basaglias'] body of work is normally attributed, at least in terms of the substance of the analysis, to Franco alone. In some ways this tendency was self-created. The posthumously published *Scritti* are interesting in this regard,[18] and the assignation of *The Negated Institution* as 'edited by Franco Basaglia' was a key moment. Moreover, as we have noted, Franca was never an official (employed) part of the équipe either in Gorizia or Trieste, and was far less present physically in the latter city after returning to Venice in 1969. She did set up an institution in Venice in the 1970s called the 'Centro Critica della Istituzioni',[19] but its initial fervour quickly faded, and few of its ambitious plans for publications, activities and research projects came to fruition.

In many ways, Franca Ongaro really came into her own after the shock of Franco's death in 1980. She was twice elected to the Italian Senate as an independent left candidate (1984–91) and worked tirelessly for the full implementation of the 1978 law while campaigning against the numerous attempts at counter-reform. She also continued to publish books and articles under her own name after 1980, as well as editing the two volumes of Basaglia's *Scritti* published by Einaudi. Her own output of texts and introductions was prolific, and she travelled up and down the country and across the world campaigning for psychiatric reform up until her death.

It is striking how those who have written about Franca Ongaro very rarely provide any personal information or even anecdotes about her life. The obituaries after her death in 2005 were largely dry and factual, providing little that could not be gleaned from already available biographical notes. One exception to this rule was Massimo Cacciari, who spoke at Franca's funeral in 2005. But even then, that one (albeit

---

18   The posthumous works tend to be assigned to Franco, almost as if they were monuments to him from his widow. More specifically, the covers carry just the name 'Basaglia', while the inside cover has the sole author of the pieces as Franco Basaglia. Overall, however, the two volumes are edited by Franca Ongaro Basaglia.

19   Which was also known as '*Critica delle Istituzioni*'. *Centro Internazionale di Studi e Ricerche*. Franco Basaglia and Franca Ongaro Basaglia, eds, *Crimini di pace. Ricerche sugli intellettuali e sui tecnici come addetti all'oppressione*, Milan: Baldini Castoldi Dalai, 2009 (Einaudi, 1975), p. 10.

revealing) quote from one of Franca's few autobiographical reflections (cited above) has often been used without any further explanation or analysis and begs more questions than it answers. Surely, as well, the shock of Franco Basaglia's early death was profound and painful, above all for Franca, Alberta and Enrico. Franca rarely if ever wrote about herself or connected her work with her own autobiography. For her, at least publicly, the personal was not political. To reconstruct her private life, we need to read between the lines.

ii. Antonio Slavich (1962–69)

Of the like-minded psychiatrists and others who came to work in Gorizia, most, at least in the early stages, arrived thanks to direct connections to Basaglia himself. In the 1967 photo, Slavich is smoking a pipe, leaning forward. The first to turn up, in February or March 1962, was Basaglia's colleague Antonio Slavich from Padua University. He had not yet qualified as a doctor and was younger than Basaglia. Slavich and Basaglia were friends and long-term colleagues, but their relationship was also a formal one. Over time, Slavich was perhaps the most loyal of Basaglia's lieutenants, but he also had his own ideas and was willing to argue his corner. In his account of his time in Ferrara (1971–78) Slavich describes frequent conflicts with Basaglia and 'arguments in Veneto dialect' between them. The two men had a lot of history together. They had shared the early pioneering period in the hospital, alone (it seemed) against the rest of the world.[20]

Slavich was born in Fiume, Istria, in 1935, a port city that was then in Italy but which became part of Yugoslavia after 1947 and is now in Croatia (and now called Rijeka). He grew up in Bolzano on the northern edge of Italy and did some of his training in Germany. Slavich was close to Basaglia in terms of his phenomenological approach to psychiatry, although he was critical of Sartre. Like Basaglia, Slavich found that his

---

20   Antonio Slavich, *La scopa meravigliante. Preparativi per la legge 180 a Ferrara e dintorni 1971–1978*, Rome: Riuniti, 2003, p. 149. Slavich can be seen in the documentary *Eccoli*; see Stefano Ricci, Jacobo Quadri, Giacomo Piermatti, *Eccoli*, Bologna: Mamiverlag, 2014.

university career in Padua was going nowhere after ten years as an assistant. He later described 'the subordinate and lowly state of psychiatry in the University of Padua'.[21] He shared the whole Gorizian experience with Basaglia right up to 1969. In that 1965 photo, Slavich is the only other doctor to be seen.

Slavich was a tough character who was not afraid of standing up to Basaglia. They argued frequently. As Vincenzo Pastore, a Gorizian from the second phase later said, 'Antonio never let anything go. He was an argumentative person'.[22] It is said that Slavich always used the formal *Lei* address whenever he spoke to Basaglia. After 1971, Slavich worked in Ferrara and then in Genoa. His independence led him away from Trieste after the experience in Colorno. Many other members of the original équipe continued to work under Basaglia.

Slavich was not a radical, politically, when he came to Gorizia. He has been described as a 'liberal-social democrat' who 'read *Il Corriere della Sera*'.[23] He moved quickly to the far left around 1968 (he claimed to have been Maoist for a while) and later joined the Italian Communist Party and its offshoots.[24] Slavich was given crucial responsibilities right from the off in Gorizia. He was in sole charge of two wards (with over 100 patients) and the hours were exhausting.[25] Occasionally, Slavich would have to work for over seventy hours a week and was often the only doctor in the entire asylum.

Basaglia, Franca Ongaro and Slavich formed a kind of mini-équipe from 1961 to 1965, along with other psychiatrists who spent time

---

21   Interview in Silvia Balconi, *L'esperienza Goriziana dal '61 al '72 . Un percorso paradigmatico di valorizzazione della professionalità in ambito psichiatrico*, unpublished thesis, Università degli studi di Torino, 1997–98, p. 495.

22   Vincenzo Pastore, in Paolo Tranchina, 'Passioni, radicalità. Un ricordi di Vieri Marzi e Antonio Slavich', personaedanno.it.

23   See Jervis, *Il buon rieducatore*, pp. 22–3, and this interview with Domenico Casagrande: Michele Loreto, 'Intervista a Nico Casagrande. Basagli gli anni di Gorizia', 7 February, 2010, micheleloreto.blogspot.co.uk.

24   He had an active political career throughout his life and was elected as a local councillor (from 1988 to 1990) in Genoa and served as an elected provincial representative for the Communist Party and some of its later incarnations in the same city. Slavich died in Bolzano in 2009.

25   Slavich in Balconi, *L'esperienza Goriziana dal '61 al '72*, p. 496. Some accounts have him in sole charge of 200 patients at this time: 'Passioni, radicalità'.

in Gorizia (and have attracted little or no attention from historians and those studying Basaglia) such as Leopoldo Tesi and a young graduate called Maria Pia Bombonato. There was also a doctor from Varese who was violently opposed to all of the Basaglia reforms, Vittorio Alì. This anti-Basaglian (said to have held neo-fascist sympathies) did all he could to block or ignore what Basaglia was trying to do in Gorizia. Alì was to play a key part in the dramatic events of 1968.[26]

Over time, younger nurses were taken on and volunteers were encouraged to work with the patients in new and innovative ways. The make-up of the hospital slowly changed. 1965 was a key year, a year of radical change, when the balance began to shift. In that year a number of important figures arrived in Gorizia, and the Socialist health minister Luigi Mariotti made an important speech in Milan (in September).[27] Mariotti made a stark comparison in that speech: 'Our hospitals today are like German concentration camps, Dantesque chambers of hell.' This comparison led to protests from the official psychiatry association.

In that same year, a Communist politician in Parma called Mario Tommasini discovered Gorizia, and in Perugia politicians and doctors began to transform the city's psychiatric hospital. Gorizia was no longer out on a limb. Suddenly, it had political support that reached right to the heart of government. Its ideas were also having an effect within more moderate psychiatric circles. A national debate began about the future of Italy's psychiatric hospitals. Gorizia was being held up as an example of change. Other asylums were described as 'concentration camps'. By 1966 a proper, working équipe was now in place. Things were beginning to move, and with some speed.

---

26   Slavich described Alì as 'active, invasive, authoritarian and violent' in Antonio Slavich, *All'ombra dei ciliegi giapponesi,* unpublished manuscript, p. 11, and as a 'fascist', p. 19.

27   20 September 1965. Cited in Babini, *Liberi tutti,* p. 207. See also David Forgacs, *Italy's Margins,* p. 199, and Angelo Del Boca, *Manicomi come lager,* Turin: Edizioni dell'albero, 1966.

iii. Agostino Pirella (1965–71)

Agostino Pirella (born 1930), the fourth member of the core équipe, arrived in Gorizia in 1965. Pirella graduated in medicine from the University of Parma in 1954 and had moved on to the grim psychiatric hospital in Mantua in August 1955. He seems to have first come across Basaglia in that same year.[28] Pirella had tried to introduce mild changes within the asylum in Mantua (such as untying patients and freeing up wards), but he felt frustrated and isolated. On return from holiday, he found that everything he had done had simply been reversed. Pirella has given us this description of Mantua's *asylum* in the 1950s:

> It was a well-organized hospital, like a concentration camp. The director would tour the hospital in his boots and with his dogs, talking to the patients in a rude and sarcastic way . . . the idea of the concentration camp was ever present at that time, for someone like me, young and well aware of these kinds of issues.[29]

In 1957, Pirella, Basaglia and others had tried, without success, to set up an alternative association of psychiatrists. They were frustrated at the lack of new ideas circulating within official circles and organizations. Many of those who were interested in transforming the deeply conservative world of Italian psychiatry gravitated towards Pier Francesco Galli in Milan. Galli was a psychoanalyst who organized a series of meetings and seminars (the Gruppo Milanese per lo sviluppo della psicoterapia) from the early 1960s onwards, mainly in Milan.[30]

Basaglia and Pirella developed a close friendship, and unlike with

---

28   Pirella may also have known Slavich and had been on a trip with Slavich and Basaglia to visit asylums in Germany in 1963. The politician responsible for the health sector for the Province of Gorizia at the time, Luigi Marchesini, also went on this trip. Agostino Pirella, 'E a Gorizia? Nascita di un'alternativa alla segregazione manicomiale', *Territorio. Bollettino* 10, November 1984, p. 32. See also Basaglia et al., *La nave che affonda*, pp. 93–4, and Agostino Pirella, 'Il giovane Basaglia e la critica della scienza', *Sapere* 851, November–December 1982, pp. 4–9. For Luigi Marchesini (a doctor and DC politician who supported Basaglia and his team) see Slavich, *All'ombra*. Marchesini died in 1966. See also 'Ricordo di Luigi Marchesini', *Iniziativa Isontina* 26, 1966. Marchesini was on the committee that appointed Basaglia in 1961.

29   Pirella interview in Balconi, *L'esperienza Goriziana dal '61 al '72*, p. 459.

30   For Galli see Babini, *Liberi tutti*, pp. 232–9.

Slavich, Pirella and Basaglia used the informal *tu* form of address. Pirella was active in the PSIUP (a left-of-centre party founded in 1964) and secretary of its local party section in Mantua in 1964–65. This was another line of connection with Basaglia, who was close to the Socialists for a time (at university) and was never a member of the Communist Party. Pirella was the only member of the équipe who had extensive previous experience in psychiatric hospitals, where he had worked for ten years or so. In the 1967 photo, he is sitting between Giovanni Jervis and Letizia Comba, smiling broadly.

Pirella has often been written out of the Basaglia story, or confined to a supporting role. This was in part a reflection of his personality, which was far more reserved than Basaglia's. Moreover, while Pirella was quite prolific, he tended to publish in scholarly journals, although he did contribute to both *What Is Psychiatry?* and *The Negated Institution*. His work in any case was not as obviously political as that of Basaglia, and less theoretical. Pirella was a formidable organizer and quietly charismatic. He was not a man for a rabble-rousing public meeting or TV appearance. He did clash with Basaglia, but these disputes usually only had one winner.[31]

Pirella, however, was also a leader, although of a different kind to his mentor. He was instrumental in the creation of a second équipe in Gorizia after 1969 and also directed one of the most important and influential examples of institutional change in the 1970s, in Arezzo. Paolo Tranchina, who worked with Pirella in Gorizia and Arezzo, wrote of his 'analytical and careful sense of judgement' and of his 'ability to manage a team, his acute sense of being able to understand madness without collusion with its regressive aspects, the solid nature of his idea of therapy'.[32]

Basaglia first invited Pirella to Gorizia in the early 1960s, but a proper job (as a *primario*, a post only available after a public competition) did not come up until August 1965. A *primario* was a doctor who ran a

---

31 Of course, there are different versions here as well (Pirella later said this in Balconi: 'My relationship with Franco was always marvellous. I remember a couple of discussions about patients, or some problems, but the climate was always one of collaboration and understanding', in Balconi, *L'esperienza Goriziana dal '61 al '72, p. 462,* but see also Jervis, *Il buon rieducatore,* p. 25.

32 Paolo Tranchina, ed., 'Fogli d'informazione, lotte antistituzionali, Legge 180', *Fogli d'informazione,* 5–6, 3rd series, 1 June 2008, pp. 56–7.

whole ward in a hospital, and this was a position that carried a certain amount of prestige. This whole process was extremely long-winded, but Basaglia felt that he needed Pirella to have a powerful institutional role in the hospital. The fact that Pirella was willing to wait was another sign of the hierarchies in place at that time. After 1965, Pirella quickly became a key member of the équipe, Basaglia's number two or his right-hand man (a role also played at times by Slavich, particularly in the 1962–65 period). On his arrival, Pirella found a hospital where some of the wards had already been opened up. He was given the tricky task of doing the same with wards that were still closed, those with the most difficult patients of all. He soon struck up a strong working alliance with a young psychiatrist called Domenico Casagrande, who also started working in Gorizia in 1965, and with Basaglia himself.

Pirella officially became the director of the Gorizian asylum in 1969, although he took on this role for much of 1968 as well (when Basaglia started to drift away from the city). However, he was already being courted by other cities and provincial administrations interested in reforming their own institutions, and he left to become director of the *ospedale psichiatrico* in Arezzo in 1971. After 1968, offers for all the Basaglians came flooding in. The Arezzo experience under Pirella would go on to become one of the most interesting and radical in Italy in the 1970s, and of all the post-Basaglian institutions it probably came closest to being 'another Gorizia'. Arezzo in the 1970s inspired a series of studies – books, photographic accounts, films. Pirella never had the sparkling charm of Basaglia, nor did his written work reach a mass audience. He was content, it seems, to play a supporting role in the movement. Nonetheless, his anti-institutional activity (from *within* institutions) in Mantua, Gorizia, Arezzo and later Turin was coherent, revolutionary, and has been extremely well documented. Of all the Gorizians, Pirella's later experiences remained close to his work in the 1960s. This Gorizianism would also lead to debates within the movement, and with other strands of radical psychiatry.[33]

---

33 The definition of the terms 'Gorizian' and 'Gorizianism' is contested. On the one hand, there was a strong sense of a group with a common aim and identity and shared sets of theories of practices. On the other, this sense of group identity was also used against those who had 'betrayed' the line, such as Giovanni Jervis. Finally, 'Gorizianism' was also used within the movement to criticize a sense that the Gorizians were attempting to dominate things. See Slavich, *La scopa meravigliante*, who uses the term 'we "Gorizians"' (p. 12) and later questions whether

iv. Domenico Casagrande (1965–72)

Domenico Casagrande (born 1939) started in Gorizia as a volunteer in 1965. He was only twenty-five at the time and had studied in Bologna, Milan and Switzerland. Casagrande was from Emilia-Romagna, but the link to Basaglia came from his hometown – his family had worked with the Basaglia family. He was taken on full-time in 1966 and would be the last director of the Basaglian asylum in Gorizia in 1971–72 after the departure of Pirella. Casagrande was a true loyalist, very close to the Basaglian line throughout his time in Gorizia (and afterwards). His contributions to the discussions in *The Negated Institution* were mainly of a practical nature. He was not a theorist but adept and a hard worker. Like the other Gorizians, he would go on to close down and reform other asylums after leaving Gorizia, in Trieste and then in Venice. In the 1967 photo, he looks the youngest of the bunch, sitting with folded arms between the two longest-serving members of the équipe: Basaglia and Slavich.

v. Giovanni 'Gionni' Jervis (1966–69)

'I never idolized him and it soon became clear that we didn't agree.'

Jervis on Basaglia[34]

'For more than a decade – when they were both alive – and right up to the present day, now that Gionni is also no longer with us, people have speculated on a presumed and deep-rooted disagreement between the two men [Basaglia and Jervis].'

Stefano Mistura[35]

Jervis 'could or wanted to still consider himself as a "Gorizian"' (p. 13). Slavich also refers to the accusation of 'Gorizian hegemonic practices' within the movement in the 1970s, pp. 136, 138–9. Finally, in a footnote, he complains about the attribution to him of the phrase 'Gorizianism', p. 265. 'Gorizianism' also sometimes implied an insistence on working to close down the asylums as a priority over all other activities. Mario Colucci and Pierangelo Di Vittorio, *Franco Basaglia*, Milan: Bruno Mondadori, 2001, p. 243, n. 74.

34   Mario Baudino, 'Jervis, l'altra faccia dell'antipsichiatria', *La Stampa*, 3 August 2009.

35   Stefano Mistura, 'Giovanni Jervis. La forza di passioni condivise', *Il Manifesto*, 5 August 2009

'Those things he wrote, for us they make no sense, because they aren't true.'

Franco Basaglia[36]

A year after Pirella's arrival, Giovanni Jervis (born 1933) became part of the équipe alongside his wife, Letizia Comba.[37] Unlike the other members of the group, with the possible exception of Pirella, Jervis was a formidable intellectual in his own right, who had worked with the celebrated ethnographer Ernesto De Martino and had connections to important left-wing thinkers in Italy and abroad as well as key protagonists of new psychiatric thought. He was a published writer and an experienced researcher, highly knowledgeable in new forms of psychiatry and psychoanalytic thought. He was also politically astute and well connected, with a wide range of cultural references to draw on. He had written extensive introductions for Einaudi to the influential work of Marcuse, Hollingshead and Redlich, and he would go on to write a new introduction to the Italian children's classic, *Pinocchio*.[38]

As a young man, Giovanni Jervis had taken part in a collective research project inspired and directed by the Ernesto De Martino. This was a first foray into what would later become known as the field of ethnopsychiatry. De Martino had become interested in the phenomenon of was known as Tarantism, an ancient rite in the deep south of Italy whereby women (in the main) would claim to have been bitten by a tarantula. What usually followed was a kind of popular exorcism involving

---

36   Basaglia et al., *La nave che affonda*, p. 99.

37   Comba's post was approved by the province in January 1967. See the official document in the Archivio Basaglia, 11 January 1967, where her gross annual income was fixed at 1,607,000 *lire*.

38   Giovanni Jervis, 'Prefazione' in Carl Gustav Jung, *Il problema dell'inconscio nella psicologia moderna*, Turin: Einaudi, 1959; Giovanni Jervis, 'Considerazioni neuropsichiatriche sul tarantismo', in Ernesto De Martino, *La terra del rimorso. Contributo a una storia religiosa del Sud*, Milan: Il Saggiatore, 1961, translated by Dorothy Louise Zinn as 'Neuropsychiatric Considerations on Tarantism' in Ernesto De Martino, *The Land of Remorse. A Study of Southern Italian Tarantism*, London: Free Association, 2005, pp. 259–68; 'Prefazione', Herbert Marcuse, *Eros e civiltà*, Turin: Einaudi, 1964; 'Introduzione' in August Hollingshead, Fredrick Redlich, *Classi sociali e malattie mentali*, Turin: Einaudi, 1965, pp. xi–l (*Social class and mental illness*, New York: Wiley, 1958, also translated by Jervis); 'Prefazione' a Carlo Collodi, *Le avventure di Pinocchio*, Turin: Einaudi, 1968, pp. vii–xxii.

wild dancing and music that went on for days. De Martino studied this rite in its social and cultural context, and Jervis was part of the team that worked on the original, fascinating and highly influential book that came out of the collective project, which was published in 1961 with the title *La terra del rimorso (The Land of Remorse)*.

The arrival of Jervis in Gorizia would help take the Basaglian experiment to a new level. The two key books based on Gorizia were published between 1966 and 1968, with the beginning of a working relationship between the Einaudi publishing house and Franco Basaglia. Jervis was heavily involved in all of these projects. His contribution was intellectual, political and practical. His voice is ever-present in both books, and his background put him in competition with Basaglia for the leadership of the équipe. Sergio Piro later argued that there had been a 'deep clash between the two men' and that Jervis and Basaglia 'had the same way of writing, the same type of egocentrism – which is what probably leads to success'.[39]

Jervis was partly English. His great grandfather was an English officer called Thomas Jervis who had fought alongside Garibaldi, and hence his nickname, which was written in various ways as 'Johnny', 'Gionni' or 'Gioni'. He hailed from the small religious Valdese community in upper Piedmont, although he was born in Florence. This isolated Protestant area (where the community was scattered across remote mountainous valleys) was a kind of enclave that had survived despite hundreds of years of persecution.

Giovanni's father was Willy Jervis, an engineer and manager with the enlightened Olivetti Company in Ivrea. Willy was active in the anti-fascist resistance during the war. After his name was forced out of another anti-fascist (Emanuele Artom) through torture, he was arrested and brutally beaten by the Nazis in March 1944 and executed on 5 August of that year. The Nazis then dragged his body (and those of four other partisans, three of whom have never been identified) by rope to the main square of Villar Pellice by truck (in the heart of the Valdese area) and strung them from trees, lamp-posts and balconies as a warning to

---

39 Sergio Piro and Candida Carrino, *Quando ho i soldi mi compro un pianoforte. Conversazioni con un protagonista della psichiatria del '900*, Naples: Liguori Editore, 2010, p. 67.

others.[40] Willy Jervis became a quasi-legendary martyr (for the Valdesians and for the anti-fascist movement in general) and was awarded a post-humous Gold Medal for Military Valour in 1950.[41] Squares, streets and two mountain refuges were named after him. Misquotes from some of his last messages to his wife were later published in one of the mythical texts of Italian anti-fascism, the *Letters from those condemned to death from the Italian Resistance,* including one of the most famous citations of all: 'Don't cry for me, don't dub me a "poor" person. I am going to die for having followed an idea'.[42] All this happened just as Gionni reached his teenage years.[43]

His background may well have given Giovanni Jervis a sense that he was one of the 'chosen people' and was certainly part of a kind of left-wing aristocracy, in stark contrast to the world Franco Basaglia came from, despite the fact that both men had important anti-fascist creden-tials. The Valdesians were a strong cultural influence in Piedmont and in Turin in particular, although after the war Giovanni's mother took her three children back to her native city of Florence, where Gionni was educated, and where she taught English literature. Summers were still often spent in the big family home in Torre Pellice, in the heart of Valdesian country.[44] Thin and angular, Jervis is right in the middle of the 1967 équipe photo, between Slavich and Pirella.

Gionni Jervis's first full account of his time in Gorizia came out in

---

40   Giovanni De Luna, 'Introduzione' in Willy Jervis, Lucilla Jervis Rochat, Giorgio Agosti, *Un filo tenace. Lettere e memorie 1944–1969,* Turin: Bollati Boringhieri, 2008. (1st ed., 1998, La Nuova Italia), pp. 7–16; see also Luciano Boccalatte, 'Premessa' in ibid., pp. 46–7.

41   The medal was awarded during a public ceremony in Ivrea in the presence of such anti-fascist luminaries as Gaetano Salvemini, Adriano Olivetti and Ferruccio Parri. Ibid., pp. 226–7.

42   Pietro Malvezzi e Giovanni Pirelli, eds, *Lettere di condannati a morte della Resistenza italiana (8 settembre 1943–25 aprile 1945),* Turin: Einaudi, 1952, p. 117.

43   For the story of the life and death of Guglielmo Jervis see Willy Jervis, Rochat, Agosti, *Un filo tenace;* see also Giovanni Jervis, 'Un ricordo di quegli anni', pp. 229–39; and the account of Willy's death written by Lucilla for her children, 'Per Gionni e Paola', pp. 130–4. Gionni was clearly a precocious child, who grew up very quickly and was a fervent reader of all kinds of historical books, political texts and fiction from an early age.

44   See ibid. for the family background here. This is presumably where Gionni and Letizia Comba met. The two were married before they worked together on the De Martino project in 1959. Slavich claimed that Letizia Comba was the daughter of the 'head of the Torre Pellice community . . . Parson Comba', in *All'ombra.*

1977, in an introduction to a collection of his essays, published by Feltrinelli. This was a text that made public the divisions with Basaglia and the Basaglians that had been fermenting behind the scenes for years. The introduction was a long semi-autobiographical essay, entitled (ironically) 'Il buon rieducatore' (The good re-educator). It was a mixture of the personal and the political, of history and hearsay, and was unusual for the time despite the personal-is-political mantra of 1968 and the 1970s. It was also a kind of confession. Every word was weighed very carefully. As with all accounts of Gorizia, we need to be careful in taking Jervis's narrative at face value. By the time the book, also called *Il buon rieducatore,* came out, Jervis had broken with the Basaglian group and there were deep tensions between the various factions within Italian 'new psychiatry'. This battle, which was in part around ideas but was also to do with personality, power, ambition and recognition, became extremely bitter and caused serious problems, for example, within the Psichiatria Democratica movement.

'Il buon rieducatore' took these divisions into the public sphere and formalized the existence of an anti-Basaglian or non-Basaglia current *within* the movement. The essay was explosive. Jervis had broken rank (a process which began in 1969 when he left for Reggio Emilia, but which began to take root in the early to mid-1970s). He had lifted the lid on a powerful myth – the Basaglian revolution in Gorizia. An alternative version of the past was now available. After that, for the Basaglians, he was persona non grata.[45] Jervis began to be written out of the history of the movement. The past was contested territory, even the very recent past. As Matteo Fiorani argued, this 'conflict' was 'fixed in time'.[46] Radical psychiatry also created a divided memory.[47]

In 'Il buon rieducatore' Jervis recounted his time studying medicine in Florence, his work with De Martino in the south of Italy and his growing interest as a young man in new forms of psychiatry. By the 1960s, like Basaglia, Jervis had become frustrated with traditional Italian

---

45   I will return to these debates and accusations at various times in this book. Slavich charges Jervis with 'clear intellectual dishonesty' with regard to that book in *La scopa meravigliante,* p. 263.

46   *Bibliografia di storia della psichiatria italiana, 1991–2010,* Florence: Firenze University Press, 2010, p. 10.

47   John Foot, *Italy's Divided Memory,* New York: Palgrave, 2010.

psychiatry. He had also taken up an important paid role as a consultant with the Einaudi publishing house in Turin, and he would visit that city on a weekly basis for the legendary Wednesday meetings of the editorial committee. In the 1960s Johnny went on what he called a 'psycho-tour' of those places that were experimenting with new forms of mental health care, and attended seminars and discussions in Milan run by Pier Francesco Galli. After meeting Agostino Pirella, Jervis soon became aware of what was happening in Gorizia, something that appeared to him to be both 'stimulating and promising'.[48] After meeting Basaglia he also gave up his private practice in Rome and took his whole family to Gorizia. It was September 1966. Jervis was thirty-three and had three small children. He had decided to throw in his lot with the Gorizian experiment.

Jervis's job in Gorizia was badly paid, with few professional prospects and back-breaking in terms of the work involved. Unlike Pirella, he was not taken on at a high level after a *concorso* (competition). But Jervis had a plan. He had not gone to Gorizia simply to be just another member of the équipe. He seems to have promised Einaudi a book on the Gorizian experiment (a series of books were originally proposed) and his arrival there would bring the Turinese publishing house and Franco Basaglia together, to the benefit of both. Jervis's wife, Letizia Comba, was also taken on in the hospital as a psychologist at the same time. The first historic Basaglian équipe was now complete.

Looking back, it had been a difficult beginning, as it had been for Basaglia in 1961–62. As Jervis remembered (nearly ten years later): 'I got to Gorizia with a high fever and under the pouring rain, driving a removal lorry with great care, with the kids silent in the back seat, and with the car packed with stuff, including even a fish tank'. It was, Jervis recalled, like being 'at the edge of the world'.[49] The sense of isolation was overwhelming. But Jervis and Letizia Comba were soon plunged straight into the daily routine, debates and work of the Gorizian therapeutic community.

Gorizia was, for Jervis, 'an attempt to despecialize and de-psychiatrize the reform of the asylum . . . a place of important political and cultural

---

48   Jervis, *Il buon rieducatore*, p. 18.
49   Ibid., p. 19.

ideas, which took on a central role for the renewal of institutional psychiatry in Italy after 1967'. The years up to 1968 in Gorizia were, Jervis wrote, 'the richest and best of my life'.[50] Lasting relationships were built with patients and nurses as the younger nurses came over to the thinking inspired by the Basaglian revolution. It was a heady time. The world was changing, and Gorizia was at the forefront of those changes.

But that period was also extremely difficult for everyone concerned. The work was hard, the hours were endless (with twenty-four-hour or forty-eight-hour shifts) and the pay was meagre. The personal and the political were indeed merged into one. In addition, Jervis, Letizia and all the others were working full-time on various projects for Einaudi as well as travelling extensively. It was a constant battle against time and tiredness. The Gorizians felt as if they were in a state of siege.

Jervis painted a very different picture of Basaglia from that of many other members of the équipe, especially those in the inner circle – describing him as someone who would not tolerate dissent, and as highly ambitious.[51] But he also lavished him with praise. 'Basaglia', he wrote,

> led [Gorizia] with enormous commitment and passion – with anger and with courage which – I believe – nobody else would have been capable of in Italy at that time, in a local context which was politically and culturally unfavourable to change, he had decided to make Gorizia into a model project, an experiment.[52]

Despite the picture of unity presented to the outside world, Jervis wrote that the équipe was marked by conflicts and continual debate, but he also argued that 'the Gorizian group worked well, and remained united, until 1968'.[53]

For a time (1966–68), the two men worked together and were the two dominant personalities inside the équipe. They were clearly friends for a brief period. It was a time of great creativity and productivity for

---

50 Ibid., p. 20.

51 'Basaglia's leadership was noticeably authoritarian.' Ibid., p. 24.

52 Ibid., pp. 19–20.

53 Ibid., p. 21. Later, Jervis went further, arguing that Basaglia had become 'prisoner of his own myth' and that 'a cult of personality [had developed] from which he was unable or unwilling to free himself'. Simonetta Fiori, 'Jervis contro Basaglia', *La Repubblica*, 31 May 2008.

the entire group, with seemingly endless debates (inside and outside the asylum, many of which were reproduced in printed form), meetings, offers of work and experiments with the patients and the nurses themselves. This moment came to an end in 1968, with the publication of *The Negated Institution* and the carving out of a privileged role for Basaglia with regard to Einaudi. In 1969, the two men's paths moved in different directions (although what they actually did in their work was very similar). Basaglia left Gorizia for Colorno and then Trieste, whereas Jervis went to Reggio Emilia and then to an academic job in Rome. In 1977, Jervis went public with 'Il buon rieducatore'. After that, Jervis carried forward with a different version of the Basaglia-Gorizia story (he rarely mentioned Trieste) and was progressively excised from 'official' histories. He is relegated to a footnote in some accounts, and in others he is ignored altogether.[54] These divisions were to continue for years and, to some extent, remain in place even today. Nonetheless, any serious historian of the movement, of Gorizia, and of what happened *after* Gorizia, needs to take into account the role of both men at that time, and afterwards. There are no more political battles to be fought. It is time for an historical truce.

After 1968, Jervis felt to some extent that he had been usurped, although he never admitted this publicly. He saw *The Negated Institution* as, at least in part, *his* project, but Giulio Bollati and Basaglia had found a strong personal bond from the start, and Jervis was marginalized, becoming a mere member of the équipe (at least in terms of the general public). At the same time, *The Negated Institution* became a bestseller, leading to a whole series of books by Basaglia and Franca Ongaro for Einaudi. This story will be told in full later on in this chapter.

For Jervis, the publication of *The Negated Institution* was the beginning of the end. Basaglia gained fame, as did the whole Gorizian experiment. Political issues (and divisions) became more and more important. The

---

54   But this petty point-scoring was by no means one-sided. One book, for example, makes no mention of Basaglia: Antonio Maria Ferro and Giovanni Jervis, eds, *La bottega della psichiatria. Dialoghi sull'operare psichiatrico a vent'anni dalla legge 180*, Turin: Bollati Boringhieri, 1999. Sectarianism ran through the movement, despite the fact that the final aims and the practical work of the various currents were often very close if not indistinguishable. Seen in hindsight, much of this seems absurd today. But the damage done to the movement as a whole was immense.

'incident' took place. In April 1969, Jervis received an offer from the Province of Reggio Emilia to set up and run a new network of non-asylum-based mental health services, and he left in June of that year (with his wife and children). His stay in Gorizia had been brief, stressful and productive, but also frustrating and difficult. It had proved costly in terms of his relationship with Einaudi, which began to change. After 1969, he became established as an alternative figure to Basaglia, a charismatic leader but one who was destined to play a supporting role at least in the mind of the public, who would have his own following and power base. Also, after 1969, the idea that Jervis was in some way a traitor, an enemy of the Basaglians, began to take root. He was seen by some as, in his own words, 'a traitor of the Gorizian "line" linked to the therapeutic community'.[55] Jervis also published a book that would rival *L'istituzione negata* in terms of its influence on a generation of young psychiatrists from the 1970s.[56]

vi. Letizia Comba (Jervis) (1966–69)

Letizia Comba Jervis was the only woman officially employed in the Gorizian asylum as part of the équipe. In the 1967 photo, she is sitting between Pirella and the head nurse, surrounded by seven men. Comba was born in Torre Pellice in 1932, and thus also came from inside the Valdesian community. She had studied existentialist philosophy, had taken a master in experimental psychology in the USA in the 1950s and had also worked with Ernesto De Martino at the end of that decade.[57] Comba was taken on in Gorizia as a psychologist, the only person with that title in the asylum at that time. There were no psychoanalysts in Gorizia before 1968.[58] Letizia Comba was particularly interested in the work of R. D. Laing, and she became the intermediary for some of Laing's most important work in Italy, writing the introduction to both *The*

---

55   Jervis, *Il buon rieducatore*, p. 27.

56   Giovanni Jervis, *Manuale critico di psichiatria*, 10th ed., Milan: Feltrinelli, 1980 (1975).

57   Caterina Spillari et al., eds, *Letizia Comba. Tessere. Scritti. 1967–2000*, Milan: Il Saggiatore, 2011; Letizia Jervis-Comba, 'Problemi di psicologia nello studio del tarantismo' in De Martino, *La terra del rimorso*, pp. 320–43.

58   Apart from Michele Risso, who was not an official part of the équipe. Paolo Tranchina, who would be associated with Gorizia in the late 1960s, was a trained psychoanalyst.

Divided Self and *The Politics of the Family*. Comba contributed important pieces to both *What Is Psychiatry?* and *The Negated Institution*.[59]

The équipe thus contained two couples from 1966 to 1968 – the Basaglias and the Jervises, both of whom had small children. Family life always took second place to the intense work commitments that both couples made (this was true of all the members of the équipe), and this took its toll on the Jervis family in particular. Letizia Comba went on to take part in the Reggio Emilia experiment alongside Gionni until the early 1970s, and then she took up a post at the University of Urbino before moving to Verona University in 1986.

vii. Lucio Schittar (1966–69)

'When I got to Gorizia I knew had no practical experience with psychiatry, and I knew little of psychiatric theory. I had always been interested in psychiatry – but I was a medical doctor at that time – an assistant in a pneumology division of a general hospital, and I had already begun to work as a general practitioner, without much enthusiasm for what I was doing.'

Lucio Schittar, *L'istituzione negata* (1968)[60]

Lucio Schittar graduated with a degree in medicine from the University of Padua in 1964 (where both Basaglia and Slavich had been based).[61] In the 1967 photo, he is opposite Basaglia, on the far right of the circle. He was from the Veneto region, like Basaglia and Casagrande.[62] After working for a brief period in the general hospital in Mestre, he became

---

59   Letizia Comba, 'Prefazione' in R. D. Laing, *L'io diviso*, Turin: Einaudi, 1969, pp. 7–11; 'Prefazione' in Ronald D. Laing and Aaron Esterson, *Normalità e follia della famiglia*, ed. Letizia Comba, Turin: Einaudi, 1977, pp. vii–xxxi.

60   Franco Basaglia, ed., *L'istituzione negata*, Turin: Einaudi, 1968, p. 86.

61   Lucio Schittar was a specialist in pneumology and mental illness and nervous diseases. His time in the Mestre hospital was as an assistant in the pneumology department. See 'Dal manicomio alla 180 e oltre. Intervista a Lucio Schittar' in Augusto Casasola and Francesco Stoppa, eds, *L'Ippogrifo* 1, 1998, pp. 13–14.

62   He was born in the small town of Cesiomaggiore (Belluno) in 1937, about 80 kilometres from Venice. I have not been able to find information on his early life beyond this.

part of the Gorizian équipe in 1966. Schittar started in Gorizia as a volunteer, as did Casagrande. The beginnings of this relationship were pretty spontaneous, typical of the times and of the workings of Gorizia itself. Schittar drove a FIAT 500 to Gorizia and met up with Basaglia, who told him he could start working there on a voluntary basis and that he would then try and get him taken on as a ward doctor. The two men seemed to hit it off from the start; Schittar wrote:

> When I went to meet him, I was used to listening in silence to the outbursts from the senior doctor in the hospital, and I was surprised by Basaglia's spontaneity, his way of bringing the best out of everyone . . . his informality, and the fact that he was entirely lacking in the haughtiness which distinguished most senior doctors at the time.[63]

The presence of people like Schittar, Franca Ongaro and Letizia Comba in and around the équipe showed how uninterested Basaglia was in the technical aspects of psychiatric training. It also showed how important it was to seize the moment in that period. Anything was possible.

In an interview in *L'istituzione negata*, Schittar put his decision to go to Gorizia partly down to 'an emotional reaction to the type of work which I would have had to carry out as a medical doctor'.[64] Gorizia was not just about psychiatry or anti-psychiatry. It was also about medicine in general and the role of authority in society as a whole. As Schittar argued, the situation in Gorizia was very different to that of a normal, medical institution:

> In Gorizia . . . we are trying to create a different kind of relationship which goes beyond authoritarianism, including in terms of our links to patients and nurses . . . There is a tendency to reduce the role of the doctor to that of a technician – it's not a nice word but it is clear – a technician of health, not necessarily of mental health, where 'technicians' are seen globally as doctors, nurses, patients.[65]

---

63 In Augusto Casasola and Francesco Stoppa, eds, 'Dal manicomio alla 180', p. 14.
64 Basaglia, *L'istituzione negata* (1968), p. 86.
65 Ibid., p. 87.

Gorizia was a place of continual discussion, a site of 'a daily battle of ideas'.[66]

Given that he could speak some English, Schittar spent a few days in Dingleton, Scotland, studying the Maxwell Jones–inspired therapeutic community there. Despite the fact that he had no qualifications in psychiatry, he was caught up in the excitement of the Gorizian experiment soon after his arrival. In early 1969 he went on to Colorno as part of the vanguard who were sent to prepare the ground for Basaglia's arrival (with the other member of the advance party, Slavich). He remained in Parma until 1972, working closely with Mario Tommasini. Schittar contributed to the discussions and publications during the most fertile period of the Gorizian experiment. He has left little in the way of reflections about Gorizia after that time, although he continued the work begun there in Colorno and later set up networks of psychiatric services in the new Province of Pordenone (1972–81).

Beyond the Équipe. Allies and Friends

The core équipe – all those people around the table in the 1967 photo, plus Franca Ongaro – was thus in situ by the end of 1966. Basaglia, finally, had a strong team with which he could work – inside and outside of the hospital. It was this group that would set up and oversee the extension of the Gorizian therapeutic community and which produced the two published texts that emerged from the Gorizian experiment in 1967 and 1968. The équipe worked as a close-knit team, meeting on a daily basis to discuss individual patients as well as to process outcomes of general and ward meetings. Basaglia demanded total commitment from everyone, both in terms of time and a more generalized enthusiasm for their work. It was much, much more than a job, and all seemed happy to oblige. Nobody had forced them to be there. They were in Gorizia because they believed in what Basaglia was doing and in the possibilities of radical change within the world of psychiatry. They were converts who worked with zeal. This commitment was not confined to the working day but continued well into the night in Basaglia's flat in the city or in

---

66   Ibid.

restaurants and elsewhere, especially during the putting together of *What Is Psychiatry?* and *The Negated Institution*, which were produced in a period that ran almost continually through 1967.

Yet, the équipe was also divided and conflictual. This conflict was in part personal and in part political. There were frequent disagreements over strategy, over tactics, over points of principle and over substance. How far should things be pushed? When exactly should the doors be unlocked? How much responsibility should be given to the patients? What was to be done about the relationship with local politicians? Which political line should the movement take? These debates were accepted as a key aspect of Basaglian strategy and were reported in great detail in *The Negated Institution*. Far from being hidden from the general public, they were a crucial part of the understanding of that experience. But there were also petty jealousies, problems of leadership and questions of authorship and control. Basaglia was always in charge, but he did not always have things his own way.

In February 1969 Basaglia wrote to his close friend Hrayr Terzian. He said that he was 'depressed' and added that 'the group (if it ever existed) is divided and broken . . . everyone is looking for their own personal ambitions to be satisfied'. His crisis was also a political one. 'I am not interested', Basaglia wrote, 'in being seen as a reformist psychiatrist . . . I wanted to negate what I had created with my previous negation, but I found myself isolated and alone'. 'The anti-institutional struggle in Gorizia', he concluded, 'is merely a political excuse'.[67]

In addition to the internal members of the équipe, a number of external figures took a keen interest in what was happening in Gorizia. A key 'extra' member of the équipe was Michele Risso. A Swiss-trained psychiatrist and psychoanalyst, Risso had been born in the small town of Boves, Piedmont. As a young man he narrowly escaped the infamous Nazi massacre there in late 1943 (and there is now a Via Dottor Michele Risso in Boves). Like Jervis, Risso was inspired by the work of De Martino,[68] and Risso later

67   1 February 1969, 'Archivio Basaglia, Corrispondenza 1969'.

68   Jervis and Risso wrote an article together in 1967 on rituals and myths linked to spider's bites and healing in Sardinia: Giovanni Jervis and Michele Risso, 'Contributi sociopsichiatrico all'interpretazione dell'argismo sardo' in Clara Gallini, ed., *I rituali dell'Argia*, Padua: Cedam, 1967, pp. 273–89.

carried out pioneering research into the mental health of Italian immigrants in Switzerland.[69] This work would come to be seen as ground-breaking in terms of a discipline now known as ethno-psychiatry. Basaglia and Risso, it seems, met in Rome around 1965, and soon afterwards they began to work together in various ways. Risso never based himself in Gorizia (although Basaglia would have happily accepted him as a full-time member of the équipe), but he contributed to discussions there and wrote a piece for *What Is Psychiatry?* He later became a key member of the Psichiatria Democratica organization, set up by Basaglia in the early 1970s.

Other important fellow travellers from the Gorizia period (whom we will meet later) included the Communist politician Mario Tommasini, the academics Gianfranco Minguzzi and Fabio Visintini, as well as the minister of health Luigi Mariotti. The publisher Giulio Bollati might also be considered a fellow traveller.[70] In addition, numerous journalists, photographers and filmmakers became interested in what was going on in Gorizia. There were also other psychiatrists, doctors and radical students who gravitated around Gorizia (especially during and after 1967–68) and are rarely present in the official versions of its history. These included Leopoldo Tesi, who came to Gorizia in 1962 and stayed until 1965, and then returned, it seems, in 1969; Maria Pia Bombonato, a young graduate who also started in 1962; and Giorgio Antonucci, who was invited to work in Gorizia for a short time later in the 1960s.[71]

---

69   Michele Risso and Wolfgang Böker, *Sortilegio e delirio. Psicopatologia dell'emigrazione in prospettiva transculturale*, Naples: Liguori, 1992; Michele Risso and Delia Frigessi Castelnuovo, *A mezza parete. Emigrazione, nostalgia, malattia mentale*, Turin: Einaudi, 1982.

70   See Fabio Visintini, *Memorie di un cittadino psichiatra (1902–1982)*, Naples: Edizioni Scientifiche Italiane, 1983; Franco Ongaro Basaglia, 'L'incontro di Fabio Visintini con Franco Basaglia', in Vittorino Andreoli et al., *L'utopia dell'eguaglianza. Ricordo di Fabio Visintini*, Naples: Edizioni Scientifiche, 2006, pp. 19–22. Mariotti was a member of the Socialist Party and served as minister of health from 22 November 1964 to 24 June 1968. For Tommasini see Bruno Rossi, *Mario Tommasini. Eretico per amore*, Reggio Emilia: Diabasis, 2006, and Franca Ongaro Basaglia, *Vita e carriera di Mario Tommasini burocrate proprio scomodo narrate da lui medesimo*, Rome: Riuniti, 1991.

71   Tesi was to go on to be the last director of Pistoia's mental hospital, which was known as Villa Sbertoli, as well as the last director of the huge asylum outside Lucca (Maggiano). Other figures around Gorizia at this time included student radicals such as Giancarlo Stisi, Luca Fontana, Silvana Pisa and Carlos Lobato from Bologna, Gianni Scalia (a teacher, also from Bologna) and many others.

Beyond the core équipe, the concept of 'group work' was extended to nurses, patients and, in theory, to the whole hospital. In each of these categories, there was a handful of leaders ('Furio' and 'Carla' among the patients, Andrian and a few others among the nurses) some enthusiastic followers, some violent detractors and a mass of the undecided or apathetic in the middle. The balance of power between these various groups changed over time. A number of nurses (some of whom were already there, while others were taken on in the 1960s) became passionate about the Basaglian revolution (usually after an initial period of opposition). It is no surprise that the 1967 group photo also includes a nurse. And among the patients there were some key personalities, above all 'Furio' (real name: Mario) Furlan, but also a number of others.[72] A strategy of 'vanguardism' was also used to win over and mobilize the patients, as it had been with the doctors and nurses. This was a slow process, and even by the end of the 1960s not all of the nursing staff or patients had been won over. Some would never be convinced.

By the late 1960s, then, many of the key thinkers and practitioners in what might be called New Italian Psychiatry were grouped around the Gorizian asylum and were coming under the influence of the theory and practice of Franco Basaglia and his équipe. Others were linked to the Perugian experience that we will also examine in this book. Experiments in reform were blossoming or had been attempted in Varese, Venice, Naples, Nocera Superiore in the south, Parma, Bologna, Padua and elsewhere. It was a fertile time, and ideas were undergoing rapid change. These were frantic and exhausting years, packed with meetings, reading, discussions, cigarettes and alcohol, sex and jealousy, rifts and arguments, loyalties and betrayals.

Yet 1968–69 was also the time when the core or historic Basaglian équipe began to break up.[73] Its golden period had lasted for an intense two years or so. At the peak of Gorizia's fame and fortune, the équipe

---

72   Slavich recounts that after Furlan's third (failed) suicide attempt in 1962, Slavich and Basaglia listened to him as he told his whole life story. Slavich, *La scopa meravigliante*, p. 59 (see also p. 58). For 'Furio' see also the long interview in Basaglia, *L'istituzione negata* (1968), pp. 88–107. Furlan kept in contact with Basaglia; see for example his letter to Basaglia in the 'Archivio Basaglia' (1969).

73   By 1970 only Pirella and Casagrande would be left in Gorizia from the 1966 équipe.

disintegrated. But this was, in part, a planned disintegration, a hard-nosed strategy, an attempt to spread the word, to create 'ninety-four Gorizias'.[74] Meanwhile, Gorizia continued to attract attention as never before. Many other psychiatrists, nurses, volunteers and students would turn up to take part in the revolution in the years to come. From 1968 to 1972, as most of the original Gorizians fanned out across Italy, bringing their methods and experience out to numerous cities and provinces, a new équipe would quickly take root in Gorizia. The seeds of change were planted there, and over the next ten years they would move out to the rest of the country and to Europe and beyond. A lot had happened in the years after 1961. From those humble beginnings, a movement had been born.

---

74 Antonio Slavich, 'Creare quattro, cinque, novantaquattro Gorizie' in *Fogli d'informazione* 27–8, January–February 1976, pp. 1–6.

SIX

Manicomio = Lager:
History and Politics of an Analogy

INTERVIEWER: 'You have had a very difficult and complicated life
. . . you were also in a concentration camp.'
CARLA: 'In my camp there was also the poor princess Mafalda.'[1]
INTERVIEWER: 'But, which camp was it?'
CARLA: 'Auschwitz.'[2]

L'istituzione negata (1968)

'Today, our [mental] hospitals are like German concentration
camps, or Dantesque chambers of hell.'

Luigi Mariotti, Milan (20 September 1965)[3]

'The institution cannot live on in a certain way while society changes
in another, while man has gone to the moon, and science is developing
in certain new ways, and society sees relationships so differently, the
survival of the madhouse, this concentration camp system, is
unthinkable.'

Franco Basaglia (1979)[4]

---

1 This is a reference to Princess Mafalda of Savoy, the second daughter of King Victor
Emanuel III of Italy, who died in Buchenwald concentration camp. According to the records
we have, Carla Nardini was not in Buchenwald camp.

2 Franco Basaglia, ed., *L'istituzione negata*, Turin: Einaudi, 1968, p. 24.

3 Cited in Angelo Del Boca, *Manicomi come lager*, Turin: Edizioni dell'Albero, 1966, p. 9.

4 'Corso di aggiornamento per operatori psichiatrici, Trascrizione di due lezioni/

'*If This Is a Man* became a kind of sacred text for the Italian
anti-psychiatric movement.'

Massimo Bucciantini[5]

In 1969 the artist Piero Gilardi, who had been one of the founders
of the Arte Povera movement in Turin, produced a poster for the
Associazione per la lotta contro le malattie mentali. It was a striking
image and it carried a striking slogan: 'Manicomio = Lager. Può capitare
anche a te! Dove la repressione addossa la camicia bianca' (Asylum =
concentration camp. This could also happen to you! When repression
wears a strait jacket).[6] The analogy between concentration camps,
Nazism and the asylum system created for the mentally ill in advanced
capitalist society had been first drawn in the immediate post-war period
in France and Germany and had been repeated in Italy by an unlikely
source, Ugo Cerletti, the infamous inventor of electroshock treatment,
in the late 1940s.[7] The comparison was already there in France and
Germany in the wake of extermination policies aimed at the mentally
ill during the war.[8] The analysis was refined in the highly influential
work of Erving Goffman, and this was taken up and developed by
Basaglia in various texts in the 1960s. Basaglia had been heavily influenced, in turn, by Primo Levi, and in particular his first book, *If This Is
a Man,* which was a key text for both him and Franca Ongaro.

---

conversazioni di Franco Basaglia con gli infermieri di Trieste, lezioni intervallate da un dibattito.
1979', deistituzionalizzazione-trieste.it.

5   Massimo Bucciantini, *Esperimento Auschwitz*, Turin: Einaudi, 2011, p. 83.

6   'Piero Gilardi – Manicomio = Lager – 1069', artribune.com.

7   Ugo Cerletti, 'La fossa dei serpenti', *Il Ponte* 5: 11, 1949, pp. 1376. Cerletti painted a
bleak picture of the situation inside asylums at the time, so much so that one of the editors of
the periodical (Corrado Tumiati) intervened to moderate his tone. See also Valeria Babini, *Liberi
tutti. Manicomi e psichiatri in Italia: una storia del novecento*, Bologna: Il Mulino, 2009,
pp. 138–9.

8   See for this history Diego Fontanari and Lorenzo Toresini, eds, *Psichiatria e nazismo.
Atti del Convegno. San Servolo. 9 Ottobre 1998*, Centro di Documentazione di Pistoia
Editrice, Fondazione IRSESC, Istituto per le Ricerche e gli Studi sull'Emarginazione Sociale e
Culturale (San Servolo), Pistoia: Collana dei *Fogli d'Informazione* 27, 2002. In France, however,
some asylums had also been places where anti-fascists and others were able to find refuge from
fascism.

The asylum–concentration-camp analogy had a history in Italy. The release of the film *The Snake Pit* in 1949 had led to denunciations of the asylum system from conservatives such as Indro Montanelli in *Il Corriere della Sera* and Cerletti.[9] Following an important 1964 congress in Bologna, with its stark title 'Processo al manicomio' (The asylum on trial),[10] 1965 saw the beginnings of a public outcry in Italy over the appalling conditions inside Italy's psychiatric hospitals. It was a period of reform, with centre-left alliances in place in many Italian cities and in national government. In that year Angelo Del Boca, a talented journalist and historian, carried out a wide-ranging and influential investigation into the conditions inside Italian asylums. The title of the book published from this journalistic work was blunt and shocking: *Manicomi come lager* (Asylums as concentration camps).[11] The volume had an enormous impact. Public opinion was beginning to change. Moreover, these parallels were not just being drawn by dangerous and isolated radicals, but began to emanate from and resonate within the government itself. Del Boca also visited places that were changing, such as Varese and Gorizia. His book contained an interview with health minister Luigi Mariotti and an extended discussion of the reform proposals that would not become law until 1968. A broad debate took place over the current state and the future of the entire health system. It was a time of change, a time for reform.

In 1965 Mariotti further legitimized the comparison between concentration camps and psychiatric hospitals in a speech linked to proposals for the first radical reforms of the post-war period to the asylum system. This speech caused something of a scandal in the medical establishment and led to official protests, but Mariotti replied that the system itself was 'in crisis'. This all came before Del Boca's book was published. Mariotti also called the asylums 'a disgrace' and argued that the whole system

---

9   See Cerletti, 'La fossa dei serpenti', pp. 1371–8, and the discussion in Babini, pp. 138–9, 141.

10   24–26 April 1964, organized by the Unione Regionale della Provincie Emiliane.

11   See also David Forgacs, *Italy's Margins. Social Exclusion and Nation Formation since 1861*, Cambridge: Cambridge University Press, 2014, p. 199. Del Boca's investigations in 1966 took in asylums in Turin, Lucca and Rome. It may well have been the case that the Mariotti speech and accompanying debate provided the spark for Del Boca to carry out his journalistic 'psycho-tour'. Del Boca cites the speech at the beginning of his book, p. 9. See also Babini, *Liberi tutti*, pp. 213–17.

required radical change. Del Boca wrote that these institutions were 'completely outdated'.[12] He also cited psychiatrists who drew similar conclusions to those of Mariotti. Professor Giuseppe Aschieri from Varese told the journalist that asylums 'should not be called hospitals, or even asylums, or even shelters, rather they are reminiscent of concentration or death camps in terms of their stench and their sense of horror'.[13]

There were various strands to the many links and analogies that were drawn between concentration camps and asylums. On the one hand was the idea of the reduction of inmates to non-persons, to animals, to sub-humans, to mere bodies, a narrative that ran through Levi's work.[14] Another level was more political, the contention that a fascist-like network of institutions was at the heart of the capitalist world and was being used as dumping ground for poverty and deviancy. Thus, the critique of the asylum system could also be a powerful way of understanding capitalism itself and the way it exercised its power. History was also important: patients had been deported from most Italian asylums (usually through the selection of Jewish patients) to the camps. Fascism had used the asylum system to suppress political dissent and to silence problematic individuals (such as Mussolini's first wife and son, and many political rebels and radicals, and well as fascist dissidents).

The sense of stripping inmates in asylums of their humanity and their rights could be found in the work of many of the leading critics of traditional psychiatric methods. As R. D. Laing wrote,

> After being subjected to a degredational ceremonial known as a psychiatric examination he is bereft of his civil liberties in being imprisoned in a total institution known as a 'mental hospital'. More completely, more radically than anywhere else in our society he is invalidated as a human being.[15]

---

12   Del Boca referred to asylums as 'completely outdated institutions' and 'a disgrace'. Del Boca, *Manicomi come lager*, pp. 7 and 11.

13   Ibid., p. 12.

14   See the analysis by Giovanni De Luna of the figure of the 'Muselmann' as described by Levi in *If This Is a Man*, in 'Introduzione' in Willy Jervis, Lucilla Jervis Rochat, Giorgio Agosti, *Un filo tenace. Lettere e memorie 1944–1969*, Turin: Bollati Boringhieri, 2008 (1st ed., 1998, La Nuova Italia), p. 10.

15   'What Is Schizophrenia?', *New Left Review* I: 28, November–December 1964, p. 64.

In the 1960s and 1970s the comparison between asylums and concentration camps or death camps became part of the mainstream. Many of those who saw these institutions in action refer to them in this stark way, almost without explanation: 'It *was* a concentration camp, a *lager*.'[16] Clearly a visual, historical and political comparison is being made, often at the same time. Visually, the comparison with familiar concentration-camp imagery is clear, with its emaciated and uniformed inmates/patients, the long wards and beds, the use of numbers instead of names, as well as the presence and frequent (and routine) use of instruments of torture.

Asylums *looked* like concentration camps. They had high walls and bars, forbidding entrance-ways, long corridors, locks everywhere. They cut the hair of their inmates, took away their clothes and possessions and wedding rings, and gave them (sometimes striped) uniforms to wear. Lobotomies were routine. Inside, patients were often tortured and sometimes beaten, tied up, electrocuted, sexually abused, experimented upon, denied basic human and political rights or even killed. Historically, there are also strong features that were seen as connecting concentration camps (especially the Nazi camps) with asylums as they developed. Nazis took over asylums and systematically exterminated patients there, often in gas chambers constructed for this purpose inside psychiatric hospitals (which continued to function as such). Of course, such practices were not necessarily part of the logic behind asylums, which were much more linked to a sense of protecting society from the mad. Asylums were not there to exterminate the mad. Yet there were continuities to be drawn, especially in terms of experimentation on patients (something common to the camps and asylums), the dehumanizing of inmates (right up to the removal of parts of their brains) and the rigid hierarchies of and behaviour induced by these institutions.

Politically, the comparison with camps was a powerful one, blocking any discussion about the possible benefits of asylums or their restructuring. If asylums were death camps, then they were a public scandal and a problem that could only be resolved through their closure. They

---

16   The word *lager* is widely used in Italian to indicate a concentration camp. For this term see Robert Gordon, *The Holocaust in Italian Culture. 1944–2010*, Stanford: Stanford University Press, 2012, pp 80–1.

could *not* be reformed or made more humanitarian (or, if they could, this was merely a way of perpetuating an immoral system). Like the constant use of the word 'fascist' from that time, the concentration-camp comparison was sweeping and extreme. It was designed to end debate. It made a moral, ethical and political case, all at the same time.

Meanwhile, at a national, political level, things were moving at last. Italy had been governed by a moderate but reformist centre-left coalition from late 1963 onwards. As a result of the entry of the Socialist Party into coalition with the Christian Democrats, a Socialist minister of health was appointed in 1965: Luigi Mariotti.[17] Real reform was on the agenda for the first time since the end of the war. Mariotti had strong ideas about psychiatric hospitals. In September 1965, as mentioned, he compared Italy's asylums to Nazi concentration camps in a speech in Milan that shocked the medical establishment.[18] Mariotti commissioned a report into conditions inside these institutions and into the health system as a whole, as part of a plan for root and branch reform.[19] He quickly became aware of what was going on in Gorizia, which was becoming a model for change, even in the corridors of power in Rome. Both Mariotti and Del Boca pointed to Gorizia as an exception, but also as something that could be reproduced elsewhere. Many psychiatrists working inside asylums were shocked at Mariotti's comments, but not the Basaglians. It was a speech they themselves could have written. Mariotti rubber-stamped the Gorizian experiment in a number of ways, including through his enthusiastic preface to *What Is Psychiatry?* (a real coup for the Gorizian équipe). By 1967 Gorizia had reached right into the corridors of power. Mariotti's reforms (which finally became law in 1968)[20] opened a breach in the closed and repressive world of Italian asylums, allowing for experimentation and change to sweep across the system, as Basaglian methods and ideas became more popular.

*   *   *

---

17   Mariotti was from Florence. He was minister of health from 1964 to 1968 and then again from 1970 to 1972.

18   Part of the speech is reprinted in Giorgio Giannelli and Vito Raponi, eds, *Libro bianco sulla riforma ospedaliera*, supplemento del *Notiziario dell'Amministrazione Sanitaria*, December 1965, pp. 178–9. See also Babini, *Liberi tutti*, pp. 207–9..

19   Giannelli and Raponi, *Libro bianco sulla riforma ospedaliera*.

20   Law 431, March 1968.

The concentration-camp analogy was drawn early on in *The Negated Institution*.[21] One of the patients interviewed near the start of the book was an Auschwitz survivor, 'Carla', who also appeared in *I giardini di Abele*. As Robert Gordon wrote, 'within the anti-asylum movement, the Lager analogy was commonplace, found in everything from graffiti to pamphlets to works of serious intellectual substance'.[22]

Carla, Caterina or Carolina Nardini had indeed been in Auschwitz. She was born on 23 March 1916 in Maria Enzersdorf close to Vienna and had been arrested in Gorizia, before her deportation to Auschwitz as a political prisoner and, in October 1944, to the camp of Flossenbürg. The number tattooed on her arm was 56579. It is said that Nardini was a fascist who refused to reveal names to the Nazis. It is also said that she was placed in the brothel in Auschwitz. Finally, on her return to Gorizia, it seems that she was attacked as an ex-fascist.[23] Nardini was secretary of the patients' general assembly for some time and appeared in Sergio Zavoli's TV documentary in 1968. Nardini built up a strong friendship with Basaglia, writing him postcards and letters from inside the hospital, and referring to him as 'our beloved director'.[24] In 1968 she made an official request for a state subsidy as a deportee, through her representative, the psychiatrist Leopoldo Tesi.

Primo Levi was a constant presence in Basaglian texts from the 1960s onwards. His work was important to them. The Basaglias made sure their children read *If This Is a Man* at a young age. It was a key text for their understanding of the world, and the world they worked in. Franca Ongaro and others within the movement often used 'Levian' language to describe what happened to people once they were interned inside

---

21   Basaglia, *L'istituzione negata* (1968), p. 24.

22   Gordon, *The Holocaust in Italian Culture. 1944–2010*, p. 134 and 135.

23   *Il libro dei deportati*. Ricerca del Dipartimento di Storia dell'Università di Torino diretta da Brunello Mantelli e Nicola Tranfaglia, promossa da ANED, Vol. 2, G-P, Giovanna d'Amico, Giovanni Vilari and Francesco Cassata eds, Milan: Mursia, 2009, pp. 1506–7. See also the account of a patient in Simona Guerra, ed., *Mario Dondero*, Milan: Bruno Mondadori, 2011, p. 167.

24   'Letter to Basaglia' (on behalf of 'the community'), 17 February 1969. See also for example the postcard to Basaglia in 1968 with a photo of a dog and the message 'To be or not to be faithful', and another letter in 1969 to Basaglia from Nardini with the address 'Manicomio Maliconico [The sad madhouse]', Via Veneto 174, Gorizia.

psychiatric hospitals.[25] Goffman's work was also central here, and had a strong influence on *What Is Psychiatry?* and *The Negated Institution*. As Andrew Scull puts it, Goffman described asylums 'as irredeemably flawed "total institutions", engines of degradation, misery and oppression resembling, in their central structural features, nothing so much as concentration camps or prisons'.[26] The Basaglias brought together Goffman and Levi to create an ethical, sociological and historically based critique of the asylum system.

Massimo Bucciantini has recently carried out an extended study of the influence of Primo Levi's work on Franco and Franca Basaglia.[27] He shows how the Basaglias used Levi to understand and interpret asylums. In this way *If This Is a Man* changed its meaning, playing

> a role which was linked to memory but also in terms of criticizing an inhumane state of affairs which had been ignored, and becoming a key text, the fundamental book for a scientific and social project which also created something of a 'scandal'.[28]

The Basaglias saw Levi as a 'naturalist–anthropologist, a clinical observer of man in his maximum state of privation and abjection'. They used citations from Levi within and on the covers of their books, and in Ongaro's presentation of Goffman's *Asylums*. The fight against the *manicomio* system was thus moral, ethical *and* political. As Franca Ongaro put it in 1967,

> Goffman's analysis of patients in psychiatric hospitals or that of Franz Fanon on the condition of black people, or that of Primo Levi about

---

25   Franca Ongaro Basaglia, *Manicomio perché?* Milan: Emme Edizioni, 1982, pp. 15–16. This analogy has also been used in some of the literature on Gorizia. For example, Nancy Scheper-Hughes and Anne Lovell cite Basaglia from *L'istituzione negata* in his discussion of the way that 'the original concentration camp environment gave way to more human relationships' and write of Basaglia's 'evocative equation of asylum, prison and concentration camp' (own experiences as anti-fascist) in *Psychiatry Inside Out*, pp. 4, 6, n. 15 and pp. 305–6.

26   Andrew Scull, 'The Insanity of Place', *History of Psychiatry* 15: 4, 2004, p. 429. See also Erving Goffman, 'The Insanity of Place', in Appendix, *Relations in Public: Microstudies of the Public Order*, New York: Basic Books, 1971, p. 336.

27   Bucciantini, *Esperimento Auschwitz*, pp. 69–91.

28   Ibid, p. 69.

prisoners in Nazi death – all these texts speak the same language because they all refer to the same phenomenon.[29]

Interestingly, Primo Levi himself rejected this analogy. In an interview he gave in the year before his death, Levi said this:

> I felt a little uncomfortable when Basaglia sent me his book which cited *If This Is a Man* and where he wrote that psychiatric hospitals are concentration camps. I don't think we can go this far if not at the level of metaphor or allusion. The aim of psychiatric hospitals was to defend the mentally ill, not kill them. If they died inside it was a sad by-product, not the aim. They are probably ugly places, but made for other ends.[30]

But, as Bucciantini concludes, 'beyond its author's judgement, *If This Is a Man* ended up by assuming a symbolic value for a new generation of doctors and psychiatrists. We might say that Italian anti-psychiatry discovered its own archetype in that text'.[31]

Of course, Franco and Franca Basaglia did not believe that the asylums were *exactly the same* as concentration camps or death camps. If they had done, their position of authority inside these places would have been untenable. They would have been the equivalent of concentration-camp guards. The use of Levi was symbolic, allegorical, a powerful political and literary tool, a provocation, and, at times, a crude propaganda weapon. It was the movement, especially after 1968, which took up and simplified the message into *manicomio = lager*. Given such popular slogans, it was not surprising that Basaglia himself was often and increasingly attacked as the 1970s wore on for his role as a 'manager of concentration camps'.

In *The Negated Institution* the sense of death hung over the description of the asylum system, particularly in the opening account by Nino Vascon

---

29   Erving Goffman, *La carriera morale del malato mentale*, Annotated by Franca Basaglia Ongaro, in Franco Basaglia, ed., *Che cos'è la psichiatria?*, Milan: Baldini & Castoldi, 1998, p. 243. See also Mario Colucci and Pierangelo Di Vittorio, *Franco Basaglia*, Bruno Mondadori, Milan, 2001, p. 180.

30   1986, cited in Bucciantini, *Esperimento Auschwitz*, p. 87.

31   Ibid., p. 89.

(the part of the book which probably remained in most people's minds). There was a sense that an asylum was a place where people came to die, and that the only sure way out was in a coffin. In 1969, the concentration-camp analogy was carried further, and into the visual sphere, with *Morire di classe*. This mixed visual–textual photo-book again carried (once again) the oft-used Primo Levi quote from *What Is Psychiatry?*, but this time the quote (in stark and very large lettering) was accompanied by a black and white photo of a woman, her hair shorn, sitting on a stone bench. Her shoes were falling apart, and she seemed to be dressed in a kind of uniform. She was a patient in an asylum, but she could have been, easily, an internee in a concentration camp. Readers were left to draw their own conclusions, but the message was clear, and not particularly subtle.

In the wake of 1968, radical anti-psychiatrists used the concentration-camp–asylum comparison in order to make their points from the left, sometimes in opposition to Basaglia and his colleagues. Edelweiss Cotti, in 1968, argued that asylums were actually *worse* than concentration camps. At least people had the chance of being liberated, he said, from the Nazi camps. How can you 'manage' a concentration camp?, he asked. Despite this outlook, Cotti would end up in charge of one of the biggest and most concentration-camp-like asylums in Italy, the so-called 'L'Osservanza' complex in Imola.[32]

Cotti's book *Contro la psichiatria* (Against psychiatry),written with Roberto Vigevani, contains an extended comparison between concentration camps and the asylum system. Vigevani argued that 'the asylum can be compared to a Nazi concentration camp or a black ghetto' and psychiatrists should refuse to carry out their duties in what amounted to the management of 'concentration camps'. Moreover, therapeutic communities, he claimed, were simply a way of 'making a concentration camp a little better'.[33]

Giorgio Antonucci has made similar arguments over the years:

---

32   Edelweiss Cotti, 'La pazzia è un invenzione', Lorenza Mazzetti, ed., *Rinascita* 41, October 1968. See also Edelweiss Cotti and Roberto Vigevani, *Contro la psichiatria,* Florence: La Nuova Italia, 1970.

33   'La repressione psichiatrica' in Cotti and Vigevani, *Contro la psichiatria*, pp. 129, 190, 197.

We do not believe that you can separate the negation of psychiatric institutions from the negation of psychiatry as a science. Psychiatry built the asylums, and it would still build them, and it continues to justify their existence not only in Italy, but unfortunately in most of the countries in the world. The essence of psychiatry lies in an ideology of discrimination – and all its ideas are scientifically inconclusive and unfounded and practically damaging . . . Politically, we could draw this important parallel. You cannot start to destroy concentration camps or ghettos without denying and destroying racial ideologies, which inevitably lead to concentration camps and ghettoes.[34]

The concentration-camp analogy was a powerful one, which was a key part of the Basaglian world-view and was taken up by the movement as a whole. Nonetheless, it carried certain pitfalls, not least the danger that it would be used against those who were trying to change things from within, and not from without. In the end, the comparison was most effective in terms of its propagandistic power. As a realistic or historical analogy, it simplified what was actually going on within asylums, and might even have made the work of Basaglia and his allies more difficult. Yet the analogy also captured something central about the dehumanization processes at work within psychiatric hospitals, something that appeared so clearly to Basaglia on that first visit to Gorizia, in 1961.

Basaglia had begun to free the patients from their chains right from the start, allowing them to become human beings again. Walls were knocked down and fences removed bit by bit, the tying up of patients was discouraged and then phased out altogether, and some were even discharged as far as was possible under the 1904 legislation. Antonio Slavich later claimed that Basaglia had stopped ordering the tying up of patients immediately after his arrival, although this practice probably continued thanks to other more traditional doctors who worked in the asylum. Electroshock therapy also continued for some time under the Basaglia administration.[35] Other changes were gradually implemented. Patients

---

34   Giorgio Antonucci, *Il pregiudizio psichiatrico*, Eléuthera, 1999, eleuthera.it.

35   There are differing accounts over the use of electroconvulsive therapy in Gorizia in the 1960s, most of them based on contrasting testimonies. It seems that ECT was still being used

were encouraged to work, and not just for bartered cigarettes but for real money. The instrument was the équipe, but the aim was (in the first instance) to create a new kind of overturned institution. This new thing was given a name: the therapeutic community. Gorizia became the first attempt to build one in Italy. With time, it might be argued, Gorizia would become the most complete, radical and 'perfect' example of a therapeutic community in the world.

---

in some wards in the mid- to late 1960s, although the role of Basaglia in this is unclear. Later, the use of ECT became a key issue for the movement. On the removal of constraints see *L'istituzione negata* and Slavich in Silvia Balconi, *L'esperienza Goriziana dal '61 al '72. Un percorso paradigmatico di valorizzazione della professionalità in ambito psichiatrico*, unpublished thesis, Università degli studi di Torino, 1997–98, pp. 495–6.

SEVEN

Gorizia: The Therapeutic Community

'We do not believe that the therapeutic community is an institutional model which should be seen as a technical way of resolving conflicts.'

Franco Basaglia[1]

'Gorizia's therapeutic community exploded like a bomb in the world of Italian psychiatry . . . This explosion, which was sudden and violent, opened up a wide and deep crater which was difficult to close with new models of management and scientific support.'
Mario Colucci and Pierangelo Di Vittorio[2]

'I think that the existence of the therapeutic community in Gorizia, in the 1960s, made a crucial contribution (more than any other factor) to a change in public opinion in terms of Italian asylums – which were at the time unworthy of a civilized country – and to move Italy towards a modern psychiatric reform.'

Giovanni Jervis[3]

---

1   Franco Basaglia, ed., *L'istituzione negata*, Turin: Einaudi, 1968, p. 149.

2   Mario Colucci and Pierangelo Di Vittorio, *Franco Basaglia*, Milan: Bruno Mondadori, 2001, p. 107.

3   Cited in 'Basaglia, il cavaliere bizzarro della psichiatria', *Il Corriere della Sera*, 29 August 2000.

From the mid-1960s onwards, the Gorizian asylum was usually described as a therapeutic community and was widely viewed as the first of its kind in Italy. Giovanni Jervis first saw what was happening in Gorizia around that time, and a decade or so later he wrote that the hospital there 'when seen close-up, it looked like the therapeutic community that I had seen in Great Britain, at least in some wards'.[4]

But what *was* Gorizia's therapeutic community? Should it have been in capitals, or within quotation marks? Was it 'therapeutic' at all? Was it indeed a 'community'? Basaglia's activity in Gorizia was influenced by various examples of institutional change outside Italy which he had read about or seen first-hand, including the self-proclaimed therapeutic community in Dingleton in Scotland, the Villa 21 and Kingsley Hall experiments in England, and radical developments in France and the USA, as well as by his own experiences and philosophical outlook. By far the most important of these models was the Scottish one.

To begin to answer these questions, we need first, like Basaglia himself and Franca Ongaro in the early 1960s, to pay a visit to rural Scotland.

The Blueprint. Dingleton. Scotland

'An open system implies that anyone, including the director, can be questioned regarding his statements and actions. Clearly, it is much easier and less risky to confront a peer, or someone lower in the pecking order, than a senior. I feel that this freedom to question anyone is mandatory if an open system is to survive and to grow.'

Maxwell Jones[5]

'The classic therapeutic community, set up after 1949 by Maxwell Jones, is based on some key elements: freedom of expression, the destruction of authoritarian relationships, an understanding of the real world, permissiveness, democratization – these are all crucial

---

4   Giovanni Jervis, *Il buon rieducatore*, 1977, p. 19.
5   Maxwell Jones, *The Maturation of the Therapeutic Community. An Organic Approach to Health and Mental Health*, New York: Human Sciences Press, 1976, p. 42.

aspects of the unmasking of asylum structures, which are founded
on authoritarian structures, violence, the objectivization of the ill
patient, the absence of communication.'

Franco Basaglia

'The most difficult part of the process of change was my initial
impact with an established traditional psychiatric hospital.'

Maxwell Jones[6]

Gorizians had a model for their revolution, and it came from the UK.
It also had a name: the therapeutic community, and an inspirational
inventor/leader/prophet: the South African/American/Scottish psychiatrist Maxwell Jones. This was a fully functioning therapeutic community
that could be visited and studied, found in Dingleton, south of Edinburgh.
A number of Gorizians made the pilgrimage to Dingleton in the 1960s,
and some stayed there to observe the workings of the hospital: Franco
and Franca Basaglia, Lucio Schittar, Giovanni Jervis. Maxwell Jones and
Basaglia became friends, and the latter promoted the former's work in
Italy. Basaglia wrote a preface to a translation of one of Jones's books into
Italian and attempted, through Jervis and also directly, to recommend
some of his other work to Einaudi.[7]

What was going on in Dingleton Hospital in the 1960s? This forbidding asylum had been built on the moors outside a small Scottish border
town in 1872. Dingleton had a history of liberal administration. A previous medical superintendent, George Macdonald Bell, implemented
an open-door policy there after 1945. By 1949 all the wards had been
opened up. Maxwell Jones called Dingleton 'the first totally open mental
hospital in the English-speaking world'. This was an institution that was
already a model for others, and the perfect place for further experimentation in new forms of treatment and asylum organization. But Maxwell
Jones was to go much, much further than a simple open-door policy.

---

6   Maxwell Jones, *The Process of Change*, London: Routledge and Kegan Paul, 1982,
p. 5.

7   Franco Basaglia and Franca Ongaro Basaglia, 'Prefazione' to Maxwell Jones, *Ideologia e
Practica della Psichiatria sociale*, Etas Compass, 1970, now in Franco Basaglia, *Scritti. II. 1968-1980*,
ed. Franca Ongaro Basaglia, Turin: Einaudi, 1982, pp. 105–25. Nonetheless this preface was
extremely critical of Maxwell Jones's ideas and the whole idea of the therapeutic community.

Jones had been trained in Edinburgh but was of South African origin. He had been extensively involved in therapeutic communities and innovative forms of mental health care in the UK before, during and after World War Two and had published some of the key texts on the subject. In 1947 he put some of his new ideas into practice at Belmont Hospital in Surrey, and this experience provided the basis for a fuller outline of the theory and practice of future therapeutic communities.

Jones took over at Dingleton in 1962 (around the same time that Basaglia arrived in Gorizia) and began to create what he called a therapeutic community. Patients were encouraged to work in the real world, outside the hospital, and there were regular, daily meetings and discussions and general, hospital-wide meetings on Wednesdays. Visits were actively promoted and barriers of all kinds were removed, including the hospital's gates in 1969, when Jones returned to the USA (and Basaglia left Gorizia). He argued for a form of *social psychiatry*, which 'includes all social, psychological, anthropological, philosophical and research factors, which may modify psychiatric practice towards a more equilibrated society with less mental illness' (1969).[8]

During meetings, chairs were placed in a circle, doctors mixed with patients and Maxwell Jones was referred to as 'Max'. In addition, other visible signs of authority and hierarchy – white coats, titles, medical paraphernalia – were toned down or removed altogether. But the therapeutic community was not merely a list of features. It was more than that, being almost a new institution *within* an institution, with its own (written and unwritten) rules, regulations and customs. All of these features were to be taken up and reproduced in Gorizia, although they were never simply copied. Jones's policies were radically different to traditional views of what psychiatric hospitals were for, but they were also in line with previous open-door policies and attitudes in Dingleton. As Jones's predecessor George Macdonald Bell argued, 'The only way to obtain security in a mental hospital and in the surrounding community is to open the doors and leave them open.'[9] Paolo Tranchina later wrote: 'The atmosphere in Dingleton Hospital . . . was interesting and open.

---

8   Cited in Anonymous, *The Story of a Community: Dingleton Hospital, Melrose*, Melrose: Chiefswood Publications, 2000, p. 124.

9   Cited in ibid., p. 79.

As well as the criticizing of institutional structures, in the debate on education a strong emphasis was placed on emotional problems, which are crucial in terms of new therapeutic relationships'.[10]

The aim in Dingleton was to 'create a genuine "community spirit"'.[11] Hence the 'importance given to communication, to commitment in relationships and to communal pursuits, not to mention the steps taken to reduce the distance between patients and the medical team by suppressing traditional attributes of authority'.[12] Dennie Lynn Briggs wrote about Dingleton:

> It is difficult sometimes for newcomers to realize just who is staff and who is patient in this treatment setting. This is perhaps one measure of the success of the methods that have been consciously employed to level the authoritarian atmosphere found in most hospitals. When symbols of status are removed, it is indeed difficult for a staff member to revert to and maintain an authoritarian role 'over' a patient.[13]

This power shift was difficult for many doctors and nurses to accept, and there was considerable resistance to change, even in a place like Dingleton, well known for its liberal policies. Maxwell Jones's plan called into question the specific role of doctors, nurses and patients. It aimed at creating real, human relationships between all those inside the hospital. Dingleton was, in many ways, a place where the institution itself (and the logic behind it) was being 'negated'. It was a living example of an overturned institution.

Therapeutic communities demanded total commitment to the cause from their staff, as well as sensitive and hard-nosed political and institutional support. David Clark, who set up and ran another celebrated therapeutic community in Cambridge, wrote,

---

10   Paolo Tranchina, 'Fogli d'informazione, lotte antistituzionali, Legge 180', *Fogli d'informazione* 5–6, 3rd series, 1 June 2008, psychiatryonline.it.

11   Catherine Fussinger, '"Therapeutic Community", Psychiatry's Reformers and Anti-psychiatrists: Reconsidering Changes in the Field of Psychiatry after World War II', *History of Psychiatry* 22: 2, 2011, p. 150.

12   Ibid., p. 150.

13   Dennie Briggs, 'Social Psychiatry in Great Britain', *American Journal of Nursing* 59: 2, 1959, p. 218, cited in Fussinger, 'Therapeutic Community', p. 150.

a therapeutic community is an excellent system in which troubled people can come to understand and modify their disturbed and disturbing behaviour. It works well when it meets a major social need and has a flexible management to support it. But it does make great demands on the staff and often causes difficulties and embarrassments for managers.[14]

Other features of the therapeutic community were not necessarily part of the original plan, such as the charismatic and hegemonic role of the community 'leader', and a tendency to overplay the formal, visual aspects of change. A key question for the proponents of therapeutic communities was this: who was really in charge? Other crucial questions went even further: Should asylums be abolished altogether? Was the therapeutic community an end in itself, or a means to an end? Were social psychiatrists reformists, or revolutionaries?

Translating Dingleton and Other Models of Change

'The first experiences started by Maxwell Jones had an enormous importance, especially as they started out with the idea that it was possible to overturn the terms of the argument. He began with practical issues, in line with the English pragmatic tradition, and reacted to the reality which he saw in front of him – and this led to immediate forms of practice, outside of the realm of all technical and scientific prejudices which would have trapped him within a sense of codification or rigid definitions.'

Franco Basaglia (1970)

How did the Gorizians import this idea of a therapeutic community to Italy? As we have seen, in such practice, regular community meetings were established. These were open to all, but attendance was not obligatory. Jones had also used meetings of this kind in his previous attempts to create therapeutic communities. In Dingleton the regular meetings

---

14   David Clark, *The Story of a Mental Hospital. Fulbourn 1858–1983*, London: Process Press, 1996, Chapter 5, human-nature.com.

were on Fridays at 3pm and Maxwell Jones himself was a constant presence. This model would be transplanted, at least in part, to Gorizia.

Word spread fast about Dingleton (as it would later on with Gorizia) and those interested in changing things turned up looking for work or simply to observe and learn from a different system. Dingleton was extensively filmed and studied: it became famous, and not just amongst psychiatrists.[15] A sprinkling of more radical experiments were seen in other parts of the UK in the 1960s, including the work of David Cooper and R. D. Laing inside traditional psychiatric hospitals (the Rumpus Room in Gartneval Hospital in Glasgow[16] and Villa 21) and the later setting up of an entirely new, alternative and private space for therapy, in Kingsley Hall in East London in 1965. R. D. Laing had also visited Dingleton. Basaglia went to Kingsley Hall in the late 1960s and was in contact with Laing and Cooper, as were other members of the équipe. These experiments fed off each other, and experiences were often shared. We have already looked at the Rumpus Room. It is now time to examine the Villa 21 experiment.

Villa 21: 'An Experiment in Anti-psychiatry'?[17]

According to his own version of events, outlined in his classic and influential book *Psychiatry and Anti-psychiatry* (1967), David Cooper started his experimental work in January 1962 in a special unit known as Villa 21 within a large mental hospital just outside London (Shenley Hospital, near Radlett in Hertfordshire, 1934–88). Cooper was a senior registrar in the hospital. South African–born (1931), he had moved to London in the mid-1950s and had met Laing in 1958. He described himself as

---

15   Other well-known experimental therapeutic communities in the UK in the 1950s and 1960s included those in Mapperley Hospital, Nottingham and Warlingham Park Hospital in Croydon.

16   Jonathan Andrews, 'R. D. Laing in Scotland: Facts and Fictions of the "Rumpus Room" and Interpersonal Psychiatry' in Gijswjt-Hofstra and Porter, eds, *Cultures of Psychiatry*, pp. 121–50; Allan Beveridge, *Portrait of the Psychiatrist as a Young Man. The Early Writing and Work of R. D. Laing, 1927–1960*, Oxford: Oxford University Press, 2011, pp. xv–xvi, 153, 199–223.

17   David Cooper, *Psychiatry and Anti-psychiatry*, London: Tavistock, 1967, pp. 73–104.

an 'existential Marxist' and went on to write a book with Laing, published in 1964, about the work of Sartre.[18]

The Villa 21 unit only took young male patients, most of whom had been diagnosed as schizophrenics and were at the early stages of a supposed breakdown. It was a small ward (initially there were nineteen beds with some twenty to twenty-five patients[19]). Only three doctors worked in the unit. At first, there were meetings and numerous activities laid out for the patients. As Cooper wrote, 'The original programme of the unit was deliberately a highly structured one, not unlike that of the "classical" therapeutic community'.[20] As in Dingleton and Gorizia, a series of regular meetings were held there. The language used by Cooper in his later analysis of Villa 21 was very similar to that of *The Negated Institution*. Debates were continual; everything was up for grabs. For Cooper 'there was a progressive blurring of role between nurses, doctor, occupational therapist, and patients'.[21] This phrase could have been taken straight from a combination Maxwell Jones and Basaglia, although it referred only to one unit within a huge psychiatric hospital, and not to a whole asylum.

Villa 21 was also put under constant pressure thanks largely to the increasing hostility of the authorities to the experimentation there. However, we only have Cooper's version of what went on, and he was of course interested in presenting Villa 21 in the best possible light, although he was also clear about the limitations of the experimental work there. Clancy Sigal's highly entertaining novel, *Zone of the Interior*, based in part on his experiences in Villa 21, paints a somewhat different picture of daily life in the unit, although the overall feel is a positive one. Later testimonies gathered from nurses who worked in Villa 21 were much more nuanced in their memories.[22] Cooper dealt with the attitude of

---

18   Jean-Paul Sartre, *Reason and Violence. A Decade of Sartre's Philosophy*, London: Routledge, 1964.

19   There is a lot of confusion in the existing literature about the number of patients inside Villa 21. Some writers make the mistake of taking the figure in the academic article published by Cooper, Esterson and Laing, which talks of forty-two patients in two mental hospitals, and applying that figure to Villa 21 itself.

20   Cooper, *Psychiatry and Anti-psychiatry*, p. 86.

21   Ibid., p. 92.

22   It is well known that Laing attempted, successfully, to prevent the publication of this novel in the UK. It finally appeared as Clancy Sigal, *Zone of the Interior*. Pomona: Hebden Bridge, 2005.

the various nurses and doctors on the unit in some detail in his analysis in *Psychiatry and Anti-psychiatry*. Cooper was also very clear about the limits of such work inside state institutions:

> We have had many pipe-dreams about the ideal psychiatric, or rather anti-psychiatric, community, but I believe we have now, by a process of demystification, sufficiently delineated the true nature of psychiatric madness and sufficiently worked out our practical needs to take a step forward. And a step forward means ultimately a step out of the mental hospital into the community.[23]

There were significant differences between Gorizia and Villa 21. Cooper was, for example, much more critical than the Gorizians about the use of anti-psychotic drugs, or the 'value' of work. Activities were provided for the patients in Villa 21, but they were also left to their own devices. Above all, Cooper and his colleagues (Laing, Aaron Esterson and others) were interested in understanding schizophrenia as 'part of a network of extremely disturbed and disturbing patterns of communication' and in developing 'a form of therapy' which did 'not focus on the individual patient but on the group or system of communications of which he is part, whether within his family or within the mental hospital'.[24] The experiment seems to have been a success in terms of discharging a number of patients from hospital, and especially in lowering readmission rates. Cooper, Laing and Esterson also made clear that simply returning patients to their families was by no means a solution to any of the issues they were trying to deal with. On the contrary, this approach was anathema to their whole approach to mental illness. They wrote, 'We try to help the patient and his family to be less disturbing to each other by intensive work with the whole family, including the patient during his stay in hospital.'[25] This attention to the family appears to have been of far less importance for the Gorizians.

---

23 Cooper, *Psychiatry and Anti-psychiatry*, p. 104.

24 Aaron Esterson, David Cooper, R. D. Laing, 'Results of Family-Orientated Therapy with Hospitalized Schizophrenics', *British Medical Journal* 2, 1965, p. 1462.

25 Esterson, Cooper, Laing, 'Results of Family-Orientated Therapy', p. 1465. See also R. D. Laing and Aaron Esterson, *Sanity, Madness, and the Family. Vol. 1. Families of Schizophrenics*, London: Tavistock, 1964.

But, as well as presenting their results in the form of a serious, scientific paper, with statistics, footnotes, formal titles and so on, Cooper, Laing and Esterson were also interested in making links with counter-cultural and political experiments elsewhere. In a *New Society* article penned by Cooper entitled 'The Anti-hospital' (published in 1965, and surely the first time that the 'anti' label was used by Cooper), Villa 21 was described as 'a revolutionary experiment' where 'traditional notions of authority have been upended' and which had led people 'seriously to question whether this invalid is in fact invalid or invalidated'.[26] 'Schizophrenia', Cooper argued, was not a disease, 'but rather a crazy way in which whole families function'. Labelling of one family member often takes place, which can lead to their diagnosis and hospitalization. What follows is 'progressive violence . . . perpetrated, in the name of treatment, against the labelled patient'. The Villa 21 experiment had been an eye-opener for all involved, but it was constrained by its institutional setting. Cooper concluded that there was 'the need for a fully autonomous unit . . . free of conventional institutional conformist pressures and their subtle violence'.[27] This was the analysis that would lead to Kingsley Hall. In fact, Villa 21 was described by Cooper as a blueprint for a place like Kingsley Hall, in order 'to establish a viable prototype for a small autonomous unit which could function in a large house in the community, outside the psychiatric institutional context'.[28]

The experiment at Villa 21 continued until Cooper left in 1966 (when Kingsley Hall was already up and running) and the unit was closed.[29] Many of those who worked there remember the filth which piled up everywhere towards the end of the experimental period. The authorities were anxious to wipe out the memory of Villa 21, so much so that it was

---

26   David Cooper, 'The Anti-hospital: An Experiment in Psychiatry', *New Society*, 11 March 1965, p. 11.

27   Ibid. This was also the conclusion of his account of Villa 21 in Cooper, *Psychiatry and Anti-psychiatry.*

28   Cooper, *Psychiatry and Anti-psychiatry*, p. 84.

29   The main source for Cooper's work in Villa 21 tends to be Cooper himself. This is also true of most studies that analyse Villa 21 in some way, although some do take a more critical approach to these sources, such as Fussinger, 'Therapeutic Community', pp. 151, 153–9. Original research does seem, at last, to be taking place into the Villa 21 experience; see Oisin Wall, 'The Birth and Death of Villa 21', *History of Psychiatry* 24: 3, 2013, pp. 326–40.

apparently renamed Villa 20A. It also appears that the archives relating to that time have disappeared.

By 1966, Villa 21 appeared to have made progress in ways that could be compared to Gorizia, but on a much smaller scale, and Cooper was well aware of the limitations of what had gone on there. Cooper's published account of Villa 21 that came out in 1967 was highly significant across the world of radical psychiatry. In conclusion, Cooper felt that his experimentation had gone as far as it could inside a public institution:

> Mental hospitals were invented to 'look after' or (in rasher moments) to 'cure' sick persons. If the 'sickness' is called in question, and if the isolation of one patient-person from the more truly sick family system is shown to be a fallacy, then we are in an area of most radical questioning indeed.[30]

This conclusion led Cooper, Laing and others to set up an entirely new space for people with mental health issues, outside of state institutions altogether, in 1965. This place was called Kingsley Hall.

Kingsley Hall: Introduction

R. D. Laing set up the Philadelphia Association in 1965 (with David Cooper, Aaron Esterson, Sid Briskin, Clancy Sigal and others), and Kingsley Hall was opened in the same year. Kingsley Hall was a large community space/building in East London where Gandhi had once stayed. The Philadelphia Association was bold in its statement of intent:

> We aim to change the way the 'facts' of 'mental health' and 'mental illness' are seen. This is more than a new hypothesis inserted into an existing field of research and therapy; it is a proposal to change the model.

In theory, there was a complete open-door and free-for-all policy at Kingsley Hall, although the practice was different, and there were

---

30 Cooper, *Psychiatry and Anti-psychiatry*, p. 103

intense debates over rules and the behaviour of residents. According to the organizers, some 130 people stayed in the building at various points and for differing periods over the five years when it was open, as well as a number of psychiatrists including Laing, Cooper, Esterson, Joe Berke, Leon Redler and others.[31] Many, many others came to visit, including Basaglia and Franca Ongaro in 1969 (just as the experiment was coming to a close). The most celebrated (non-psychiatrist) resident at Kingsley Hall was Mary Barnes, whose journey 'through madness' was told in book form and later became a West End play.[32] Kingsley Hall is (and was) often referred to as a therapeutic community, but it bore little relation to any of the other experiences we have described so far.

Many have seen it as a kind of counter-cultural commune, an experiment in an alternative form of asylum, in the real sense of the term – as a 'haven' providing 'shelter or protection from danger'. It has also been described as a 'chaotic mess'.[33] Joseph Berke later noted the 'general turmoil' in the place.[34] Some have argued that the set-up of Kingsley Hall was irresponsible and damaging for the patients there, as well as in terms of the message the place was sending out to the rest of the world. Comments have often concentrated on the more lurid aspects of the place, the drug-taking, the drinking, the sex, the bizarre behaviour, the attempted suicides, the hostility expressed by some elements of the local community. Certainly, the form and content at Kingsley Hall seem light years away from what was taking place in Gorizia at the same time, although there are more parallels with what would happen later in Trieste, perhaps, in the 1970s.

---

31   Detailed records do not appear to have been kept (in some ways they would have been against the whole spirit of the place, and who would have kept them anyway?) and, as I write, no serious historical research has been carried out with regard to the Kingsley Hall experience.

32   Franca Ongaro later advised Einaudi to publish the book, but it was not translated and published in Italian until the early 1980s, and not with Einaudi; Mary Barnes and Joseph Berke, *Viaggio attraverso la follia*, Milan: Rusconi, 1981.

33   Hugh Freeman, 'A Man Who Used to Be Ronnie Laing', *Times Higher Education Supplement*, 16 May 1997.

34   Joseph Berke, 'Trick or Treat: The Divided Self of R. D. Laing', janushead.org.

The Italian Movement and Kingley Hall

'Did Kingsley Hall succeed? It is an irrelevant question, it did no harm. It did not cure. It was simply a place where some people encountered selves, lost, distorted or forgotten. Given time, given luck, some were able to hear the beating of their hearts and elucidate the rhythm.'

Joe Berke[35]

Franco and Franca Basaglia visited Kingsley Hall in 1969, towards the end of the experiment, at a time when Laing himself was involved in other activities.[36] Basaglia was making a film at the time, and according to Paolo Tranchina, this was the first time that TV cameras had filmed the inside of Kingsley Hall.[37] Tranchina described it as 'the model for all those halfway-houses and family-homes which would be formed later'.[38] Tranchina and Basaglia also met Mary Barnes (still living there in 1969). In this account, Kingsley Hall is depicted as a 'peaceful' and 'simple' place. According to Tranchina, 'Franco was struck by the experience and he engaged in lively discussions about the possibility of using this type of structure elsewhere and its practical implications'.

Basaglia engaged at some length with the Kingsley Hall experience and the ideas of Laing and Cooper, especially after 1968 and the visit to the UK in September 1969. In *La maggioranza deviante*, the first book written by the Basaglias after *L'istituzione negata*, there is an extended discussion of the Laingian network in the UK (and in particular in London).[39] This section is a mix of interviews, debates and a description and analysis of what we might call the Laingian experience.

---

35 'Therapeutic Community Models: Kingsley Hall' in E. Jansen ed., *The Therapeutic Community: Outside the Hospital*, London: Croom Helm, 1980, p. 101.

36 The account we have of this visit is largely culled from the article by Paolo Tranchina, who was present: 'Fogli d'informazione, lotte antistituzionali, Legge 180', *Fogli d'informazione* 5–6, 3rd series, 1 June 2008, psychiatryonline.it.

37 Although there are a number of fragments of film of Kinglsey Hall, some of which have been used by Luke Fowler in his art installations, *All Divided Selves*, lux.org.uk.

38 Tranchina, 'Fogli d'informazione', pp. 52–3.

39 Franco Basaglia and Franca Ongaro Basaglia, eds, *La maggioranza deviante. L'ideologia del controllo sociale totale*, Turin: Einaudi, 1971, pp. 103–29.

The Basaglias were critical in this text of what they called

the dangers of escaping into a kind of existential consciousness which would lead to a new objectification. There is an illusion here that you can somehow 'leave the game', and attempt to create a non-organized organization which is outside of the world of 'power' and its institutions.[40]

The book also notes that many of those involved in the network (Cooper, Laing and others) had previously worked within state institutions. Basaglia also underlined the lack of a social analysis in the UK experience. But the book makes clear how interested the Basaglias were in what was going on in the UK, and shows how there was an ongoing dialogue between their own work and that of Laing, Redler and others. Basaglia was anxious for his work to be recognized in the UK, where critical psychiatry had first taken root. Laing, his theories and his practice were treated with great respect. In the long interview with Laing in *La maggioranza deviante*, there is very little analysis or even input from the editors/authors of the volume. For example, Laing is given time and space to describe, once again, his experience with the Rumpus Room in the 1950s. Yet, the Basaglian final conclusion (expressed mainly in the form of a series of questions) was certainly sceptical:

How will this network succeed in saving just one of these experiences from the totalization effect on behaviours of the capitalist system? What is different, in terms of domination, when a person declares themself not to be a therapist, or a patient says that they are a non-patient?[41]

The Basaglias also poured scorn on the anti-psychiatric idea that understood personal crises as a kind of journey.

A further long debate with Laing appeared in *Crimini di pace*, published in Italy in 1975.[42] Here the Basaglias again showed some scepticism in terms

---

40　Ibid, pp. 105–6.

41　Ibid., p. 129.

42　Franco Basaglia and Franca Basaglia Ongaro, 'Crimini di pace' in Franco Basaglia and Franca Basaglia Ongaro eds., *Crimini di pace. Ricerche sugli intellettuali e sui tecnici come addetti*

of the social and political reach of Laing's work, and his claim that he was working outside the system. They argued that 'there is no such thing as "outside of the system"'.[43] But the overall tone was one of a constructive debate, with the idea that the activities of Laing and that of the movement in Italy were 'looking for a common denominator'.[44] *Crimini di pace* also included a new piece by Laing translated by Enrico Basaglia.[45] Franca Ongaro later wrote a preface to the published script of the documentary film *Asylums*, which was a study of the community houses that were set up after Kingsley Hall.[46] For Basaglia and others, the Kingsley Hall model was important as an alternative to what had happened in Gorizia, but also (and perhaps above all) as a possible solution for care *after* asylums had been closed and emptied. In the UK, as Franca Ongaro argued, there was an attempt to prevent people from being forced into asylums in the first place (something which was also attempted in Reggio Emilia and Perugia, for example). In Italy, the Basaglian movement (or part of it) was intent, as a first priority, on destroying the whole asylum system, from the inside.

Maxwell Jones and David Clark saw their therapeutic communities as models (as did Laing and his followers, to a certain extent). The books they produced were blueprints for others, almost guides, and visitors were encouraged to reproduce these models in their own institutions. Basaglia and his équipe understood things differently (at least *in theory*). The Gorizian group, perhaps ironically, was keen that their therapeutic community was *not* to be viewed as a model, or simply reproduced elsewhere. Nonetheless, this is how it *was* seen by many of those who visited the place, by the Socialist minister of health Luigi Mariotti, by Mario Tommasini and by many of the readers of *The Negated Institution*. Later on, some psychiatrists in Italy and others attempted to create Kingsley Hall–style spaces, but only after the closure of asylums had led to patients moving back out into the community *en masse*.

---

all'oppressione, Milan: Baldini Castoldi Dalai, 2009 (Einaudi, 1975), pp. 70–80.

43   Ibid., p. 72.

44   Ibid., p. 70. See also p. 80.

45   'Considerazioni sulla psichiatria' in Basaglia and Ongaro, *Crimini di pace*, pp. 316–30.

46   Peter Robinson, *Asylum. Un film su una comunità psichiatrica di R. D. Laing*, Turin: Einaudi, 1977; 'Prefazione', Franca Ongaro Basaglia, pp. xxi–xxiv.

Gorizia and the Therapeutic Community, 1961–72

'The first outside wall was knocked down – but I remember that,
once this wall had been knocked down, there was a patient who still
walked around the courtyard and never went beyond where the wall
had been until – bit by bit – he started to place his feet across the
(ex-)divide and to look around and it took days . . . until at last he
walked past and he saw that nothing happened and so he started to
move around more. It is not enough to be given freedom back.'

Domenico Casagrande[47]

By the mid-1960s, Gorizia was an asylum that had been opened up,
physically and democratically. Power had also been handed over, in part,
to the patients. It was a place of ceaseless meetings and discussion, where
hierarchies had seemingly been dissolved and spaces for self-management
created for and by the patients (a bar, but also a club and various other
spaces). Inmates made frequent trips outside the old walls of the hospital
and organized *feste* within the grounds. Over time many were released
altogether (within the limits imposed by the law) or became 'guests' (after
the 1968 reforms). All this – the entire organizational structure – was
given the name, rather grandly, perhaps, of a therapeutic communicty.
Yet, the presence of this entity has often been accepted at face value, and
largely from a reading of *The Negated Institution* and other work by
Basaglia himself. Little or no research has been carried out into what the
therapeutic community actually did and what it did not do. Moreover,
Gorizia was not the only place in Italy where change was taking place,
although it is often presented as such.[48]

For example, there were limits to how far things had really changed,
limits of which Basaglia and his colleagues were well (and increasingly)
aware. Did the patients have real power over their lives? Yes, they could
work, and they could move around. They had a series of negative and

---

47   Interview by Michele Loreto, 'Intervista a Nico Casagrande. Basaglia gli anni di
Gorizia', 7 February 2010, micheleloreto.blogspot.co.uk.

48   Reforms and changes were also implemented by Sergio Piro and his colleagues in
Nocera Superiore (1959–69), and the Perugia experience also began in the mid-1960s. See the
later chapters on Perugia, Colorno as well as the work of Sergio Piro.

positive freedoms. They were no longer tied up, beaten and tortured, or forced to stay silent. They no longer had to go to bed at a certain time. Most were free from treatment being forced upon them. Some could even leave the hospital, at least for a brief time, but most could not (without some form of permission) and, until July 1967, many were still in locked wards. Gorizia had moved further than any other asylum in Italy, but it was an incomplete experiment. By the time *The Negated Institution* was written, the équipe themselves were intensely critical of what they had created. Structural differences remained, which were linked to power, the law, to class, to society itself.

The term 'therapeutic community' was taken directly from Maxwell Jones. It was an import, but in its Gorizian guise, and in the context in which it was constructed, Basaglia's therapeutic community took on a more radical (at least in theory) and at the same time a more ephemeral form.[49] Whereas British therapeutic community models generally aimed at transformation within the context of an asylum, Basaglia, by the mid-1960s, was convinced that the aim of his work, and *the only way to proceed*, was to *destroy these institutions altogether*.[50] But this was also true for those involved in the Perugian experience, and later of Tommasini's activities in Parma. All over Italy, psychiatrists and others were becoming convinced that asylums had no future. They had to be closed down. The debate became one about means, and not necessarily ends. Michael Donnelly wrote, 'The mental hospital had often been criticized, but in the 1950s and 1960s it was in many ways completely discredited.'[51] In Britain, however, the exponents of therapeutic communities did not argue for the suppression of the entire asylum system. A more radical wing, linked to Laing and Cooper, had moved outside the system altogether.

---

49   For example, some of the descriptions of Dingleton seem to make claims which go beyond the situation inside Gorizia, 'By 1963 we had arrived at a position whereby the hierarchy had been truly flattened to make a democratic organisation which provided open communications to all levels and one in which authority could be openly questioned in a constructive way by everyone in the community.' D. W. Millard, 'Maxwell Jones and the Therapeutic Community' in Hugh Freeman and German Berrios, eds, *150 Years of British Psychiatry. Vol. 2. The Aftermath*, London: Athlone, 1996, p. 598.

50   It appears that this conviction was there in Basaglia's mind right from 1961, but it was only expressed publicly (outside of Gorizia) from 1964 onwards.

51   Michael Donnelly, *The Politics of Mental Health in Italy*, London: Tavistock, 1992, p. ix.

For the Basaglian équipe, the means towards this destruction was at the centre of debate. One first step was to try to overturn the internal logic of the institution itself, from within. In a therapeutic community, everyone worked together: patients, doctors and nurses, towards a common end. Hierarchies were dissolved (or 'placed in brackets') in order to construct real relationships where people could understand and relate to one another.[52] Patients were listened to, as individuals, for the first time. Their life stories *mattered*. But the therapeutic community would also highlight (and help to provoke) its own contradictions as well as those of society as a whole. In some ways, these aims appear contradictory in themselves. On the one hand the hospital as a whole was acting as if it was a community, and on the other Basaglia was trying to create conflicts and tensions between patients, staff and society, undermining that same community.

Taken strictly on its own terms, the Basaglian therapeutic community improved the lives of patients, doctors (this aspect, perhaps, was debatable) and nurses. It made non-people into real people again, with a history, an identity and a voice, and it freed doctors and nurses from purely repressive activity. The therapeutic community, in itself, also became a powerful means of promoting reform, a 'concrete' or 'working' utopia that could be displayed to outsiders and publicized. It could be visited, recorded and photographed. It even became part of the 'society of the spectacle'. But it could only go so far. It was perfect yet also trapped by and within its own perfection, within the walls/non-walls of the asylum. Some even claimed that the hospital had become such an exciting and stimulating place that patients preferred it to the outside world. It could have gone on for ever as it was, but it had also reached the end of the line. For Basaglia, things needed to go forward, or be closed down.[53] Others disagreed.

---

52   This sense of communication with the patients comes out very strongly from the interviews with nurses who worked in Gorizia, collected by Silvia Balconi and transcribed in her unpublished thesis, *L'esperienza Goriziana dal '61 al '72*.

53   Perhaps this was because the 'therapeutic' aspects of the therapeutic community in Basaglian terms were played down, while they were central to Dingleton and Cambridge as well as Kingsley Hall. It is also true that these therapeutic aspects were conceived in an entirely different way by Basaglia and Maxwell Jones, although there were some overlaps between the two. In the UK-type, the patients or residents were meant to 'get better' in some way through group therapy and changes to the hospital from the inside (while, in the case of Kingsley Hall,

Followers and Leaders, Theory and Practice

Many of Basaglia's followers were transformed by a visit to Gorizia, or by reading *The Negated Institution* (which was a way of 'visiting' Gorizia in text form) or *Morire di classe* (or watching *I giardini di Abele*). For a number of people Gorizia worked almost like a religious conversion, a kind of a miracle. It was as if they had seen the light. People's lives were changed by a visit to Gorizia. They came across a place where a revolution seemed to have taken place. And this revolution could be repeated elsewhere, in other asylums, in other institutions and even within the family itself. Every institution, however small, could be overturned.[54] But by the time the movement discovered Gorizia, Basaglia had already moved on, both theoretically and in many cases physically. The therapeutic community had already passed its creative peak and was coming under fierce criticism from the very people who had created it. But this criticism was often overlooked or ignored by those who were 'converted' by Gorizia. The Basaglians were the vanguard, while all the others were far behind. Gorizia had become, for the Basaglians, a 'golden cage', a beautiful trap. But the masses that discovered Gorizia in 1968 saw it as the Promised Land.

By 1968–69, Basaglians were already moving out across Italy to take things further. Some did set up classic therapeutic communities elsewhere, but others skipped that specific phase altogether. The 1968 reforms and the Gorizian experience had moved forward the possibility of institutional *and* revolutionary change. It was now time to speed things up. The slow, laborious and perhaps (in the end) futile construction of a new entity *within* the old *manicomio* system, a therapeutic community, was no longer necessary.

Basaglia himself was very clear on this:

In Gorizia the opening up of the asylum, and the creation of relationships between people within the institution, the setting up of a therapeutic

---

the whole spectrum of better and worse was being overturned). This concept was there in Gorizia, but it was not seen (necessarily) as an outcome of the classic aspects of the therapeutic community, but more to do with power and social change.

54 As Antonio Slavich wrote, imagining a guide-book which was never written, 'Free yourselves from your own asylums: public, private or personal', *La scopa meravigliante. Preparativi per la legge 180 a Ferrara e dintorni 1971–1978*, Rome: Riuniti, 2003, p. 5.

community, was the end; in Trieste we were aiming to go beyond the asylum because we had already lived through those experiences which, yes, had been interesting at a human level . . . the therapeutic community [in Gorizia] was like a kind of reform of a ghetto, a nicer ghetto, but a psychiatric ghetto . . . where the main aim was social control.[55]

In Gorizia, the hostility of the 'territory' (politically and culturally) led to the creation of a therapeutic community that stretched its influence across Italy and the world, but had very little effect in Gorizia itself (the city, *outside* of the hospital). The inability to break out into the local context led to a 'perfect' therapeutic community in Gorizia, but one with very few connections with the city where it happened to be located. Things would be very different in Trieste after 1971, as well as in Arezzo, Ferrara and elsewhere. Perugia, meanwhile, had *already* shown that a different road towards radical psychiatric reform was possible.

Limits and Glories of Gorizia's Therapeutic Community

'The "limits" of the therapeutic community in Gorizia were that we opened up the hospital in a city which was a closed reality. That which surrounded the hospital was a place which was conservative and quiet – and it reacted badly to the new policies introduced in the psychiatric hospital and its director.'

Lucio Schittar[56]

'It is nothing like any other psychiatric hospital in the world, and it is not even like the "therapeutic communities" in England.'

Fabrizio Dentice[57]

---

55   'Corso di aggiornamento per operatori psichiatrici. Trascrizione di due lezioni/conversazioni di Franco Basaglia con gli infermieri di Trieste, lezioni intervallate da un dibattito. 1979', deistituzionalizzazione-trieste.it.

56   Matteo Impagnatiello and Piero Colussi, 'Intervista a Lucio Schittar. Presente, passato e futuro nelle parole di un protagonista del cambiamento' in Azienda per i Servizi Sanitari n. 6 Friuli Occidentale, *Venti'anni dalla 180. L'esperienza del DSM di Pordenone*, Pordenone: Azienda per i Servizi Sanitari n. 6 Friuli Occidentale , Booksei 2, 1998, p. 24.

57   'Una Montessori per i matti', *L'Espresso*, 3 March 1968.

Gorizia was the first therapeutic community to be seen in Italy inside an asylum, even though it was closely followed (and mirrored) by the experience in Perugia. But Gorizia's therapeutic community was not created overnight. The process took years. The first ward to be called a therapeutic community in Gorizia contained just fifty patients. By 1967–68, all the components of the Basaglian therapeutic community (meetings, self-management, discussions, elimination of hierarchies, open wards) had been extended to the entire hospital.

Franco Basaglia was intensely aware of the conservative impact of models and ideologies. He liked to cite Sartre on this very point.[58] Yet Gorizia's therapeutic community was undoubtedly a model and an inspiration for many people across Italy and the world. It was also intended as such. It was *displayed*. But Basaglia was uncomfortable with this use of Gorizia. Later, he wrote that

> the experience of Gorizia needed to be physically eliminated, because it could not be allowed to be seen as a new technical model, like Maxwell Jones's therapeutic community in England or the Thirteenth Arrondissement in France, which are psychiatric shop windows where you can see new products to consume.[59]

However, this was exactly what had taken place with Gorizia. Journalists and photographers were often invited to visit and report on the asylum, Zavoli shot his programme there, *The Negated Institution* became a bestseller. It appeared at times as if the équipe were doing everything they could to promote awareness of what was happening in Gorizia. Basaglia argued that 'we refuse to put forward the therapeutic

---

58   'Ideologies signify freedom while they are being made, but oppression when they are finished'. Basaglia and Ongaro, *Crimini di pace*, p. 50.

59   Basaglia and Ongaro, *Crimini di pace*, in Basaglia, *Scritti. II*, pp. 268–9. The critical approach to therapeutic communities hardened considerably in the 1970s. Sometimes, you get the feeling that Basaglia was continually frustrated by the mistakes of his followers – the over-enthusiastic journalists and students, those who simply wanted to re-propose the therapeutic community, or the anti-psychiatrists. Few seemed to really understand what Basaglia was trying to say, in part because his theories were a complicated mix of statements and concepts.

community as an institutional model',[60] but this is what happened, especially during and after 1968.

Gorizia: Models and Original Features of the Therapeutic Community

Gorizia developed into a hybrid therapeutic community, with a mix of elements from the classic Maxwell Jones model along with others from more radical experimental communities, plus specific Basaglian details and additional aspects from France. The Dingleton model was not simply imported but filtered into the Italian system and through the particular world-view of the équipe. Basaglia did not merely copy or reproduce what he had seen on his travels. The general meetings, for example, were very different in Gorizia from those in Dingleton. As Scheper-Hughes and Lovell have written,

> The assemblea [in Gorizia] are not to be confused with the general meetings that are part of the therapeutic community model of Maxwell Jones and his followers. Basaglia's assembleas were disorganized, uncontrolled, and open to anger, passion and unreason. They were anything other than 'safe' places for the 'controlled' venting of inter-personal or intra-psychic problems.[61]

It should be noted that this kind of assessment is based on Basaglia's own claims in terms of Gorizia, and not on any systematic research into the Dingleton experience. We should be wary of simply accepting at face value the Basaglian analysis of Dingleton and other therapeutic communities.

The 'therapeutic' aspect of Gorizia was not that of Maxwell Jones's model community in Scotland. Gorizia's therapeutic community rarely discussed specific forms of therapy and was more interested instead in practical and social issues, although the progress of individual patients

---

60   Basaglia, *L'istituzione negata* (1968), p. 149.

61   Nancy Scheper-Hughes and Anne Lovell, 'Breaking the Circuit of Social Control: Lessons in Public Psychiatry from Italy and Franco Basaglia', *Social Science & Medicine* 23: 2, 1986, p. 165.

was often debated collectively. Obviously, these discussions touched on mental illness itself, but this was largely something that remained, as Basaglia put it, inside brackets. A key feature of the therapeutic community in Gorizia was the sense of collective responsibility it supposedly instilled inside the institution, something that, it was argued, stretched from the director to the nurses and the patients, but the therapeutic community in Gorizia was clearly a 'means to an end', 'a transitional phase'.[62]

As we have seen, the general public, and the 'movement', discovered Gorizia in 1968. But, by then, the very people who had built the therapeutic community were distancing themselves from their own creation. In the book that revealed to the world the triumph of a model that had been set up in Gorizia (*The Negated Institution*), Lucio Schittar wrote that that very model was in fact, a 'failure'. He argued that the therapeutic community was simply a more sophisticated way of managing society and of enforcing control. A therapeutic community had only one useful function for those who really wanted to change things: it could help to expose the contradictions in the system, provoking rebellion and revolt amongst those who had been oppressed.[63] Because of the social nature that Basaglia saw as underlying the role of the asylum, the overturning of the institution through a therapeutic community was by no means enough. The movement needed to reach the outside world, beyond the asylum walls. Gorizia was seen as an example of reformism. Trieste would be where the revolution would take place.

Gorizia was not the only example of a therapeutic community in Italy, as there were also attempts to create similar institutions in asylums in Nocera Superiore with Sergio Piro and in Perugia.[64] But these other

---

62 Franco Basaglia, ed., *Che cos'è la psichiatria?* [*What Is Psychiatry?*], Milan: Baldini & Castoldi, 1998, p. 26. The phrase is repeated in the new 1997 'Prefazione' by Franca Ongaro Basaglia, p. 6.

63 'L'ideologia della comunità terapeutica' in Basaglia, *L'istituzione negata* (1968), pp. 153–78. The word 'failure' is used on p. 168. Basaglia had already made this point in Basaglia, *Che cos'è la psichiatria?*, pp. 46–7.

64 Perugia saw the creation of what was called a therapeutic community inside the asylum in the mid-1960s. See Francesco Scotti and Carlo Brutti, *Quale psichiatria? 1. Strategie per la trasformazione dei servizi psichiatrici. Storia e documenti*, Rome: Borla, 1980, and Michel Legrand,

therapeutic communities never came close to Gorizia in terms of their visibility or influence. They remained as local and limited experiments, even when they went further than in Gorizia. The Basaglian équipe's 'negated institution' achieved national and international fame. It attracted visitors, students, volunteers, militants, journalists, photographers, film directors, TV documentary makers, politicians. It sold books. Its protagonists became stars, celebrities, potential leaders, gurus. None of this was true in Perugia or Nocera Superiore. Gorizia was the place that became the *byword* for change, during and after 1968.

La psychiatrie alternative italienne, La psichiatrie alternative italienne, Toulouse: Editions Privat, 1988, pp. 209–35. The experience in Perugia is usually given a perfunctory mention in books about Basaglia.

EIGHT

Il Picchio: *The Voice of the Patients and the 'Archive of the Revolution'*

'The hospital is like a small village with all the needs and demands of a community. The population inside undergo continual change – some come in, some go out. And those who come in should find an environment which helps them to react, to struggle and to succeed.'

Il Picchio (8 March 1963)

A key part of the early activity in Gorizia was the production of a magazine by the patients themselves, alongside Basaglia. *Il Picchio* (the woodpecker), whose title was presumably a play on words linked to the local paper *Il Piccolo*, first came out in August 1962, soon after Basaglia's arrival.[1] The first issue stretched to a mere three pages. With time, *Il Picchio* became longer and more interesting, particularly in terms of its verbatim reports on meetings inside the hospital. Much of its content pre-empted that of the collective books produced by the Gorizian équipe in 1967–68. The overall feel of *Il Picchio* was straightforward and practical: there was very little theory here. The magazine/newsletter gave the patients, or some of them, a voice and raised a series of everyday issues that were subject to debate within the

---

1 Franco Basaglia, ed., *L'istituzione negata*, Milan: Baldini & Castoldi, 1998, p. 88.

burgeoning therapeutic community. Sometimes, Basaglia himself wrote directly for *Il Picchio*, and his voice was also often present in the pages of the magazine, either in debates or in editorials.

The magazine was described as 'edited and put together by the patients of the Provincial Psychiatric Hospital in Gorizia'. The address given was Basaglia's flat, and Basaglia himself was the editor or managing editor, but the magazine was produced by the patients in the hospital itself (after all, that was the point) using a makeshift printing press. *Il Picchio*, as its name suggested, was

> born as a polemical magazine . . . and it aimed to collect together and stimulate the personal protests of the patients in order to create a real sense of a leadership group around which the life of all could converge as a community.[2]

A key figure in the production of *Il Picchio* was 'Furio' (Mario) Furlan who was one of the patient leaders in the hospital – perhaps *the* patient leader. Furio became identified strongly with the production of and content in *Il Picchio*.[3] One of the ideas behind *Il Picchio* was precisely the formation of a group of patient leaders from within the community – a kind of patient vanguard. *Il Picchio* was produced above all for the patients of the hospital in Gorizia, but there were plans to distribute it more widely in the city, and even to sell it in newsagents. Antonio Slavich later described Furio as Mario Furlan – 'the creative, concrete and constant support given to us in a spontaneous way by an unforgettable personality – Mario Furlan (Furio) – in all the phases of this socio-therapeutic activity and for the whole duration of the Gorizian experience'.[4]

Il Picchio documented the way the hospital was changing, describing the gradual, public and collective dismantling of fences, walls, gates and other barriers. In March 1963 *Il Picchio* revealed that 'the fences around the courtyards are coming down bit by bit' (they were to be

---

2   'Ripresa', *Il Picchio* 40, v, 6 July 1966, p. 2.

3   Franco Basaglia, ed., *L'istituzione negata,* Turin: Einaudi, 1968, pp. 88, 95–6. As Furio himself stated, 'The paper rested almost entirely on my shoulders and my friends tended to identify "Il Picchio" with Furio', p. 96.

4   Antonio Slavich, *All'ombra dei ciliegi giapponesi,* unpublished manuscript, p. 31.

replaced by bushes and flowers). A month later the magazine reported that 'the destruction of the fences has begun . . . we are convinced that in a few years this hospital will be unrecognizable, it will be a real place where people are cured'. Many years later, a nurse called Enzo Quai remembered those exhilarating moments: 'Basaglia had the fences which separated the wards knocked down by the patients . . . he was overjoyed. I can still see him now. He was laughing and clapping as he looked on'.[5] These moments were considered 'festivals of the oppressed'.[6] They were also unique. Nobody had done this before, anywhere in the world. *Il Picchio* reported, however, that some patients wanted more and demanded a greater speed of change. 'Why had all such barriers not been taken down?' they asked.[7] In March 1963, a patient called Federico Z. acknowledged that 'many of the metal grates have been removed', but he also complained that 'there are still others in place and why haven't these been taken down?' The process was gradual and collective. It was not simply a case of freedom being handed down from above: it was also being taken from below. Yet some patients demanded more freedom, and faster.

The hospital was opening up, and even the worst wards were changing. Although they remained closed to the outside world, the infamous C Wards were being transformed from the inside. As one patient reported in November 1963,

> In our ward there are doors which are open, and which we were used to seeing closed. We can move freely around . . . but years of forced immobility have left their mark. Now that we can move we must do so – not remain for hours curled up in the corner.

---

5 'L'infermiere della rivoluzione', *L'Unità*, 8 December 1996.

6 'Revolutions are the festivals of the oppressed and the exploited. At no other time are the masses of the people in a position to come forward so actively as creators of a new social order as at a time of revolution. At such times the people are capable of performing miracles, if judged by the narrow, philistine scale of gradual progress.' Vladimir Lenin, *Two Tactics of Social-Democracy*, Moscow: Progress, 1988, p. 5.

7 In *The Negated Institution* Furio said that this was a deliberate tactic. Some barriers would be removed, and then there would be a pause in order to observe the reaction of the patients. Basaglia, *L'istituzione negata* (1968), pp. 89, 91–2. Later on, one of these public removals was filmed by a local amateur film-maker, and in 1968–69 Sergio Zavoli used a clip of this event for his *I giardini di Abele*.

This comment highlighted something that had also been noted by David Cooper in Villa 21, and by Domenico Casagrande in Gorizia. The possibility of freedom was not a guarantee of a desire for freedom. Many patients were institutionalized. Many did not want to leave their wards. It would take years for mobilization across the hospital to have an effect.[8]

These processes were collective. As *Il Picchio* added, in a kind of call to arms, 'This hospital is changing and all of us must take part in helping to make this transformation work.' In March and April 1964 *Il Picchio* reported:

> The wall which held up the grate which was demolished last year has been knocked down in the B Ward . . . We saw how the demolition squad under the leadership of our friend Francesco C. worked hard and – above all – with joy in removing any sign of containment.

These public destructions of barriers were to be repeated in Gorizia until all such signs of the past were gone, and the tactic was later replicated in Trieste, Imola, Colorno, Rome and many other institutions. It was a revolutionary moment, something unimaginable under the previous regime. The 'mad' were dismantling their own chains.

New institutions, services and spaces were added to the hospital: a bar (in a converted wood-store), a patients' club called 'Aiutiamoci a guarire' (Help us to get better), a football pitch, a ping-pong table, televisions, radios, new daytime rooms, a day hospital, a mental health centre in the grounds of the hospital (opened in May 1963), a hairdresser's salon and a library. The hospital developed into something like a small town, and one where people could freely move around. The new hairdresser told *Il Picchio* that many of the patients had not had their hair cut professionally for a long time, and some were even frightened of his tools. The service was so popular that appointments were soon required. Mirrors and combs were also being introduced on

---

8   For institutionalization, see Erving Goffman, *Asylums: Essays on the Social Situation of Mental Patients and Other Inmates*. New York: Doubleday, 1961. This point was later made by Basaglia in Franca Ongaro Basaglia and Maria Grazia Giannichedda, eds, *Conferenze brasiliane*, Milan: Raffaello Cortina Editore, 2000, p. 10.

the wards for the first time. Several patients had not even seen their own faces for years. Patients were reclaiming their dignity, their bodies, their identities. There was also a series of organized events: trips, parties and festivals (inside and outside the hospital), football matches, film screenings. Subsequently, much discussion and debate among the patients focused on the running of these institutions (especially the bar) but also on food, on work and pay – the nitty-gritty of daily organization. The fact that *Il Picchio* existed at all was testimony to the rich life being introduced in Gorizia's therapeutic community. The patients were documenting and discussing the transformation of the institution where they were interned. Their voices were being heard. Years of silence had been broken.

Il Picchio also carried 'normal' articles written by patients, many of which had nothing to do with the hospital or its reform. Some expressed the simple pleasure of being able to walk in the park behind the hospital. Others revealed how things were changing for them and everyone else. In the past, one patient wrote, 'we were always locked away and nobody could discuss anything'. A patient who had arrived from another asylum described himself as 'someone who has gone from hell to heaven' (Gaetano T.).

Occasionally, the stories were heartbreaking. Another patient, referred to as Doralice C., had not left the hospital at all for nearly thirty years: 'I haven't seen Gorizia since 1935.' Some argued that they were not ill at all and asked why they could not simply return home. 'Our friend S. . . . experienced an outpouring of emotion because he considers himself to be cured and he can't leave because somebody refuses to sign for his release [presumably a family member].'

With time, *Il Picchio* also began to underline the contradictions in the therapeutic community project, the constant sense of one step forward, two steps back. Many patients, for example, saw meetings as a waste of time. Attendance was often poor and personal arguments and petty disputes delayed debate. *Il Picchio* itself was also criticized in its own pages. Basaglia warned the patients about the liberties inside Gorizia: 'Our freedom is relative.'

A key structural problem emerged in the mid-1960s: the closed wards (which were the male and female C Wards). This issue also dominated discussions in *The Negated Institution*. According to *Il Picchio* these wards 'are still very reminiscent of the asylum'. The fact that some wards were still closed was something that hung like a cloud above the hospital and led to intense discussion. Debates at general and ward meetings began to explore the best way to integrate the 'friends' from the C Wards. In 1965 it was clear that there was still work to be done:

> Our friend S. . . . expressed the opinion (which was shared by the majority of those present) – that the fences in that wing shouldn't be taken down all in one go, but gradually because we need to GET TO KNOW the people there: we need to talk to them using good manners and give them advice, playing cards or taking part in other activities with them. In short, we need to get to know each other and create friendships which will help those patients have hope in a better future.

The patients in the C Wards were not ready to be freed. The 'advanced' patients volunteered to help with this work of integration. At times, *Il Picchio* also dealt with more philosophical questions. What was mental illness? Why was there such a stigma in the outside world against the mad?

A further key issue for *Il Picchio*, but one that was rarely brought out into the open, was the relationship between Basaglia himself and the magazine. Basaglia wrote directly for *Il Picchio* on occasion, and his voice was also present in debates and discussions with patients that were reported in the journal. The language in these pieces was very different to that of Basaglia's academic work, or that of his contributions to *L'istituzione negata*. It was clearer, more straightforward and more practical. We can also detect a sense of deference to Basaglia in the magazine (something which would also be noted in *What Is Psychiatry?*). In July 1966, *Il Picchio* reported that 'the Assembly broke out in warm applause for the director who is back from holiday'. Postcards from Basaglia were read out, and when he was away, things were clearly different. His absence was felt. Moreover, the running of the magazine was hard work. It was not easy to get patients to collaborate with *Il Picchio*, as Furio admitted in an interview which was published in 1968 in *The Negated Institution*.

There was also a sense in *Il Picchio* that Gorizia was becoming a model for other places, as well as somewhere that was visited by journalists and others. The asylum saw visitors from Imola, Pordenone and Florence in the 1962–65 period, as well as numerous journalists, documentary makers from the RAI and photographers. Local politicians also made occasional appearances to talk to the patients. *Il Picchio* was closed in 1965–66, having reached the end of its useful life.[9]

The experience of Gorizia would soon appear in two full-length books (1967–68). As the experiment moved on, *Il Picchio* became part of the past. It disappeared, almost literally so. After 1966 nobody seems to have kept a full set, not even the asylum itself, and Gorizia's local library had to appeal for copies in the twenty-first century (they have a partial set now). In 1996 a journalist from *L'Unità* interviewed Enzo Quai, a psychiatric nurse who still lived in the grounds of the ex-hospital in Gorizia:

Downstairs I have kept the memorabilia of the revolution – the old issues of *Il Picchio*, the magazine which the patients wrote and printed on their own. I remember the stories, the experiences, the poetry, the jokes, the first demands: 'A TV with two channels in every ward.' 'Why don't we give shoes to the women workers?' 'Why has the demolition of the fences stopped?'

Il Picchio had become a (semi-lost) fragment of the past, a melancholic reminder of a movement (and an institution) that no longer existed.

---

9   'It is no longer produced because the liberalization of the hospital has meant that mediated instruments of communication are no longer required.' Basaglia, *L'istituzione negata* (1968), p. 88.

NINE

Anti-Psychiatry, Italian Style

'Mental illness does not exist and in my experience I have never come across a single case which shows otherwise.'

Edelweiss Cotti[1]

I taly, in the 1960s and 1970s, developed a group of non-psychiatrists or self-confessed anti-psychiatrists, who positioned themselves to the left of Basaglia, Jervis and the Gorizians. They argued that psychiatry was part of the problem, not the solution. They were also explicit, in many cases, about their belief that mental illness itself was a myth or simply did not exist. This type of position was common among followers of the movement as a whole, especially after 1968. A number of those attracted by the Gorizian and Triestian experiments, and by the writings of R. D. Laing and David Cooper, were much more radical (at least in theory) than those who were in charge of those projects. Students and others often bought into classic non- or anti-psychiatric ideas such as those propagated by Thomas Szasz or Cooper, whose books circulated widely before, during and particularly after 1968.

Edelweiss Cotti (1923–98) began to apply his radical ideas in a section

---

1 Cited in Libero Medina, 'Se ti ribelli sei matto', *A-Rivista anarchica*, vol. 1 no. 3, April 1971, at xoomer.virgilio.it.

of Bologna's psychiatric hospital in the mid-1960s. Giorgio Antonucci later claimed that Cotti was a 'follower of Szasz' at that time, but he was also influenced by developments in France and had visited the Saint Alban clinic in 1965.[2] Cotti began to open up a ward along the lines of Cooper's Villa 21 model and in parallel with the Gorizian experiment, in a separate building known as Villa Olimpia. This experiment ran from 1964 to 1967. Very little has been written about Villa Olimpia and, once again, as so often in this book, we are forced to rely largely upon the accounts of the protagonists of the reform.[3] Many of the reforms applied in Villa Olimpia were similar to those seen in Gorizia and Perugia: the abandonment of white coats and status, constant meetings, an opening-up of wards, the use of an équipe-type approach and the end of repressive treatment of patients. Two features of Cotti's theories seem to distinguish what he was doing from the work of the Basaglians: an increasing belief that mental illness was a myth, and a refusal to use sedatives or anti-psychotic drugs. Villa Olimpia was closed down, for 'political' reasons according to Cotti, in 1967.

The Cividale Experiment, 1968

'This is not an asylum, but a centre for human relations.'

Edelweiss Cotti[4]

A key early moment for this disparate group of Italian anti-psychiatrists came in 1968 in a tiny place very near to Gorizia: Cividale in Friuli. In this small, conservative town, Cotti was given space to open and direct a new ward or unit for psychiatric patients within a general hospital's grounds. The ward opened in January 1968. Cotti and his team, which included a young psychiatrist called Giorgio Antonucci and another psychiatrist who had worked with Basaglia in Gorizia (Leopoldo Tesi),

---

2   Georgio Antonucci, *Il pregiudizio psichiatrico*, Eléuthera, 1999, eleuthera.it.

3   Edelweiss Cotti and Roberto Vigevani, *Contro la psichiatria*, Florence: La Nuova Italia, 1970, pp. 31–75. A lot of material and analysis can now be found in Libero Bestighi et al., eds, *Specialista in relazioni umane. L'esperienza professionale di Edelweiss Cotti*, Bologna: Pendragon, 2001. For Villa Olimpia, see pp. 89–165.

4   'Medici e malati di mente si barricano in ospedale', *La Stampa*, 3 September 1968.

used the space given them to put various methods drawn from R. D. Laing, David Cooper *and* Gorizia to the test. Basaglia was also linked to this project. Cotti claimed that Basaglia had found him the job in Cividale, and this same assertion was later repeated by Antonucci and Tesi.[5] Basaglia reportedly visited the centre in Cividale on a number of occasions.

The experimental unit was renamed as a 'Centro di Relazioni Umane' (Centre for human relations). For Christian De Vito this ward worked

in complete opposition with traditional medical-psychiatric practice and in line with radical critiques of the whole concept of mental illness. For the first time in a public health institution, a centre was born which was outside of the traditional and official scientific parameters, breaking with the gradualism which had marked change in the Gorizian experience.[6]

Cividale was modelled on the Gorizian experiment, but it moved too fast for the local authorities. Unlike with the Basaglian équipe and in other areas, the slow and boring groundwork had not been done. Cotti wanted to go straight towards a revolution. Patients, in a sense, were free to leave (in some accounts this seems to be qualified as 'at certain times of the day') and were given a high degree of personal autonomy in the unit (as in Villa 21 or Kingsley Hall). In his reports on his patients, Cotti stuck to his principles, avoiding all use of words like 'schizophrenia'. The aim was the following: 'We do not accept in any way current definitions of mental illness.'[7]

De Vito further described the ward:

At the centre of the Cividale experience were some principles which were strong alternatives to those of traditional psychiatry: a refusal to use containment and anti-psychotic drugs, the complete freedom of

---

5   See Bestighi, *Specialista in relazioni umane,* p. 189, and for the whole experience see pp. 167–93.

6   Christian De Vito, 'I "tecnici ragazzini". Operatori sociali, medici e tecnici nei movimenti degli anni Settanta a Reggio Emilia', Tesi di perfezionamento, Scuola Normale di Pisa, 2008, p. 97.

7   Cotti and Vigevani, *Contro la psichiatria,* p. 73.

patients in terms of movement, day and night; a continual dialogue and collective discussion as the only ways to act; the conviction that 'people should never weaken their relationships with civil life'. Those working in the centre were encouraged to have a relationship with the outside world instead of remaining on the wards, to be a part of society, not escape from it into what [Antonucci] described as 'sad monuments of a failed civilization, where people are ferocious with themselves and with others, because they can no longer understand the meaning of life'.[8]

There were no violent incidents as a result of the short-lived open ward and open-door policy in Cividale, although some accounts talk of a patient suicide. But the visible presence of these patients in this small town apparently led to protests from part of the local population, and there were disciplinary procedures from the authorities. The increasing fame of Cotti and probably of Gorizia in 1968 may well have had an influence on the decisions taken by local politicians. They did not want another Gorizia on their doorstep.

Tensions between the authorities and the doctors running the unit soon reached a breaking point, leading to one of the most extraordinary episodes in the history of the radical psychiatry movement. In June 1968 it was announced that the experiment was to be closed down (the official justification was linked to the costs of the unit). Official letters were sent to the families of the patients announcing this move. This was met with dismay from the doctors working there, and a campaign started to save the ward. A stand-off ensued, but no more patients were referred there. At the end of August 1968 Cotti and some of his team (as well as the twelve remaining patients) decided to occupy their own building in protest at its imminent closure.[9] The occupation lasted three days and nights, and prefigured that of the asylum in Parma (an event which is much more well known) in 1969.[10] In the face of the occupation, the

---

8   De Vito, 'I "tecnici ragazzini"', pp. 97–8.

9   Cotti also claimed that the closure of the Cividale experiment was due to his refusal to create a separate psychiatric section for richer patients, something he said he refused to do.

10   See Itala Rossi, '"Pericoloso a sé e agli altri e di pubblico scandalo". L'occupazione del Manicomio di Colorno. Una lotta contro la violenza istituzionalizzata' in Margherita Becchetti

authorities decided to use force. Police and carabinieri surrounded Cividale's hospital in early September 1968 and the experiment was shut down.[11] The phone lines were cut off and a chain was placed across the door of the unit (which was then cut by the occupants). The authorities referred to the occupiers as 'invaders'. Eventually, Cotti gave in and left the unit.[12] The whole incident became a cause célèbre, although, as a *La Stampa* journalist later pointed out, the 'barricades' in Cividale had been more symbolic than real.[13]

The Cividale incident provided Cotti and his colleagues with a fair amount of kudos on the left, and a lot of press coverage. Their ideas were given a hearing and a platform. In October 1968 Cotti gave an interview to the Communist Party monthly magazine *Rinascita* that caused something of a scandal. The title of the piece was stark: 'Mental illness does not exist'.[14] Cotti claimed that 'madness is an invention. Madness is completely normal in the face of abnormal situations', and compared asylums to concentration camps. In fact, Cotti said that asylums were worse than concentration camps. He also drew a powerful link between asylum inmates and 'slaves who needed to be liberated'.

In 1969, Cotti made similar points at an important meeting of psychiatrists and activists in Rome, organized by the Italian Communist Party. In his intervention there, Cotti repeated his claim that 'there is nothing worthwhile in our field if we don't contest mental illness itself . . . let's be clear. For me, mental illness does not exist'. He described what was seen as 'mental illness' as 'a behavioural situation which is not pathological, in a medical sense'.[15] Cotti also openly questioned how far the Gorizian experiment had gone.

A number of the leading players in the Cividale episode were investigated and eventually brought to trial by the Italian state. Cotti, Tesi

et al., *Parma dentro la rivolta. Tradizione e radicalità nelle lotte sociali e politiche di una città dell'Emilia rossa 1968–1969*, Milan: Edizioni Punto Rosso, 2000, pp. 175–215.

11   Roberto Vigevani, 'Assalto a Cividale', *Il Ponte*, 9 September 1968, pp. 1261–3.

12   'Si è arreso il primario barricato nell'ospedale', *La Stampa*, 3 September 1968.

13   Gigi Ghirotti, 'Amnistiato il medico di Cividale che dava la libera uscita ai pazzi', *La Stampa*, 11 March 1971.

14   'La pazzia è una invenzione'. Lorenza Mazzetti, ed., *Rinascita* 41, 18 October 1968.

15   Edelweiss Cotti in Istituto Gramsci, *Psicologia psichiatria e rapporti di potere. Roma, 28–30 Giugno 1969*, Rome: Riuniti, 1974, p. 83.

and two other assistants from Cividale were charged with 'forcible entry, aggravated damage, usurpment of public duties' during the period of the occupation (31 August to 2 September 1968). In 1971, a judge decided not to proceed to a trial (against the wishes of Cotti and his lawyer) due to an amnesty passed after the strike wave of 1969.[16] Cotti had been 'defending his workplace', it was argued.[17] Cotti was described by a *La Stampa* journalist as 'a lively forty-seven-year-old with a beard like that of Karl Marx'. For Cotti, 'Basaglia never made clear his position on the existence, or otherwise, of mental illness. For me, above all after the Cividale experience, I am convinced that it doesn't exist . . . we need to fight the idea that mental illness exists.' He also emphasized his rapid shift to the left: 'I used to be a liberal, now I am to the left of Mao.'

Yet, Cividale was a drop in the ocean in comparison with what had already happened in Gorizia and Perugia, or what would take place later in Trieste, Arezzo and Ferrara. It was a short-lived experiment that was quickly shut down, and became (in)famous largely for the repressive way it ended rather than its successes while it was open. Cotti himself made some exaggerated and rhetorical claims about the achievements in Cividale in a manifesto-book for Italian anti-psychiatry, published in 1970 with the evocative title *Against Psychiatry*. For example, he argued that the work in Cividale 'showed that mental illness and so-called psychosis should not be called an illness'.[18] In the end, however, he thought that a revolution was required in order to create 'a completely different society, in which real democracy and socialism eliminate fear, and where we won't need psychiatrists'.[19] This book set up an alternative and supposedly more radical position to that of the Gorizians, who were described as reformists and as part of the system. The second part of *Against Psychiatry*, written by the sociologist Roberto Vigevani, extended the parallels between Nazi concentration camps and asylums, and criticized any attempt to 'manage' such institutions. Nonetheless, despite these ideas and proclamations, Antonucci, Cotti and other non-psychiatrists

---

16   See Mario Passi, 'A giudizio uno psichiatra che cura le origini sociali della malattia', *L'Unità*, 8 March 1971; Mario Passi, 'L'attacco alla nuova psichiatria', *L'Unità*, 5 July 1972; and Concetto Testai, 'Città e fabbrica nella battaglia per la salute', *L'Unità*, 26 October 1968.

17   Ghirotti, 'Amnistiato il medico di Cividale che dava la libera uscita ai pazzi'.

18   Cotti and Vigevani, *Contro la psichiatria*, p. 81.

19   Ibid., p. 115.

continued to work *within* the asylum system throughout the 1970s. In practice, their activities were similar to those of the Basaglians.

Cotti became director of the huge provincial asylum in Imola (L'osservanza) from 1973 onwards, a position he would hold until 1986. Imola's gargantuan hospital employed over 500 nurses. Antonucci was also employed at Imola for some of that time. Meanwhile, the Basaglians ignored Cividale. No mention is made of the experiment in the Basaglian literature, although relations remained cordial at a personal and a professional level. In practical and political terms, the Cividale incident was a small-scale and short-lived experiment that was vulnerable to swift and over-the-top state repression. Its long-term effects were minimal, and its place in the history of the movement can only be a marginal one. Cividale was perhaps a brave experiment, but it also showed the dangers of moving too fast without the hard, grinding work of preparation which had been put in by Basaglia and by those in Perugia in the early 1960s.

TEN

One of the Wonders of the World: The General Meeting

'In Gorizia, as in Arezzo, the words of the patients contain much more truth than those to be found in psychiatric tracts.'

Agostino Pirella[1]

'A long silence'
  Comment from transcription of a meeting, *L'istituzione negata*[2]

'The assemblies of Franco Basaglia's "mad" patients were the most moving and most powerful demonstrations of democracy [in the 1960s] and its regenerative power.'

Anna Bravo[3]

Under Basaglia's stewardship, democracy came to the mental asylum in Gorizia, a place that had never experienced any sense of free speech. From an institution which was the very essence of non-democracy and exclusion, where the mad were locked up and

---

1 Agostino Pirella, 'Prefazione. Chi ha paura dell'Assemblea Generale? La verifica della psichiatria' in Gigi Attenasio and Gisella Filippi, eds, *Parola di matti e anche nostra*, Verona: Bertani, p. 18.

2 Franco Basaglia, ed., *L'istituzione negata*, Turin: Einaudi, 1968, p. 39.

3 Anna Bravo, *A colpi di cuore. Storie del sessantotto*, Bari: Laterza, 2008, p. 101.

silenced, and became non-people, without an identity, a past or a future, Gorizia's asylum developed into a school for democracy, a place people would visit to see new forms of democracy *in action*. This was the 'overturning', the 'negation' that was discussed so often by the Basaglian équipe. Gorizia was a wonder of the 1968 world, something to visit and be amazed by, a vision of change that transformed people's lives: a kind of miracle.

General meetings, which were open to the whole hospital population, began in earnest in 1965, although meetings involving patients had been a part of the Basaglian project from the very beginning.[4] Mario Dondero took a series of photos of a smaller ward meeting (with Basaglia present) in 1964. From November 1965 onwards, however, regular hospital-wide *assemblee* were held inside the asylum, at about ten every morning.[5] Everyone was welcome to attend: nurses, doctors, patients and even their families. Complete outsiders also began to turn up: students, filmmakers, journalists, activists, psychiatry students. The patients ran these meetings and kept the minutes. This was a process that was in part lifted from classic therapeutic communities in Scotland and elsewhere, where meetings had been observed by members of the Gorizian équipe. In the beginning, things took time to get going. In the smoke-filled room, with its simple wooden chairs and table, the first meetings were often marked by pandemonium, or by long uncomfortable silences. They were occasionally captured on film, and more often by photographers who flocked to Gorizia in 1968.[6]

But amid the foggy haze of cigarettes, the arguing and the babble of

---

4   Pirella later wrote, 'I took part in the first general assembly held in an Italian psychiatric hospital, following the techniques used by the therapeutic community, in November 1965.' Pirella, 'Prefazione', p. 13. There are reports of various kinds of meetings in *Il Picchio* from 1962 to 1965.

5   For a lucid analysis of the question of power inside Gorizia and a detailed account of the development of the therapeutic community see Antonio Slavich, 'Mito e realtà del autogoverno', in Basaglia, *L'istituzione negata* (1968), pp. 179–203.

6   See Sandro Parmiggiani, ed., *Il volto della follia. Cent'anni di immagini del dolore*, Milan: Skira, 2005; Eric Hobsbawm and Marc Weitzmann, eds, *1968. Magnum throughout the World*, Malakoff Cedex: Hazan, 1988, magnumphotos.com. See also the photo of a meeting in Franco Pierini, 'Se il matto è un uomo', *L'Europeo* 34, 24 August 1967, p. 14–15. Film of a general meeting shot by the Finnish documentary film-maker Pirkko Peltonen (August 1968) can be seen on video.repubblica.it

voices, and the interminable and embarrassing pauses when nobody said anything at all, these chaotic events took shape and prefigured 1968 itself. In many ways they *were* 1968. Patients shouted and grumbled, came and went as they pleased and talked amongst themselves. Some simply sat there and watched, especially at first. A large number did not attend at all. The doctors present were dressed normally, usually without white coats (these were finally abolished in 1964, although it is said that some doctors continued to wear them in protest *against* Basaglian reforms, as a sign of their 'non-Basaglian' nature), and mingled with their patients. The members of the équipe spoke very little during these general meetings, although afterwards there were regular feedback sessions and yet more meetings where the previous meeting's events were analysed. Meetings about meetings followed meetings. Gorizia was verbal, spoken, loud and often long-winded. But slowly, inexorably, the patients began to discuss those things that affected their lives on a daily basis. They began, to some extent, to take control.

Franco Pierini, a journalist from the magazine *L'Europeo*, visited Gorizia in 1967. He took a photographer with him. This was his description of the general assembly:

> Their discussions are held in community groups. We spent two days in Gorizia and heard speeches by both women and men; they discussed matters of concern to them, such as why Ward D had not been on an outing for a long time, why the women in the dressmaking shop opposed the transfer of the dining room to their workroom, why it was pointless to worry every time there was a grass snake in the park: 'Signora Giovanna spoke with a lady who works in the fields; she said she had seen a grass snake, but a grass snake is not venomous.' It would be wrong, very wrong, to report that these men and women talk like us and can argue like us. *They do it better*. Their way of discussing things, their dialectic of opposing views, their skill in reaching conclusions without scapegoating or making anyone feel defeated, is superior to ours [my italics].[7]

---

7   Pierini, 'Se il matto è un uomo', p. 14. This translation is from Hobsbawm and Weitzmann, *1968. Magnum throughout the world*, p. 68.

Previous rigid hierarchies were flouted, overturned, ignored and undermined. The *assemblea* was the practical demonstration of Basaglia's claim to have placed mental illness 'in brackets' when dealing with patients. During these encounters, some patients would cause trouble, and it was difficult to concentrate on the matter in hand, and often frustrating. But Basaglia saw patient disturbances as part of the process of change, as signs of (welcome) rebellion. His work, he claimed, was intended to open up contradictions in the system. A community was being formed, which would be able, in time, to act in a collective way.

Gradually, the meetings began to take shape. More and more patients turned up. Silences were shorter and shorter. 'Words ran freely, rebounded, captured the attention of nurses and doctors, but required an audience which helped them to move forward'.[8] Votes were counted and decisions were taken. Documents were produced. Real responsibilities were transferred to the patients, including institutional and financial powers. Discussion was usually around what appeared to be the most boring and mundane issues of all: food, cigarettes, pay for work done (for the first time), day trips. But there were also bigger questions at stake. Who could be allowed out into the wider world? Was it safe or useful to open the locked wards? What exactly was wrong with certain patients, if anything? And all of this touched upon even bigger problems, which went to the heart of the total institution where these meetings were taking place. What *was* madness? Why *were* they all inside an asylum? Who had put them there? Who were they?

Patients were taking back some control over their lives and over those of their fellow inmates. They were becoming people again, even citizens, with responsibilities and rights. All of this was exhausting, but also exhilarating and fascinating. The powerless were being given power, and in this process, form was as important as the content. The fact that these meetings were even taking place was revolutionary. Hours would be spent discussing the cleanliness of wards, or the management of the meetings themselves, but this was democracy in action: real, direct democracy, almost unmediated by others. The disappeared people of the asylums, those who had been shut away from real life, without rights and without identities,

---

8   Giuliana Kantzà, 'Il punto d'impasse', *La psicoanalisi. Rivista del campo Freudiano* 25, January–June 1999, p. 73.

emerged from the darkness. They showed that they could think for themselves and organize their own lives. Whatever was said was really not that important. The exciting thing was that *something* was being said, in public. Detailed records were kept of some of these meetings and then used in publications that outlined the Gorizian experiment. These minutes form a kind of transcribed oral history of the movement, which was analysed at the time and can be looked at again with the benefit of hindsight. The meetings were the core, the living heartbeat, of the Basaglian project.

These general meetings, especially in 1968, gave Basaglia's experiment an extremely radical tinge. It had become clear to Basaglia and the others from the start that asylum patients were not just part of a group called 'the mad', they were also very often from extremely poor backgrounds. Their faces were marked and shaped with deprivation and by their time in the institution, their clothes were the clothes of the poor. The social analysis of the asylum was confirmed, it seems, by the physical appearance of the participants at the general meetings.

Never before had the mad been given the chance to speak out (and Sergio Zavoli later gave some of them a voice on camera, on national TV). So these meetings appeared to be both therapeutic and revolutionary at the same time. But this process was also held back by the setting: *inside* the asylum. By the mid-1960s, Basaglia was already beginning to argue that a therapeutic community was extremely limited in the progress it could make. It was the institution itself that was the problem. Reform could be dangerous, a trap. Internal change and the arrival of humanitarian improvements might actually prolong the life of total institutions. A humane asylum could help the system adapt to a rapidly changing society, making it more acceptable. The Basaglians needed to be careful. They might become 'useful idiots' who, by making asylums more tolerable, prevented their destruction. Basaglia also highlighted what he saw as another danger: that Gorizia would simply be copied by others, becoming a new, conservative form of ideology. Others were more explicit. The meetings were projecting an idea of false democracy. Antonio Slavich, in his analysis of the reformed hospital in *L'istituzione negata*, put democracy in quotation marks.[9]

---

9   Slavich, 'Mito e realtà', p. 180. See also Fabrizio Dentice, 'Una Montessori per i matti', *L'Espresso*, 3 March 1968.

Gorizia: Voices from the 'Assemblea Generale'

'Basaglia was able to overturn his own situation of dependency, freeing himself from his institutional role and creating a new culture which was destined, right from the start, to appear as a "counter-culture".'

Edoardo Balduzzi[10]

'[There were] endless meetings.'

Zbigniew Kotowicz[11]

'If somebody were to attend our meetings from the outside, they would see that, even here, there are people who are able to think for themselves.'

'Verzegnassi'[12]

'They don't come to the meetings because things take too long, and they say that nothing is ever decided.'

Danieli, discussing those who didn't come to meetings.[13]

The Gorizians saw these meetings from various angles: in part, they were viewed as therapeutic in themselves (although this was rarely acknowledged, and sometimes explicitly denied). But the meetings were also understood as material to be studied and analysed, almost as though they were a kind of ongoing research project. The patients were willing participants in an anthropological and political study of institutions undergoing change. Finally, the meetings were spontaneous 'happenings', events which helped to spread the message that the mad could govern themselves and take up the reins of power, if they were only given the chance to do so.

The first book published about Gorizia (by the Gorizians), *What Is*

---

10   Edoardo Balduzzi, *L'albero della cuccagna. 1964–1978. Gli anni della psichiatria italiana*, Rovereto: Edizioni Stella, Nicolodi Editore, 2006, p. 38.

11   Zbigniew Kotowicz, *R. D. Laing and the Paths of Anti-psychiatry*, London: Routledge, 1997, p. 82.

12   Franco Basaglia ed., *Che cos'è la psichiatria?*, Milan: Baldini & Castoldi, 1997, p. 142.

13   Ibid., p. 144.

Psychiatry? (1967), gave its readers a precious insight into the world of the general meeting. During meetings,

> roles are indistinct and tend to become confused at the level of reciprocal protest; this is the moment when the culture of the hospital begins to understand its own existence and sets itself up as a meeting point where the various ward-based cultures and the social subsystems of the hospital come together.[14]

What Is Psychiatry? printed transcripts of two general meetings from January 1967, and this use of transcription was later repeated in *The Negated Institution*, which came out in 1968. Both of these were, in part, 'spoken books'. The two meetings from Gorizia which appeared in *What Is Psychiatry?* were dominated by debate over the issues of pay and work. The patients had run up a deficit and needed to do something about it, and so it was decided that pay had to be cut. *But whose pay, and how?* And what about those who did not work at all, or could not do so? Of course, in many ways, these meetings were repetitive, and dealt with minor and irrelevant issues (the pay of a few people inside one mental hospital). But they also went to the heart of some key issues. Could the patients govern themselves? Were they able to live normal lives? Were they capable of acting collectively, in the interests of their own community? Did the community extend to all the patients in the hospital, even those who never left their beds?[15]

General meetings had some real muscle; they were one way of negating the logic of total institutions from the inside. In most asylums, in the world beyond Gorizia, the director exercised absolute power, and patients were excluded from any kind of decision-making. They were both silenced and powerless, objects of treatment or violence. Their very identity had been taken away from them, alongside their freedom, their clothes, their possessions, their wedding rings, their shoelaces and their hair. In Gorizia, none of this was the case (apart from the central question, of course, of individual freedom: the patients were *not* free, on the

---

14   Ibid., p. 147.
15   In the end this debt was paid off by the Gorizian Provincial Council. The debate had no practical consequences of note.

whole, to simply leave the hospital altogether). In Gorizia, patients wore
their own clothes, they decided when to go to bed and when to get up
(in many asylums, patients were forced to go to bed at 5.30 pm and get
up at 6 am, whatever the season, something which was hated by most
patients). Gorizian inmates also had the power to express an opinion
about who would be let out and who would not (although the final
decision was left up to the medical staff and the director, at least in a
technical sense). In theory, and increasingly in practice, the problems of
the individual became the problems of everyone.

This was a community that appeared to be acting collectively, in the
interests of all, and used the language of community. And, as we have
seen, spaces were opened up which were then handed over to the patients
to run. A small building in the grounds of the Gorizia asylum was set
up as a bar, with its own juke-box, managed by the patients. Anyone
could walk in off the street and have a coffee or a beer there. This would
later become the norm in many other psychiatric hospitals, including,
most famously, in Trieste in the 1970s.

The first *assemblea* recorded in *What Is Psychiatry?* (from 7 February
1967) was attended by sixty-eight patients, eight nurses, five *monitori*
(observers), four social workers, five doctors and one psychologist. A
patient always chaired the hour-long meetings (and the chair was changed
regularly). There were also regular ward meetings with smaller numbers
(on a daily basis in the observational wards, and every two weeks in the
areas with long-term patients) as well as feedback discussions, meetings
about meetings.[16]

But it was one thing to hold meetings in this way, quite another to
dispense entirely with imbalances of power. These conversations and
debates also revealed the way that subtle hierarchies still worked in the
hospital, as well as hinting at the powerful role of Basaglia himself,
something of which the équipe was well aware. As Slavich and Letizia
Comba wrote in their commentary about one of the meetings, 'The
charismatic figure of the director is here reclaimed as a "good man", and
thus comes to be seen in terms of paternalistic reassurance.'[17]

---

16   These smaller meetings often dealt with issues linked to individual patients, and were
more medical and technical than the general meetings.

17   Basaglia, *Che cos'è la psichiatria?* pp. 141, 147.

Elsewhere in *What Is Psychiatry?* this danger was described as a kind of 'cult of personality'.[18] However reformed, this was still a divided institution, with wide social and intellectual differences among doctors, nurses and patients. Real institutional power lay with the doctors and the nurses. Interestingly, these critical comments around the transcriptions of general meetings were largely absent from *The Negated Institution*, which was aimed at a much wider audience than *What Is Psychiatry?* and brought out by a commercial publisher.

On the surface, then, there were no hierarchies within the therapeutic community (or the hierarchies were *among* the patients) but in reality, real power still resided largely with the doctors and the nurses, and with politicians and judges in the outside world. These hierarchies could also be seen in the language that was used. Basaglia, for example, is often referred to as 'Il Direttore' in meetings and elsewhere. This was also true of the équipe itself. Basaglia was clearly the leader of the Gorizians, the others his followers (although not always willingly, or particularly deferentially, as with Jervis). But this certainly did not mean that there was no debate. On the contrary – Gorizia was a place of permanent discussion. But the *line*, the final word, was (generally) Basaglia's.

Of course, these inevitable hierarchies and power structures inside the Gorizian asylum were nothing compared to almost every other total institution in Italy. Basaglia sat in normal clothes in the meetings, and usually in silence. He occasionally intervened to ask a question or make a point, and usually in a subtle way. If you did not know already, you would have found it difficult to guess that he was the director of the entire institution, with near-absolute power over almost everyone inside that place.[19] Pirella later reminisced about the role of Basaglia during these meetings:

I remember Franco during those first general meetings. He was interested in trying to understand every element of novelty, and he was

---

18   Giovanni Jervis and Lucio Schittar, 'Storia e politica in psichiatria. Alcune proposte di studio' in ibid., p. 195.

19   Not everyone came to these meetings, and sometimes the discussion touched on those who were not there. Attendance was not obligatory, for the patients. For the doctors and the équipe, it was a different story. *They* had to justify their absence.

committed in follow-up meetings to try and understand what has happened and what could happen and how we should organize ourselves. He was both inflexible and ironic, and inspired by a generous spirit, and I would like him to be remembered in this way by all the Gorizians, despite everything.[20]

Total dedication

'The climate of work in Gorizia was one of perpetual mobilization, in a way which was close to volunteerism.'

Giovanni Jervis[21]

'We started at eight in the morning and we would leave at four in the morning, and at eight we would be there again.'

Domenico Casagrande

For the members of the équipe and volunteers, life and work (although the separation was minimal) in Gorizia put enormous strain on them and their families. Hours were long and the work was highly demanding, quite apart from the numerous meetings that the équipe was expected to attend. The transition period carried huge risks and responsibilities. It was conducive to sleepless nights. Nobody thought of what they were doing as only a job, and many were badly paid (or not paid at all) and without career prospects. As Domenico Casagrande later wrote, 'They were great years, but also very hard . . . there were very few of us.' Looking back at that period, it is difficult to see when the participants in the Basaglian revolution ever ate or slept.

One of the key aspects of the Basaglian revolution was actually very mundane: doctors were expected to stay in their workplace *all the time*. Edoardo Balduzzi later referred to the 'continual presence of staff' in Gorizia and argued that

---

20   Agostino Pirella, 'E a Gorizia? Nascita di un'alternativa alla segregazione manicomiale', *Territorio. Bollettino* 10, November 1984, p. 36.

21   Giovanni Jervis, *Il buon rieducatore*, 1977, p. 20.

the real new feature with respect to practice at the time was that the doctors were there from the morning to the evening, and were a constant reference point – this was a kind of . . . 'shock therapy' . . . carried out by five doctors and two psychologists who broke with the habits of the two older doctors . . . the new doctors were seen as models with which every person and aspect of the institution should, in every moment, identify.[22]

In other places, doctors were rarely seen, while in Gorizia they were ever-present. Moreover, discussions and problems were constant, and debates continued well into the night in Basaglia's flat or in bars and restaurants. All the members of the équipe lived within a short walk of each other. It was almost a kind of collective life. There was a strong risk of burn-out. The movement demanded complete dedication to the cause, as did Basaglia himself. Meetings were followed by other meetings and yet more meetings. Patients also now expected attention, all the time. And there was the constant fear of violence and suicide, both inside and outside the hospital. Before the open-door policy, such events would be hushed up or barely noticed. Nobody really cared. Now all eyes were on Gorizia. This was a place under the microscope.

Meetings, meetings, meetings: in Gorizia's asylum there were more than fifty of them a week, of various kinds. Many of the protagonists of the Gorizian experiment wrote of the intense nature of the work there, the pressure, the long shifts, the stress of being alone in the hospital all night. For the équipe (and their families) Gorizia was a totalizing experience. The demands on everyone involved, and on their families, were extremely high, physically and mentally. Marriages broke up under the strain, children were neglected, social life was reduced to a bare minimum, holidays were frowned upon. The working day usually began around eight thirty, with a meeting involving nurses, social workers and doctors. From nine to ten the doctors visited the wards (as in a traditional hospital). At ten there was the general assembly, with seats in a kind of disorderly semicircle, no fixed places and where patients ran the show (at least formally), chaired the *assemblea*, took the minutes and so on. Then: more meetings. At every moment, during every meeting, the idea

---

22   Balduzzi, *L'albero della cuccagna*, p. 39.

was that the needs of the whole community had to be taken into account. After the general assembly there was a feedback discussion, *about* the previous meeting, with doctors, nurses and patient community leaders (which was an interesting idea in itself). From about 11.15 to 1.15 there was a break, a rare period without meetings. At 1.15 the next shift started. Afternoons were largely taken up with more meetings, this time on the wards. And then there were the various committees.

One of the great differences between Gorizia and other asylums at the time, as we have seen, was that doctors were ever-present in the hospital and available to talk to patients. Slavich referred to this as 'the continual presence and their "ubiquitousness" in the wards'.[23] This was not the case in most asylums, where doctors would usually do the bare mini-mum.[24] The sense of endless debate was particularly intense during the 'golden age' in Gorizia, from 1966 to 1968, with the production of two books, a film and numerous other initiatives. In Gorizia, moreover, the meetings were not confined to the asylum. Discussions within the équipe continued in Basaglia's flat deep into the night, or over dinner.

The contradictions were clear, at least for the équipe. Basaglia used the meetings to draw supporters in, and to spread the word about what was happening in Gorizia. But at the same time, the équipe explained how the patients were, at the end of the day, powerless. Other observa-tions might also be made of the general meetings. Were they voyeuristic? Were the patients on show? The inmates were, in some sense, being displayed (as they also were in photographs taken of them, or in films). There was a fascination with the physical ravages that the asylum had created, and with mad behaviour, a kind of 'attraction-repulsion' (which the journalist Nino Vascon admitted to in *L'istituzione negata*).[25]

There was also a risk of paternalism. Basaglia and his team had 'given' the patients their freedom, they had opened the locked wards, they signed the permits that allowed some of the inmates to leave (usually accom-panied, and with an obligation to return). Despite the rhetoric of 'we put the key in the door, and they turned it', the Gorizian experiment

---

23   Basaglia, *L'istituzione negata* (1968), p. 187.

24   Balduzzi, *L'albero della cuccagna*, p. 39.

25   See also David Forgacs, *Italy's Margins. Social Exclusion and Nation Formation since 1861*, Cambridge: Cambridge University Press, 2014, pp. 239–43.

was in the hands of the équipe. They were free, the patients were not. They had the keys, the patients did not. Once the Basaglians had resigned in 1972, normal service was resumed (to some extent). In this sense, Basaglia was right. The asylum could not be reformed. It had to be destroyed.

By 1967 the Gorizian experiment was well known in psychiatric circles. The équipe had published their first book and a steady stream of visitors turned up to see what was happening there. But in 1968 Gorizia, and Basaglia, became famous. The key instrument of this fame was a book published by Einaudi in March 1968, a book which would become the 'bible' for a whole generation. The book's title was significant in itself: *L'istituzione negata*.

ELEVEN

The Genesis of The Negated Institution

'Your book . . . is one of those rare examples of a book which builds on itself, it lives through the tensions which it produces within itself and it sustains itself through its own self-destructive tendencies.'
Giulio Bollati to Franco Basaglia (26 January 1968)

Giovanni Jervis and Einaudi

There are various stories of the genesis, production and birth of the book that became *The Negated Institution*. Everyone agrees, however, that it was Giovanni Jervis who provided the connection between the Gorizians and the book's publisher: Einaudi.[1] 'Gionni' Jervis had worked for Einaudi on a temporary basis from the 1960s onwards. His role in that early period (as an external consultant and an intermediary with Ernesto De Martino) had been briefly threatened for a time by his friendship with Renato Solmi and Raniero Panzieri, after a notorious split over the publication of Goffredo Fofi's book on southern immigration to Turin led to the sacking of the two 'workerist' intellectuals from the company's editorial committee in November 1963.

Jervis started to make regular appearances at the celebrated Wednesday

---

1 This link is, however, often played down or entirely ignored in some accounts, probably as a result of the long-running disputes and bitterness between Jervis, the other Gorizians and the Basaglians post-Gorizia.

meetings of Einaudi's editorial committee (consiglio editoriale) in the spring of 1965 (a presence which was strictly by invitation only). These meetings in Turin were presided over by Giulio Einaudi and Giulio Bollati, and were the arena where book proposals and published books were discussed and editorial plans laid down. Gionni had already been commissioned by Einaudi to write an extended introduction to Marcuse's *Eros and Civilization* (he was first given this work in 1962), and by the mid-1960s he had become the in-house expert on psychology, psychiatry and psychoanalysis (areas which were attracting the increasing attention of publishers and readers).[2] Jervis also translated books from English and was invited to write an introduction to a new edition of the children's classic *Pinocchio*. His star was on the rise, and he was often one of the first people to speak at these meetings.

Jervis was given a vast amount of material to read and report back on and was invited even further into Einaudi's inner-inner circle, and in particular the regular summer editorial get-together in the Valle d'Aosta (Jervis attended in 1965, 1966, 1967, 1970 and 1971). His angular figure can be spotted in group photos from those years, alongside Italo Calvino and others. In 1967, he was put on a permanent retainer by Einaudi (with pay of 150,000 *lire* a month). It had been a long slog, but he had made it.

This was the context in which Jervis decided to move to Gorizia to join the Basaglian team in 1966. In October of that year he wrote to Einaudi giving his new address as 'Gorizia, Ospedale Psichiatrico Provinciale', and in the same month he referred in another letter to 'my colleague and friend Franco Basaglia'.[3] Part of Jervis's reasoning for joining the équipe was to connect Einaudi with the most exciting experiment in Italy at that time in terms of mental health reform and radical psychiatry. Soon before his departure for Gorizia, plans were hatched for a series of books based on what was happening there, and Jervis reported back on all this to Einaudi.[4] We have seen that Jervis quickly

---

2   He also translated and wrote a long introduction to the influential and much-cited book by August Hollingshead and Frederick Redlich, *Social Class and Mental Illness (Classi sociali e malattie mentali)*.

3   Letter, 31 October 1966, Jervis to Fossati. Einaudi Archive.

4   It seems likely that Jervis met up with Basaglia in the latter's holiday home in the mountains of Trentino, in the summer of 1966, to discuss these plans.

became a key member of the équipe and contributed to the first collective book about Gorizia, published in Parma in 1967. That book (*What Is Psychiatry?*) turned out to be a kind of trial run for *The Negated Institution*, and the two volumes are similar in terms of their structure, content, style and tone. Einaudi later bought up the rights for *What Is Psychiatry?* (which they reprinted in 1973).

The connections between Einaudi and Gorizia were built up in a number of ways, at first through the presence of Jervis. As anti-psychiatry quickly became fashionable and marketable, Einaudi (after suggestions from Jervis, some of which had their origins in Gorizia) took up options for books by R. D. Laing, Erving Goffman and others, and some of the translation and editorial work involved was assigned to members of the équipe in Gorizia, including Letizia Comba and Franca Ongaro. Books that were important for Basaglia and the équipe were proposed to Einaudi for translation, via Jervis, such as those by Maxwell Jones and Foucault. In this way Einaudi, in the wake of *The Negated Institution*, published almost all the key texts for the Gorizian team. A Basaglian library, a *set of texts*, was built up after 1968.

The book which would become *The Negated Institution* was cited in February 1967 by Jervis as what 'we are creating in Gorizia'.[5] It was also clear at that point that this book was intended for the Nuovo Politecnico series where it eventually was to appear. What this also tells us is that work must have started on *The Negated Institution* soon after Jervis's arrival in Gorizia in 1966, or even before that date. The original Einaudi plan was for at least two books linked to Gorizia: one was to be called 'Psychiatry and Power', and another was to be specifically about the asylum.[6]

Jervis was responsible for bringing Basaglia and Einaudi into direct contact. There were also signs that other publishers were beginning to court the director of the Gorizian asylum. As Jervis warned in April 1967,

A collection based on experiences in Parma and Gorizia is due to come out . . . we are already talking about it . . . and Basaglia has been contacted by Filippini in terms of future publications with generous

5   1 February 1967, editorial committee, memo.
6   5 April 1967, editorial committee, memo.

financial offers. For other books, Basaglia will go with the best offer he receives.

This was a reference, presumably, to Enrico Filippini, who worked for the Feltrinelli publishing house in Milan. It was at this point that Jervis added the fatal words: 'I could bring Basaglia with me'.[7] Up to that point, Basaglia had not been in direct touch with anybody in the Einaudi publishing house, but things would soon change. This would be an encounter that would have hugely important consequences: for Jervis, Basaglia, Bollati, Einaudi and Gorizia.[8]

In April 1967, then, Jervis suggested that he bring Franco Basaglia to Turin to meet Giulio Bollati and others. The meeting duly took place on 17 May, and the two men (Bollati and Basaglia) hit it off from the beginning. A further connection was provided by the role and interests of Bollati's wife, Piera Piatti, who would set up an organization working on similar themes to Basaglia called the Associazione per la Lotta contro le Malattie Mentali in Turin in late 1967. Bollati was immediately seduced by Basaglia's intelligence and radical passion. It was friendship at first sight.[9] Basaglia, moreover, was not interested in a career inside Einaudi itself, unlike Jervis. Both Bollati and Basaglia were intellectuals, but both were interested in getting things done, in the real world, and

---

7 Letter, 22 April 1967, to Paolo Fossati. With pen: 'I will come to Turin on 17 May, with Basaglia. Is that OK? Tell Bollati, perhaps'. The meeting with Bollati was not confirmed until the last minute: 'I would like to know if Bollati will be in Turin next Wednesday and if he is available to meet Basaglia. In any case I will be there.' This is Jervis's later version: 'I thought that a book of this kind could be very interesting before I moved from Rome to Gorizia in 1966 and I discussed this with Giulio Bollati and put forward a project to him. I also discussed this with Basaglia and after a few months I took him with me to Turin . . . I thus was able to insist that the contract for the book was signed by both of us and not by me alone, and that the front cover carried the phrase "edited by Franco Basaglia"', *La razionalità negata*, p. 86.

8 In 1968, after the publication of *L'istituzione negata*, Filippini wrote to Basaglia congratulating him on the book and reminding him of their discussion about the project over a year earlier. His letter had a sting in the tail: 'I would be a hypocrite, however . . . if I did not tell you honestly, and in terms of any future relationship between us, that this is not the correct way to do things' (21 February 1968). Basaglia replied with a partial apology. Filippini had been in discussions with Basaglia about a book in 1967, as the letters between them show.

9 Basaglia wrote to Bollati after he had visited Gorizia in 1967 that 'I had the clear and pleasurable impression from our meeting that this could be the beginning of a friendship between us'. Basaglia Archive.

not just in abstract theorizing. Bollati was also a man with real power, and Basaglia understood how power worked.

In the aftermath of this meeting, Bollati and Piatti visited Gorizia and Venice on a number of occasions, and Basaglia began to make regular trips to Turin. A correspondence started which also included Franca Ongaro, who also struck up a friendship with Bollati. The three would remain close until Basaglia's death in 1980. Bollati was then in constant contact with Franca Ongaro until his own death in 1996.

The friendship between Basaglia and Bollati quickly took hold, as their letters show. On 15 June 1967 Basaglia wrote to Bollati about that first meeting: 'It was a great pleasure to meet you.'[10] A channel of communication was established in this way that by-passed the previous (and only) intermediary between Einaudi and Gorizia: Jervis. Basaglia continued, 'I am happy about the editorial possibilities which are opening up for me and for my équipe with the Einaudi publishing house.'[11] That first meeting in Turin also included direct discussions over work on what was to become *The Negated Institution*. Einaudi, through Bollati, agreed to pay for the costs of recording and transcribing general meetings in Gorizia. This was a key idea/source behind the book, which was also referred to as a 'spoken book'.[12] From May 1967 onwards, Bollati became Basaglia's 'minder' within Einaudi. Jervis was slowly side-lined, although he continued to report back to the editorial meetings. Proposals also arrived directly through Basaglia and Bollati and were discussed with Giulio Einaudi. Jervis was no longer the lone spokesman for the Gorizian experience with the publishing house, although it took him some time to realize what was happening. Editorially, the Bollati–Basaglia–Ongaro connection would lead to a number of books by the Basaglias or on their recommendation.[13]

---

10   Letter, 15 June 1967, Einaudi Archive. Basaglia Folder.

11   Ibid.

12   18 June 1967, Einaudi Archive. Basaglia Folder.

13   Directly by the Basaglias, beyond the numerous editions of *L'istituzione negata* (1968), *Morire di classe* (1969), *La maggioranza deviante* (1971), a new edition of *Che cos'è la psichiatria?* (1973), *Crimini di pace* (1975) and the two volumes of the *Scritti* published posthumously in 1981, should be added a number of introductions, prefaces and translations, plus a series of projects that never saw the light of day. A new collection of Basaglia's writings was published in 2005 by Einaudi, Franca Ongaro Basaglia ed., *Franco Basaglia. L'utopia della realtà*.

Bollati's letters to Basaglia were also those of a friend, with an informal tone (very different to that which Bollati used with Jervis). For example, this is from 10 November 1967:

> I would like to thank you from the bottom of my heart for the reception you offered me in Gorizia, and I would also like to thank your wife. I hope we can meet again soon, maybe in Turin. In any case I am certain that Piera will make sure that we keep in touch, something which I am very committed to, not only as a publisher, but as a friend.[14]

The two men worked closely together on the publications being prepared in Gorizia. In July 1967 Basaglia wrote to Bollati about the various projects emerging there. The first was provisionally entitled *Practical Overturnings: Report from a Therapeutic Community*. Basaglia wrote that 'the title, it seems to me, corresponds perfectly with the conceptual meaning of the book'.[15] For Basaglia it was important that the book was *not* seen or presented as psychiatric in any way: 'Nothing about psychiatry should be included on the cover . . . given the overall "anti-psychiatric" or "anti-scientific" stamp of the whole work.'[16] The second book proposed was a collection of Basaglia's writings. Its provisional title was *L'istituzione negata* (The Negated Institution) while the third was a more analytical book called *Psichiatria e potere* (Psychiatry and power). The volume that came out in 1968 was a combination of all three of these proposals. These discussions continued in parallel with those involving Jervis at the editorial committee. It is not clear to what extent Jervis was aware of the importance of this direct line of communication. There is no doubt that his previous key role was undermined after May 1967.

In May 1967 Bollati reported back to the editorial committee on his meeting with Jervis and Basaglia in a non-committal way: 'Jervis and

---

14   10 November 1967, Bollati to Basaglia. Einaudi Archive.

15   Further information on the development of the title can be gleaned from the material in the Archivio Basaglia. The idea was still to have two books in November 1967. As Basaglia wrote to Bollatti on 6 November 1967, 'Given that we will all be there I suggest the title "L'istituzione negata" should be used for the spoken book.'

16   18 July 1967, Basaglia to Bollati. Einaudi Archive.

Basaglia came to Turin to talk about the two books born from their experience in Gorizia.' Jervis added that

> the first was dedicated to *Psychiatry and Power*, and is in development. The one which is more urgent and more ready is for the Nuovo Politecnico series and is an analysis of the life and problems of a therapeutic community, with an editorial commentary, in the wake of the volume which came out with the Provincial Administration of Parma. This book will be informative, but also stimulating. It will be ready in about three months.[17]

What Is Psychiatry? had been published by a small ad hoc publisher, with a limited circulation. *The Negated Institution* would be a different operation altogether. Gorizia was about to hit the big time. In the end, as we have seen, these two ongoing projects (plus that of a collection of Basaglia's writings) were merged into *The Negated Institution*, and the volume which was to be called *Psichiatria e potere* never appeared.[18] A complete, two-volume edition of Basaglia and Franca Ongaro's writings would appear after the former's death in 1980.[19]

But who was the author of *The Negated Institution*? This was a book unlike any other, a true collective work, with a plurality of voices, authors, editors and inputs. Its pages contained a range of statements, conversations and debates involving patients, doctors, nurses and the journalist Nino Vascon, as well as chapters by every member of the core équipe plus Franca Ongaro. Large sections were given over to the patients. In 1967–68 there was a key debate about whose name or names would appear on the cover of *The Negated Institution*. Who would be seen as the book's author or editor? This was not merely a practical issue, but also a philosophical and political one. Did the book actually *have* an author or an editor? The issue of authorship was seen as crucial. Basaglia originally wanted no name at all on the cover, or a collective term. He saw the book as a truly shared effort and was worried about the possibility

---

17   24 May 1967, 404, memo, Einaudi Archive.

18   Giovanni Berlinguer published a book with the title *Psichiatria e potere* in 1969 (Rome: Riuniti).

19   Franco Basaglia, *Scritti*, 2 volumes, Turin: Einaudi, 1981–82.

of the appropriation and identification of the volume's author by the 'cultural industry'. But Bollati appears to have convinced him to change his mind. The experienced publisher argued that 'the system' would identify an author in any case and that an anonymous book would just be seen as 'Einaudi's': 'Even if you are not the official author of the book, or Jervis, or Pirella, some of the public will still know that the book is yours, or Jervis's, or Pirella's.'[20]

Interestingly, this letter also shows that there were other possible authors/editors of *The Negated Institution*. Clearly, the book *was* a collective effort, with input from the entire extended équipe plus journalists, patients and others. It is also obvious that Jervis played a significant editing role, as did Bollati, Basaglia, Franca Ongaro and others. Much later, Luca Baranelli (an Einaudi editor at the time) would argue that Jervis had been the 'real editor' of *The Negated Institution*.[21] But Gorizia itself would never have happened without Basaglia. It was his creation, and he was clearly its leader. His ideas ran right through the book. There was also a fear of (mis)appropriation, the worry that Gorizia would become fashionable and be made toothless by the power of cultural consumption. It might be eaten up by the 'society of the spectacle'. Basaglia was particularly aware of this, hence his hesitation about the authorship of the volume, or the identification of the book with a single author.[22]

In the end, the book was published with the byline 'Edited by Franco Basaglia', and *was* identified immediately with Basaglia himself, as was (and is) the whole Gorizian experience. On occasions, *The Negated Institution* is attributed to one author alone, as if it was literally '*By* Franco Basaglia'. In some ways, then, Basaglia's fears were justified. However, from a publishing point of view, and from that of the movement as a whole, Bollati's intuitions were correct. This was a decisive moment, especially for Jervis. After all, without Jervis, Einaudi might well have missed out on *The Negated Institution*, as well as a series of subsequent

---

20   18 December 1967, Bollati to Basaglia. Einaudi Archive. Basaglia Folder.

21   See also the version given by Jervis in his last published book, *La razionalità negata*, pp. 86–7.

22   The question of authorship was a delicate one, however. After a piece in the magazine *L'Espresso* highlighted the role of Jervis, Basaglia wrote to the magazine to complain.

volumes by Basaglia and Franca Ongaro. And without the interplay between Basaglia, Bollati and Jervis, would *The Negated Institution* have been a bestseller at all? They shaped the book into something perfectly in tune with its times.

The contract for *L'istituzione negata* was signed jointly by Jervis and Basaglia in February 1968, with all royalties going to the patients' club in Gorizia. It came out in March 1968. Antonio Slavich later wrote of the day when Giovanni Jervis arrived back in Gorizia with a pile of new books, which smelt of ink. He then proceeded to hand them out among the équipe. Basaglia himself, it seems, had taken the manuscript to Turin. Nobody expected this technical, dense and multi-authored book about an asylum in Gorizia to become a bestseller, although the publishers were well aware of its importance and power, and the clear links to the explosion of worldwide protest in 1967–68. An extensive promotional tour was organized involving various members of the équipe, and the book was reviewed all across Italy, in a wide variety of publications, including many linked to the Catholic world. As Einaudi editor Paolo Fossati wrote to Jervis in February 1968, 'This book is urgently required.'[23]

With the unexpected success of *The Negated Institution*, a whole world opened up for Franco Basaglia and the other Gorizians. The book's timing was perfect; its appearance 'at a crucial juncture in the great social mobilizations of the late 1960s, quite suddenly made the Gorizia experience famous'.[24] It also made Basaglia into a celebrity, a star, one of the acknowledged leaders of 1968. Gorizia both reflected and helped to produce the Italian 1968 movement. *The Negated Institution* became one of the key texts from that time, 'the first major publication of the new psychiatry'[25] to be found on the shelves of all self-respecting *sessantottini*

---

23   There was also discussion, it seems, over the possible addition of a selection of letters that had been received. But this idea was not taken up. For the second edition, which was published in April 1968, the Basaglias added two articles as an appendix (one by Franco Basaglia and Franca Ongaro Basaglia, 'Il problema dell'*incidente*', pp. 363–9 and one by Franco Basaglia alone, 'Il problema della *gestione*', pp. 370–80). Since then, the text has remained the same. A new edition was published by Baldini & Castoldi in 1998 with a new 'Nota introduttiva' by Franca Ongaro Basaglia and a new cover (a photo by Carla Cerati from *Morire di classe*).

24   Michael Donnelly, *The Politics of Mental Health in Italy*, London: Tavistock, 1992, p. 48, Jervis used more or less the same phrase in 1977, 'Gorizia suddenly became famous.' *Il buon rieducatore*, p. 23.

25   Donnelly, *The Politics of Mental Health in Italy*, p. xiii.

('68ers). When Antonio Slavich started work in Ferrara in 1971, he found that most of his team knew the book well: 'Everyone had read it, and they were still passing copies around.'[26] *L'istituzione negata* quickly became the central historical source for understanding what had happened in Gorizia.[27]

Basaglia personally thanked Bollati for his help on behalf of his équipe and the patients ('I want to thank you for all you have done for me and for all the Gorizians'). The publicity campaign linked to the book was highly successful, with packed crowds across Italy, but also difficult and tiring. In some ways these events confirmed Basaglia's worst fears. Gorizia had become a product, something that was being consumed and sold. 'With *L'istituzione negata*', Basaglia wrote, 'I am moving around Italy like a travelling salesman'.[28] There was a danger of things being simplified or put forward in a banal sense as models for others to follow. When the book won a special prestigious Viareggio Literary Prize in the summer of 1968, this danger was underlined once again, and the équipe was divided over whether to accept the award or not.[29]

The Basaglia-Bollati relationship was fatal, in the end, for Jervis and his role within Einaudi. Although it seems that Basaglia never became a paid consultant as Jervis had been, his direct contact with Bollati meant that the latter took his ideas directly to the committee, or to Giulio Einaudi himself. Jervis was marginalized. His own work had no chance of being published with Einaudi. A proposal for a critical book on psychiatry, based partly on Jervis's work post-Gorizia in Reggio Emilia, ended up with Feltrinelli in 1975.[30] Basaglia had no more need of an intermediary within Einaudi. Quickly, after 1968, Jervis and Basaglia had gone from being friends and close colleagues to rivals. Jervis continued working with the publisher in Turin, as did his wife Letizia Comba, but it was clear that his days there were numbered. By the end

---

26   Antonio Slavich, *La scopa meravigliante. Preparativi per la legge 180 a Ferrara e dintorni 1971–1978*, Rome: Riuniti, 2003, p. 21.

27   Donnelly, *The Politics of Mental Health in Italy*, p. 130.

28   Some of the details of the tour with *L'istituzione negata* can be gleaned from the correspondence in the Basaglia archive.

29   See the following chapter for more details on this award and the debate that followed.

30   Jervis, 24 May 1967, 404, memo. Einaudi Archive.

of 1971, Jervis's time with Einaudi was over. His bitterness over this experience would be laid out fully in his frank account of his life (up to that point), which would be published in 1977.[31]

The final title of *The Negated Institution* was decided at the last minute, and probably not until early 1968. There is some controversy over who came up with the phrase *L'istituzione negata*. Some cite Pirella,[32] others Jervis, others Basaglia himself.[33] One earlier suggestion was for 'The Practice of Overturning', and Basaglia used the term *l'istituzione negata* with reference to a collection of his own work that he proposed to Bollati in June 1967, which is in indication that he at least had a part in choosing the term.[34]

The book itself was written in parts, discussed and put together in Basaglia's flat in Gorizia and in the hospital in the city with input from the whole équipe as well as Franca Ongaro, Michele Risso, Giulio Bollati and others. Nobody has ever written in detail about this process. It was like a jigsaw, made up of voices, articles, debates. Basaglia's own writings were cut and pasted into the book at various points. Each member of the équipe had their own piece in the volume, and there were also outsiders involved in key roles, such as the RAI journalist Nino Vascon and the sociologist Gian Antonio Gilli. This working model had already been used with *What Is Psychiatry?* in 1966–67.

The Negated Institution was the right book at the right time, a book whose time had come. It flew off the shelves, going through 'eight

---

31   This particular story was not told by Jervis in that text. See also *La razionalità negata*, pp. 86–7.

32   'When *Che cos'è la psichiatria?* came out, the Gorizians were already working on a new book, whose title came from an insight by Pirella. Maria Grazia Giannichedda, 'Introduzione' to Franca Ongaro Basaglia, ed., *Franco Basaglia. L'utopia della realtà*, Turin: Einaudi, 2005, p. xxv. Jervis provides a different version of events: 'Obviously we talked about the title, and perhaps it is symptomatic of things that a couple of years later Basaglia told me that I had chosen the title, while I seemed to recall that it had been suggested by him. Maybe nobody wanted to take responsibility for it . . . we both felt a little uneasy . . . because the book's title had become a little too triumphalist and too promotional.' *La razionalità negata*, p. 88. From the letters I have seen between Bollati and Basaglia the title was part of a discussion between them and the équipe.

33   Oreste Pivetta, *Franco Basaglia. Il dottore dei matti. La biografia*, Milan: Dalai, 2012, p. 180.

34   18 July 1967, Basaglia to Bollati. Einaudi Archive.

editions of which two during 1968 and 60,000 copies sold in Italy of which 50,000 between 1968 and 1972'.[35] *The Negated Institution* sold 12,500 copies in 1968 alone, making 690,000 *lire* for the authors, all of which was donated to the patients' club in Gorizia (and thus went directly to the patients), once the publisher's costs had been deducted. *The Negated Institution* told people what they wanted to hear, but it also created new currents of opinion. Its title was perfect: a slogan, a call to arms, and not just for psychiatrists (and perhaps not for them at all). Suddenly, Gorizia was headline news, a mecca for the 1968 generation, a place with its own bible.

The Negated Institution both produced and reflected 1968.[36] Journalists flocked to Gorizia to write pieces for all kinds of magazines and newspapers, and other visitors simply turned up to see things with their own eyes: the miracle-spectacle of the mad discussing how to manage their own hospital, the spectacle of a group of lunatics who really had taken over an asylum, as their doctors sat around without white coats and made occasional comments. Sergio Zavoli's powerful documentary, *I giardini di Abele*, aired on national TV in early 1969 and watched by millions, was the icing on the cake. A gloomy mental asylum in the middle of nowhere had, unexpectedly, become one of the key sites of the 1968 movement in Italy, and to some extent in Europe.

After *The Negated Institution* Basaglia could do no wrong as far as Einaudi were concerned. He was given a whopping 2.5 million *lire* in advance to visit a series of South American countries in 1969 in order to carry out research into anti-institutional movements there. The book that was promised about this trip never appeared.[37] By 1969, Basaglia was

---

35   Giannichedda, 'Introduzione', p. xxv. The publisher reported a sales figure of 12,500 for the first three editions of the book in 1968. By the end of 1972 this figure had risen to around 27,000 copies, through five editions (Einaudi Archive). In December 1975 sales of a further 25,000 or so copies was reported, giving a total of over 52,000 in seven years and seven editions. This gets us close to the overall total of 60,000 that is often given as the official sales figure for Einaudi over eight editions up to 1974.

36   See the section on 1968 below, as well as Robert Gildea, James Mark and Anette Warring, eds, *Europe's 1968. Voices of Revolt*, Oxford: Oxford University Press, 2013.

37   Although a short article based on Basaglia's experiences in the USA appears to have been published by Einaudi in 1969: *Lettera da New York. Il malato artificiale* (see the bibliography to *Franco Basaglia. L'utopia della realtà*, p. 323). I have never been able to find a physical copy of this book.

becoming more interested in what he saw as the anti-institutional struggle in general, and not in anti-psychiatry or radical psychiatry *per se*. He would later, for example, decide not to produce a *Negated Institution Two* about Trieste in the 1970s. It seems that there was an original plan to put together a book of this kind, concentrating on Trieste, but that this eventually turned into a much more theoretical and wide-ranging text which was published by Einaudi in 1975 with the title *Crimini di pace*.[38]

---

38   This is from the introduction to *Crimini di pace* by Franco Basaglia and Franca Ongaro Basaglia; the book was originally intended to be 'the first analysis of a local psychiatric hospital with testimonies and documents from another experience . . . but it has become, bit by bit, a work of collective research into the role of the intellectual and specialist as part of the system of oppression'. Franco Basaglia and Franca Ongaro Basaglia, eds, *Crimini di pace. Ricerche sugli intellettuali e sui tecnici come addetti all'oppressione*, Milan: Baldini Castoldi Dalai, 2009 (Einaudi, 1975), p. 7. There is little or nothing directly about Trieste in this volume. Basaglia was upset about the reception which this book received. See the letter to Ruggiero Romano in the Einaudi Archive (n.d. but almost certainly 1975).

TWELVE

The Negated Institution:
The 'Bible' of 1968

'A hospital starts to have a history – we could say that history enters the hospital – when society enters in the hospital, and breaks its isolation.'

Letizia Comba[1]

'If a revolution requires violence, our violence is the opening of a ward.'

Franco Basaglia[2]

'We have started to work together on a project which is outside of all scientific parameters. We have come up with a practical hypothesis – that an institution of that kind had no right to exist – and we have started to work in that direction.'

Agostino Pirella[3]

'The reality of the asylum has been overcome . . . and we do not know what will happen next.'

Franco Basaglia[4]

---

1 Franco Basaglia, ed., *L'istituzione negata,* Turin: Einaudi, 1968, pp. 237–8.

2 Ibid., p. 269.

3 Franco Basaglia, Franca Ongaro Basaglia, Agostino Pirella, Salvatore Taverna, *La nave che affonda. Psichiatria e antipsichiatria a dieci anni da 'L'istituzione negata'. Un dibattito,* Rome: Savelli, 1978, pp. 103–4.

4 Basaglia, *L'istituzione negata* (1968), p. 8.

*T*he *Negated Institution* was a book with a plurality of voices, a kind of babble, a chorus, a patchwork, a work in progress. In many ways it was indeed a 'spoken book'. Inside, on its pages, there were patients of all kinds, doctors, nurses, psychologists, journalists and others in a variety of settings – meetings, one-to-one interviews. It contained real characters, with names, genuine life experiences, discussions transcribed verbatim. The book reproduced the sense and the dynamism of life within the therapeutic community, with its lively and yet interminable debates, dialogues, confessions and high levels, of verbosity. It was also a collage of texts, which ranged from near-impenetrable high theory to graphic accounts of torture. Much of the book was obscurely written, highly theoretical and complicated; other parts were hard-hitting and straightforward. Some sections were deliberately shocking and graphic. Parts of the book made little reference to Gorizia itself. There were no historical studies of the patients, their origins or of the context in which the hospital had been built and had functioned until the 1960s. *L'istituzione negata* was also intended as a text that would lead to extra study. It carried its own bibliography as a guide to further reading. This was a text like no other. It had no overarching narrative and its very form was that of the 1968 movement, the *assemblea*. In some ways, Gorizia invented the *assemblea*. It transmitted a sense of radical change, change that was actually happening (or had already happened) here and now. It sold so fast that Einaudi could hardly keep up with demand.

'This is no longer an asylum.'

Fabio Isman[5]

'Our only rule, in here, is linked to our practice, to the lived experience of reality.'

Franco Basaglia[6]

---

5   'I medici senza camicie bianco simbolo dell'esperimento do Basaglia', *Il Piccolo*, 27 October 1968.

6   Quoted in Fabio Isman, 'Hanno discusso tranquilli in assemblea come adoperare il milione del "Viareggio"', *Il Piccolo*, 20 October 1968.

The journalist Nino Vascon[7] set the scene. Gorizia's psychiatric hospital was a complex made up of nine buildings set in a huge and beautiful wooded park, which also contained a small church, a bar, a farm. Inside, there were 500 or so patients, 150 nurses and nine doctors (plus a chaplain, a number of nuns, a psychologist, some social workers and some volunteers). In certain ways, it was a strangely beautiful place: 'This park is something which cannot be described – beautiful, magnificent.'[8] The asylum was on the edge of this small city, opposite the enormous mass of the city hospital. A large building opposite the main gates housed the offices of the staff, the park stretched out behind. When Basaglia arrived the area was rigidly divided by gender: men on the left, women on the right. But this was an asylum which was, by 1968, 'open to all . . . once you are through the gates, which are never closed, the occasional visitor walks through the avenues of the park'. This hypothetical visitor, according to Vascon, would have been unable to tell the patients from the 'normal' people. 'There aren't dangerous people here', wrote Vascon (slightly optimistically, perhaps, in the light of events to come that year).

Was this a psychiatric hospital at all, or something very different, something new, revolutionary even? There were no 'gates, strait jackets, coercive methods which create violence'.[9] Vascon then plunged the reader straight into something that seemed very strange in a psychiatric hospital: a mass meeting of patients. And this was not an isolated or purely symbolic event: 'The entire life of the hospital is marked by meetings.'[10] Vascon was describing a place that seemed unique.[11] This psychiatric hospital was open, it had no visiting hours, most of the patients moved freely in the grounds, and they could even go out into the city itself. The patients also had their own bar, which they ran themselves. Few of the doctors wore white coats, or even described themselves *as* doctors. The patients were paid with real money for work. None of the wards were locked at this stage (the last closed wards had been opened by the end of 1967). General, ward and other meetings decided on the

---

7 Basaglia knew Vascon from his school days.

8· Isman, 'Hanno discusso tranquilli in assemblea'.

9 Basaglia, *L'istituzione negata* (1968), p. 26.

10 Ibid., p. 28.

11 Although experiments had been attempted in various places, and were ongoing in Perugia.

key issues involving the management of the hospital, as well as on outside visits. *Everything* was discussed, openly and at great length.

Gorizia's asylum appeared to Vascon as a place where mental illness had been 'placed in brackets', and where the roles of doctor, patient and nurse had also, to some extent, been put on hold. Everyone inside the institution was well aware of their objective status, but most were trying to free themselves of their prejudices and of their past. As one psychologist wrote about herself: 'I am trying to free myself from the tendency to objectify ill people'.[12] This was one of the key ideas in the book, and of the movement itself. The mad were real people, like you and me, and the aim of the staff was to 'make contact directly with mental hospital inmates'.[13] One of the other messages coming out of Gorizia was this: ordinary people needed to be listened to, as people, not as schizophrenics or alcoholics. As Pirella put it, there was a constant sense of 'the confrontation with reality'.[14] Interestingly, this was not a lesson that the 1968 generation was always able or willing to follow. The practical lessons of Gorizia were often ignored or overlooked in favour of its theorizing. Sartre had said that 'if you want to see a place where practical knowledge is being formed, go to Gorizia',[15] but this was not necessarily the way that Gorizia was read or understood. The fragmented nature of *L'istituzione negata* allowed for many different readings of this text. This was not a book that was read cover to cover.

Only a smattering of people (most of them specialists) had heard about what was happening in Gorizia before 1968. Yet, by the time *The Negated Institution* came out, many of the protagonists of that experiment were on the verge of leaving. They had also come to the conclusion that what they were doing had reached something of a dead end. While *The Negated Institution* was a revelation for those who read it, for the Gorizians themselves it marked the beginning of the end. These aspects of the book were often ignored, as Colucci and Di Vittorio wrote: 'It is also – and perhaps above all – a book written against the idea of the therapeutic community

---

12   Basaglia, *L'istituzione negata* (1968), p. 69.
13   Michael Donnelly, *The Politics of Mental Health in Italy,* London: Tavistock, 1992, p. xiii.
14   Basaglia, *L'istituzione negata* (1968), p. 228.
15   Cited in Babini, *Liberi tutti,* p. 178.

and attempts at "institutional reform", but this aspect has remained somewhat in the shadows.'[16]

Thus, at the same time as the very success of *The Negated Institution* set Gorizia up as a model (despite the book's claims that 'we refuse to put forward the therapeutic community as an institutional model'),[17] most of the Gorizians had already moved on. In fact, they saw what they had done there, in part, as a trap, a 'golden cage', a way of providing a sophisticated and humane veil to mask new forms of oppression. There was a deep ambiguity at the heart of this book and the furore that surrounded it. The revolution in mental health care would be carried forward elsewhere, close to Gorizia itself, in Trieste, but also in other cities across Italy. It was a 'book which discusses a crisis and which brought the Gorizia experience to a point of crisis – this is what makes it original, a sense of genius',[18] but this is not how most people read or understood it.

The Text

'The material collected in this book is a set of documents and notes which aim to present a concrete vision of an institutional reality which is being overturned, and with all the contradictions implicit in this experience.'

Franco Basaglia[19]

Basaglia's piece in the first edition of the *The Negated Institution*, which opened the volume, was the most radical and '68esque of all the material in the book, and the most far-reaching. It was almost a manifesto for what 1968 would become, with the contestation of *all* institutions linked to the exercise of power – a declaration of intent for an anti-institutional and anti-authoritarian movement. Called 'The institutions of violence',

---

16   Mario Colucci and Pierangelo Di Vittorio, *Franco Basaglia*, Milan: Bruno Mondadori, 2001, p. 179.

17   Basaglia, *L'istituzione negata* (1968) p. 149.

18   Colucci and Di Vittorio, *Franco Basaglia*, p. 179.

19   Basaglia, *L'istituzione negata* (1968), p. 7.

Basaglia's piece linked up a series of social and political organizations: 'Family, school, factory, university, hospital: these are all institutions based on the clear separation of roles.'[20] This piece was a collage of Basaglia's writings from 1964 to 1967, a sort of primer that also outlined the evolution of his ideas. For Basaglia, 'Violence and exclusion stand at the basis of every relationship within our society.'[21] Patients were seen here, starkly, as victims of institutional violence. The movement everywhere, like that in Gorizia, needed to move forward, or it would simply create new forms of these institutions, or help them to survive. 'We are forced', Basaglia wrote, 'to carry out continual checks and leaps forward'.[22] This article was clearly connected in spirit to the radical critique of the school system which had been developed by a priest in rural Tuscany, and which led to another key Italian text from 1968, *Letter to a schoolteacher*, and to Cooper's *The Death of the Family*.[23] 'The publication of *L'istituzione negata* had a formidable impact on public opinion . . . The book became a reference point for the whole movement.'[24]

Basaglia was providing a blueprint for action and his language was revolutionary. Moreover, he was not simply indulging in empty rhetoric. Change *had* really happened in Gorizia. It could be seen there *and* (by contrast) in every other asylum in Italy (or most of them, with a few notable exceptions) that had *not* changed *at all*. Theory and practice were working hand in hand. Something could be done, through the work of a tiny vanguard of intellectuals and militants. A few dedicated people could change the world, even in a place like Gorizia. Yet, there were dangers in this message. The idea of the revolutionary vanguard was abused time and again as the decade wore on, as was the sense that all state institutions (plus the family) were to be contested *tout court*. *The Negated Institution* told its readers that you did not need a mass movement to overturn any institution. Sheer will-power and ideas could be enough. But this strategy could only get you so far. After 1968, there

---

20   Ibid., p. 115.

21   Ibid.

22   Ibid., p. 150.

23   David Cooper, *The Death of the Family*, London: Penguin, 1971, translated into Italian as *La morte della famiglia*, Turin: Einaudi, 1972. Don Milani, *Lettera a una professoressa*, Scuola di Barbiana, Florence: Libreria Editrice Fiorentina, 1967.

24   Colucci and Di Vittorio, *Franco Basaglia*, p. 207.

was a lot of talk about 'engaged intellectuals' and 'organic intellectuals', but very few actually got their hands dirty, as the Gorizians had done.

The Negated Institution was thus a patchwork and collective work, similar in form to *What Is Psychiatry?* (but more traditional, less academic and more populist). It appeared as Number 19 in the Nuovo Politecnico series published by Einaudi, which had been set up by Giulio Bollati in 1965 (and was run by him). The first edition came out in March 1968, with a second edition in April of the same year (with a new appendix).[25] Previous books in this series included works by Barthes, Gombrich and Benjamin, and Nuovo Politecnico would later host classic texts by R. D. Laing as well as numerous books by Basaglia himself written with Franca Ongaro. Many of the volumes in this series were explicitly linked to the ideas and movements of the student revolt, such as Hal Draper's *Berkeley: The New Student Revolt*[26] or Marcuse's crucial '1968' text *One-Dimensional Man*.[27] *L'istituzione negata* was not a short book: its first edition ran to over 350 pages. The Nuovo Politecnico series would become strongly associated with Basaglia and radical psychiatry – and in short, with 1968 itself, which it prefigured and shaped. This was a series with a strong identity and mission, not simply a list of books.

The Nuovo Politecnico series (a title which harked back to Elio Vittorini's *Il Politecnico*, an influential cultural magazine which had been closed down by the Italian Communist Party after running from 1945 to 1947) had a precise set of objectives:

It was born from the need to give quick answers – and perhaps only in an intuitive or hypothetical way, but always in a well-informed and intelligent sense, to the questions posed by a society undergoing rapid

---

25 *L'istituzione negata* cost 1,000 *lire*. The Nuovo Politecnico series closed in 1989. See the comments of fellow Einaudi editor, Guido Davico Bonino in 'Leggere come editare', *BAIG* 4, Supplemento settembre 2011, p. 10, associazioneitalianagermanistica.it, and in 'All'Einaudi con Giulio Bollati' in Rosa Tamborrino, ed., *Giulio Bollati. Intermittenze del ricordo. Immagini di cultura italiana*, Edizioni Fondazione Torino Musei, 2006, p. 138.

26 Hal Draper, *Berkeley. The New Student Revolt,* New York: Grove Press, 1965. Published in Italian as *La rivolta di Berkeley. Il movimento studentesco negli stati uniti,* Turin: Einaudi, 1966.

27 Herbert Marcuse, *One-Dimensional Man. Studies in the Ideology of Advanced Industrial Society*, Boston: Beacon Press, 1964. Published in Italian as *L'uomo a una dimensione. L'ideologia della società industriale avanzata,* Turin: Einaudi, 1967. According to Maria Grazia Giannichedda this book sold an incredible 220,000 copies in Italy.

evolution. There were militant essays, or books written 'in shirt-sleeves', but with strong ideas, as attempts to ask the right questions and to try and reach towards the first answers – in any field – and they were always aimed at a kind of ideal reader, someone with an encyclopaedic knowledge, almost a utopian personality – but someone we have always worked towards – we were convinced that we were working towards the modernization of the country.[28]

Birth of a Text

The cover was simple and stark, and would remain the same for the whole series (a small red square on a white background). The subtitle was direct and effective: *Rapporto da un ospedale psichiatrico* (Report from a psychiatric hospital).[29] Basaglia was named as the editor on the cover, although the work was presented as *collective*: as that of the équipe as a whole, plus the patients themselves, as well as outsiders such as Nino Vascon. The title also made a direct reference to the very first book in the Nuovo Politecnico series, the celebrated study *Report from a Chinese Village* (Rapporto da un villaggio cinese. Inchiesta in una comune agricola dello Shensi).[30] *The Negated Institution* was a combination of all the key traits of Italy's 1968. It was an account of radical anti-institutional practice mixed with large doses of revolutionary and Marxist rhetoric, plus some obscure philosophical language and a sense of 'counter-information' ('The Report'). It also intended to give a voice to the oppressed (the patients). The whole series had a Maoist tint to it, as in the famous slogan 'Chi non fa inchiesta non ha diritto di parola' (No investigation, no right to speak – Unless you have investigated a problem, you will be deprived of the right to speak on it) and the idea of 'barefoot doctors'.[31]

---

28   Giulio Einaudi, *Tutti i nostri mercoledi*, Bellinzona: Casagrande, 2001, pp. 117–18.

29   Basaglia and other Gorizians were clearly influenced by Maoist thought at this time. See the next chapter, on 1968.

30   Jan Myrdal, *Report from a Chinese Village*, New York: Pantheon Books, 1965 (first published in Swedish in 1963; published in Italian by Einaudi in 1966). Basaglia had noted the similarity between the two titles in an 18 July 1967 letter to Bollati, Einaudi Archive. This was almost certainly not a coincidence. Myrdal's book went through seven editions by 1977.

31   Mao Tse-tung, 'Oppose Book Worship', 1930, in *Selected Works of Mao Tsetung*, Vol. 6, marxists.org.

The Negated Institution is (and was), for a kind of bible or 'book-man-ifesto', difficult to read. Its 356 pages in the first edition are made up of various sections: historical and sociological studies, philosophical accounts, analyses of *assemblee* from Gorizia, as well as reflections on the work of others. It was fragmentary, even in its structure, a kind of free-form play where various actors, narrators and others took the stage and then left.

Basaglia's very brief introduction ('Presentation') hinted at how this celebrated volume had been put together. It began with a radical and bold statement of intent. This was a work in progress, an ongoing project, a manifesto, something that was unfinished. What kind of institution were we dealing with? 'A reality which can only be violently rejected: the madhouse.'[32] There was no need for debate (at least on this issue) and no room for compromise. This asylum (and all asylums) simply *had to be destroyed*, as Basaglia had first written back in 1964.[33] There was no other way forward.

In many ways, the form of the book was like 1968 itself: patchy, experimental, open-ended, a weapon in the hands of the movement. It used collective terms – 'we' – and was inspired by a collective movement, which included the patients of a psychiatric hospital. The words them-selves were also that of 1968: 'contestation', 'institutional violence', 'anti-psychiatry'.

And the method outlined in *The Negated Institution* was not just applicable to asylums. It could also be applied to a whole series of insti-tutions. In fact, Basaglia argued that this extension of the struggle, the battle against institutions, was absolutely necessary. Institutions such as the asylum needed to be overturned, rejected, revolutionized, and in Gorizia *this had already taken place*. *The Negated Institution* was a theo-retical and practical blueprint for radicals, a guide for how to change the world.

The Negated Institution was music to the ears of a growing movement

32   Basaglia, 'Presentazione' in *L'istituzione negata* (1968) p. 7.

33   This paper was originally given in English in London (at the Quintin Kynaston school in North London) and later published in Italian: 'La distruzione dell'ospedale psichiatrico come luogo di istituzionalizzazione. Mortificazioni e libertà dello "spazio chiuso". Considerazioni sul sistema "open door"', *Annali di neurologia e psichiatria* 49: I, 1965, now in *Franco Basaglia. L'utopia della realtà*, pp. 17–26, and in Franco Basaglia, *Scritti. I*, pp. 249–57.

beyond Gorizia (and beyond Italy). Institutions were violent and oppressive. They could be overcome, contested, negated; and 'we' were all in this struggle together: intellectuals, doctors, teachers, pupils, psychiatrists, patients, prisoners, nurses, the working class, the 'sick' and the 'well' (whatever those terms meant). Moreover, it was not enough just to destroy these institutions, but society itself (which had produced and sustained the *manicomio* system) needed to be transformed. As Basaglia argued, 'How can we not move from the excluded to the excluder?'[34]

The language was also that of the speakers of the Dialectics of Liberation conference held in London in 1967, of Bateson, Laing and Ginsberg. The final sentence of the introduction was a kick in the teeth for the psychiatric profession:

> It is easy for the psychiatric *establishment* to define our work as unserious and lacking in scientific respectability. But we can only be proud of such judgements, given that they bring us together – at last – with the unserious and respectability always afforded to the mentally ill and all the excluded.[35]

Basaglia and his équipe were happy to be seen as outsiders. They identified with their patients (and with all the excluded). Psychiatrists, if they acted as psychiatrists had always acted, were part of the problem, not the solution. The same was true of university lecturers, teachers and others. Power should only be exercised in order to negate *that* power.

The first words, significantly, were given to a patient, a blind man called Andrea who had experienced the hospital before Basaglia's arrival: 'Before, those who were here asked only to die.' *Then*, it had been a place without hope, where the only possibility of getting out was death itself (or escape, which never worked). Nino Vascon had recorded Andrea's words and carried out research, interviews and oral history, inside the asylum. He also produced a documentary about the hospital for the RAI.[36] Vascon confessed that he had continued to visit Gorizia after his

---

34 Basaglia, *L'istituzione negata* (1968), p. 8.
35 Ibid., p. 9.
36 I have not been able to locate this radio documentary, nor discover when it was aired.

Franco Basaglia and Franca Ongaro, Venice, 1949

Franca Ongaro and an unidentified patient in Gorizia, 1960s

General meeting, Gorizia Psychiatric Hospital, 1960s. Giovanni Jervis is standing with his hand on his head. Agostino Pirella is in the middle of the photo towards the back

Franco Basaglia sitting among patients, Gorizia, 1960s

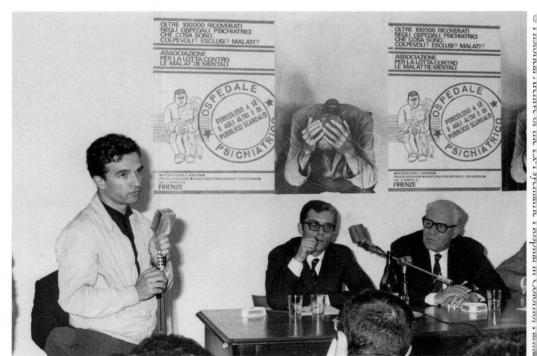

Debate on 'Psychiatry and Public Opinion', 19 June 1969. Antonio Slavich is sitting on the left

Franco Basaglia at the Réseau, a congress of radical psychiatrists, Trieste, 1977

Regina, an ex-asylum patient, Trieste, 1970s. *Marco Cavallo* is in the background

Franco Basaglia at the Réseau, Trieste, 1977. Michele Risso is to his left, and
Domenico Casagrande behind him

'Freedom is Therapeutic', painted on Ospedale Psichiatrico San Giovanni, Trieste

Marco Cavallo, 1973

Marco Cavallo, papier maché sculpture, San Giovanni, Trieste, 2011

documentary had been transmitted, although he found the place difficult and disturbing. He was 'pushed by a kind of attraction-repulsion for this subject-matter'.[37] The established media, as well, was working here at the service of the revolution.

Andrea, a kind of patient leader, underlined how much the hospital had changed. During the early *assemblee* (of which he was one of the first presidents), nobody had had the courage to speak. Andrea also described how Antonio Slavich would take some of the patients from C Ward for trips outside the hospital. This was the first time many of these inmates had left the *manicomio* (or even their wards) since their internment. A film showing patients leaving the hospital was later included in Sergio Zavoli's 1968 documentary about the hospital. Vascon's study was angry and powerful, and the words were those of the patients themselves. As with Zavoli's film, this in itself was a revolutionary act. The excluded, the invisible were being heard for the first time. *They* were the real protagonists of *The Negated Institution* (in theory).

Other patients told of the removal of barriers, of an end to physical restrictions. There were stories from the past of torture, of forms of waterboarding (*le maschere,* a wet cloth placed over the mouth to simulate suffocation), of strait jackets, of cages with locks placed over beds. All the patients who spoke out insisted on the sweeping changes that had taken place inside the asylum, and were grateful to Basaglia and his équipe for this transformation. One particular patient, referred to in the book as 'Margherita', was adopted in a certain sense by Basaglia and Franca Ongaro and helped out in their flat at times. Margherita was able to work for the first time in the 1960s (inside the hospital). In the two-part TV film made in 2010 of the Basaglia story, Margherita was a key figure.[38] *L'istituzione negata* also included an interview with Carla, a patient who was also an Auschwitz survivor. This interview underlined again the link between Basaglia and Primo Levi, of whose work he was a great admirer, and the connection between the idea of the total institution and that of the concentration camp.

---

37 Basaglia, *L'istituzione negata* (1968), p. 16.

38 See Elena Bucaccio, Katja Colja, Alessandro Sermoneta, Marco Turco, *C'era una volta la città dei matti. Un film di Marco Turco: dal soggetto alla sceneggiatura,* ed. Barbara Grubissa, Merano: Edizioni AlphabetaVerlag, 2011.

Most of these testimonies were permeated by a feeling of radical change, and this was true of doctors and nurses, as well as the patients. A nurse summed up this sense of transformation:

When we see that a patient comes here and seems lost and needs to be looked after all the time – and we look after them – and then we can say, finally, they can survive on their own. This is a great satisfaction for us.[39]

Gorizia was completely different to most other psychiatric hospitals:

Here a young doctor can work at two levels, with his work, and with the participation in numerous meetings at all levels. There is the professional activity, and a daily battle in terms of ideas – and the latter is certainly more satisfying than the former![40]

The Negated Institution let the patients speak, as well as the nurses. Its voices were those of the hospital/community itself, although the theoretical insights and the studies were provided by the équipe, who all had their own pieces in the volume.

The Negated Institution was not an abstract, theoretical text (like so many others which were to emerge in the late 1960s and throughout the 1970s), but it did contain sections that verged on the incomprehensible. Much of the book *was* immersed in the reality of Gorizia's asylum, in the words of its patients, in the rituals of its institutionalized and de-institutionalized practices. The nitty-gritty was important. A key feature of the negation of the institution idea was that those involved should 'never tire of a confrontation with reality' (Pirella).[41] Gorizia also showed the power which activists and technicians could wield. An institution could indeed be overturned without new laws or outside support. But there were also moments of high theory, and the level of the writing was uneven. Much of the book was hard-going to read, and the more theoretical sections, not surprisingly, seem dated today.

---

39   Basaglia, *L'istituzione negata* (1968), p. 71.
40   Ibid., p. 87.
41   Ibid., p. 228.

The debate over the opening up of the last closed wards inside the hospital, which dominated a large part of the book, showed how different positions were taken up within the équipe.[42] Slavich was more pragmatic. What was the point of opening up the wards? What were they trying to achieve? Basaglia, meanwhile, wanted to push forward and *then* judge the consequences and outcomes. There was no point waiting any longer. Other équipe members took up various intermediate positions. By the time the book came out, these wards had been entirely opened up.

A Bestseller

'One of the most important medical books from the post-war period'
Giulio Alfredo Maccacaro on *L'istituzione negata*[43]

Basaglia was suddenly big business. Thousands of copies sold for a book of this kind was something of a miracle. It was widely reviewed in a whole series of publications. Basaglia and Gorizia had become a brand. The difficulties presented by this sudden fame could also be seen in the reaction to the Viareggio Prize results later in 1968. A special Viareggio Prize was awarded to *The Negated Institution* in July 1968.[44] The jury had decided that the prize for a first work for poetry was not to be awarded, and with the money left over (a million *lire*) an extra *Premio Speciale* was assigned to *L'istituzione negata* and to the entire équipe (a decision which bent the rules for the prize, which was meant to go to individual authors). The jury wrote that the

---

42   Ibid., p. 249–73

43   'Lettera al Presidente dell'Ordine' in Giulio Alfredo Maccacaro, *L'umanità di uno scienziato*, ed. Enzo Ferrara, Rome: edizioni dell'asino, 2011, p. 146. (Originally in Jean-Claude Polack, *La medicina del capitale*, Milan: Feltrinelli, 1972).

44   This was not the main non-fiction prize, which went to Giuliano Procacci's book *Storia degli italiani*. Subsequent accounts have ignored the arguments around the prize, and usually simply state that *L'isituzione negata* won the *saggistica* (essay) prize at the Premio Viareggio. See for example, Maria Grazia Giannichedda, 'Introduzione' in Franca Ongaro Basaglia, ed., *Franco Basaglia. L'utopia della realtà*, Turin: Einaudi, 2005, p. xxv, and E. Venturini et al., *Il folle reato. Il rapporto tra la responsabilità dello psichiatra e la imputabilità del paziente*, Milan: Franco Angeli, 2010, pp. 122, 171.

book was 'a kind of critical diary where documents, testimonies, debates all come together alongside practical reflections, and dialectical considerations'.[45]

There was a fierce debate inside the équipe about whether to accept the prize, and a further discussion over what to do with the million *lire* which came with it (which was eventually handed straight over to the patients).[46] This discussion was complicated by the fact that Italo Calvino, Einaudi author (and key Einaudi consultant) and man of the left, had turned down his own Viareggio Prize with a polemical telegram, throwing the whole idea of literary awards into crisis. This was 1968 after all, a period when the entire cultural industry was under attack from the left. The opening of Venice's Biennale in June 1968 had been met by protests, occupations and police violence.[47] Calvino's telegram arrived just as the preparations for the prize distribution were being finalized in Viareggio. It read as follows:

> Given that I believe that the epoch of prizes is over, for ever, I do not intend to accept this prize because I do not want to provide support for these institutional forms which are completely lacking in meaning. In my desire to avoid any press sensation, please do not announce my name as one of the winners. In friendship, Calvino. [48]

The organizers of the Premio Viareggio were furious (at first they thought the whole thing was a joke) and the affair was extremely embarrassing. After all, the prize winners had already been announced to the

---

45   Gabriella Sobrino, Francesca Romana de'Angelis, *Storie del premio viareggio*, Florence: Mauro Pagliai, 2008, p. 83.

46   See Isman, 'Hanno discusso tranquilli in assemblea come adoperare il milione del "Viareggio"'.

47   The protestors included Franco Basaglia's cousin, Vittorio. Gianni Beregno Gardini took a series of extraordinary photos of the violence in Piazza San Marco in the centre of Venice. For a general critique of literary prizes at the time see 'La crisi dei "premi"', *L'Unità*, 16 July 1968.

48   Sobrino, *Storie del premio viareggio*, pp. 84–5; Renzo Ricchi, 'Premi contestati e qualcosa da fare', *Il Ponte* 24: 8, 31 August 1968, and 24: 9, 30 September 1968, pp. 1091–3. See also Santino Salerno, *A Leonida Rapaci. Dediche del '900*, Soveria Mannelli: Rubbettino, 2003; *Viareggio. 50 anni di cultura italiana*, Rome: Edizioni delle autonomie, 1979; and 'Calvino premiato rifiuta il "Viareggio"', *L'Unità*, 13 July 1968.

press,[49] and Einaudi had submitted the book for a prize in the first place. The organizers then issued a press statement where they called Calvino's actions 'demagogic and an insult to his own dignity and that of the other candidates'.[50] Calvino's refusal (his prize was worth 3 million *lire*) was front-page news and put pressure on the Gorizian équipe. His choice of words was radical. It appeared that anyone who accepted a prize was a sell-out. Renzo Ricchi wrote:

> The fact of being given a prize created a sensation of being amongst the conservatives, and an accomplice in terms of the power of the publishers, and these prizes ended up being a problem rather than a pleasure.[51]

In the end, the idea of such a large sum of money going straight to the patients was decisive, and a somewhat grudging telegram was sent to Viareggio 'in which it was written that the équipe who edited the book *L'istituzione negata* heard about their victory "with great surprise" and had decided to hand over the money to the poor patients'.[52] The telegram also said that the *premio* had 'not been asked for' by the authors. This was later dubbed a 'non-refusal'.[53] Pitrelli wrote that

> At first, Basaglia and his team decided to refuse the award, but later they changed their mind and accepted it. These disagreements had important consequences for the équipe – and are probably part of the reason why Basaglia left Gorizia, which is one of the most difficult questions to resolve in historical terms.[54]

---

49   This led to a somewhat farcical series of articles and corrections. See Armando La Torre, 'A Calvino, Procacci e Vigolo la 39a edizione del "Viareggio"' and 'Ultim'ora: Il premio a Bigiaretti', *L'Unità*, 13 July 1968.

50   Sobrino, *Storie del premio viareggio*, p. 85.

51   Ricchi, 'Premi contestati', p. 1091.

52   Ibid., p. 1091.

53   *L'Espresso* wrote that Basaglia 'refused' the prize and simply 'sent the cheque' to the patients ('Una Montessori per i matti', *L'Espresso*, 3 March 1968).

54   Nico Pitrelli, *L'uomo che restituì la parola ai matti. Franco Basaglia, la comunicazione e la fine dei manicomi*, Rome: Riuniti, 2004, p. 82. However, Pitrelli does not cite any source for this affirmation.

Once again, the organizers of the award were incandescent with rage. They issued yet another press release which accused Basaglia of a publicity stunt.

> The doctors in Gorizia . . . led by Franco Basaglia, by justifying their non-refusal of the award with a desire to help the poor economic conditions of their patients, show that they want to take with one hand what they have refused with the other. Franco Basaglia, by taking part in the ongoing protests with such a low sense of expediency and measure, has created this doubt in our mind: perhaps his scientific merits are not immune from the desire to court publicity.[55]

The president of the jury, Leonida Rèpaci, repeated his accusations during the ceremony itself, arguing that the Gorizia telegram was written with 'poison ink'.[56] A cheque for a million *lire* was sent to Gorizia. The reply was minimalist: 'We have received the million *lire* – a letter will follow – The Director of the Hospital'.

In some ways, this award confirmed some of Basaglia's worst fears about the book. It was *too popular*. Gorizia's fame had its own downside, as Basaglia told a journalist in September 1968: 'Many people come and visit us, we are trendy, a centre of attraction and curiosity. This is not what we are interested in.'[57]

---

55   Sobrino, *Storie del premio viareggio*, p. 87.

56   Ibid. According to Sobrino and de'Angelis, Calvino later admitted that he had refused the *premio* under pressure from Giulio Einaudi: 'We were in 1968, in the middle of the student protests', cited in ibid. See also *Italo Calvino. Letters. 1941–1985*, trans. Martin McLaughlin, Princeton and Oxford: Princeton University Press, 2013, pp. 359–61, 579.

57   Isman, 'Hanno discusso tranquilli in assemblea come adoperare il milione del "Viareggio"'.

THIRTEEN

Gorizia and 1968, Gorizia as 1968

'The psychiatric protests of 1968 identified the madhouse as the symbol of everything that was static, hostile, repressive.'

Fulvio Marone[1]

'The struggle against the exclusion of the mad and for the closure of the asylums had numerous points of contact with the anti-authoritarian struggle carried out by the student movement, and the latter took on these demands as part of its own programme and ideology.'

Marcello Flores and Alberto De Bernardi[2]

'There were high levels of ideology, strong contradictions, simplifications and confused ideas which pushed the best intentions of the movement to the limit. But there was also an extraordinary desire to know more.'

Patrizia Guarnieri[3]

---

1 Fulvio Marone, 'La psichiatria alternativa italiana', *La psicoanalisi. Rivista del campo Freudiano* 25, January–June 1999, p. 102.

2 Marcello Flores and Alberto De Bernardi, *Il Sessantotto*, Bologna: Il Mulino, 2003, p. 226.

3 Patrizia Guarnieri, *La storia della psichiatria. Un secolo di studi in Italia*, Florence: Olschki Editore, 1991, p. 25.

Basaglia, the Gorizians and other radical psychiatrists helped to create 1968 and were very much part of the movement. They radicalized people, their writings and activity were extremely far-reaching and the movement also gave *them* strength and power. But they were also victims of the worst excesses of the movement: the over-powering rhetoric, a tendency towards simplification and sloganeering, the excessive verbosity. Gorizia's assemblies were models for the open-style meetings that would dominate 1968 – from the universities to factories to housing estates to schools. It was a simple message: everyone had a right to speak, and for as long as they liked. As Agostino Pirella later wrote: 'For the first time, meetings and assemblies were held with all the representatives of the "institutional field" (beginning with the patients themselves) and were seen as an alternative to the madhouse and its hierarchical-repressive and "total" rules.'[4]

These meetings were also a prototype for 1968 as spectacle, as an event which could be recounted, photographed, filmed, recorded, transcribed, studied and, eventually, also sold as a commodity. Everything was to take place in public, all would be observed. General assemblies also prefigured the chaos and spontaneity of 1968, especially its early phase. They were long-winded, boring, frustrating, and at the same time they could be exhilarating and exciting, even sexy. They were also (and *always*) smoke-filled. Cigarettes were a key visual and physical feature of 1968. They often served as money inside asylums and provided patients with one of their few comforts during the long, boring days where nothing happened at all.

Gorizia was one of the stepping-stones for the long march through *and* at the same time *against* institutions, which would soon take in a whole series of other organizations, from universities and schools to the judiciary and the medical world in general. These changes tapped into themes that had emerged from a reading of the Cultural Revolution in China, with its supposed overturning of power structures and humiliation of those who

---

4   Agostino Pirella, 'Franco Basaglia, o della critica pratica alla psichiatria istituzionale' in Diego Giachetti, ed., *Per il Sessantotto. Studi e ricerche*, Bolsena: Massari Editore/CDP, 1998, p. 120. A longer version of this article can be found in Vinzia Fiorino, ed., *Rivoltare il mondo, abolire la miseria. Un itinerario dentro l'utopia di Franco Basaglia. 1953–1980*, Pisa: Edizioni ETS, 1994, pp. 27–40.

held authority.[5] Basaglian thought and practice exposed the brutal workings of the state machine, the repression of deviancy (especially the deviant poor), and extended this analysis to an entire group of institutions, beginning with psychiatric hospitals and expanding to the rest of society. It was a powerful, angry and all-encompassing world-view, and its slogans became the buzzwords for the movement. Roles were questioned, power was undermined, white coats were thrown away, symbolically and in practice. Connections were thus quickly made between 1968 and the Gorizian experiment. The two movements were a natural fit. In many ways they were one and the same.

Gorizia seemed to show that a tiny vanguard of people, a handful of determined individuals, could change the world. It was important, however, that this small group worked together, collectively, as a group: an équipe. In the process of two-way translation between Gorizia and the movement, much of what was actually being said and done was lost. *L'istituzione negata* was one of the bibles of 1968, but it is unclear how carefully it was read, if at all. Generally, the biting critique by the Gorizians of what they had created in Gorizia was *not* taken up by the movement. And this was also because the Gorizians sent out a series of conflicting messages: from warnings about the creation of a 'neo-reformist . . . golden cage' to (ironic) calls to create 'four, fifty, ninety-four Gorizias'.[6] *What was the message of Gorizia?* This was never made entirely clear. In fact, Gorizia sent out many signals at the same time, many of them contradictory. Were psychiatric hospitals really the same as concentration camps? Had genuine change taken place in Gorizia? Was the therapeutic community a trap, or a goal to which people should aspire? Was it the institution that was the problem, or society itself?

---

5   The theme of Maoism has rarely been cited with regard to the Basaglias and the movement as a whole, but it was clearly important at the time, both in terms of the language used and in the sense of some of the theoretical and political concepts utilized. See for an analysis of the idea of the 'cultural revolution' in 1968, Robert Lumley, *States of Emergency. Cultures of Revolt in Italy from 1968 to 1978*, London: Verso, 1990, pp. 119–43 as well as Antonio Slavich himself, *La scopa meravigliante. Preparativi per la legge 180 a Ferrara e dintorni 1971–1978*, Rome: Riuniti, 2003, pp. 258, 266–7. See also Jervis on the lessons of the 'cultural revolution', *Il buon rieducatore*, p. 128.

6   Antonio Slavich, 'Creare quattro, cinque, novantaquattro Gorizie', *Fogli d'informazione* 27/28, January–February 1976, pp. 1–6.

Quite quickly and unexpectedly, asylums themselves became key sites for the organization and expression of 1968 itself. From closed and secretive areas, often on the edge of cities, many asylums opened up to the outside world, developing into places of discussion, meetings, networks of activism and cultural activity. People just turned up and took part, listened, spoke, were employed as volunteers or taken on to do jobs that they were not qualified to do. Basaglia was open to the student movement, and contact was made with student leaders from Bologna and elsewhere. As the asylums opened up towards the cities they had served, these links formed a dual purpose, breaking down stigmas towards the mentally ill and creating connections between social change, urban change and psychiatric reform.

Suddenly, there was an 'explosion of interest in anti-psychiatry'.[7] Books about psychiatry (and against psychiatry) flew off the shelves. 'Medicine had become a crucial metaphor for the exercise of power in modern capitalist societies' and 'conflicts over the control of the body and over definitions of normalcy and deviancy suddenly grew in importance'.[8] People wanted to know about the issues, to study them, to understand them. Madness became fascinating, almost fashionable, and ideas around normality were also questioned. A system which was able to drop napalm on Vietnamese children was surely, in some way, sick or crazy.

The desire to know and to act was attractive both to the students from the movement itself and to those working as technicians within these institutions. This led to 'liberal professionals, intellectuals and informed people engaging critically on the basis of their own expertise rather than in the name of generalized criteria such as "revolution" or "justice"'.[9] However, this could also lead to a fair amount of sloganeering and superficiality. Many of the texts produced in the 1970s were, as Jervis wrote, 'drunk with intellectualism, generic, lacking in concreteness'.[10] There

---

7   Julian Bourg, *From Revolution to Ethics. May 1968 and Contemporary French Thought*, London: McGill-Queens University Press, 2007, p. 108.

8   Lumley, *States of Emergency*, p. 136.

9   Bourg, *From Revolution to Ethics*, p. 48.

10   Giovanni Jervis, *Manuale critico di psichiatria*, 10th ed., 1980 (1975), p. 18. See also the rest of the caustic analysis by Jervis, pp. 11–25 (and in particular p. 21). Jervis drew a useful distinction here between a 'critique of psychiatry' and 'critical psychiatry', pp. 18–19.

was a real danger of the co-option of the movement. 'The end result is that psychiatry remains strong because it is negated verbally, but not seriously studied or criticized in terms of its practice and theory.'[11] Jervis argued that in order to criticize psychiatry you needed to understand it first. Mere catch phrases were not enough.

As the 1970s progressed, the links between radical psychiatry and the movement became even stronger. In Arezzo, Ferrara, Trieste, Perugia, Parma-Colorno, Rome, Turin, Reggio Emilia and many other Italian cities, students and others set up local Psichiatria Democratica groups. Others worked with umbrella movements such as the Associazione per la Lotta contro le Malattie Mentali (The association for the struggle against mental illness), which brought together patients, psychiatrists and local activists. In Turin, this association (run for a time by Giulio Bollati's wife at the time, Piera Piatti) was particularly important in its opposition to the construction of a new asylum, and through its radical documentation of the state of the psychiatric hospitals in the city.

Other more negative aspects of Gorizia also heralded what 1968 would become: the occasional pomposity, the sectarianism (Gorizia was a valuable commodity, and its history soon became the object of discussion and division, as well as myth-making), the hyper-orality, the central role of the charismatic leader, the marginalization of women.[12] As De Bernardi and Flores have argued, the movement 'created its own myths and its own hypocrisies at the same time as it demolished those which were already there'.[13]

---

11   Ibid., p. 22.

12   For many of these aspects of 1968, and its memory, see the brilliant work of Luisa Passerini, *Autoritratto di gruppo*, Florence: Giunti, 2008. Women did play a strong role in Gorizia, including women patients, as well as, of course, Franca Ongaro and Letizia Comba Jervis. But it was men who dominated the movement as a whole, and in particular Psichiatria Democratica. In part, this was a reflection of Italy itself. There were very few qualified female psychiatrists at the time in Italy.

13   Flores and De Bernardi, *Il Sessantotto*, p. xv. One of these myths (and a counter-negative myth) is linked to Basaglia himself. See Benedetto Saraceno, 'Franco Basaglia. Una teoria e una pratica per la trasformazione', *Sapere* 851, November–December 1982, p. 3.

The Historians, Radical Psychiatry and 1968

In many of the histories and studies on 1968 that have appeared at various moments over the last forty-five years, the role of radical psychiatry has often been played down or ignored altogether. Arthur Marwick's monumental study *The Sixties* only devotes two pages to R. D. Laing, while the subject is passed over completely in a number of other volumes.[14] Basaglia usually gets a perfunctory citation in a number of texts devoted to 1968, and this is often done in a superficial way and without any real analysis of the connections among 1968, radical psychiatry, *The Negated Institution* and the Gorizian experience. Why is this?

One of the reasons for this underplaying of critical psychiatry may well have been the backlash against anti-psychiatry, which had already begun in the 1970s and proceeded apace in the 1980s and 1990s.[15] Even the protagonists of those very experiences began to turn their backs on some of the ideas they had unleashed or inspired. A second explanation has to do with the lack of historical and sociological work on Gorizia. The movement moved on. It did not look back. This was also an issue with 1968 in general, as I have argued elsewhere.[16] A third reason was certainly linked to the divisions within the movement, which led to bitter and often personalized squabbles and sectarian tribalism. The movement began to look in on itself, in the way it told its own story, instead of outwards, towards the rest of the world. Much of this seems inexplicable today, but it took up a lot of time and effort on all sides in the 1970s and 1980s (and continues in part today). A final explanation has to do with the very different paths taken by the leaders of the radical psychiatry after the boom of the late 1960s and 1970s. Some went towards mysticism (such as Laing himself) or were seduced by fame and cultural industries, others went (or went back) into the university system and some remained part of the movement itself. Finally, 1968 and Gorizia,

---

14   Arthur Marwick, *The Sixties. Cultural Revolution in Britain, France, Italy and the United States, c.1958–c.1974*, Oxford: Oxford University Press, 1998, pp. 313–4.

15   See Michael Staub, *Madness Is Civilization: When the Diagnosis Was Social, 1948–1980*, Chicago and London: University of Chicago Press, 2011, pp. 167–94.

16   John Foot, 'Looking back on Italy's 'Long "68"'. Public, Private and Divided Memories' in Ingo Cornils and Sarah Waters, eds, *Memories of 1968. International Perspectives*, Oxford: Peter Lang, 2011, pp. 103–30.

as we have argued already, demanded complete commitment. Many were quickly burnt out by the experience. Nobody could continue that kind of commitment for long. Several died young, while others moved on to a less totalizing form of activism. It was unsustainable, in the long run. The Gorizians were radical psychiatrists twenty-four hours a day, seven days a week. The stress levels were high, and they took their toll. They had put their careers, their lives, their bodies on the line, and it could not last.

The gap between the space and analysis dedicated to radical psychiatry and the importance of these ideas within the series of movements which come under the broad umbrella of '1968' is huge.[17] Radical psychiatry was at the heart of what 1968 was all about. Its texts were the texts of the movement – *The Divided Self, The Politics of Experience, The Dialectics of Experience, Anti-Oedipus, Asylums, The Wretched of the Earth, Morire di classe, Madness and Civilization, The Death of the Family, Psychiatry and Anti-psychiatry, Not Made of Wood, What Is Psychiatry?, The Negated Institution.* Its messages were the messages of the movement: anti-authoritarianism, a combination of radical theorizing and practical change (you could go and visit the revolution in Gorizia and be welcomed with open arms – Gorizia was extremely permeable and open), direct democracy (the general assembly, which you could also see with your own eyes) and a wide-ranging social critique of capitalism and its institutions. Radical psychiatric ideas and practice could be applied to other institutions – schools, the family, universities, hospitals, prisons. Everyone could then try and overturn their own institutions – by contesting *their* own parents, *their* teachers, *their* professors, *their* prison officers, *their* generals, *their* psychiatrists. Radical psychiatry provided a kind of guide to how to be a '68er, but it was also practical, not just hot air, as Gorizia showed.

Historical Questions and the 'Schizophrenia' of 1968: Managing or Overturning Institutions?

'The psychiatrist and the doctor find themselves immersed in a reality in which they are in part complicit and in part victims,

---

17   Foot, 'Looking back on Italy's 'Long "68"'.

forced by our current social system to declare themselves as protec-
tors of an order which they want to destroy.'

Franco and Franca Basaglia[18]

'A revolution is underway, but the revolutionaries are pessimistic.'

Michele Tito[19]

There was – in 1968 but throughout the 1970s as well – a constant
contradiction in the relationship between the movement and public
institutions. Many 'militants' worked within these institutions in order
to change them, while acknowledging that in an ideal world, some of
these organizations would not even exist. This was the point of view of
Franco Basaglia, expressed so eloquently in his writings about his work
in Gorizia and Trieste in the 1960s and 1970s. But these contradictions
also emerged in the universities, in hospitals and in prisons. Capitalism
– it was argued – had created all these things, and they needed to be
abolished, but, in the meantime, technicians would work from within
to subvert, change, transform or destroy them.

This attitude was most elegantly put by the Basaglias in *L'istituzione
negata*. For Franco Basaglia the presence of institutions presented 'an
impasse' which was at the same time 'theoretical and practical'. His work
was an attempt to 'understand how an anti-institutional act can con-
cretely affect structures'. Citing Frantz Fanon, who resigned as a
psychiatrist to take up the popular cause, Basaglia concluded that

> Fanon was able to choose the revolution. But we, for obvious objective
> reasons, cannot do so. Our situation is that we are forced to live
> through the contradictions of a system which creates us, managing an
> institution we deny/negate, carrying out therapy which we refuse to
> acknowledge as useful, denying the fact that our institution – which
> has become, thanks to us, an institution where violence is hidden and
> masked – does not continue to be functional to the system, trying to
> resist the temptations provided by new scientific solutions which tend

18   Basaglia, *L'istituzione negata* (1968), p. 368.
19   Michele Tito, 'Il viaggio dentro la follia. Gli ospedali psichiatrici, case di cure o pri-
gioni?', *La Stampa*, 2 March 1971.

to crush the contradictions which our work makes explicit; well aware
that we are attempting the impossible in trying to uphold values while
non-rights, equality and the daily death of man are part of the very
legal system itself.[20]

Was it possible, therefore, to overturn and work within state institutions at the same time?

Basaglia and the Gorizians also carried forward a critical and ethical
approach to the society of which they were a part. They came from a
new, post-war generation who refused to accept the ways things had been
done in the past, and the word of their teachers and supposed 'masters'.
They lifted the veil on the horrors that were an intrinsic part of a democratic society, the 'peace crimes' they had seen with their own eyes, and
which they refused to accept as normal. The old ways were not acceptable,
for them, and they were not content with a refusal to simply do things
as they had been done in the past, but wanted the rest of society to share
their outrage and desire for change.

Gorizia as a Symbol: Gorizia as a Model

By 1968, Goriza's asylum became a symbol, a place to visit, a model to
imitate. In the early 1960s, Basaglia was more interested in studying
what was happening elsewhere and trying to import other models to
Gorizia. Things changed from 1965 onwards, as other experiments also
took hold. The first and most important connections were made with
Parma after 1966. Mario Tommasini provided political and financial
support, putting on exhibitions, setting up talks and congresses and
publishing the first book on Gorizia. The Parma and Gorizian experiments moved in parallel after 1966, with the exchange of ideas, experiences
and solidarity, as well as of people. Meanwhile, Perugia had begun to
carry out its own radical reform of mental health services. With 1967–68
came the Mariotti law, the publication of *The Negated Institution* and
the explosion of anti-institutional and anti-authoritarian protest across
Italy and in the rest of the world. Anti-psychiatric texts began to circulate

---

20   Basaglia, *L'istituzione negata* (1968), pp. 377, 379–80.

in Italy, and Laing and Cooper were translated. At that point, even with the departure of Basaglia, Gorizia remained as a key example of change. Numerous journalists, photographers and film-makers turned up to document Gorizia, which was afforded special spreads in weekly magazines and dailies.

For example, Fabrizio Dentice in *L'Espresso* described Basaglia as 'The Montessori of the mad' in March 1968, in a long piece accompanied by photographs, and called Basaglia's methods 'revolutionary'. For Dentice,

> The psychiatric hospital which runs, through its beautiful park, along the border with Yugoslavia – is like something from another planet. It wasn't like any other psychiatric hospital in the world, and not even to the 'therapeutic communities' realized in England, with which it has some methods in common which capture the imagination.[21]

One of the interesting points about this article is that Dentice assumed that his readers had no idea who Franco Basaglia was. By the end of the year, such introductions would no longer be necessary. Basaglia was anxious that Gorizia should not become a model, but he was too late. It was about to become precisely that, just as Basaglia himself was ready to move on and beyond the therapeutic community. The irony was that just as journalists, the media in general and militants were discovering and celebrating Gorizia, the Gorizians themselves were in a different place and had come to reject what they had created. For Dentice, 'Gorizia wanted to present itself only as stimulus, a germ, an example of one of the possible subversive situations which can be created within an unjust system, and proliferate.'

Suddenly, Gorizia was famous. This provincial backwater had become one of the key sites of 1968, and *The Negated Institution* was on every '68er's bookshelf. In this way, perhaps more than in any other country, the fight against asylums spread like wildfire and caught the popular imagination. Young psychiatrists, nurses, patients, intellectuals, journalists and militants all started to define themselves as Basaglians. A heady mix of anti-authoritarianism, liberation theories, self-analysis and ideas of alternatives to the family found a mass audience. Suddenly, asylums

---

21   Fabrizio Dentice, 'Una Montessori per i matti', *L'Espresso*, 3 March 1968.

were opened up and documented. Photos taken of patients shocked people. This was a scandal that could not be allowed to continue – 100,000 'slaves' were waiting to be liberated. And there were people willing to change things. Basaglians and other reformers took over asylums all over Italy and looked to close them down and transform them as had happened in Gorizia. It was a movement which moved with enormous speed and which gathered together a hybrid and diverse group of people, from artists, actors and theatre directors to student militants, psychiatrists and sociologists, as well as the patients themselves. A number of important local politicians gave solid support to these changes, and they soon found allies at a national level.

Smascheramento: Critical Psychiatry and Public Institutions

Radical psychiatry also performed another crucial function in terms of the movement. As Flores and De Bernardi argued:

> This was probably the most original aspect of 1968 and of the legacy it left to society as a whole. There was a transformation of public space, and the end of a clear separation between public and private space – and this was a change which could not be cancelled out.

The critical psychiatry movement in Italy performed this task. It 'unmasked and revealed to the masses that which was previously only available to the élite'.[22] The 1968 phenomenon was at the same time 'revolution/revelation and revolution/change'. Parts of *The Negated Institution* were examples of counter-information, another product of the movement in the later 1960s and early 1970s.

The Gorizians made visible what had, for so long, been invisible, and at the same time promoted individual and collective rights. They also questioned the institutional roles played by so many at that time, including those of the Gorizians themselves. For Flores and De Bernardi, 'and it was this unmasking of the true nature of power – in the often infantile but effective form of "the emperor has no clothes" – that

---

22   Flores and De Bernardi, *Il sessantotto,* p. xv.

represented the most lasting and effective legacy of the 1960s'.[23] At the
same time, by attempting radical change, psychiatrists learnt about what
it is they were changing and could modify their theory and working
methods accordingly. It was a case of 'to know something in order to
change it . . . but also change things in order to know them'.[24] Research
methods themselves were radicalized. Real people became an object of
study. The movement took on board the classic instruments of the wider
student movement – occupations (most notably of the asylum in
Colorno, in 1969, but also in Turin, Trieste and elsewhere), demonstrations and strikes, counter-information, leaflets and, increasingly in the
1970s, artistic and musical happenings of various kinds.[25]

Radical Psychiatrists and Organic Intellectuals

Radical psychiatrists attempted to 'negate' their own role and tried to
undermine institutions where they exercised power, having a particular
affinity with the 1968 movements.[26] These psychiatrists came close to
Gramsci's older idea of the 'organic intellectual'. As Ortoleva wrote:

> The critical psychiatrists were perhaps the first category of intellectuals
> who chose to enter into dialogue with the student movement, accepting
> it not only as their pupil, and in some cases as an apprentice, for the
> transmission of their own theoretical and practical ideas and methods,
> but also as a motivator and interlocutor, able to give political weight to
> an activity which, otherwise, ran the risk of remaining isolated.[27]

The radical critique of total institutions, which was initiated by critical
psychiatrists, struck a chord with the students who were taking on the
power of the university barons. The unmasking of total institutions

---

23   Ibid., p. xvii.

24   Ibid., p. 188.

25   For Colorno and Turin, see Sergio Dalmasso, 'Il sessantotto e la psichiatria', in Francesco
Cassata and Massimo Moraglio, eds, *Manicomio, Società e politica. Storia, memoria e cultura della
devianza mentale dal Piemonte all'Italia*, Pisa: BFS Edizioni, 2005, pp. 45–58.

26   Jervis was highly critical of this concept later in the 1970s.

27   Ortoleva, *I movimenti del '68 in Europa e in America*. Rome: Riuniti, 1998, p. 223.

exposed the brutal inner workings of the capitalist system. 'In the total institutions it was possible to read a pure, non-hypocritical, unveiled form of social "complexity", the institutional, social and psychological ways in which authority and oppression worked'.[28] In this situation, no compromise was possible.

> The total institutions were at the same time a reality and a metaphor of the entire system: they showed the relentless contraposition between oppression and liberation ... oppressed and oppressors, victims and butchers, they were all there [in the asylum] in their clearest expression, and it was impossible to mediate, or to avoid choosing sides.[29]

The excluded, the deviant, the waste products of capitalism, 'the wretched of the earth' were to be found there, living and breathing – inside the asylums, the prisons, the orphanages. Critical psychiatrists exposed how these institutions really worked and built alliances with the students and the workers from the movement.[30] These alliances (their form and their content) also tied in with another key slogan from the time, Rudi Dutschke's 'long march through the institutions'. Such was the symbiosis of theory and practice that radical psychiatrists became the ideological and, at times, political leaders of the entire movement.[31] Radical psychiatry (at least at first) was able to combine an ethical and moral critique of capitalism and the system with a clear idea of what was to be done, and how. With time, all this would become more difficult. But in 1968, at least, the movement was pushing in the same direction. Doors were opening and barriers were broken down, both literally and metaphorically.

---

28 Ibid., p. 223.

29 Ibid., pp. 223-4.

30 Hence Basaglia's success in 1968 itself and afterwards, when the students flocked to his courses in Parma and *L'istituzione negata* was read and passed around; as Ortoleva argues, 'It is interesting that the anti-psychiatrists, more than any other professionals, were recognized as experts, with some authority, within alternative university courses in various cities.' Ibid., p. 282.

31 This type of leadership was of various kinds, ranging from 'archaic forms of relationships between the leader–professor (the guru, the sect)' to 'the timid idealization of the figure of the "expert", who was usually not a university professor but a professional who had "negated their own role" in their "march through the institutions" and this role was attributed – in the struggle against total institutions – to the anti-psychiatrists'. Ibid., p. 115.

FOURTEEN

The Incident

'In any case this much is clear, the Miklus case will not go away.'

Giorgio Verbi[1]

'Within a reality which is being overturned . . . a false step or an error could confirm – in the face of public opinion – the impossibility of an action.'

Franco and Franca Basaglia[2]

'Can we, because of someone who goes too far, condemn thousands of people to a civil death, and can we give up our practice which tries to cure people, can we go back to being the merciless jailors of fragile people, at the behest of a method which doesn't like problems?'

Franco Basaglia[3]

'This small group of protestors and subversives who release murderers'

Neo-fascist poster, Gorizia (1968)[4]

1　Giorgio Verbi, 'Superato il clima di paura rimangono gli interrogativi', *Il Piccolo*, 30 September 1968.

2　Franco Basaglia and Franco Ongaro Basaglia, 'Il problema dell'incidente', Appendix in Franco Basaglia, ed., *L'istituzione negata*, 2nd ed., April 1968, p. 362.

3　Michele Tito, 'Lo psichiatra accusato: se mi condannano, la camicia di forza tornerà nei manicomi', *La Stampa*, 24 February 1971.

4　Cited in Tito, 'Lo psichiatria accusato'.

I t was their worst nightmare. Basaglia and his équipe lived in constant fear of an 'incident': a suicide or an outbreak of violence, which they thought would then be used against the whole system they had built up with such care. The second edition of *The Negated Institution* in April 1968 (printed on 13 April 1968) added an appendix that included a celebrated essay by Basaglia and Franca Ongaro entitled 'The problem of the incident'.[5] It was almost as if the Basaglias could see into the future.[6]

The Basaglias outlined a lucid and original analysis of incidents that occurred in asylums involving patients and how they were interpreted. 'Any incident which takes place in a psychiatric institution is usually blamed on the illness, which is identified as the only possible explanation for the unpredictability of the patient's behaviour'.[7] Given this logic (which was also that of the magistrates and judges in Gorizia after the incident had taken place), the only outcome, for the state and society, was that patients should be locked up to protect 'normal' people from them, and to protect them from themselves. In this kind of system, nobody was responsible for anything. These people were ill and incurable. In a closed hospital, therefore, 'the only possible future is death'.[8] Death was the only way to escape, the only way out of the asylum. But, in an open institution, things were different. Here an incident might be the result of the 'lack of support given by the institution' of the patient.

In an open institution, the *psychiatrists* were trapped within a contradiction: 'constrained by our current social system to declare themselves to be the guarantors of an order which they want to destroy'. In an open hospital there was a need to move towards the

---

5   Basaglia and Ongaro, 'Il problema dell'incidente', pp. 363–9. (The article is signed by Franco and Franca Basaglia and also carries the extra information, Gorizia, 28 March 1968).

6   See Mario Colucci and Pierangelo Di Vittorio, *Franco Basaglia*, Milan: Bruno Mondadori, 2001, pp. 208–10, who call the article 'prophetic' (p. 208). However, some of the analysis in Ernesto Venturini, Domenico Casagrande and Lorenzo Toresini, *Il folle reato. Il rapporto tra la responsabilità dello psichiatra e la imputabilità del paziente*, Milan: Franco Angeli, 2010, seems to indicate that the authors believe the piece was written in response to the Miklus incident.

7   Basaglia and Ongaro, 'Il problema dell'incidente', p. 363.

8   Ibid., p. 365.

outside world, but that world was a difficult place, 'with its own violent rules, discriminations and tyrannies, which continue to represent the refusal, negation and exclusion of mentally ill people as one of the many elements which disturb things'. And at this point, who was responsible for an incident? What choice does a patient have? 'What can they do apart from kill themselves or kill anyone who, for them, depicts the face of the violence which they are subject to? In this process can we really, honestly, just talk about illness?' This radical, searing article was both a critical look at society and at the link between illness and violence. There were no easy answers. Opening up the hospital was only part of the story, and it could even make things worse.[9]

The Negated Institution was well aware of the ever-present risk of patient violence. In some ways, this issue had patterned the decisions taken by the équipe from the start, with the opening of wards and the pulling down of barriers. Everything had been done with extreme care. Every time doors were opened or walls knocked down, the doctors waited to see what would take place. But nothing had happened of note before 1968. It seemed as if an incident might not happen after all. In another section of the book, 'Furio' said that 'I don't think a patient dismissed from our hospital will commit an act of violence without justification'.[10] The worst was over, or so it appeared.

When it finally came, the incident was a deeply shocking moment, an event that changed the relationship between Gorizia and the Basaglians for ever, and in particular that with Basaglia himself. It was a moment that gave the local state and authorities, many of whom had never been supportive of the Gorizian experiment, the chance to strike back. In some ways, it was also the moment when many ordinary Gorizians first sat up and took notice of what had been happening in their local asylum. That moment of truth arrived in September 1968 – at the peak of Gorizia's fame. The worst fears of the general public and of those politicians and élites hostile to the Basaglian experiment (as well as of the équipe themselves) were confirmed in a horrific way.

---

9   Ibid., pp. 367, 368, 369.
10   Basaglia, *L'istituzione negata* (1968), p. 100.

It was front-page news, and not just locally. An 'incident' had occurred.[11]

Giovanni (Alberto) Miklus (born 1906) had worked as a rural labourer. A married man with three children, he had been an anti-fascist partisan during the war for three long, hard years. After the war he had received blackmail letters (apparently linked to events during the war) and was threatened by armed men in his own home. One of the perpetrators of this violence had been sent to jail but had then visited Miklus again on his release. It was after these events that Miklus began to appear ill. He had been in and out of Gorizia's asylum since December 1951, when he had been interned after a suicide attempt.[12] He had received electroshock treatment on numerous occasions. Miklus's origins were on the Yugoslavian side of the Cold War divide, as his surname indicated. The Cold War in Gorizia was also a continuation of the bitter divisions of the inter-war and war years.

Witnesses said that Miklus had threatened his wife, Milena Kristiancic, on a number of occasions, once with a bayonet, and that he blamed her for his confinement in the asylum. These accounts and stories were all contested at the trials that followed the incident. He denied that he was ill at all and had made numerous escape attempts over the years (on at least seven occasions). He had often been picked up in Yugoslavia and returned back over the border to Italy. Everybody who had dealt with Miklus agreed that he had shown signs of improvement during the Basaglian period, and he had participated in discussions during meetings inside the hospital. By the late 1960s, doctors and the wider community in the asylum felt that it was time for him to make contact with his family again. Antonio Slavich described Miklus as 'a big man with white hair, kind and reserved . . . he thought he had a lot of enemies, some from within his own family, whom he blamed for his detention'.[13]

---

11   The only extensive study of the Miklus case is in Domenico Casagrande, 'L'incidente di Gorizia' in Venturini, Casagrande, Toresini, *Il folle reato,* pp. 104–28. This book also contains a series of documents relating to the Miklus case.

12   Officially, he was diagnosed as a paranoid schizophrenic. Miklus had not been in the asylum continually since 1951, according to judicial documents, but had been released on various occasions between 1951 and 1953. Ibid., pp. 107–19.

13   Antonio Slavich, *All'ombra dei ciliegi giapponesi,* unpublished manuscript, p. 76. Slavich

Miklus was housed in the last closed ward: the C Ward. These male and female wards, as mentioned, were the subjects of constant debate within the therapeutic community and in *The Negated Institution*. They had finally been opened up in 1967. The incident would close these wards again, at least for a brief period. This was a crisis that went to the very heart of the Basaglian community and which undermined part of the power of *L'istituzione negata*. Nothing was definitive. A 'negated institution' could easily reappear in its traditional guise. Reforms were reversible. Negation could be negated. The gains of the Basaglian period were fragile and vulnerable to outside pressure.

On at least one occasion before the incident in 1968, Miklus had been given permission to go home for a day, and the visit seems to have passed without any problems. This time, however, things would be very different. Doctors and nurses (and not the general meeting, it seems[14]) discussed whether Miklus could be allowed home again, although the exact circumstances surrounding the actual decision over his day release would be the subject of protracted legal proceedings. The release permit for Miklus was signed by a doctor called Vittorio Alì, who was probably the most anti-Basaglian of all those on the medical staff in Gorizia. Slavich may have been present at the meeting, while Basaglia was abroad at a conference at the time (in Germany). Agostino Pirella (who ran the C Wards) was also absent in the key meeting.[15]

Miklus was duly driven home by a male nurse called Ivan Klasnicek on the morning of 26 September 1968, and that same nurse was due to pick Miklus up at nine o'clock that evening and take him back to the asylum. 'Home' was a farm-house near a small rural village called San Floriano del Collio very close to the border with Yugoslavia. Despite the ongoing problems over the years with her absent husband, Kristiancic had managed to bring up their three children alone.

Early that afternoon at about two, Miklus got into an argument with

---

recounts a visit to the Miklus family home in 1965.

14   This confusion between the daily organizational meetings involving staff and the daily general assemblies ran through the investigations by the magistrates in Gorizia. It was clear that they had heard a lot about these general meetings, but they did not really know how the Basaglian hospital worked.

15   Key, that is, from a bureaucratic and legal point of view. These issues were not important to the Basaglians, in any political or moral sense.

his wife while their two sons were out at work in local vineyards.[16] According to *Il Piccolo*, Kristiancic had asked not to be left alone with her husband. Miklus then grabbed a 'worker's hammer', turned it around and struck her on the head with it.[17] One fatal blow left a fifteen-centimetre-wide gash, although it appears that Kristiancic was hit at least five times. Miklus then hurried off into the woods surrounding the house. Neighbours heard screams and saw Miklus make his escape. Marjan Miklus found his mother's body about fifteen minutes later and raised the alarm.

Wild stories started to appear in the press, including one claiming that Miklus had started a fire nearby to delay the return of his sons from work. People abandoned their homes in the surrounding area as the search intensified. Gorizia was transfixed. A 'madman' was on the loose, armed with an 'axe'. According to *Il Piccolo*, which did not hesitate to fan the flames, 'the disgust about the murder remains strong', and people were living through 'real moments of terror' and 'a nightmare'.[18] 'The murder had huge repercussions at a national level, and the Gorizia experience ended up in the eye of the storm'.[19]

The hunt for Miklus took in both sides of the iron curtain. Miklus reportedly knew the zone well from his childhood and was able to find hiding places in the thick forest. During his previous escapes, he had usually been picked up pretty quickly, including on one occasion in 1963 when the Yugoslav authorities handed him over at the so-called 'Casa Rossa' Cold War frontier post. This was also an area that had seen fierce fighting during World War One, and was thus criss-crossed by trenches and caves.[20] Miklus had been removed from normal life for two decades or so, behind the walls of the asylum. The only photo of him the authorities were able to find had been taken some twenty-two years before the murder. He had become invisible. As the manhunt

---

16 The couple's daughter was not home at the time.

17 There are various descriptions of the murder weapon: 'axe', 'hammer', 'worker's hammer'.

18 Giorgio Verbi, 'E finita l'incubo di S. Floriano. Resta lo sgomento per l'accaduto', *Il Piccolo*, 29 September 1968.

19 Colucci and Di Vittorio, *Franco Basaglia*, p. 209.

20 'Ancora senza esito le ricerche del folle uxoricida di S. Floriano', *Il Piccolo*, 28 September 1968.

continued, police and carabinieri stood guard at the house and in the surrounding area.

After two days of intensive police searches with dogs brought in especially from another city, roadblocks and contacts with the Yugoslav authorities, Miklus was found in the woods at about 11.30 am on 28 September. A press photographer managed to snap a photo as he was taken away.[21] He claimed that he was unsure whether he had killed his wife or not, and that he had tried to return to the house. Miklus was sent to a criminal asylum in Reggio Emilia after a period in the local prison in Gorizia. He never returned to the city and died, it seems, a few years later.[22] At his trial he was found to be 'unfit to stand trial due to complete mental incapacity' and sentenced to a criminal asylum for a minimum five-year term. The psychiatrist appointed by the public prosecutor, however, supported the équipe through his conclusion that 'the murder could not have been foreseen' while concluding that Miklus 'is a socially dangerous person'.[23]

In the wake of the murder, *Il Piccolo* launched a violent attack on what it saw as 'those responsible' for the tragedy. How had this been allowed to happen? 'Nobody', the paper wrote on 29 September, 'is able to explain how a man who is a real danger to the public can be freed – even temporarily'.[24] But this article was nothing in comparison with what was to come. On 30 September, journalist Giorgio Verbi made a direct call for judicial action in *Il Piccolo*:

Public opinion is awaiting measures on the part of the judicial authorities after the psychiatrist's evaluation . . . But – and this is the question

---

21   'Catturato nei pressi di casa il folle uxoricida goriziano', *Il Piccolo*, 29 September 1968

22   Enzo Quai later stated that Miklus died 'shortly afterwards' (Michele Sartori, 'L'infermiere della rivoluzione'. *L'Unità*, 8 December 1996). Casagrande points out that 'Miklus disappeared as a story and as an individual' (Casagrande, 'L'incidente di Gorizia', p. 127). However, Slavich writes that 'a few weeks later he hung himself' (Slavich, *All'ombra*, p. 13). He also claims that he was surprised that Miklus had been allowed home on his own in 1968.

23   Casagrande, 'L'incidente di Gorizia', p. 114. The official psychiatric expert was Francesco Coppola from Bologna. Basaglia and Slavich had a counter-analysis carried out on Miklus on behalf of the defence by Fabio Visintini, who cast doubt on the conclusions drawn by Coppola about Miklus's condition.

24   Verbi, 'È finita l'incubo di S. Floriano', *Il Piccolo*, 29 September 1968.

which is on everyone's lips – who is to blame, given that the mental state of Miklus has been well known for years?

Verbi claimed here to be speaking in the name of a kind of 'silent majority', 'public opinion' and even 'everyone'. In this world-view, the Basaglians were a tiny minority. He was almost certainly right, in the Gorizian context.

Patients held within asylums were often violent, and this violence could increase with the toning down or complete removal of physical controls. In some ways, the unleashing of violence (verbal and/or physical) was also part of Basaglia's overall strategy, a sign of the 'opening up of contradictions' within the system which he had called for on various occasions. In this sense, the Basaglians were indeed playing with fire. They took huge risks, all the time, of which they were well aware. These very risks were debated openly in *L'istituzione negata*.

In the wake of the murder, Basaglia gathered together the équipe and argued that the whole Gorizian experiment should be closed down, or handed over to reformist psychiatrists (in another version of events). According to Jervis, there was a fiery debate among the staff over this plan.[25] Basaglia himself was tempted to give up altogether, and it took all of Franca Ongaro's powers of persuasion to stop him from doing so. According to one journalist, writing in the wake of developments in the case in 1971, Basaglia 'is troubled, he knows he is at the centre of a drama which is also a social drama'.[26] Basaglia later stated, it 'was a moment of crisis, that is for sure, because it threatened the whole movement which was beginning to grow'.[27]

---

25   Pirella confirms this debate in Franco Basaglia, Franca Ongaro Basaglia, Agostino Pirella, Salvatore Taverna, *La nave che affonda. Psichiatria e antipsichiatria a dieci anni da 'L'istituzione negata'. Un dibattito,* Rome: Savelli, 1978, p. 101. Jervis later wrote that Basaglia argued that the whole hospital should be closed down for an 'indefinite period'. Giovanni Jervis, *Il buon rieducatore*, p. 21. Jervis sees the Miklus case as a turning-point, but in a different sense, arguing that it pushed Basaglia towards a more conservative position. Both Pirella and Jervis agree that this was the moment when Basaglia began to argue that the Gorizian experiment had, in some sense, 'failed'.

26   Tito, 'Lo psichiatra accusato'.

27   Basaglia et al., *La nave che affonda*, p. 99.

Miklus's ward (the famous C Ward, whose opening up was discussed at length in *The Negated Institution*) was reclosed for a time in the wake of the murder, although it was then reopened.[28] The incident also had repercussions for the therapeutic community as a whole. According to the standard version of this story, the general meeting found it impossible to deal with the aftermath of the Miklus incident. Silence fell. The issue was too painful to air in public: 'For fifteen days nobody in the assembly was able to mention it.'[29] The clock was turned back. Everyone felt responsible. Franca Ongaro later wrote that

> There was a terrible sense of anxiety . . . every patient felt responsible, guilty of that which M. had done. Alongside the nurses and doctors the patients identified with a gesture which seemed to signal the failure of everything we had hoped to achieve.[30]

The community had no words with which to describe what had happened. Then, it is said, a discussion finally started, and the question came out into the open. It was as if a kind of collective trauma had taken place. This process was later recreated in the TV fiction film aired in 2010.[31]

Beyond Gorizia, the impact of the incident was enormous, with *The Negated Institution* in the bookshops and Basaglia already a household name among the 1968 generation. The book had also just won a major literary prize. In Gorizia there was near panic. Moreover, the fact that Miklus was a Slav and an ex-partisan, who had lived right on the border with Yugoslavia, was an added and potent factor in this deeply divided town. His wife was from an area that had been assigned to Yugoslavia after the war. Miklus's life story was a complicated one, bound up with those very divisions. It was closely connected with the lacerating events

---

28   See Pirella's account in ibid., pp. 100–1.

29   Franca Ongaro in ibid., p. 101.

30   Ibid., p. 101.

31   Although the fictional version takes liberties with the murder itself, which became accidental in the final version; see Elena Bucaccio et al., *C'era una volta la città dei matti. Un film di Marco Turco. Dal soggetto alla sceneggiatura*, Merano: Edizioni Alphabeta Verlag, 2011, pp. 120–7, 304–6, 315–9. The audience for this programme was well over 5 million on both nights it was first aired.

of the war and post-war period, and the tensions in the city and across the border between Italians and Yugoslavs.

Basaglia reacted very badly to the incident. He felt that his whole project was doomed. It was a dark time. Years of work seemed to have been thrown away. After the incident, the relationship between the Basaglians and the city would never be the same. Much later, Vincenzo Pastore, who was working in Gorizia at the time, spoke of 'the great crisis after the Miklus case'.[32] It was a moment of a 'loss of innocence'. The Gorizians (finally) discovered that a revolution had been going on, right under their noses. Most of them didn't like what they saw. It scared them; it seemed dangerous and subversive, and they wanted it to end. In the wake of the incident, the full force of the state was brought to bear on the Gorizians, beginning with Basaglia himself.

The Legal Process and the Miklus Trial, 1968–72

It took just a matter of days for the 'judicial measures' called for by *Il Piccolo* to materialize. On 13 October 1968 Franco Basaglia was formally placed under investigation for manslaughter (*omicidio colposo*) and had been questioned by Bruno Pascoli, Gorizia's *pubblico ministero/procuratore* (investigating magistrate).[33] Under Italy's legal system at the time, an investigation was carried out by a public prosecutor, who then passed it on (with recommendations) to a different kind of Judge to decide whether a trial should be held or not. In this case the prosecutor (Pascoli) recommended a trial for both Basaglia and Slavich for 'assisting with manslaughter' after a long investigation (January 1971). In May 1971 the *giudice istruttore* (Raul Cenisi) cleared Basaglia (given his absence at the time of the decision, 'and in partial disagreement with the requests of the public prosecutor')[34] while sending Slavich on for trial. At the subsequent trial, as we shall see, the judges criticized the previous investigation, and cleared Slavich of all charges.

---

32   Interview in Silvia Balconi, *L'esperienza Goriziana dal '61 al '72. Un percorso paradig-matico di valorizzazione della professionalità in ambito psichiatrico,* Unpublished thesis, Università degli studi di Torino, 1997–98, p. 455.

33   'Accusato d'omicidio colposo per il crimine di un paziente', *Il Piccolo,* 14 October 1968.

34   Casagrande, 'L'incidente di Gorizia', p. 120.

Basaglia appointed two lawyers to his defence: one was the well-known Socialist deputy Loris Fortuna (an anti-fascist and ex-partisan from Gorizia who would go on to be a key mover in the first successful divorce law to be passed in Italy) and Cesare Devetag (who was also the politician responsible for health policies in the Region at the time). Later on a Communist provincial councillor in Gorizia, Nereo Battello, would become a key member of Basaglia's legal team.

Despite evidence to the contrary (including the fact that Basaglia was not even in Italy when the decision to release Miklus was taken), these charges were confirmed. It was clear, however, that Basaglia was being investigated because of the methods he had introduced within the Gorizian asylum. According to the Judge, Basaglia had introduced,

> in the Psychiatric Hospital of Gorizia, of which he was director, the practice of releasing in an experimental way the patients before they had reached a level of improvement as regulated by Article 66 of the rules governing the asylum.

Basaglian practices were on trial, more than any specific set of facts connected to a single crime. Antonio Slavich, meanwhile, was accused of having played a key part in the Miklus release at the general meeting that had allegedly discussed the patient's case. The leader of the Gorizian revolution, and the man who had joined him there in 1962, were both under judicial investigation. It was a highly symbolic moment, a frontal attack on what had happened in the Gorizian hospital over the previous six years.

In a decision that shocked many, Basaglia and Slavich were formally charged with manslaughter in October 1968.[35] Divisions also opened up within the hospital as at least one nurse testified against the Basaglians. The atmosphere inside the asylum was poisoned. Slavich (the main judicial victim in the case) would later refer to nurse Felice Minardi in

---

35   The judicial authorities wrote to the hospital asking for Miklus's clinical records (Pascoli, 2 October 1968, Basaglia Archive). Originally, a new appendix to *L'istituzione negata* called *Anatomia di una istruttoria* (Anatomy of an investigation) relating to Miklus was prepared. A copy is held in the Basaglia archive. But in the end, this edition was never issued. The police also wrote to Basaglia asking for details on the numbers of suicides in and escapes from the hospital. The Basaglia archive contains important material regarding this case.

particular as 'devious, a spy'.[36] Once this decision was made public, Basaglia received numerous letters in his support from across the world.

The case dragged on and on. In May 1971, Basaglia's case was dropped before coming to court, while Antonio Slavich was sent forward for trial. Neither man was based in Gorizia by that time. The evidence against Slavich, that he had expressed an opinion favourable to Miklus's release during a general meeting, was exceptionally thin. The whole case smacked of political propaganda and persecution, and despite taking years, the investigation was not particularly thorough. Only fourteen people were interviewed, and their testimonies seemed to contradict each other on various important points. Key members of the équipe who had been present at most of the important meetings under investigation (such as Jervis, Lucio Schittar and Casagrande) were never even questioned by the prosecutors.[37] As Casagrande concludes, 'The whole enquiry . . . has been aimed, in short, at supporting the sense of custodial practice over cure.'[38]

Journalists reporting on the case argued that new forms of psychiatry were themselves on trial. They appeared to be correct. The legal process was a sort of test case way beyond Gorizia itself. The magistrate claimed that Miklus was 'dangerous' and 'incurable', and thus it was manslaughter to allow him out into the outside world. Such arguments effectively meant that people like Miklus were to be closed away in asylums, for life. There was also some confusion about previous acts of violence and threats linked to Miklus and his wife and other patients.

The Trial: February 1972

Slavich was duly tried for manslaughter in Gorizia in February 1972.[39]

---

36   Slavich in Balconi, *L'esperienza Goriziana dal '61 al '72*, p. 501. Nurse Minardi appears in the debates in *Che cos'è la psichiatria?*

37   See Antonio Slavich, *La scopa meravigliante. Preparativi per la legge 180 a Ferrara e dintorni 1971–1978*, Rome: Riuniti, 2003, p. 264, n. 3.

38   Venturini, Casagrande, Toresini, *Il folle reato*, p. 124.

39   'Prosciolto Basaglia ma sotto accusa il manicomio senza sbarre', *L'Unità*, 23 May 1971; Rino Maddalozzo, 'La nuova psichiatria al vaglio dei giudici', *L'Unità*, 19 February 1972; Mario

The trial itself was extremely brief. After two days of hearings, the judges took just thirteen minutes to clear Slavich of all charges. Three and a half years had passed since the incident itself.[40] After a series of testimonies and statements from the prosecution and the defence, as well as from a number of witnesses (including Casagrande, Pirella and two of Miklus's children), the judges returned to the courtroom in Gorizia just before midnight to announce that Slavich was not guilty 'because he did not commit the act in question'. Only Miklus would pay in legal terms for the murder of his wife.

Slavich had been accused of 'non-observation of the law, negligence and professional inexperience due to having authorized the "experimental" dismissal of a patient from the psychiatric hospital'. But the case against him was weak at best, and it was clear that he had been charged as Basaglia's number two. If Basaglia had been in Italy at the time of the murder, he would probably also have gone on trial. Slavich claimed that he had only discussed Miklus at a meeting on the morning of the twenty-sixth, the day of the murder, and that the debate had been largely technical. The process by which the two men had been initially charged appeared to be political and ideological, and they were cleared on the basis of the (lack of) evidence against them. The law had not been broken.

The case exposed and created divisions within the therapeutic community and the city itself. Another nurse in the hospital testified that Slavich had taken the decision to release Miklus on his own. Meanwhile, Miklus's sons confirmed that permits for their father's release had been signed on 15 and 26 September. Basaglia was present at the trial, while the anti-Basaglian doctor Vittorio Alì (who had actually signed the Miklus temporary release permit) had died in the meantime. As Slavich was cleared, the packed courtroom broke into cheers and applause.

Two separate psychiatric examinations of Miklus were carried out as part of the investigation. One concluded that he was a 'paranoid schizophrenic' and 'socially dangerous', but also that the murder could not have been premeditated and that Miklus had shown signs of

---

Passi, 'Processo contro un medico della "nuova psichiatria"', *L'Unità*, 14 February 1972; Sartori, 'L'infermiere della rivoluzione', *L'Unità*, 8 December 1996; Rino Maddalozzo, 'Condannata la teoria della camicia di forza', *L'Unità*, 20 February 1972.

40   'Piena assoluzione al prof. Slavich', *Il Piccolo*, 19 February 1972.

improvement before 1968. The other examination of Miklus, carried out by Basaglia's friend Fabio Visintini for the defence, was a much more sophisticated document.[41]

The Aftermath: Gorizia, Il Piccolo, the Incident and the Basaglian Experiment

In the wake of the Miklus murder, *Il Piccolo*, which had more or less ignored the asylum and Basaglia for much of the previous six years, launched a cutting critique of the new methods being employed there. It was as if Gorizia, the city, had finally discovered the Basaglian revolution on its doorstep, after seven years. This was no ordinary murder. Quickly, almost immediately, it had become a case: 'il caso Miklus'.

But *Il Piccolo* was quick to draw a connection between the murder and Basaglian methods. Patients in the asylum, the paper wrote, 'enjoy extraordinary levels of freedom, which is also something that is, obviously, extremely dangerous'. Examples emerged of families who had supposedly been 'forced' to look after their relatives. One woman claimed that her husband 'comes and goes from the psychiatric hospital as if he were in a hotel'. Later, a pro-Basaglian nurse evoked 'the siege-like atmosphere surrounding the hospital'. It was as if the murder was the false step that the enemies of the Basaglia project had been waiting for.[42]

Il Piccolo presented Miklus as a monster, 'the madman', 'the crazy wife-murderer', 'the insane person'. The paper also declared that Miklus had *planned* to murder his wife. His was a 'wicked criminal plan', wrote one journalist, who added (contradicting himself), 'We should not talk about premeditation.'[43] The city itself was depicted as terrified of

---

41   Both reports are now in Casagrande, 'L'incidente di Gorizia', pp. 107–19.

42   Gino Accurso in Venturini ed., *Il giardino dei gelsi*, p. 34, cited in Colucci and Di Vittorio, *Franco Basaglia*, pp. 208–9. Franco and Franca Basaglia later referred to the judicial action as a series of 'incriminations and . . . trials instigated by the most backward parts of the state'. Franco Basaglia and Franca Ongaro Basaglia, eds, *Crimini di pace. Ricerche sugli intellettuali e sui tecnici come addetti all'oppressione*, Milan: Baldini Castoldi Dalai, 2009 (Einaudi, 1975), pp. 15–16.

43   Antonio Cattalini, 'Ammazza la moglie a tradimento un pazzo in permesso dal manicomio', *Il Piccolo*, 27 September 1968. The court later ruled out any idea that the murder had been premeditated.

further incidents. Journalists wrote that the whole of Gorizia had been 'horrified' by the Miklus murder and that 'public opinion' had been 'shaken'. The supposed danger emanating from the psychiatric hospital with its open-door policies was 'the question that is increasingly worrying Gorizia and disturbing its usual tranquillity', and these issues were 'on everyone's lips'. But had the Miklus murder simply confirmed the worst fears of 'normal' Gorizians, or had it exposed something of which people were unaware? So violent were these attacks that Franco Basaglia was prompted to write a letter of protest to *Il Piccolo*.[44] Later, in 1971, Basaglia pointed out that 'Italian asylums are full of neglected stories of murders, suicides and injuries due to the aggravation of punitive systems'. Should we return to systems used in the past, Basaglia argued, simply because of one horrific event?[45] Nurse Enzo Quai later made a similar point: 'This is what I think, if you look at the negative aspects of what happened, you also need to look at the positive developments. Something bad happened, but hundreds of people were reborn thanks to Basaglia.'[46]

The judicial and (local) journalistic assault on the Basaglian model in Gorizia was also accompanied by political condemnation, particularly from the neo-fascist party that had such a strong presence in the city. Eno Pascoli, provincial councillor for the Italian Social Movement (MSI), was particularly active in this campaign.[47] He called Basaglia's methods 'total madness' and made frequent critical speeches relating to the new asylum regime. In a debate at the Provincial Council he attacked the 'anarchy within the hospital, which people have gossiped about for years'. For Pascoli there had been too many escapes which 'put the whole city in danger'. Pascoli was clear, almost threatening: 'This anarchy must come to an end . . . those patients free to go to bars and who return to hospital drunk.'[48] The (tiny) local Communist Party defended Basaglia, and referred to a 'campaign of denigration'. This was also the case with

44   'Significati e prospettive dell'innovazione terapeutica', *Il Piccolo*, 12 October 1968.

45   Tito, 'Lo psichiatra accusato'.

46   Sartori, 'L'infermiere della rivoluzione', *L'Unità*, 8 December 1996.

47   Slavich confuses the magistrate Bruno Pascoli with the MSI politician Eno Pascoli in *La scopa meravigliante*, p. 264.

48   'Ampio dibattito al Consiglio Provinciale dopo le "reserve" mosse al dott. Basaglia', *Il Piccolo*, 16 October 1968.

the Socialists and the Christian Democrats, although their support was far more tepid.

On 20 October, Miklus's three children (Marjan, Davide and Giuseppina Miklus) wrote a letter to *Il Piccolo*. It was a powerful document, in which they claimed that they had been 'terrified' of their father. They also wrote that they had been put under pressure by the asylum authorities to accept his visits.

> The pressure to have him back at home, above all in recent times, went beyond our ability to receive him safely . . . We don't have psychiatric congresses who give us support, nor doctors' organizations, nor trade union or political movements, nor a group of famous lawyers.

This was a reference to the support received by Basaglia from various official bodies after the judicial investigation had been made public.

The Miklus children went on to discuss the mental health of their father:

> He was and he is ill, and we have lived with the nightmare of his phobias, and we have had moments of sheer terror after his escapes from the hospital . . . We are victims of his illness, just as he is, and we are not angry with him – but only have feelings of compassion and love towards him . . . We would like to send this message as ordinary people to those ordinary people who work humbly and anonymously in the hospital where our father was a patient and who were able to get to know his activities and reactions and who could testify with honesty about the facts of those tragic days.[49]

This letter led to further attacks on Basaglian methods in the asylum, including a call for an administrative enquiry into what was going on there from at least one councillor. Political pressure was rising.

The Miklus case was a moment of crisis for the therapeutic community. For years, the fear of an incident of this kind had hung over the hospital like a dark shadow. In seven years, nothing of the kind had happened. But Miklus marked a loss of innocence. Parts of the state

---

49 'Sollecitata allo 'Psichiatrico' un'inchiesta amministrativa', *Il Piccolo*, 18 October 1968.

machine and the local media turned against the Basaglians. It was a siege, a war, which isolated the hospital even further in the context of the city. Basaglia saw the case as a personal and political turning-point. Gorizia had reached an impasse, and he wanted to move on in a place where the political machine would support the movement, not block all attempts to progress further.

Gorizia and the Peteano Bomb, 1972

It is worth taking a little time to examine the judicial authorities in Gorizia around the time when the Miklus case was a live issue (1968–72). The public prosecutor in the city for much of that time was Bruno Pascoli, and Raul Cenisi was the *giudice istruttore* when the Miklus murder took place.

Let us look at one infamous case. On 31 May 1972 (at about 10.35 pm) a telephone call alerted the carabinieri in Gorizia to a supposed incident involving gunshots in a small place called Peteano, which lay between Gorizia and the huge World War One memorial in Redipuglia. On arrival, the carabinieri found an abandoned car – a white FIAT 500. The car appeared to have two bullet-holes in its side. When the carabinieri tried to open the car bonnet at eleven thirty that evening, a bomb exploded which killed three officers and injured two others. All the dead were southern immigrants; one was Sicilian, another Lucano, and another from Lecce (they were thirty-one, thirty-three and twenty-three years old): Antonio Ferraro (*brigadiere*), Donato Poveromo (carabiniere) and Franco Dongiovanni (carabiniere).[50]

This event was the most shocking in a series of violent incidents in the Gorizia area, including an attempted hijacking at Gorizia's airport on 6 October 1972. Years later, it would turn out that the Peteano bomb was placed by neo-fascists as part of the 'strategy of tension', an attempt to destabilize Italy and force the authorities into an authoritarian crack-down on the left. Elements of the secret services were also involved in this conspiracy. But the judicial authorities in Gorizia ignored any

---

50   The early part of the story is told in Gian Pietro Testa, *La strage di Peteano*, Turin: Einaudi, 1976.

possibility of a right-wing plot. Instead, they looked first to the left and then tried to frame a group of common criminals thanks to an incredible series of lies and false confessions. Two men were in charge of this investigation: Raul Cenisi and Bruno Pascoli. Some politicians even tried to link the Peteano bomb with the Basaglian experiment.[51] A series of trials related to the Peteano bomb took place between 1973–79 that ended with all the criminals being cleared. Many of those involved in various ways in this investigation and trial were linked to the MSI in Gorizia.[52] It would take years for the truth to emerge, largely thanks to the confession of one of the neo-fascists involved, Vincenzo Vinciguerra, in 1984. Cenisi, meanwhile, moved to Trieste. He would soon come across Basaglia again.

Gorizia was a place of plots, right-wing conspiracies and political violence. In 1962 a bomb had been thrown at the Communist Party offices in the city. Gladio, a secret, paramilitary organization formed to 'defend' Italy from Communism, was active in the city and the surrounding area. The Peteano case was striking, even in the 1970s in Italy, for its association with false trails, cover-ups, lies, wilful distortions, set-ups and framings. Much of this was politically motivated, and this kind of activity infected the judiciary in that part of Italy, that same judiciary which investigated the Miklus case.[53]

51   Such as the MSI deputy Renzo de' Vidovich who supposedly made this link in a speech in Parliament. For this speech see Lucio Schittar: 'A clear sign of how the area responded was to be seen at the time of the Peteano massacre when a Parliamentary question by the Honourable de' Vidovich asked, more or less, if it was well know that Peteano was close to Gorizia, where Professor Basaglia had tranformed the patients into "human bombs".' Matteo Impagnatiello and Piero Colussi, 'Intervista a Lucio Schittar. Presente, passato e futuro nelle parole di un protagonista del cambiamento' in *Venti'anni dalla 180. L'esperienza del DSM di Pordenone*, Pordenone: Azienda per i Servizi Sanitari n. 6 Friuli Occidentale , Booksei 2, 1998, p. 24.

52   'Peteano: avvocato fascista per uno degli indiziati', *L'Unità*, 27 March 1973.

53   Slavich, *La scopa meravigliante*, p. 264, n. 3. Slavich argues that the decision of the prosecutor not to appeal his case was because of the effects of the Peteano bomb.

FIFTEEN

I giardini di Abele *and* Morire di classe:
Gorizia on Television and the Role of Photography

'Gorizia. I am here for the psychiatric hospital. In short, the madhouse.'

Sergio Zavoli, *I giardini di Abele* (1969)

SERGIO ZAVOLI: 'Professor Basaglia, people say that this hospital is more of an example of civil denunciation rather than a psychiatric proposal.'
BASAGLIA: 'Absolutely. I completely agree.'

I giardini di Abele

ZAVOLI: 'Then, one day, this hospital was opened up. What changed?'
PATIENT ('Carla'): 'Everything!'

Interview in Gorizia (1968)

A TV camera is moving down a long flat road, mounted on a car. The place is an anonymous one. It could be anywhere, any city. A voice-over starts in the background. It is a well-known voice in Italy, that of Sergio Zavoli, 'God's socialist', a film-maker and journalist who had also created and presented popular and innovative sports programmes on national television, as well as a series of celebrated documentaries and reports.[1] Here, in 1968, he is in Gorizia. The voice-over continues:[2]

> The mentally ill are always found at the end of a street on the edge of the city, perhaps because in this way they do not disturb us too much. In Gorizia I'm right on the extreme limit of the city – a wall around the hospital runs along the border between the Italian state and that of Yugoslavia. I have tried to get to know this asylum because its recent history has attracted the attention of scientists and people of cultures from all across the world, but in Italy it runs the risk of being understood only because of a piece of bad news.[3]

The camera turns into a side road and goes through the open gates towards the asylum itself. Soon, we will see patients leaving via these same gates. Zavoli's voice-over is in the first person, although he never appears physically in the film beyond his voice. He had chosen to visit Gorizia, he says, because it had become famous. People were talking about what was happening there.

The next shot is from a photo by Carla Cerati of a man holding his head in his hands: a psychiatric patient from the asylum in Colorno. This photo would be reproduced time and time again by the Basaglian

---

1   Zavoli was a left-wing Catholic. He had become famous thanks to his hosting of *Il Processo alla Tappa*, which covered Italy's annual cycling race, the *Giro d'Italia*. For this programme, see John Foot, *Pedalare! Pedalare! A History of Italian Cycling*, London: Bloomsbury, 2011, pp. 202, 308.

2   There are various published versions of the script for *I giardini di Abele*, many of which differ from that which was actually transmitted. These quotes are based, unless otherwise stated, on the film transmitted in 1969. See for edited versions of the script, Sergio Zavoli, *Viaggio intorno all'uomo*, Turin: Società Editrice Internazionale, 1969, 'I giardini di Abele', pp. 237–48; Sergio Zavoli, 'I giardini di Abele, i giardini dei fratelli scomodi' in Parmiggiani, ed., *Il volto della follia*, pp. 81–2; Sergio Zavoli, *Diario di un cronista. Lungo viaggio nella memoria*, Rome: Rai-Eri, 2002, pp. 363–78. For a more detailed analysis of this documentary see John Foot, 'Television Documentary, History and Memory: An Analysis of Sergio Zavoli's *The Gardens of Abel* (1969)', *Journal of Modern Italian Studies*, 19, 5, 2014, pp. 603–24.

3   This was a direct reference to the Miklus case. In the published script this section has since been changed (in one version) to 'while in Italy, in some haste, many have argued that the Gorizia experiment was scandalous'. Zavoli, *Viaggio intorno all'uomo*, p. 237.

movement in the years to come.[4] It would appear soon afterwards in the celebrated photo-book *Morire di classe* and had already been seen on posters and in exhibitions. Cosimo Schinaia later referred to it as 'the symbol of the marginality imposed by the asylum'.[5] The film also mentions, obliquely, the recent controversy over the Miklus case, which it referred to as a 'piece of bad news'. The Miklus case had possibly led to the postponement of the screening of the film, which had been shot and edited in 1968.[6]

Sergio Zavoli's TV film, called *I giardini di Abele*, was screened on 3 January 1969.[7] It went out at about 9.25 pm on a Friday night, on RAI Uno, after the news. This was a good slot: prime time, and just after Christmas when many families would have been at home. *I giardini di Abele* was key in putting the Gorizia experiment on the national map. At that time, there were only two TV channels available in Italy. The documentary was shown as part of a popular weekly news-documentary magazine programme called *TV7*, which usually contained two or three separate short films. *TV7* ran on a weekly basis from 1963 to 1971. From 1967 the show aired on Friday evenings.

---

4   The photo was first published in *Morire di classe*, 1969, where it was reproduced twice as a double-page spread, in order to increase its effect on the reader. It was promoted to the cover of a new but much-changed edition in 1998, *Per non dimenticare. 1968, la realtà manicomiale di 'Morire di classe'*, Turin: Edizioni Gruppo Abele, 1998. It also made the cover of *Psychiatry in Transition*, where it was wrongly attributed to Berengo Gardin.

5   'Sui rapporti tra fotografia e psichiatria' in Parmiggiani, *Il volto della follia*, p. 41. The photo itself is reproduced in the same volume on p. 213.

6   A recent book claims that Zavoli came to shoot the documentary in December 1968 (Elena Bucaccio et al., *C'era una volta la città. Un film di Marco Turco. Dal soggetto alla sceneggiatura*, Merano: Edizioni Alphabeta Verlag, 2011, p. 96) *after* Miklus. But this is clearly not the case. The film was transmitted on 3 January 1969 and was months in the making. Zavoli was in Gorizia in the spring of 1968. We do not have precise details about exactly when the documentary was shot, but the garden interviews do not seem to be from the winter. Certainly, the commentary was changed or recorded after Miklus, as it makes reference to the case.

7   The date of this transmission is often mistakenly cited as 1968, or sometimes as 1967. Oreste Pivetta, *Franco Basaglia. Il dottore dei matti. La biografia*, Milan: Dalai Editore, 2012, pp. 625, 1727. The film was made in 1968. But there are some signs that the preparation went back to 1966. Maria Grazia Giannichedda, for example, seems to suggest that the film was shown before *L'istituzione negata* was published. 'Introduzione' in Franca Ongaro Basaglia ed., *Franco Basaglia. L'utopia della realtà*, Turin: Einaudi, 2005, p. xxxi–xxxii.

Zavoli's film has since become a key part of the way Gorizia is narrated and remembered. It is shown frequently at anniversary events and has appeared fairly often on television. It is also available in various versions on the Internet. The film contains most of the common elements of the standard Gorizia story: the charismatic role of Basaglia himself, the contrast between closed and open institutions, a connection between mental illness and social class, and between mental health *treatment* and wealth, the voice given to the patients, the resistance to change which needed to be overcome, the horror and torture as features of the old asylums. But it also added other, original and different elements: visual depictions of Gorizia and the patients, the voice and face of Basaglia himself and a specific 'Zavolian' social and quasi-religious reading of what was going on in Gorizia and the issues the experiment there raised.

For Zavoli, throughout the film, the issue was not to do with mental illness, but with society. *Everyone* was responsible for what was going on. This was not a film aimed at psychiatrists or patients, but at Italians in general. As Valeria Babini argues, the film was not merely a report on what was going on in Gorizia, it was also concerned with people's attitudes to mental patients and to mental illness. It was a film about the sane as much as it was about the mad: 'Zavoli's voice (and he is always out of shot) has the calm but authoritative tone of a moral conscience: like it or not, the *Gardens of Abel* also tell us about Cain'.[8]

The third act of the documentary takes us into the gardens of the asylum, gardens that had been cited in the opening prologue. The camera swoops and floats through the gardens, hiding among the trees. Finally, the title of the programme is explained, with its biblical connotations.

In these parks with their ancient kinds of beauty, so vast and hospitable, we can see much of the hypocrisy with which we normally absolve ourselves in cases of conscience. The orderly park where, having gone through the gates, we can see the free and serene lives of the mentally ill play themselves out, are in reality the gardens of our uncomfortable brothers – the gardens of Abel.[9]

---

8   Valeria Babini, *Liberi tutti. Manicomi e psichiatri in Italia. Una storia del novecento*, Bologna: Il Mulino, 2009, p. 8.

9   Zavoli, *Viaggio intorno all'uomo*, p. 241 (slight differences in printed text).

The slow motion and music[10] are used to prick the emotions of the audience, as patients walk around the grounds of the hospital, sometimes accompanied by nurses.

For Zavoli, the whole issue of mental illness and its treatment forced us to look deep into ourselves. His programme served, he thought, to highlight this contradiction, to underline the presence 'at the edges of our cities' of these 'problematic brothers and sisters'.

In the penultimate and final acts of the film, the patients come into sharp focus. They are given a voice. Zavoli introduces the four one-to-one interviews as 'a series of dialogues I filmed in Gorizia's asylum' with 'ill people'. Extracts from the interviews are then shown, with the patients sitting on simple chairs in the garden. Once again, Zavoli is out of shot.

In the second dialogue, a woman described how she had been treated in the 'closed' asylum. It was a story of institutionalized violence: 'They tied me up, they beat me, they wanted to carry out electroshock treatment and I was terrified.' This was 'Carla', an important figure in the Basaglian hospital, the secretary for the general meetings and the Auschwitz survivor who was interviewed early on in *L'istituzione negata*, where she was described as 'one of the most listened-to patients in the hospital'.[11] Carla's interview was much more staccato, with much shorter answers.

What is a closed hospital?

Closed? Prison.

Did you experience closed hospitals?

Yes.

Carla's interview touched on a series of issues: the relationship with the outside world, her illness, her treatment in the total institution that had been there before Basaglia's arrival.

How do the people outside see you?

Well, they know me. I am from Gorizia. It's not as if I am a monster.

Carla seemed both strong and fragile at the same time. She claimed that she 'didn't care' what people thought, but she also claimed that, in

---

10   Gustav Mahler, Symphony no. 1 (*Titan*), second movement.

11   Franco Basaglia, ed., *L'istituzione negata*, Turin: Einaudi, 1968, p. 24. 'Carla' can be seen sitting next to Basaglia in a photo by Berengo Gardin taken inside Gorizia in 1968. Parmiggiani, *Il volto della follia*, p. 200.

life, she was 'all alone'. At one point she burst into tears, and her crying was captured and highlighted by the camera, as was her smoking. It was, despite Zavoli's earlier raising of the issue, a voyeuristic moment. She also defended the 'open' hospital, underlining the fact that 'everyone' there was paid.

Zavoli's film was Basaglian and Zavolian. It discussed prejudice, it drew comparisons between concentration camps and asylums, it treated the patients as real people, it analysed social class. Moreover, it looked at stigma and at resistance to change. The film placed the viewer in a stark relationship with the inside of a psychiatric hospital, and with patients and ex-patients. For Zavoli, all this was *our* problem, *everybody's* problem, and it was also a social problem, not a medical one. Basaglia himself had 'no idea' what mental illness was, and he was much more interested in the 'ill' in any case. Onto these Basaglian traits, Zavoli added the poetry that came from the combination of the images and the words being spoken, both in the voice-over and by the interviewees. He also ended the film with shots of patients walking out of the hospital and onto a river bank (with a close-up of one person's shoes to, once again, underline their poverty), and included shots (taken from other films) of patients knocking down walls, and archived ones of others being tied up.

Finally, Zavoli gave the whole programme a religious edge and religious language – from the title onwards. It was as if Basaglia was carrying out a kind of mission. It was didactic – the message was rammed home – moralistic, a history lesson, but also powerful and revolutionary, perhaps as much, if not more so, than *The Negated Institution* itself. Millions of Italians saw images that were radically different to any previous visual study of psychiatric hospitals. They saw Basaglia and heard his voice. Gorizia entered the living rooms of Italy.

But by the time *I giardini di Abele* was transmitted, things had changed in Gorizia. Basaglia had left the city for ever, along with many members of the original équipe. The film captured a moment in the asylum's history that was already part of the past. It was a historical document, even as it was transmitted.

Morire di classe: *Images from within the Total Institution*

Morire di classe had a striking lilac cover and a bold title. It had a different form than normal books, in size and shape, and inside, in terms of its content. Its images screamed out at you from the pages. It used the techniques of modern advertising. It was part of the society of the spectacle, a product of that same society. But its message was radical.

On the right, underneath the title, there was a long (unattributed) quote from the Basaglias:

> At the end of this process of dehumanization, the patient is handed over to a psychiatric hospital to be cured – he no longer exists – he is absorbed and incorporated into the rules which determine his existence. He is a closed case. Labelled in an irreversible way – he is never able to cancel out the signs which have defined him as something less than human, without the possibility of appeal.

Right from its cover page, this book, entitled *To Die Because of Your Class: The Asylum Condition Photographed by Carla Cerati and Gianni Berengo Gardin* (edited by Franco and Franca Basaglia),[12] presented itself as a different sort of publication. Not a collection of texts, debates and documents, this was a design object, a political and sociological photo-book, to be looked at (or away from) as much as read. As well as attempting to revolutionize mental health care, the Basaglias (along with Einaudi and Giulio Bollati) were also struggling to transform the world of publishing and political campaigning. It was a memorable moment in the history of the movement.

The photos in the book came from three different asylums (in Gorizia, Parma and Florence) and were taken between April and October 1968.[13] The book itself did not indicate which images were taken by which photographer, nor from which asylum they came. All of these asylums

---

12   Franco Basaglia and Franca Ongara Basaglia, eds, *Morire di classe,* Serie politica, 10, Turin: Einaudi, 1969.

13   Further details on these visits and various exhibitions, including the original publicity leaflets, can be found in the Basaglia Archive. For a more detailed analysis of this volume and the images within it see 'Photography and Radical Psychiatry in Italy in the 1960s: The Case of the Photobook *Morire di Classe* (1969)', *History of Psychiatry*, 26, 1, 2015, pp. 19–35

were undergoing some sort of change (and therefore were by no means the worst total institutions in Italy). The two photographers also visited the asylum in Ferrara.[14] Basaglia helped the photographers gain access in Gorizia and in Parma. In Gorizia they were given the run of the hospital. In Florence, however, according to Cerati, the authorities were opposed to any photography, and they were only allowed in on one occasion thanks to the help of two psychiatrists working there.

> The experience inside the psychiatric hospital in Florence was the most traumatic for me . . . they told us that we were in luck as they had just cleaned up and usually there was a metre of excrement in the corridors . . . but it was terrible in any case to witness the suffering of those people.[15]

Cerati later argued that

> during this work I felt the limits of the camera for this first time – I was not able to capture the obsessive repetition of gestures, the voices, the cries, the laments . . . but at the same time the impact of a still image is much stronger than that of the moving image which we all watch with indifference on the small screen.[16]

Things were certainly easier in Colorno, thanks to Mario Tommasini and Basaglia, but not entirely straightforward once the photographers were inside. Not all the nurses in Parma were interested in reform (and this is also clear from the history of change in Colorno), and some nurses tried to seize the film taken by Cerati and Berengo Gardin. According to Cerati, Berengo Gardin fooled them by handing over blank film.

The photos taken were important for their context, for the environment in which the patients were to be found (bars, gates, concrete courtyards), but above all because of the way that the patient's bodies and faces betrayed the signs of poverty and institutionalization, pain,

---

14   Cerati has said that they were not allowed to take photographs within Ferrara's asylum, but an image from Ferrara taken by Berengo Gardin appears in Parmiggiani, *Il volto della follia*.

15   See photographers.it/articoli/carlacerati.htm.

16   Massimo Mussini, *Carla Cerati*, ed. Gloria Bianchino, Milan: Skira, 2007, p. 162.

suffering and the rules imposed within the asylum. Numerous other photos of various kinds were taken inside the asylums, especially in Gorizia, including those that documented the changes that had happened there. Berengo Gardin, for example, took shots of Basaglia himself, and of the general meetings, but these were not published in *Morire di classe*.[17] That book did not aim to underline that any change was going within asylums. Its goal was, in part, to shock. It was a political volume, a violent statement of a state of affairs that, for its authors, had been allowed to continue for far too long.

Basaglia had been interested in the use of visual media alongside texts and had utilized cartoons and drawings by his childhood friend Hugo Pratt in earlier propaganda and publications.[18] With time, *Morire di classe* became a classic work of Italian photography, cited in most histories of the discipline. As it quickly went out of print, it was also more cited than read.

Maria Grazia Giannichedda described *Morire di classe* as 'a cultural operation with a high level of originality and impact – a small book which was also a model for others ... with a sophisticated graphic design'. She continued,

> This book is a kind of rational catalogue of images of institutionalization collected in the psychiatric hospitals of Gorizia, Parma and Firenze, by two great photographers who used a measured, clean type of visual language, which was always respectful and never scandalous, to represent the bodies and the spaces of the asylum.[19]

---

17   Other photos from the series have turned up in various publications over the years; see for example the photos of a meeting and of students in Gorizia, and of Franco Basaglia in Parmiggiani, *Il volto della follia*, pp. 200–1. There are plans currently in place to publish a fuller set of Berengo Gardin's asylum photos.

18   Giulio Bollati played a key role in *Morire di classe*, as he had with *L'istituzione negata*. He was interested in photography and its relationship with history and was also a photographer himself. See Carlo Bertelli and Giulio Bollati, eds., *L'immagine fotografica (1845–1945)*, 2 vols, Turin: Einaudi, 1979; Bollati's piece 'Note su fotografia e storia', pp. 3–55; and his *L'Italiano. Il carattere nazionale come storia e come invenzione*, Turin: Einaudi, 2011, pp. 128–85.

19   Giannichedda, 'Introduzione', *Franco Basaglia. L'utopia della realtà*, p. xxxi. It is not true that each photo carried a brief comment in the original volume. Also, Giannichedda makes no reference to the photos that were not taken inside asylums.

Morire di classe was also a little bit of a fake, designed to work above all for reasons of politics and propaganda. For example, the fact that a number of the images were taken in Gorizia in 1968 was somewhat strange, for a book of this kind. After all, this was an open hospital, without fences and gates where nobody was tied up any more. Yet, the photos were taken (or chosen) in such a way as if they were from an old-style *manicomio*. None of the photos showed the patients taking part in the activities associated with the therapeutic community, or the general meetings that many other photographers came to Gorizia in order to document. This book depowered patients; it put them back into a passive state, a state from which many (in Gorizia) had escaped. It re-victimized them in order to serve the movement's needs. Of course, the photographers were also documenting or representing the institutional effects on patient's bodies of years of internment in the asylum, but it was clear that the photos chosen from Gorizia were of a particular kind. They showed a past, not the Gorizian present (when they were taken).

By depicting patients as objects and not subjects, something that was profoundly anti-Basaglian, *Morire di classe* presented a problematic vision of what was going on in Gorizia. It is perhaps for this reason that no images were chosen of the movement itself, or of meetings, and also that the places where the photos were taken were not indicated in the original volume. *Morire di classe* was not a book that provided images of hope, or of change. Its message was blunt: *close these places down*.

SIXTEEN

The End of an Era:
Basaglia Leaves Gorizia

'I have decided to leave Gorizia for ever at the beginning of next year, in January, and I have already discussed this with the provincial administration.'

Franco Basaglia to Giulio Bollati (n.d. but 1968)[1]

'We have been able to carry forward a set of practices which demonstrate a certain set of values for others and have helped spread the possibility of a different relationship between people.'

Basaglia's resignation letter (20 November 1972)[2]

L'*istituzione negata*, 1968 and the incident marked the beginning of the end for the Gorizian experiment, but Basaglians continued to work there until 1972. Just as Gorizia reached the height of its fame, in 1968–69, Basaglia, Franca Ongaro, Antonio Slavich, Lucio Schittar, Letizia Comba and Giovanni Jervis all left the city. It was clear that relationships within the équipe had been in crisis for some time.

---

1   Letter 16. Einaudi Archive. Basaglia folder.
2   Republished in Franco Basaglia and Franca Ongaro Basaglia, eds, *Crimini di pace. Ricerche sugli intellettuali e sui tecnici come addetti all'oppressione*, Milan: Baldini Castoldi Dalai, 2009 (Einaudi 1975), pp. 37–9. The whole letter was also published in *Fogli d'Informazione* 3 November 1972, pp. 7–9. This letter was also sent to the patients in the hospital.

Basaglia had been plotting his departure from Gorizia in 1968, *before* the Miklus murder, and his reasons were both political and personal. On the one hand, the équipe was no longer working as a cohesive group. And, on the other, the difficult relationship with the provincial administration was preventing the experiment in Gorizia from going any further.[3] Basaglia also expressed concerns about the political direction of the movement. In January 1968, for example, Basaglia wrote to Maxwell Jones. He said that he was 'personally interested in moving from Gorizia' and added that

> I am in crisis too, about the internal meaning of my job . . . I feel that increasingly my job appears to be supportive of the current political and economic system – a system which I disagree with – and I must look for a different path, otherwise I will not see any sense in my work.[4]

Divisions within the équipe had begun to appear in 1967, when Basaglia wrote that 'the Gorizian experience is getting worse by the day (there are oppositional forces everywhere) . . . as well as in terms of the deterioration of internal relationships which by now seem irreconcilable'. For a time it appeared as if Basaglia would be going to Bologna. He wrote in a letter in 1968:

> I will be quite surely moving from Gorizia to Bologna during the summer . . . I want to start something completely different from Gorizia, as I realized that revolutionary situations are immediately consumed by 'power' as a new solution to its own contradictions, and I don't want to be part of a social system which I don't like.[5]

---

3 The relationship with the provincial administrators in Gorizia was a rocky one from the beginning. There were continual requests, for example, for Basaglia to pay for his phone calls. Frequently, the provincial administrators wrote to Basaglia to remind him that they were in charge, and these issues went way back. In 1963, for example, the president Bruno Chientaroli wrote to Basaglia to admonish him and underlined that 'sometimes you do not take into account that the Institute directed by yourself belongs to and is under the control of an Administration' (29 July 1963). In 1967, Chientaroli complained again after there were reports of sexual relations between patients in the hospital grounds. He told Basaglia about rumours that 'illicit relationships between patients of both sexes continue to take place, despite the complaints in this case'.

4 28 January 1968, Basaglia Archive.

5 Basaglia was wary of new psychiatric trends becoming 'fashionable'. As he wrote to David Cooper in August 1968 (Basaglia Archive): 'Psychiatric problems are in fashion now in

But the Bologna solution did not work out. Basaglia finished a distant fourth in the competition there, a clear sign that the city's Communist Party did not want him.

Further evidence of this crisis is provided by the letters of Michele Risso, who was a close observer of the Gorizia experience and friends with a number of members of the équipe. At the end of 1968 Risso wrote to Basaglia from Rome. He had recently met up with Giovanni Jervis and Letizia Comba, who were his friends at that time. His analysis of the situation in the équipe was lucid and negative. The writing was on the wall:

> I fear that in the end you will leave each other as enemies, without having understood anything . . . haunted by ghosts . . . continuing your recriminations and writing in order to justify your recriminations . . . It's all going badly . . . You are becoming enemies . . . If you carry on like this you will end up writing and talking as enemies . . . I have heard that Gorizia ends up destroying those who work there, and I don't doubt that this is the case.

He concluded that 'the équipe is breaking up'. But he added that Basaglia needed to understand that this break-up had implications which went way beyond the fate of the individual members of the group: 'You are now aware of the importance of Gorizia.' He was afraid that 'the experience of Gorizia will end with the negation of Gorizia'. Risso had already warned Basaglia about these problems at the beginning of 1968, when he noted a 'sterile, useless, damaging and stupid competition' within the équipe.[6]

Italy and I have already had some horrible experience on television where they are interested to show new things, without facing the new problems [they are] just interested in showing the most famous people in this field and I did not accept to do [sic.] their game.'

6   18 January 1968, Basaglia Archive.

PART II

BEYOND GORIZIA: THE LONG MARCH

SEVENTEEN

Perugia: The 'Perfect' Example, 1965–78

'The only experience which was able to marry sectoral reforms with the politics of the anti-institutional movement, an experience which wasn't boycotted by the local political forces and which managed to produce visible and concrete results, facts and not opinions',

Edoardo Balduzzi[1]

'The experience of Perugia was one of the most important, complex, rich and difficult, but also the most forgotten.'

Ferruccio Giacanelli[2]

After 1965 Perugia was the setting for one of the most successful movements for the reform of mental health care in Italy, and perhaps in the world. An alliance of politicians, nurses, patients and psychiatrists managed not only to transform Perugia's huge asylum system, but also to set up alternatives to that system across the Umbrian region. In addition, this process of rapid and radical change was accomplished with the active participation of the citizens of the city and the region.

---

1 Edoardo Balduzzi, *L'albero della cuccagna. 1964–1978. Gli anni della psichiatria italiana*, Edizioni Stella, Nicolodi Editore, 2006, p. 7.

2 Sabrina Flamini and Chiara Polcri, eds, 'Atti del seminario di avvio collettivo del progetto di ricerca sulla storia delle politiche psichiatriche in Umbria', Fondazione Angelo Celli, per una cultura della salute. Perugia, 16 April 2003, antropologiamedica.it.

The Perugian experience was so far ahead of its time that the 1978 'Basaglia Law' was seen as a kind of backward step in the Umbrian region.[3] Yet despite its extraordinary achievements and local legacy, the Perugian reform movement never gained the same notoriety as the experiments in Gorizia, Parma or Trieste.

This near-invisibility is an historical error that needs redressing. The history of Italy's radical psychiatric movement in the 1960s and 1970s cannot be written without strong and central reference to Perugia. For this reason, the labelling of this movement as Basaglian is a misnomer.[4] The movement, as this book has tried to show, was polycentric, complicated, multifaceted and always influenced by local factors – historically, politically, culturally and institutionally.

Those involved in the movement in Perugia were interested, above all, in changing their own region and its approach to mental health, and in practical solutions to real problems. They *had* theories (lots of them) but these ideas were always linked to actual change. They also took a global approach to total institutions, as did Mario Tommasini in Parma. Thus, they saw the asylum as part of a network of institutions and semi-institutional practices which needed to be replaced – orphanages, old people's homes, special classes for disabled or unruly children, sanatoria and so on. In an area where the Communist Party was extremely powerful, there was an emphasis on public debate and discussion, but also a heavily politicized understanding of change and its management.

The city of Perugia is perched on a crest running through the Umbrian hills. It is the capital of a region of small hill towns, each with their own identities and long municipal histories. The area had been under papal control since the mid-sixteenth century, and only the unification of Italy in 1860 finally liberated the city from the direct rule of the pope.

After 1945, the city's politics were controlled by the left, and in

---

3   Carlo Manuali in Luigi Onnis and Giuditta Lo Russo, eds, *Dove va la psichiatria? Pareri a confronto su salute mentale e manicomi in Italia dopo la nuova legge*, Milan: Feltrinelli, 1980.

4   Basaglia was well aware of what was happening in Perugia and visited the city on a number of occasions. Giovanni Jervis was also a vistor. Basaglia was in correspondence with Aldo Capitini and Ilvano Rasimelli, and thanked Rasimelli in *What Is Psychiatry?* Both men had been active in the Resistance and were both born in 1924.

particular the Communist and Socialist parties. In the elections of 1965, the left fell back a little across the region but remained in control in Perugia itself. Umbria had seen strong migratory movements to its cities throughout the post-war period, but the region as a whole was still an area of emigration until the 1980s.

In 1971, the overall population in Umbria had fallen by nearly 20,000 in the ten years since the previous census. This was the period when the peasant population of the region began to fall with some speed: from 193,000 in 1951 to just 55,000 twenty years later. It was an epochal change: a whole way of life was disappearing. More than half of the population changed their jobs or roles in ten years.[5] Villages emptied, churches were closed, fields were left fallow. Umbria was changing, forever.

Much of the Umbria region had been marked, for hundreds of years, by a system of farming known as share-cropping. These ancient systems began to break down in the post-war period, and many peasants migrated to the cities in search of different kinds of work. Perugia's population rose from 95,000 in 1951 to nearly 130,000 in 1971. Many of the inmates in the asylums and other institutions were of rural origins. But the world they had known was soon to become part of the past.

Perugia's vast Santa Margherita asylum complex was spread out in hilly parkland just below the historic centre of the city, with its beautiful Corso Vannucci and spectacular views across to Assisi. A mental asylum of kinds had been in the Santa Margherita area of the city since 1824 (where there had once been a Benedictine Monastery). In 1901 the provincial government took over the running of the psychiatric hospital. Other cities in the region also had their own, smaller asylums. Perugia's *manicomio* was made up of a series of vast buildings set in this large park, with farm-houses, farm-land, workshops and space for more than a 1,000 patients. It was, like many other asylums in Italy and across the world, a city within a city, almost self-sufficient and cut off from Perugia itself by gates and walls.

The asylum was an important institution in the city of Perugia, and

---

5   Giuseppe Micheli, *I nuovi Catari. Analisi di un'esperienza psichiatrica avanzata*, Bologna: Il Mulino, 1982, p. 61.

its management was almost a family affair. Cesare Agostini became director in 1904, and the Agostini family would remain in charge of the institution until 1965, when Giulio Agostini (Cesare's son) retired. Giulio had been nominated director in the place of his father in 1928, an appointment confirmed by a public competition in 1931. He would serve as director of the asylum for the next thirty-four years.

Ilvano Rasimelli and the First 'No'

'Perugia began with a strong political slant. The Perugian experience was extremely rapid.'

Gianni Lungarotti

'For me our responsibility as councillors is to understand the city not as a group of roads, squares and buildings, but as a collectivity of men and women.'

Ilvano Rasimelli, Perugia (1970)

As with Gorizia and Colorno, it all started with a 'no'. The push behind the Perugian anti-asylum movement was both political and moral. In 1965, as in Parma, a new breed of politicians took over the provincial government. These politicians created alliances with radical psychiatrists, ordinary citizens, activists and administrators. They also built support for change across the political spectrum, and only the neo-fascists opposed the reforms. Like Basaglia in 1961, and Tommasini in 1965, in Perugia one man simply refused to be fobbed off. He was convinced about one thing: *that* state of affairs was unacceptable. It was a 'no' that was to lead in a series of different directions. Rasimelli was no ordinary politician. As he later said, 'I wanted to administrate not for the system but against the system, and I must say that today the understanding of the so-called psychiatric phenomenon has helped make us more angry and ready to fight.'[6]

It was Carlo Manuali (1931–93), a psychiatrist working inside the asylum and a close friend of Rasimelli's, who had advised him to take a

---

6   Cited in 'A conti fatti' in Paolo Lupattelli ed., *I Basagliati. Percorsi di libertà*, Perugia: CRACE, 2009, p. 27.

look. Manuali was a short man with big and unruly hair. He was undoubtedly charismatic, and his modus operandi was the public meeting or private debate.[7] He wrote relatively little (and even less of his work was published), and when he did his arguments were often difficult to decipher. Perugia never produced any texts to rival *The Negated Institution, What Is Psychiatry?* or Jervis's *Manuale critico*. Although the example of Perugia was important to others in the movement, the Perugian experience never tried to spread its revolution in mental health care beyond its own region. This was both a strength and a weakness.

Ilvano Rasimelli was elected as president of the Perugian provincial government in the 1964 elections and took office in January 1965. One of his first acts as president was to visit the asylum that had just come under his control. As with Tommasini in Parma, it was a shocking moment. Rasimelli had only been in power for two days when he arranged an official visit to the asylum. During this first tour he was accompanied by the then director of the hospital, Giulio Agostini. Not satisfied with the cosmetic vision of reality they had presented, Rasimelli returned early the next morning (6 am), alone in his car, and simply rang the bell. The head nurse did not want to let him in, but he insisted, inviting the nurse to inform Agostini of his presence.

Like Tommasini around the same time in Parma, Rasimelli was soon faced with a vision of hell. In one small room, there were around sixty women 'who were screaming and rolling around on the ground, sometimes in their own excrement'.[8] Rasimelli was 'deeply affected' by what he had seen. He concluded quickly, as had Tommasini, that he could not 'carry out his functions as president of the province with dignity' if he 'ignored a situation of this kind'. He decided to act. It was the first 'no' in Perugia. Many others would soon follow.

---

7   Manuali became the official voice of the Perugian movement, along with Tullio Seppilli, Ferruccio Giacanelli and Rasimelli, Francesco Scotti, Carlo Brutti and others. For Manuali see Francesco Scotti, 'Carlo Manuali. Scritti sulla malattia mentale', *Umbria contemporanea* 4, June 2005, pp. 34–46.

8   Cited in 'A conti fatti' in *I Basagliati*, p. 23; Ferruccio Giacanelli, 'L'ospedale psichiatrico di Colorno nella storia della psichiatria di Parma', *Psicoterapia e Scienze Umane* 46, 2012, p. 579.

Rasimelli was born in Perugia in 1924 in a secular and Communist family. He could count the celebrated pacifist thinker and activist Aldo Capitini amongst his friends (they went to school together).[9] After failing his school exams he trained as a priest in a Salesian college. But he did not become a priest and went back to school to finish his studies. In 1943, while at university in Rome, he was (twice) arrested for anti-fascist activities. He would go on to become a partisan and an anti-fascist commander. After the war he completed a degree in engineering in Pisa and then went into politics in the 1950s. He was elected to the province in 1964 after serving on the city council for more than ten years and became president of the province in 1965, a role he covered until 1970. In the 1980s he became a Communist Party senator.

Rasimelli was not the kind of politician to give up. A sense of his personality can be gauged from the title of his autobiography, *Un romp-iscatole* (A ball-breaker).[10] Rasimelli felt that he could not just ignore the situation he had seen. He was incapable of simply *managing* an institution of that kind. A new director of the asylum – Francesco Sediari – was appointed in June 1965 (finally ending the seemingly endless Agostini family dynasty). Sediari was open to the ideas coming from the reformers. That summer, a tied-up patient died. Such events were commonplace within asylums. Usually, nobody even noticed. But Sediari went to the magistrates and spoke out. It was an unprecedented act, another important 'no'. The local press took up the case.

In September of that year (1965) Rasimelli organized a public meeting to decry the situation inside the *ospedale psichiatrico*, complete with a slide show and shocking testimonies.[11] Things would never be the same again. The Perugian revolution in mental health had begun. Another member of the Provincial Council also went public with their experiences of what they had seen inside the asylum.

---

9   Domenico Casagrande described Rasimelli to me in 2013 as 'Basaglia in the form of a politician'.

10   Ilvano Rasimelli, *Un rompiscatole. Tra le novità di un'epoca*, Perugia: Benucci Editore, 2007.

11   'I remember when Rasimelli, as president of the province, made his first speech about the asylum in 1965. It was in the Provincial Council chamber and the slides he displayed showed disgusting things – it created a scandal – it showed an asylum in a terrible state!', Ferruccio Giacanelli in Flamini and Polcri, 'Atti del seminario ', p. 40.

My first encounter with the psychiatric hospital . . . was last winter with a visit to the 'Neri' female ward – also known as la Vigilanza. It was a deeply dramatic encounter and it left me with a sense of guilt and social co-responsibility which I think would affect anyone in a similar way in the face of such a reality . . . after passing through some dark and squalid corridors . . . I reached the so-called refectory, which looked like a slaughterhouse with its marble-topped tables, wooden benches and grey and crumbling walls. Then I entered a big room where over the course of the day some sixty patients, in the company of some nurses, passed most of their time. When the door was opened I saw dozens of women sitting down, lying down, partly dressed or naked, who were crying out or talking incoherently in a fetid and unplastered room, without furniture – or rather with just some hard benches fixed to the walks – which did not allow somebody, even if they wanted to, to sit down.[12]

The Perugian Provincial Council had an immediate problem to face. In 1953 a plan for an entirely new psychiatric hospital had been approved. Work on the new building was due to start in 1966. Such a project flew in the face of the sense that it was the institution *itself* that was the issue here, not the kind of building it was housed in. In the end, this proposal was abandoned (as were similar plans in Turin, Parma and elsewhere). The rambling and ramshackle Santa Margherita hospital complex would be Perugia's last mental asylum.

As in Parma and Gorizia, it was crucial that the reformists had the nurses on their side, so one of the first measures taken was to reduce their working hours. Very quickly, other changes were introduced inside the asylum itself: doors were opened, visiting hours liberalized and walls knocked down. The city and the asylum were brought closer together. Some of these changes appeared minor, even trivial, and in themselves they meant very little. But their symbolic value was inestimable. This was true, for example, of the introduction of real cutlery for the first time (so that the patients did not have to eat with their hands).

Patients were increasingly seen in town, and some became well known

---

12   Clara Roscini (September 1965). Cited in Chiara Polcri and Sabrina Flamini, 'La ricerca sul movimento umbro di auto riforma', Perugia: Fondazione Angelo Celli per una Cultura della Salute, antropologiamedica.it.

for their eccentric behaviour (although this may have been mythologized later on). Occasionally, patients became part of the city's fabric itself and were missed if they were not there. In some cases, later on in this process, the return of a patient to his or her hometown became a memorable, public event. With time, some journalists began to take an interest in Perugia, and a series of pieces appeared in the national press.

Rasimelli would later use his rhetorical power to paint mental patients as part of a 'community of the exploited'. As he said at a huge public meeting, held in the beautiful surroundings of the Sala dei Notari in the centre of Perugia in 1970:

> From the depths of the old segregationist hospital a cry of revolt against the ills of society arose. We discovered a kind of hotline which brought together those segregated people inside the psychiatric hospital with the exploited, the humiliated, the oppressed of the world.[13]

Rasimelli would pay a price for his unorthodox way of doing things, which included sending a telegram to the Soviet embassy in protest at the invasion of Czechoslovakia in 1968. He was also seen as too popular by elements within the Communist Party. As a result he was shifted away from the presidency of the province and became a simple city councillor in 1970 (and not the mayor, a post for which he would have been a strong candidate, given the high number of preference votes he won in that election). After that, he started working as an engineer again, leaving full-time politics. The glorious period of radical reform of the asylum had come to an end. A different phase was about to begin.

The Movement

> 'The overcoming of the madhouse is not an administrative act, or something to do with psychiatry. It is the fruit of civilization.'
>
> Francesco Scotti[14]

---

13   Cited in Rasimelli, 'A conti fatti'.

14   Francesco Scotti, 'Trenta anni di psichiatria in Umbria: 1965–1995' in Provincia di Perugia, *I luoghi della follia dalla "Cittadella dei Pazzi" al territorio. Percorsi della psichiatria in*

'Mental illness is not a problem for doctors.'

Carlo Manuali[15]

In the 1960s, as we have seen, Umbria itself was changing – from a peasant society to an urban and industrial society. This momentous transformation also created a new political class. Modernity was on the march. But the Communists in Perugia were far less conservative than many of their comrades, and in any case the Italian Communist Party (PCI) was never a monolithic bloc. Some of the Communist leaders in Perugia were mavericks like Rasimelli. These factors were part of the context that explains the success of the reform process in Perugia.

The Perugian movement was intensely practical (despite Manuali's interest in philosophy and high theory in his writings). Its overall aim (after killing off the asylum) was to 'bring back to the territory – where they were born – specific problems – and look for their meaning and their origins through collective work, and to change forms of medical work in favour of new forms of intervention.'[16]

The movement in Perugia acted in advance of the 1968 Mariotti law and was extremely successful in shifting patients out of the *manicomio* (much more so than Gorizia) as well as closing down a number of total institutions altogether. A network of mental health centres (known as *Centri di igiene mentali* or CIM) were then set up across the region. Long public debates discussed the rules governing these institutions.[17] The CIM were run by highly motivated young psychiatrists and supported by the local political and judicial system, as well as, for a time at least, by the population as a whole, although this high level of approval would quickly fade. As a result, the main asylum population was reduced to a residual number of patients by the middle of the 1970s (before Trieste).

Umbria dal '700 ad oggi, Perugia: Arnaud Editore, 1995, p. 84.

15   Cited in Ferruccio Giacanelli, 'Carlo Manuali protagonista moderno della riforma psichiatrica a Perugia' in Lupattelli, *I Basagliati*, p. 39.

16   Balduzzi, *L'albero della cuccagna*, p. 18.

17   Graziella Guaitini, ed., 'Le assemblee popolari sulla politica psichiatrica dell'Amministrazione Provinciale di Perugia', *Annali di neurologia e psichiatria e annali ospedale psichiatrico di Perugia* 1–2, 1974. The regulations can be found in Carlo Brutti and Francesco Scotti, *Quale psichiatria? 1. Strategie per la trasformazione dei Servizi Psichiatrici. Storia e documenti*, Rome: Borla, 1980, pp. 152–9.

By 1980 there were only 252 people left inside the asylum in Perugia, most of them unmoveable for various reasons.[18]

There was a permanent level of micro-conflict within the movement in Perugia and across Umbria, which has been commented upon by many observers of the movement (from the inside and the outside). Nonetheless, these conflicts were largely contained *within* a strategy that was firmly aimed towards work in the 'territory'. Debate was endless but never seen as an end in itself. Commitment was total, dominating the lives of all those involved (as in Gorizia). The Perugians were all intent on moving swiftly beyond the asylum towards new and alternative institutions. They had no real interest (in the long run) in transforming the asylum itself. The asylum was part of the past. The quicker it was left behind, the better. It was an irrelevance.

In Perugia, some of the asylum nurses put up significant resistance to change. But this resistance did little to halt the alliance of other nurses, psychiatrists and politicians in their desire and ability to get things done, and with speed. Opposition was brushed aside. The power lay with the reformers – politically, culturally and medically. As in Gorizia and Parma, the nurses were divided, and some were radicalized quickly – becoming part of the vanguard themselves.[19] In Perugia (and perhaps only there) the 180 Law represented a step backwards, not least because of the way that emergency care centres were placed inside general hospitals. Perugia had already moved beyond such a medicalized model by 1978.

Humanizing the Asylum

'When it was a matter of giving the nurses more elegant uniforms, even the conservatives and the "old fogies" were in agreement, because it was like restoring your own house, and making it nicer to live in. Then there were the first real changes in terms of the nurse's working hours – all these first measures caused little controversy.

---

18   Marcello Panettoni and Filippo Mario Stirati, 'Presentazione' in Provincia di Perugia, *I luoghi della follia*, p. 6.

19   A key figure here was the nurse Adamo Sollevanti, who went on to work in the CIM and later became mayor of the small town of Lisciano Niccone.

They were signs of a more modern, more civilized, more acceptable
and more rational hospital . . . The real clashes came afterwards.'

Ferruccio Giacanelli

There were various phases to the movement in Perugia. The early period,
as we have seen, concentrated on work within the asylum (up until 1968).
Then there was a short time when the idea of the therapeutic community
was in vogue. After 1970, decentralized mental health services were
opened across the region, which gained more autonomy in the period
running up to the Basaglia law, in 1978.

The first phase aimed simply to make the asylum a 'human' place.[20]
Meetings were used, as in Gorizia, to break down hierarchies. The
appointment of a new director in May 1965 was an important moment.
Sediari was a reformer, open to change being propagated from within
and outside of the asylum. The continuity with fascism was broken, at
last. Meetings became more radical and open to outsiders, as 1968 pen-
etrated Perugia's asylum. Giacanelli later argued that the phase of
humanization of the hospital gained widespread public support.

In February 1970 a working group was set up to organize the first
mental health centre, with a doctor (Francesco Scotti who, with Carlo
Brutti, would later write a penetrating study of the movement of which
he was part), a social worker and twelve nurses. A second, similar group
began work in August of the same year. In the end, ten such centres were
opened. Popular debates (known as assemblies) were staged to discuss
the rules that would govern these centres.

A key principle of those involved in the movement was that people
should be treated – as far as possible – *outside* a hospital/medicalized
setting. The approach to people who came to them with various kinds
of problems was holistic, social and therapeutic at the same time. It saw
them as *people*, not patients. This outlook was called 'the politics of
non-admission'. Another key idea was the search for the roots of mental
illness – in schools in particular, but also in the family and the social
setting. 'Strange' behaviour was tolerated, as far as possible. Each and

---

20 'It was a space of the city, inside the city but at the same time on the outside'. Giacanelli
in Flamini and Polcri, 'Atti del seminario', p. 20. For the humanization of the hospital see also
p. 11.

every person had a right to dignity and to personalized treatment (in every sense of the word).

One feature of the mental health centres was the sense of autonomy they enjoyed, which was connected with the views and outlook of the doctors who ran individual centres. There were considerable differences, above all, between the outlooks of the centres under the control of Brutti and Scotti (who would go on to become the chroniclers and historians of their own movement) and those under the influence of Carlo Manuali. Legrand's study analyses these divisions.[21] Giuseppe Micheli (whose work concentrates on the strategy adopted by Manuali) argues that the Scotti and Brutti centre was more conservative and that the two institutions worked as separate entities within the same overall system.[22] Scotti and Brutti were also more interested in psychoanalysis. Manuali argued that you needed to begin early in terms of institutional work. The slogan was 'get there first', and the idea was to 'get a grip on psychiatric problems before they became defined institutionally'.[23]

The first phase of change was similar to the events inside the asylum in Gorizia after 1961. The hospital was humanized. Ferruccio Giacanelli wrote,

> In this early phase the aim was 'simply' to create dignified living and working conditions for everyone, giving the patients back a sense of human dignity and the nurses an idea of the real importance of their role – and to recreate the links with the patient's families – to create a climate of freedom – and to open up the hospital to the city.[24]

---

21   Michel Legrand, *La psychiatrie alternative italienne*, pp. 209–42.

22   Micheli, *I nuovi Catari*, and *Il vento in faccia. Storie passate e sfide presenti di una psichiatria senza manicomio*, Milan: Franco Angeli, 2013. Micheli's full-length and 'external' study of the workings of the mental health centres in Perugia and Umbria (a rarity in both senses) was hampered by its somewhat obscure title, and a series of minor mistakes in the initial section (which were seized upon by critics of the book). It was viewed by the participants with some disdain and suspicion, not least because of its critical approach to their work.

23   Micheli, *I nuovi Catari*, p. 39.

24   Giacanelli, 'Carlo Manuali', p. 36.

This would become Perugia's own therapeutic community, with its ward and general meetings. The humanization process started with the worst wards and worked down (or up). As in Gorizia, democracy was being introduced in a place that had never had a glimpse of it, and as in Gorizia, people changed, got their lives back, became *people* again. Uniforms were abolished and hair was allowed to grow. In the past, on entering the asylum, patients would have their identities stripped away from them – having to give up their possessions and even wedding rings. All this was stopped. Change was rapid: 'In a few weeks the hospital was unrecognizable and it then became a reference point for all those who were struggling for psychiatric reform alongside Basaglia'.[25]

By the end of the 1960s, Santa Margherita was the site for a variety of meetings, where decisions were made and debates raged. For the journalist Felice Chilanti, who reported from Perugia back to his newspaper *Paese Sera* in 1968, 'The assembly is the self-government of the therapeutic community – wards are effectively "governed" by the assembly.' The difference in Perugia was that this phase was brief and never became an end in itself. The Perugians were always looking to move out of the hospital, into the real world outside. Meetings and exhibitions were also organized in the city. They were often packed.

At the same time, the area of the hospital opened up to the city. Francesco Scotti later remembered how

at that time the psychiatric hospital was opening up, but in an almost anarchic way, as a park, a 'space of freedom'. A lot of people – above all students – would hang around there, in the pavilions which had few patients left – and it wasn't always clear what they were doing there and why.[26]

---

25 Cited in 'Attività della Provincia di Perugia nel periodo del presidente Ilvano Rasimelli (1964–70)' in Mario Tosti, ed., *Tra comuni e stato. Storia della Provincia di Perugia e dei suoi amministratori dall'Unità a oggi*, Perugia: Quattroemme, 2009, p. 2006.

26 Flamini and Polcri, 'Atti del seminario', p. 27.

Outside: Umbria's Mental Health Centres

'The first set of rules for a Centre of Mental Hygiene was ours. We were the only province which had given up its power and decentralized services. This unique nature of our reforms should be underlined.'

Pino Pannacci[27]

'At the end of the 1960s the ideology of the good hospital came to an end. A new era opened up – that of the "good territory".'

Giuseppe Micheli[28]

The real lesson from Perugia (but also from Reggio Emilia and later from many other areas) lay in the work carried out in pioneering decentralized mental health centres. These were known as Centres for Mental Hygiene (CIM), the rather antiquated term used in the 1968 Mariotti law.

The peak of the Perugian movement in terms of the general public was marked by a series of meetings held in the 1973–74 period across the province, which ended up with the approval of a set of radical rules governing the mental health centres. These meetings were packed and addressed by politicians, psychiatrists, students (Perugia is a student town), members of the public and journalists. The rooms were always thick with the smoke of hundreds of cigarettes. Debate was fierce but carried out in a civilized and calm fashion. Nobody shouted. At the heart of all this was Manuali, whose interventions were short and went straight to the point. Accounts of the meetings were published in full, and they were recorded on tape and later studied by anthropologists.

Some of these debates were staged and then filmed for a powerful documentary on the Perugian reforms that was called *Fortezze vuote. Umbria, una risposta politica alla follia.*[29] This documentary was presented in Venice at the film festival in 1975, although it is never shown today thanks to the objections of one family regarding a patient seen briefly in the film. Many of these meetings were taped and transcribed, and their content was studied

---

27 Ibid., p. 41.
28 Micheli, *I nuovi Catari*, p. 20.
29 Gianni Serra, 1975.

and discussed by anthropologists and others. In particular, Tullio Seppilli, who was part of the movement and carried out research into its history and development (work which continues to this day), organized and supervised numerous discussions around various issues linked to psychiatric reform. Much later, a beautiful documentary was made by a young film-maker which covered the entire history of the movement in Perugia.[30]

The rules themselves were a mix of statements about the principles behind the movement, specific regulations about the centres and more general principles for the future. In part these were an historical account of what had already happened in Perugia:

> The experience of the psychiatric services in the Province of Perugia was part of the struggle against psychiatric internment and segregationist institutions. This struggle has led to psychiatric work being moved from asylum-like institutions to those within society (family, school, factory).

And there were more philosophical statements (probably inspired by Manuali): 'Mental health is connected with the possibility of dominating in terms of knowledge and activity one's own existential condition and the processes which determine it.'

Writing in 1980 and looking back on the movement of which they had been a part, Scotti and Brutti were critical of these rules. They described them as a kind of monument to the movement, backward-instead of forward-looking. At the time, the rules were an extremely radical statement.

New Asylums?

> 'We need to ask ourselves this question: when a psychiatric hospital closes, what is it that opens up? For while there is a celebration about closure, and the knocking down of walls, and the throwing open of doors and gates, there is silence on what is opened up.'
>
> Brutti and Scotti[31]

---

30 *Dentro le proprie mura*, Carlo Corinaldesi, 2010.

31 Carlo Brutti and Francesco Scotti, *Psichiatria e democrazia. Metodi e obiettivi di una*

Carlo Manuali was never satisfied. He was one of the movement's leaders and its critical voice. In this way he was very similar to Basaglia himself. Manuali believed that the CIMs themselves would eventually have to disappear (as had the asylums) and that the movement needed to work within schools and factories, immersing itself ever deeper in society itself. He rejected any kind of simplistic link between society and mental illness. He also overturned traditional explanations (at the time) by arguing that it was not exclusion, but forms of *inclusion* that lay behind many cases of mental illness. The institutions themselves were the problem, from the school and the family upwards. For Manuali, 'Behind every situation linked to madness, there lies a hidden plan of failed normality.'[32] 'Mental illness', he continued, 'can be seen in the institutions who legitimate marginality'.[33]

Scotti and Brutti underlined (in their 1980 study) how they were much more than just psychiatrists. They saw their work as global, social, cultural *and* psychiatric. They were

doing what is necessary in order to be truly and correctly psychiatrists – taking care of and being interested in the lives of the patients, their economic conditions, the places where they live, the health services with which they come into contact.

Beyond the Asylum

In Perugia, the centrality of the asylum was only an issue in the mid- to late 1960s. A couple of hundred long-term patients remained there until the 1990s, but they were no longer a priority. Everyone knew that, in the end, these residual patients would either die in the asylum or be transferred elsewhere. The asylum was effectively closed. As Ferruccio Giacanelli has said with reference to 1970, 'We were ready, ready to abandon the madhouse, ready for laws which cancelled out its particular

---

politica psichiatrica alternativa Bari: De Donato, 1976, p. 32.

32   Micheli, *I nuovi Catari,* p. 35.
33   Ibid., p. 83.

nature, and ended the isolation of psychiatry from the rest of the health system.'[34]

The Perugian model was clearly very different to that of Gorizia or Parma. In the former case, the asylum itself was the main focus, and the territory around the asylum was unaffected by Basaglia and his équipe. Political hostility increased this entrenchment. In Parma, the territory was used against the asylum, which resisted change. Meanwhile, in Perugia, the asylum was quickly transformed and things shifted into the cities and towns of Umbria. Gorizia introduced democracy into the asylum, but only there. Perugia took issues linked to mental health out into the streets, cities, towns and villages of the region.

Returning the Patients

The issue of the return of ex-patients became a political one which involved the participation of local communities. Rasimelli, for example, has told the story of one well-known patient (Nello Gentili) who was returned to his hometown of Spello, a tiny, beautiful hill town some thirty kilometres east of Perugia.

> I remember the meeting held in Spello to discuss the return to the town of an ex-patient from the psychiatric hospital – a person who was a little difficult to say the least, and who had acted strangely in the past. I remember a lively debate, where a number of people spoke in opposition to the patient's return. But the speeches by Mayor Petrucci, a man of great intelligence and humanity, and by many young people, were in favour, and at the end of the meeting a big majority decided to accept back citizen Gentili.

Umbria was the setting for some quite extraordinary events at this time. The story of Nello Gentili was exemplary in this sense. At a certain point, Gentili was recommended for transfer to the criminal asylum. He did not want to go, and his position was supported by key figures such as Carlo Manuali. Gentili then staged his own highly original form of

---

34   Flamini and Polcri, 'Atti del seminario di avvio collettivo', p. 17.

protest. He climbed up an electricity pylon and refused to come down. In the end, Gentili was successful in his protests.

Votes were held at local public meetings as to the return, or otherwise, of citizens who had been interned inside psychiatric hospitals. It is not clear what happened if the citizens voted *not* to accept ex-patients. This process was highly unusual and unorthodox. Seppilli also notes that 'on occasion when a patient returned home from the psychiatric hospital the local mayor would have the bells rung in celebration'.

This key part of the Perugian strategy was the logical outcome of the decentralization and sectoral reforms they implemented. Patients were returned home, sometimes after years. Many were well known in the hill towns that mark the Umbrian landscape, and some were very unpopular with parts of the local population. This was never an easy process.

The Perugian experience, like that in Gorizia and Trieste and elsewhere, was marked by total commitment. Discussions were long and daily, and continued in the bars and restaurants of the city over dinner and coffee.[35] This commitment ran right through the asylum phase and reached its peak with the work of the CIM in the 1970s, where all kinds of technically qualified staff worked alongside psychiatrists, social workers and volunteers.

Oblivion? The Movement in Perugia: Forgotten, Ignored or Too Successful?

Historically, the Perugian experience has often been relegated to a footnote or a brief citation. Some claim that it has been completely forgotten, or simply ignored.[36] Balduzzi, for example, has emphasized how the Perugian experience has been forgotten or ignored in terms of the legacy of the anti-asylum movement. But it is a moot point if forgetting is the correct term to utilize here. Perugia never reached the same popularity or notoriety as Gorizia, Trieste or Colorno. It was already marginal within

---

35 One central restaurant was the scene of many late-night discussions. For the role of caffès and bars in general see Micheli, *I nuovi Catari*, p. 60.

36 Lucio Biagioni writes of 'a progressive and unstoppable sense of oblivion' in his introduction to a collection of Manuali's writings, 'Carlo Manuali. Scritti' in *Dossier, Salute! Umbria* 3, Dec. 2003, p. 3. This analysis is then extended to Manuali himself as well as to the entire national movement. See also Micheli, *Il vento in faccia*.

the national movement during the 1960s, and within Psichiatria Democratica in the 1970s.

Since then, the domination of Basaglian versions of the past have reinforced and cemented this marginality. Perugia is a poor fit with Basaglian narratives. The idea that Basaglia and Gorizia were isolated pioneers, for example, is undermined by the presence and achievements of the Umbrian movement. In addition, the argument that the Communist Party was an obstacle to change does not fit at all well with the Perugian experience. Moreover, in Perugia there seems to have been a successful attempt to both humanize the hospital *and* create an alternative to it at the same time.

In some ways, however, Perugia also isolated *itself*. The movement there was never particularly interested in creating a message for collective consumption, or publishing a bestseller for the rest of the world to read. The books about Perugia had little impact and are now out of print. The main publication of the Perugian movement was the technically named *Annali di neurologia e psichiatria*, which was not a journal with a wide circulation outside of a fairly restricted circle of specialists.[37]

The historical isolation and/or self-isolation of the Perugian movement has continued to the present day. Perugia in some ways *was* limited, closed, insular. It failed to communicate with other places (or simply wasn't interested in doing so). Giacanelli has spoken of 'communicative weakness'. Perugia was an almost perfect model, but within its own geographical boundaries. The key idea in Perugia was to get things done. Their aim really was to change *their* world – and that world, Umbria – was indeed changed. So one way of understanding Perugia's 'invisibility' would be through a positive frame. It was also a result of the collective nature of the movement in Perugia and Umbria, with its polycentric leadership. The mental health centres that criss-crossed the region allowed for a series of different approaches to mental health care, but one that did not easily transmit into the mass media or to popular publishing ventures.

---

37   This was the official publication of the asylum, with a history going back to Cesare Agostini in 1907. In 1965 Giulio Agostini passed the editorship of the journal onto Sediari, the new asylum director. The front page still carried the name of Agostini (who had founded it) right into the 1970s.

There were also other factors involved here. Giacanelli points to the 'progressive marginalization of our region in the demographic, proto-industrial, political and cultural context of the nation as a whole'. But surely this analysis would also apply to Gorizia and Trieste, which were anything but invisible, in psychiatric terms, in the late 1960s and 1970s? Often, intellectual laziness is at work. Few have bothered to read the significant body of material concerning the Perugian movement in the 1960s and 1970s, and not even the important books by Micheli and Legrand. The Basagliacentric story is a linear one. It is easier just to ignore everything else that was going on.

Internal conflict provides us with another possible explanation for Perugia's marginality (something which is also underlined in Micheli's book). As Tullio Seppilli has argued,

> one of the reasons for which the Perugian movement is less well known than others is that too much time was spent on internal arguments and too little on transmitting our message outside of the region and into the vast national debate which was, at the time, ongoing.

The Perugian movement was far less savvy about the use of the media than the Basaglians, and was less well connected intellectually and internationally, although journalists did come and write about what was happening there, and artists were used to produce striking logos and posters. Perugia had no Marco Cavallo phenomenon (as did Trieste), and little national TV coverage. There was no moment when 10 million Italians suddenly discovered what was going on in Perugia. In recent years an important documentary has reawakened interest in the history of the movement, but Perugia had no Basaglia, and, crucially, no Einaudi or Sergio Zavoli.

It may have been that Perugia was a victim of its own success. The total support given by the left-wing provincial government in Perugia to the dismantling of the asylum there was in stark contrast to the problems Basaglia and his followers faced in Gorizia. Basaglia was *forced* to find allies outside Gorizia; the Perugians had no need to look beyond their own city and, while there were furious debates locally, they had little or no national profile. Perugia never became a concrete utopia, nor did it look to become one. The Perugians attempted (and are still attempting) to write their own history, but in a way which is largely aimed at an internal audience. Perugia has found it difficult to break out of its own borders, and this has worked both for and against it.

Francesco Scotti argues that the Perugian strategy naturally moved away from the spectacular:

> We rejected this formidable form of iconic communication, we rejected the assemblies, we turned away from Capitini [a famous local peace activist] who would come to the general meetings in the hospital. In short, we gave up on all those symbols of power (and cultural and intellectual power). We weakened ourselves in order to provide a service for the people – carrying out forms of psychiatry which became invisible – precisely because they permeated into the local context and its needs.[38]

Conclusion

> 'The brief season of psychiatric protest now seems over.'
>
> Brutti and Scotti[39]

> 'The psychiatric hospital was an explosive feature in terms of all kinds of social structures, at a cultural level, and in terms of political activity and the understanding of public power and the general question of relationships between people, and of the ways in which the struggle against the class structure at the time could be given concrete form.'
>
> Rasimelli (1970)[40]

Patients inside the Psychiatric Hospital in Perugia:
    1961: 1,141
    1977: 394

---

38   Flamini and Polcri, 'Atti del seminario', p. 26. For further analysis see Micheli, *I nuovi Catari*, pp. 79–82.

39   Brutti and Scotti, *Psichiatria e democrazia*, p. 29.

40   Rasimelli, *Un rompiscatole*, p. 178.

Ilvano Rasimelli argues today that the 'moment' of great reform and change in the psychiatric system is 'unrepeatable'. It was strongly linked to a specific period and to particular forms of political commitment and institutional change. Perugia never had one leader or one centre. It had multiple sources of power and inspiration. Rasimelli was the key political force (until 1970 at least), and there were numerous administrators who helped the movement. Manuali provided charisma, ideas and enormous energy, while Scotti and Brutti worked with different and more main-stream ideas, and specialized in child psychiatry as well as having an interest in psychoanalysis. Other sources of leadership and inspiration came from nurses, other psychiatrists and some patients. All this meant that Perugia could never be associated with one person or one set of ideas. The movement lived through its sense of conflict and debate – a state of permanent (if friendly) discussion. The end of the asylum was only the beginning of a revolution. For Manuali, the death of the asylum did not mean 'the disappearance of madness, but [rather] a facing up to it'.[41]

---

41   Micheli, *I nuovi Catari*, p. 268.

EIGHTEEN

Parma: The Gas-Meter Reader and the Total Institution

'Who ends up in the madhouses, in the foundling hospitals, in the children's prisons, in the old people's homes? Those who don't have the economic or cultural resources in order to deal with life's problems. The response to social injustice which produces and deepens discrimination is another injustice which renders definitive a condition which requires assistance.'

Mario Tommasini (1965)

'Inside here is a reign of terror.'

Remo Bonelli to Tommasini[1]

'Sun, clean air, light, water all appeared as permanently absent from this terrifying building where the deepest squalor was to be found over decades – without any respite, no smiles, no sense of human or civil compassion or any sense that this agony and seclusion could be avoided.'

Luigi Tomasi[2]

---

1 Cited in Vincenzo Tradardi, 'La psichiatria a Parma ai tempi di Mario Tommasini e Franco Basaglia' in Giovanna Gallio, ed., 'Basaglia a Colorno', *Aut Aut* 342, Milan: Il Saggiatore, 2009, p. 197. Some of Tommasini's allies were within the asylum itself, including a patient called Remo Bonelli, who kept the assessor informed about developments from the other side of the institution's high walls. See pp. 195–8. Like another key patient–leader in Gorizia (Mario Furlan), Bonelli later committed suicide.

2 From Luigi Tomasi, *L'ospedale psichiatrico provinciale dal 1948 al 1955,* Parma: Giacomo

'In the post-war period the hospital declined in a way which seemed to testify to a kind of culture of abandonment, or rather a mental view-point which saw Colorno as a remote and unreachable place, a place of human exile where people were destined to be forgotten.'

Ferruccio Giacanelli

'The patients lived in indescribable conditions . . . with fifty, sixty or a hundred of them in filthy large rooms, badly treated, naked or semi-naked, tied up, surrounded by faeces and urine.'

Mario Tommasini[3]

P arma's asylum had a long history, which went back longer than that of Italy itself. In 1873 the asylum had been moved from the city to a formal ducal palace and convent in Colorno, a small town (with its own mayor and local council) some fifteen kilometres away to the north of the city, on the Lombard-Emilia border, close to the Po River. Colorno was originally meant to be a temporary home for the mad, and various alternatives were proposed over the years that followed. The building complex itself was a sprawling affair, with enormous gardens, but only the director of the asylum ever used the grounds, usually on his horse. Patients were restricted to a walled-in courtyard with nailed-down benches and chairs.

One of the key problems in Colorno was the terrible state of the buildings that housed the asylum (which hadn't been built to be an asylum). As the director Luigi Tomasi wrote in the mid-1950s: 'This is a hospital only in name, and thanks to some timid and failed aspirations . . . all the rest in terms of the environment, the equipment, the furniture had the sad and desolate appearance of a badly maintained prison.'[4] The provincial administration (who ran the asylum) had made some improvements to the asylum infrastructure in the 1950s. Yet the hospital

---

Ferrari & Figli, 1956, now in Ferruccio Giacanelli, 'L'ospedale psichiatrico di Colorno nella storia della psichiatria di Parma', in Pier Francesco Galli and Alberto Merini, eds, 'Tracce', *Psicoterapia e Scienze Umane* 46: 4, 2012, p. 577.

3   Franca Ongaro Basaglia, *Vita e carriera di Mario Tommasini burocrate proprio scomodo narrate da lui medesimo*, Rome: Riuniti, 1991, p. 7.

4   Tomasi, *L'ospedale psichiatrico provinciale dal 1948 al 1955*, p. 13.

population continued to increase, reaching a peak of 991 in 1964.[5] The
asylum itself was just the tip of the iceberg. Parma's local authorities
presided over a whole galaxy of institutes, ranging from orphanages to
places where handicapped, deaf, dumb and blind children and others
were sent, as well as decentralized asylums and a juvenile prison.
Historically, Parma's problems had been expelled to the north of its
province, where they could be safely hidden away.

Mario Tommasini was born into a militant anti-fascist family in Parma
in 1928. He grew up in a working-class neighbourhood called Borgo del
Naviglio. Imprisoned various times under the regime, he played a part
in the resistance despite being little more than a boy. In 1943 he became
an active member of the Italian Communist Party. During the 1950s
Tommasini was arrested more than once during local struggles against
the Democrazia Cristiana government and its police forces. He was
unemployed for a time and contemplated emigrating to Venezuela with
his wife.

Tommasini seemed to have what might be described as a critical relationship with institutions of all kinds. He was expelled from school *and*
summer school in the fascist period and even chucked out of prison after
organizing a demonstration among the prisoners.[6] This heretical nature
was extended to the Communist Party itself. Tommasini never accepted
the party line. He was described by Franca Ongaro as 'creative, passionate, honest'.[7] Tommasini eventually found work as a meter reader
for the municipal gas company.

It is difficult, if not impossible, to write about Mario Tommasini
without dealing with what we might call the 'Tommasini myth'. He is
often spoken about as if he had been a kind of lay saint, and his biogra-
pher subtitled his book 'A heretic who acted out of love'. It is also difficult,
if not impossible, to say something new about Tommasini. Despite the

---

5   There is a series of different statistics available concerning the numbers of patients in
Colorno at various times. The 991 figure is from Giacanelli, 'L'ospedale psichiatrico di Colorno',
p. 576, and is also found in Tradardi, 'La psichiatria a Parma'. Various statistics are available
concerning these numbers.

6   Paolo Migone, 'Un ricordo di Mario Tommasini', *Il Ruolo Terapeutico* 103, 2006, pp.
77–93 (and a longer version of this text at psychomedia.it).

7   Ongaro, *Vita e carriera di Mario Tommasini*, p. xi.

mass of material available, very little real research has been carried out
into his work in the 1960s and 1970s and its effects. Much of the research
that has been done concentrates on the relationship between Tommasini
and Basaglia or on the role of Basaglia in Colorno. Much of it is also
based on Tommasini's own accounts of the past. A further, related
problem is this: all of the books we have on Colorno, apart, perhaps,
from that by the journalist Bruno Rossi, are written by insiders or participants. All the other material comes from those who were involved in
some way.

Mario Tommasini was appointed assessor with responsibility for the
running of the Colorno asylum for the Province of Parma in early 1965
following provincial elections.[8] He had no competence in or knowledge
of psychiatry or mental health care, or of the asylum system. In late
February 1965 he was given official control over the psychiatric hospital
and soon afterwards he visited it for the first time.

Colorno, 1965: The Discovery of Hell

This visit has become a key component of the Tommasini myth and
has been repeated various times in print and in interviews in slightly
different versions. It is said that Tommasini put on his best clothes (a
jacket and tie), got into a Fiat 500[9] and drove the fifteen kilometres or
so out to Colorno through the winter fog. When he got inside he was
met by an unforgettable vision: *a vision of hell*. That visit was traumatic
and life-changing on a number of levels. First, the state of the building
and the way the patients were treated inside shocked him to the core
– on a basic, human level. But there was also a political and emotional
aspect to Tommasini's sense of dismay. He *knew* many of the people

---

8   His official job was as an assessor in charge of transport and the psychiatric hospital.
The province also had an assessor for health care. In 1967 these jobs were merged after the health
assessor died.

9   The car had been borrowed from the province, according to Tradardi. Tommasini
would become well known for travelling everywhere on his bike. This story contains a number
of elements from the Tommasini myth – the man of the people, the humanist, his naivety, his
image as a 'servant of the poor and the needy', his saint-like qualities, his stubbornness.

inside: 'Mario recognized people and was recognized by people.'[10] They had been his comrades in arms, both during and after the war. He had fought by their side. They were his friends, and they had ended up *there*. He *knew* they weren't mad. What was going on? How had it come to pass that 'dozens and dozens of comrades, people who used to live in my neighbourhood and who were well known to me' were locked up in such a terrible place?[11] It was heartbreaking, just twenty years after the triumph of the liberation struggle of which they had been part.

Tommasini's reaction to this vision of hell was very similar to Basaglia's in 1961, in Goriza: disgust, anger, a physical sense of nausea.

> The first time I set foot in the Colorno asylum, two days after I took over as assessor, I had to go out and throw up . . . it was carnage, naked patients, women in dressing gowns without even the belts, men sitting on the floor, their heads in their hands, others who scraped their feet on the floor . . . broken glass, it was filthy.[12]

'We were', he wrote later, 'in a place where death and violence were daily events'.[13] This immediate, semi-physical rejection of the asylum was something that would bind together Basaglia and Tommasini. The state of affairs was simply unacceptable.

Colorno was a dark, forbidding place, a labyrinth. In Colorno, as in Gorizia, the first vision of the asylum often provoked a sense of horror. Peppe Dell'Acqua, for example, later wrote of 'the smell of a closed institution, the mass of bodies, of those unclaimed and devastated people'.[14] Tommasini had been in prison, and, like Basaglia, he saw the asylum as a scandal and its inmates as people who needed to be liberated. He used the word 'kidnapped' to describe what had happened to them. The people inside were prisoners who had committed no crime.[15]

---

10   Tradardi, 'La psichiatria a Parma', p. 187.

11   Cited in Ongaro, *Vita e carriera di Mario Tommasini*, p. 7.

12   Mario Tommasini, 'Il mio rapporto con Basaglia. Intervista di Giovanna Gallio' in *Aut Aut*, 2001, p. 21. Similar accounts can be found in Ongaro, *Vita e carriera di Mario Tommasini*, and in Bruno Rossi, *Mario Tommasini. Eretico per amore*, Reggio Emilia: Diabasis, 2006.

13   Tommasini, 'Il mio rapporto con Basaglia', p. 43.

14   Peppe Dell'Acqua, 'Prima per me era solo un libro' in Gallio, *Basaglia a Colorno*, p. 15.

15   Tradardi, 'La psichiatria a Parma', p. 188.

On his way back to town, he stopped in a lay-by. It was all too much. He would have to resign. But then he changed his mind (so it is said): 'I won't give up, I will bring those people home . . . could I simply abandon them to their fate? And, are they really mad?'[16] *Something* could be done, and he had the power to change things. This 'something' would become Tommasini's mission. He used a mix of politics and sociology to explain the make-up of the inmates inside this galaxy of total institutions. He would strive to close that place down and free its 'prisoners', whatever the cost to his party. From that moment on, Tommasini dedicated his political career to that particular struggle.

The next day, the story goes, Tommasini was back in Colorno. This time he decided to make his views clear. He gathered together the four doctors and the hospital director, as well as some nuns and nurses and union leaders – and he lambasted them. He was angry. Furious. He compared the asylum to a concentration camp, and the methods used there to Nazism. According to Tommasini, a nun present at the meeting fainted in response to his words. Tommasini saw the incarceration of those in the asylum as a simple injustice – inspired by politics and social discrimination. His mission was equally straightforward, and it had nothing to do with psychiatry or mental health. He would get the people *out of there*, by any means necessary. He would save them.

Tommasini's harangue caused some controversy in the local press. Who *was* this man, they asked, this gas-meter reader? What right did he have to criticize qualified and eminent psychiatrists? Tommasini's stark position also caused disquiet in his local party. But he was unruffled. He set up a commission to study the hospital and suggest on reforms, and a debate began in the Provincial Council. It is said that Tommasini won the arguments there, in part, thanks to a speech by a neo-fascist councillor. As with Ilvano Rasimelli in Perugia in the same year, Tommasini made a simple appeal to his party and to his colleagues in the administration. The situation in the asylum was inhumane. It could not be allowed to continue: 'I will only talk about facts – what I saw with my own eyes in Colorno. You can then tell me if the situation there is humanly possible . . . if it is not your human duty to do something.' Tommasini won that debate (although he had not won the war). He was

---

16   Migone, 'Un ricordo'; Rossi, *Mario Tommasini*, p. 153.

given the task of humanizing the asylum, and he set out to find ways to get people out of there. It would be a long battle. The asylum was only finally closed in the 1990s.

The Encounter with Gorizia

'I already possessed a deep conviction and cultural and emotional reasons in terms of the emptying of the asylum in Colorno before I went to find Basaglia.'

Mario Tommasini[17]

'There was still an entire world to be untied.'

Franco Rotelli[18]

What was to be done? Tommasini asked for advice. He knew nothing about psychiatry, or asylums, or mental health. The commission he had set up included two academics – Gianfranco Minguzzi, a psychologist and psychiatrist who had studied in Bologna and also worked in Trieste, and Fabio Visintini, who ran the psychiatric clinic in Parma University – and they informed him about what was going on in Gorizia. So he picked up the phone and called Basaglia. The two men met for a coffee in Padua. Basaglia appeared bored but told Tommasini to come and see Gorizia for himself. Ten days later, he was there, with Visintini and a social worker (in Visintini's car). Like so many others, he was astounded by what he saw. The contrast with Colorno was stark. They were both places called 'psychiatric hospitals', but in every other way, they were completely different, at least on the surface. It was the beginning of a beautiful, strange and lifelong friendship, and a fruitful, if complicated, alliance.

From that moment on, the fates of Gorizia and Parma would be intertwined. This is Tommasini's description of that first visit, told from memory, years later:

17   Tommasini, 'Il mio rapporto con Basaglia', p. 18.
18   'Un borgo diventato mondo', preface to Rossi, *Mario Tommasini*, p. 10.

As soon as I entered the park, it was as if I was in a different world. There appeared to be no distinction between patients, nurses and doctors. There were no white coats. Everyone moved around as they pleased. Here and there were meetings where people were discussing various things. Anyone could speak, about everything. There were people there from outside taking photos. And Basaglia's office was packed – people were leaving and entering all the time – journalists, nurses, the mad . . . Professor Visintini was pointing at people and saying – who is that? I replied, Professor, I have no idea. I was struck by it all. And I started to feel at home there.

Tommasini was also surprised by the fact that Basaglia's office was a place where 'the door was always open'. He described Gorizia as 'a dream'.[19]

Visintini later wrote (in a much-quoted passage) that

I was saddened when I found out that Basaglia had left the university for a provincial hospital. But when I visited Gorizia with Mario Tommasini I changed my mind. It appeared to me that I was observing an extraordinary therapeutic discovery.[20]

In the years to come, and above all from 1965 to 1968, Tommasini would provide the kind of whole-hearted political support that was absent in Gorizia. Basaglia began to see the possibilities of change given the backing of the political world. In short, he began to look beyond Gorizia.

Tommasini was well aware of the importance of Gorizia, which he described as 'completely different to all other Italian hospitals'. One question which came to mind was a fundamental one: was it still a hospital at all? He was clear about what was needed in Colorno: 'We need to follow Gorizia!' From 1965–66 onwards, Tommasini helped Gorizia reach a wider audience. In 1966 Basaglia gave a public lecture in Parma, and in the same year groups of nurses from Parma visited Gorizia (and their debates were recorded and transcribed for posterity). In 1967 the

---

19   Ongaro, *Vita e carriera di Mario Tommasini*, p. 11.
20   Fabio Visintini, *Memorie di un cittadino psichiatra (1902–1982)*, p. 188.

first account of the Gorizian revolution was published directly by the Province of Parma, with texts based largely on a conference held in Parma. *What Is Psychiatry?* was later republished by Einaudi, on the back of the overwhelming success of *The Negated Institution*, in 1973. Parma also set up its own umbrella pressure-group and published other texts as part of debates around mental health care.

Gorizia and Parma began to work together as part of a growing movement for change. The two experiences were twinned. This dual experience was documented in *What Is Psychiatry?* and culminated in a series of semi-mythical and oft-recounted events: a photographic exhibition in 1968 (which would later become the basis for *Morire di classe*), a strike and protest where some nurses paraded through Parma in strait jackets, and the student-led occupation of the asylum in 1969.

In a sense, Parma became, quite quickly, the capital of the anti-asylum movement. While Gorizia had a fully functioning therapeutic community inside the asylum, Parma made great strides in terms of propaganda for the ideas of the movement and the creation of services and alternatives in the territory beyond the asylum. Perugia combined both these approaches in one place – but was far less well known outside Umbria. Tommasini began to make plans to bring Basaglia to Parma. He would only succeed in this dream, and then only briefly, in late 1970.

Emptying the Asylum

'I used to think that various kinds of health institutions were necessary. The mad in the madhouse, the abandoned kids in the orphanage, the old people in the old people's home. Basaglia taught me everything. I learned how to reject these kinds of solutions, and look for others. I began to understand the real aim of these institutions: to avoid dealing with more serious social problems. Health assistance of this kind was an alibi.'

Mario Tommasini

'The change was radical, and lacerating, and, for some, exciting – it was as if a new ethical commitment had overtaken everything else and required action without compromise.'

Ferrucio Giacanelli[21]

Mario Tommasini was clear. Conditions inside the asylum that was under his control were scandalous, intolerable. There were 1,000 patients in a structure that had enough room for just 350, and a mere six or seven doctors to 'cure' this mass of people. Gorizia, which he had visited, represented 'a real revolution in terms of the rules and methods which regulate the lives of the mentally ill inside psychiatric hospitals'.[22] Like Basaglia, Tommasini had strong ideas about total institutions. Asylums needed to be destroyed. Tommasini also extended this plan to other places of exclusion. He began to see the asylum as part of a network of institutions of exclusion, including orphanages, old people's homes and special schools. His plan was to close down all of these institutions.

Tommasini had already begun to implement a clear strategy for the emptying of the asylum well before Basaglia became director there, and this was a different approach to that employed by Basaglia in Gorizia. The idea was to provide alternatives to the asylum for many of the patients there – places of real, valuable work in the outside world. In part this approach was dictated by the difficulties and frustrations Tommasini had experienced in changing things inside the asylum. In some ways, Parma became the opposite example to Gorizia. Most of the change that took place in Parma was *outside* of the asylum. Inside, patients were still tied up and there was a grim atmosphere of violence and oppression. In Gorizia the technicians (the psychiatrists) and the patients were the agents of change, while in Parma the leading role was played by politicians. Technicians (in general) took a back seat, especially at first. Three hundred people had already been released in some way from Parma's asylum by the time Basaglia arrived in 1970.

But these two experiences can also be interpreted as two aspects of the same movement. For Giovanna Gallio, 'Gorizia was clearly the key

---

21   Giacanelli, 'L'ospedale psichiatrico di Colorno', p. 578.
22   *Che cos'è la psichiatria? Discussioni e saggi sulla realtà istituzionale*, eds Franco Basaglia and Amministrazione provinciale di Parma, Parma: Step, 1967, p. 64.

laboratory in terms of change "inside" the space of the asylum, while Parma set itself up as a laboratory where the "outside" was in opposition to the "inside".'[23] In this sense, Perugia was the place where both these processes took place almost at once, at the same time.

The fact that Tommasini had clear ideas about how and what to do did not leave a great deal of space for Basaglia to impose his own vision. Gallio wrote, 'When Basaglia arrived in Parma he found everything "already done", and he realized that there was nothing more to do, and he didn't do anything.'[24] Hundreds of people had already been liberated from the asylum, at a speed which was much greater than that in Gorizia in the 1960s. A second issue was the clear and constant pressure on Tommasini from within the administration, something that Basaglia had seen time and again in Gorizia. Tommasini was engaged in continual mediation and negotiation with the Communist and Socialist parties, the nurses and the institutional setting in general.

How did Tommasini release so many people from the asylum? The key plan was to provide them with work. Many of the patients had worked in some way before Tommasini came along – and this was something which was often presented as therapeutic – but this was usually exploitative and repetitive activity. Some patients even worked on the director's own land. Tommasini, in the face of political opposition and mumblings of discontent in the city itself, opened up alternative spaces across the province. One was a farm, another was a factory where patients restored road signs. A number of patients were taken out of the hospital on a daily basis to spend all day in these alternative spaces, which were often in the city of Parma itself. Most of these people would then return to the asylum at night. These patients became known as 'the commuters'. Antonio Slavich, a little cynically, argued that these patients had the best of both worlds: free food and board, and fruitful activities in the daytime. Why would they want to leave? Tommasini also took on a series of new staff in an attempt to change things from the inside.

Tommasini fought to create flats and houses where ex-patients could live, taking personal responsibility over their release. This process

---

23   'Colorno, occasiona mancata? Appunti da una ricerca su "Franco Basaglia e il corpo curante"' in Gallio, *Basaglia a Colorno*, p. 163.

24   Ibid., p. 159.

mirrored that which had taken place in Perugia and would be repeated in Trieste, Arezzo and elsewhere. In this way, Tommasini was able to reduce the numbers of those inside the asylum in Colorno as well as others in the province. It was a constant battle – against his own party, the local press, the nurses (at least some of them) and the bureaucrats. One outcome of this strategy was that a big split opened up between some of the young, idealistic people who worked with the patients in Tommasini's external laboratories and a number of the nurses who worked within the asylum itself. The latter group were extremely suspicious of Tommasini's new course, which they saw (quite rightly) as a threat to their well-established systems of power and privilege. They also complained that the patients who worked in the laboratories became difficult to control. Tommasini tried repeatedly to get rid of the ageing director of the Colorno asylum, Luigi Tomasi, who had been in charge since 1948. The two men did not even speak 'for years'.[25] Their methods were radically different. Tommasini hated everything about the asylum and wanted to close it down; Tomasi, on the other hand, was deeply, utterly rooted in the whole violent, repressive ethos of that total institution.

There was no therapeutic community in Colorno. Tommasini was using what was to become known as 'the territory', and his political power there, to empty the asylum, which remained impervious to internal change. In addition, he created alliances with the student movement (after 1968) to push for further and more radical change.

What Is Psychiatry? (1967)

What Is Psychiatry? was a book about a meeting of minds and a mismatch between Parma and Gorizia. It told the story of an encounter between an asylum just beginning to undergo change and one which had been totally transformed. To this end, What Is Psychiatry? included the transcript of a meeting between a group of nurses from Colorno and a more disparate group in Gorizia. The nurses from Colorno were amazed by

---

25 'Con il direttore non parlavo più da anni'. Tommasini, 'Il mio rapporto con Basaglia', p. 43.

what they saw in Gorizia, as one said to Basaglia: 'Your talk was interesting for both the male and female nurses – we understand what you are saying, up to a point. But you need to understand that all this is completely new for us.'[26]

On 20 December 1966, a group of staff from Colorno were plunged into the eccentric, democratic world of a Gorizian general assembly. They found themselves besieged by questions from staff and patients. It was clearly a coming together of two, separate worlds. For their part, the statements and questions from the Colorno staff betrayed their vision of the patients as dangerous. 'What do you do', they asked, 'when a patient becomes very agitated?' Colorno was still doing things in the old way, while Gorizia had become something else altogether.

The nurses from Colorno, an institution that was unreformed in almost every way, were held to account, and probably for the first time. The first questions came from the patients themselves. It must have been a bizarre experience; it was almost as if they could see into the future. *Why don't you have a bar? Why do you separate men and women? What therapy do you offer? Why do you tie people up?* The old, accepted rules which governed total institutions were being questioned, and in a radical way. The very fact of the meeting was proof of change. Things *could* change. They *had* to change. Many nurses in Colorno, however, would do all they could to resist reform.

Gorizia still had closed wards in 1966, and a significant minority of its patients were under lock and key.[27] But nobody was tied up, unlike in every other asylum in Italy. Meanwhile, this practice was absolutely routine in Colorno. As one nurse from Gorizia put it, the idea of tying up a patient at all was 'so far from our minds that we don't even consider doing it – we don't even know *how* to do it'.[28] In Colorno, *every* ward was closed. Nothing else had ever been contemplated or tried by 1966, despite Tommasini's pressure, anger and constant presence.

---

26 Bruno Popoli, cited in Franco Basaglia, ed., *Che cos'è la psichiatria?*, Baldini & Castoldi, Milan, 1997, p. 53.

27 Precise figures were given: Seventy-seven men were still in closed wards, 181 in open wards, while the figures for women were 100 and 180 respectively.

28 Baldassi in Basglia, *Che cos'è la psichiatria?*, p. 89.

The Occupation. 1969

'Those twenty-four hours inside the psychiatric hospital taught me more than all the university psychiatry courses I took.'

Itala Rossi[29]

'Colorno will be our Vietnam.'

Banner (1969)

'The best forty days of my life',

Mario Tommasini on the occupation[30]

It was a unique moment in the galaxy of protests, occupations and demonstrations that made up what is generically known as '1968'. A group of students and others occupied a total institution – a mental asylum – and remained there for some thirty-five days or so. This militant action was national news, connecting the student movement directly to issues around psychiatry and medicine more generally. Colorno therefore became the setting for one of the most extraordinary events of Italy's 1968.

Everything started with Tommasini, who gathered together a group of student leaders and others. In some versions of this story Basaglia and Slavich were also present, but this is almost certainly untrue. The plan was simple and yet carried a high level of risk. Radical students would occupy the asylum itself, in a way that was designed to bring the question of Colorno onto the front pages, and not just in Parma. Catholic students in Parma had already occupied the city's cathedral (in September 1968) and had been forcibly evicted.[31]

The story of the occupation has generally been told by those deeply involved in it – Tommasini (who organized the whole thing) and the student leaders, especially Vincenzo Tradardi – but we also have accounts

29   Itala Rossi, '"Pericolo a sé e agli altri di pubblico scandalo". L'occupazione del manicomio di Colorno. Una lotta contro la violenza istituzionalizzata' in Margherita Becchetti et al., *Parma dentro la rivolta. Tradizione e radicalità nelle lotte sociali e politiche di una città dell'Emilia rossa 1968–1969*, Edizioni Punto Rosso, Milan, 2000, p. 188.

30   Cited in ibid., p. 197.

31   See Brunella Manotti, '"La mia religione era un profumo". Parma e il dissenso cattolico. Il caso de I Protagonisti' in Becchetti et al., *Parma dentro la rivolta*, pp. 33–84.

from newspapers, historians and some nurses and doctors inside of the asylum, where the occupation had a divisive effect on those working within the institution. It is probably also true that the importance of the occupation – historically – has been exaggerated. It was not a turning-point, although Tommasini had clearly hoped that it would be. In some ways the occupation strengthened the position of those opposed to change within and outside of the hospital. Luigi Tomasi, the director, disappeared completely and waited for the students to leave: 'The director stayed at home and refused to show his face.'[32] They pointed to the occupation period as a spectre of what might happen if chaos and disorder were allowed to take over. In terms of changes to the hospital and treatment of those inside, other trends and long-term effects were far more important. Antonio Slavich and Lucio Schittar – who were sent from Gorizia to prepare the way for Basaglia himself – turned up in Colorno just as the occupation took hold.

The student occupiers arrived en masse on 2 February and took control of the entrance hall to the asylum. Initially, it was both exciting and confusing. There were constant meetings, discussions, debates and arguments. Tommasini was there the whole time.[33] Some bars were removed in a symbolic gesture. Factory workers from a nearby firm, threatened with closure, also turned up. Patients were given a voice. It was a fervent time, and further occupations, debates and exhibitions were to follow. A continual flow of students and others moved between Colorno and Parma. Some of the visitors and organizers were from Gorizia. A mass meeting was held in the asylum with students from all over the country on 9 February.

According to Tommasini:

We held meetings with the patients in the morning and organized the life of the asylum together. Those were the only thirty-five days when nobody committed suicide and nobody was beaten up. Every evening dozens of young people went out to churches, factories and to the university to debate with people.

32 Tommasini cited in Ongaro, *Vita e carriera di Mario Tommasini*, p. 35.
33 Tommasini: 'Io ero dentro 24 ore al giorno, perché questi ragazzi andavano anche protetti', Rossi, '"Pericoloso a sé e agli altri edi di pubblico scandalo"', p. 197.

However, it is not clear if the occupiers really did take over the asylum. For the most part they stayed in the entrance area. In the rest of the asylum life went on more or less in the same way, without the presence of most of the doctors and the director.

Most of the major parties seemed to back the occupation, although it caused disquiet among many, including the Communists themselves. The Socialist Party in Colorno was highly critical of the students. This was not surprising as their electoral base depended on those who worked within the asylum. But the opposition to the occupation was also strong. *La Gazzetta di Parma* ran a strong campaign against the movement. There were claims that patients had committed suicide as a result of the students' activities. The spectre painted was one of chaos, disorder, of a complete breakdown of rules and regulations. The occupation further split the nursing staff (who were already divided, broadly, between reformers and conservatives). Bruno Fontanesi wrote, 'The occupation did not unite people; it caused great divisions among the nurses.'[34]

This split was seen most dramatically on 28 February, when the students were thrown out by a group of nurses who also chucked mattresses and papers out of the window of the hospital. The students came in again by a side door, but the occupation was coming to an end. Various documents were produced, including one that was based on a form of historical research using material linked to inmates. These statements and documents were marked by a high dose of rhetoric.[35] A simplified class-based analysis of the asylum was propagated by the occupiers with slogans such as 'Only the poor are mad'. Three days before the end of the occupation (on 4 March), a group of neo-fascists turned up looking for a fight, and there was a violent stand-off.

Opinion is divided on the overall effects of the occupation. Some argue that the occupation was 'too successful' and that its high profile attracted hostility from some elements in the local Communist Party and raised expectations about change.[36] At the time, some even blamed

---

34   Cited in Rossi, '"Pericoloso a sé e agli altri edi di pubblico scandalo"', p. 194.

35   See the extracts in Giovanni Braidi and Bruno Fontanesi, *Se il barbone beve . . . cronache e documenti di una esperienza psichiatrica a Parma*, Parma: Libreria Feltrinelli di Parma, 1975, p. 42.

36   Gallio, 'Colorno, occasiona mancata?', pp. 160–1.

the occupation for the left's defeat in local council elections in both Colorno and Parma in 1970. It is not exactly clear what the occupation was intended to achieve. Was it meant to 'prepare the way' for Basaglia? Was it simply a method of publicizing the fight against the asylum? Was it an attempt to politicize patients and nurses? Some of this did happen (although the evidence is fairly thin and is usually taken directly from those involved in the occupation itself), but Basaglia would not come until Tomasi finally retired, in 1970, and the political effects of the occupation were short-lived and, in part, negative.

The Gorizians Arrive, 1969–71

As we have seen, the beginning of the occupation in Colorno coincided with the arrival of the advance-guard from Gorizia, in the form of two of Basaglia's most trusted allies from that time: Antonio Slavich and Lucio Schittar.[37] We have very little information about the experiences of Schittar and Slavich in Colorno, despite the two years they both spent there. In his book based on his time in Ferrara (after Colorno), Slavich was critical of Tommasini, whom he described as 'the explosive and somewhat erratic assessor'.[38] Slavich also mentioned the 'indescribable violence and squalor of that place [Colorno]' and characterized his time there as 'nightmarish'.[39] Slavich and the others all lived in Parma, and he recalled his drives out to Colorno in his Fiat 500 in the thick fog. According to Slavich, there were personality clashes between Basaglia and Tommasini. He described them as 'too different and similar . . . and it was certainly not a political or cultural question, but one linked to "character" and pride'.[40]

A much more nuanced and detailed account of the Basaglian period in Colorno can be found in Slavich's unpublished manuscript *All'ombra dei ciliegi giapponesi* (In the shade of the Japanese cherry trees). Slavich

---

37 Negotiations with Basaglia had been going on for some time. In 1967, Tommasini wrote to Basaglia asking him to 'send us someone you trust in advance' (Basaglia Archive).

38 Antonio Slavich, *La scopa meravigliante. Preparativi per la legge 180 a Ferrara e dintorni 1971–1978*, Rome: Riuniti, 2003, p. 32.

39 Ibid., p. 32.

40 Antonio Slavich, *All'ombra dei ciliegi giapponesi,* unpublished manuscript.

had moved rapidly to the left after 1968, taking up pro-Maoist positions. He was elected as an independent left councillor in Colorno in 1970 (and subsequently joined the Communist Party).[41]

The relative absence of Basaglia in the hospital itself caused a good deal of comment. Slavich makes an issue of this in his Ferrara book and his account of the Colorno period, comparing Basaglia's non-appearances on the wards in Colorno (outside of the regular morning staff meetings, which would begin at eight thirty, and which Basaglia chaired while he was director) with 'his continual presence in Gorizia'.[42]

Basaglia was clearly reluctant to spend time inside the asylum in Colorno. He explained his absence in two ways: first, there was a danger of being imprisoned and paralysed by rules and bureaucratic procedures. But, he added, 'there is another and deeper explanation here – the stress of visiting wards when you can't see any way of changing the obsessive reality of the hospital'.[43]

Even before his first trip to Gorizia, Tommasini had moved things along in Parma. He saw from the outset that he needed the nurses on his side, or at least some of them, and on 21 June 1965 he cut the working hours of the nurses in the asylum. Nonetheless, a conservative block of nurses (backed by some of the unions) would prove to be the biggest obstacle to change inside the hospital. Colorno's psychiatric hospital was a city within a city, and was a vast political and economic resource for that tiny town, able to support hundreds of jobs and services (and provide votes). In fact, it was more or less the only large-scale source of employment in Colorno itself. As Tommasini said, 'The hospital was the only source of work, the only "industry" in Colorno ... the town lived off the asylum.'[44]

A commission was quickly set up by Tommasini to look into the

---

41 A series of accounts claim that Basaglia arrived in Colorno and Parma in 1969. In reality, he was only based in the city (during the week) from October 1970 onwards, as Gallio's detailed work has shown. This correct chronology was also included in Venturini, *Il giardino dei gelsi*, p. 206.

42 Slavich, *La scopa meravigliante*, p. 175.

43 Cited in Gallio, 'Riunione di staff e di comunità. Organizzazione generale e rapporti di potere nell'ospedale psichiatrico (Parma 1970–1971)' in 'Basaglia a Colorno', p. 94.

44 Cited in Ongaro, *Vita e carriera di Mario Tommasini*, p. 18.

running of the asylum and its future. This 'Tommasini commission' produced its report in November 1965. Its first proposal for change was modest, a kind of Trojan horse. The idea was to break up the monolithic asylum through the creation of smaller institutions, decentralization and sectoral reform. In 1965-66 a fierce debate took place within the province around these proposals. But Tommasini's real aim was to abolish the asylum system altogether, or rather, more simply, to free those people imprisoned within a series of institutions.

Tommasini was often viewed with suspicion (and not least within his own party). He was seen as a maverick, boorish, undisciplined and without any real knowledge of what he was dealing with. A Communist comrade called him a 'bull in a china shop'.[45] Nonetheless, he won most of the arguments (often through sheer force of will) and change began to happen almost immediately, despite the continued presence of the director, who hung on grimly until his retirement. It was a gruelling and often frustrating battle against inertia and bureaucratic conservatism, and against the left itself, but Tommasini never gave up. He was stubborn, and he built alliances with other militants in the party, nurses, psychiatrists, patients, students, industrialists, intellectuals and others.

Alternative institutions were opened and others were closed down, flats were created for ex-patients and the doors of the asylum started to open to the outside world. Tommasini believed in self-management, that the patients should be given responsibility for their own lives. From 1968 on, he began to restore a publicly owned farm (in a place called Vigheffio) for some asylum inmates, including an ex-partisan he had met on his first 1965 visit. This farm would go on to become celebrated as a social experiment, and it would become an integral part of the Tommasini myth.[46] Slavich called Vigheffio 'a utopian masterpiece'.[47] This myth

---

45   My translation of the Italian phrase, 'An elephant in a glass shop', a phrase apparently uttered by the Communist Primo Savani and cited in Tommasini, 'Il mio rapporto con Basaglia', p. 29.

46   Stefania Parmeggiani, 'La Fattoria di Vigheffio trent'anni di "mattacchioni". A 30 anni dalla riforma Basaglia viaggio nella struttura tra le prime in Italia ad ospitare i pazienti psichiatrici sul territorio', *La Repubblica*, 8 May 2008. For Vigheffio see also 'Ieri alla fattoria di Vigheffio trattati problemi di psichiatria', *La Gazzetta di Parma*, 26 August 1979, and Rossi, *Mario Tommasini*, pp. 196–208.

47   Slavich, *All'ombra*, p. 11.

usually includes the visit of Enrico Berlinguer to the farm in 1980 (as a sort of official blessing for Tommasini's work) and his description of it as a place which 'prefigured the features of the kind of socialism we are hoping for'.

Basaglia, Tommasini and Colorno

'The co-habitation between two strong personalities like Tommasini and Basaglia was too tight and too close, and it ran the risk of holding both of them back.'

Vincenzo Tradardi[48]

'I was unable to forget the fact that Franco Basaglia left Parma because it was impossible there to move beyond the (good) management of the asylum, which was something that he did not have in mind.'

Franca Ongaro[49]

After Gorizia, Basaglia needed a break. He had spent seven years in endless meetings, fighting with colleagues, politicians and bureaucrats and talking to patients and nurses. It had been physically and mentally draining, and the Miklus incident had been traumatic for all concerned. Basaglia was already tired of Gorizia, however, before the incident took place. It had been a time of huge success, but also of long hours and interminable discussions. Basaglia became famous, and the offers came flooding in. But he was also dangerous and difficult to control, and many tried to block his progress.

Politicians from a new, younger generation who had taken over many provincial administrations looked to Basaglia to reform their mental health services. Publishers were queuing up to publish books on psychiatry after the success of *The Negated Institution*. Invitations came in for political meetings and conferences. Basaglia was much in demand. As he himself said, rather cynically, he had 'become an institution' himself.

---

48   Tradardi, 'La psichiatria', p. 201.
49   Ongaro, *Vita e carriera di Mario Tommasini,* p. xiv.

He was even given a route back into the university system, when Fabio Visintini found him a (temporary) post in Parma.[50]

After the obscurity of his clinical and academic work in Padua in the 1950s, Basaglia's courses were now absolutely packed. Everything had changed in his life. For the first and perhaps only time in his career, he decided to take a break and spent six months in New York with his family studying a huge psychiatric hospital, before embarking on a study-tour of Latin America. He was still employed by Gorizia, in theory, but he was rarely seen there.

In the meantime, Basaglia's future plans slowly took shape. Everything appeared to centre on Parma. His new university job was there, and there were strong political and personal connections with Tommasini, who was anxious for Basaglia to take over the asylum in Colorno.[51] As part of the preparation for this move, Basaglia had sent his faithful troops to Colorno in advance to prepare the ground for his arrival. A new équipe was being set up, without Giovanni Jervis and Letizia Comba, who were just down the road in Reggio Emilia. But something went wrong. Basaglia kept putting back his arrival and decided he would not live in the city on a permanent basis. During his weeks in Parma (in 1970–71) he lived in a hotel, and his presence in the asylum was on a much lower level than it had been in Gorizia, even as director. Franca, Enrico and Alberta settled in Venice. Basaglia, meanwhile, kept his options open. In Bologna he came fourth in a competition for a post, and his mysterious Ravenna plans came to nothing. His work in Parma was at a different level in terms of commitment. Why was this? Why did Basaglia seem to get cold feet about Colorno?

The over-concentration (in much of the literature) on the reasons for Basaglia's 'failure' in Colorno is an historical error. On the one hand, this kind of focus undermines and downplays the achievements of Mario Tommasini himself, and on the other it exaggerates the Basaglian version of the past, which follows Basaglia himself and ignores changes implemented or presided over by others (such as Giacanelli and Jervis). Nonetheless, we do need to pay some attention to Basaglia's supposed 'failure' in Parma.

---

50   For Visintini see his own account in *Memorie di un cittadino psichiatra*.
51   In the Basaglia Archive there are a number of letters from Tommasini to Basaglia.

The classic explanation for what happened in Colorno, where Basaglia, in the end, only spent six months as director (from October 1970 to August 1971), is a *political* one. Basaglia's revolution, it is argued, was held back by the conservatism and control-freakery of the Italian Communist Party (PCI). His attempts to reform the asylum were hampered at every turn by the unions and the party, leading to frustration and the search for a place where he could work with more freedom. This version is repeated in a number of classic accounts, including that by Franca Ongaro. It is almost a standard story. Take, for example, Maria Grazia Giannichedda's account of Colorno:

> At the end of 1969 [sic.] Basaglia went to Parma to become director of the Colorno asylum. He stayed there less than two years, suffering from the restriction on his practical anger against the institution . . . and of misunderstandings over his way of working, which was too Jacobin in terms of the Communist culture of the administrators in Emilia, too unpredictable, too risky, too conflictual.[52]

However, this is also quite a good description of the way that Tommasini himself worked. Ongaro's book (*Vita e carriera di Mario Tommasini, burocrate proprio scomodo narrate da lui medesimo* [The life and career of Mario Tommasini. A really unusual bureaucrat who didn't fit in. Narrated by himself], Editori Riuniti, 1991) is a mixed text, combining elements from a series of interviews and conversations with Tommasini, plus statistics and other material, and with two different prefaces by Ongaro herself. It is a combination of oral history and sociological enquiry: a kind of subjective and collective history of a period, a city and a movement. Gallio underlines the mythical qualities in this first-person account, which was then ghost-written by Ongaro (who alluded to this in the book's title). Gallio calls this account 'the transfiguration of a somewhat picaresque story of the hero, the noble and invincible knight'.[53] Tommasini (as

---

52   Maria Grazia Giannichedda, 'Introduzione' in Franca Ongaro Basaglia ed., *Franco Basaglia. L'utopia della realtà*, Turin: Einaudi, 2005, p. xxxviii. This analysis is repeated in Daniele Piccione, *Il pensiero lungo. Franco Basaglia e la Costituzione*, Merano: Edizioni Alphabeta Verlag, 2013, p. 71.

53   Gallio, 'Colorno, occasiona mancata?', p. 168.

interpreted by Franca Ongaro) conceded that Basaglia was right to leave, 'even if, for me, it was very hard to take on board the fact that in a province run by the left it was impossible to achieve the objectives we had in mind'.[54] But Franca Ongaro also has her say:

> I disagreed with his decision: I thought it was important that we succeeded in a red area, so that the message would penetrate into the Communist Party (something which didn't happen) . . . and I am still curious to know what would have happened if the PCI had taken on these new arguments at *that* time.[55]

But there are other possible reasons for the late beginning and premature end of Basaglia's time in Parma. The real explanation for the 'Colorno failure' was perhaps a different and more complicated one, or a combination of factors. By the time Basaglia finally turned up in Colorno, as we have seen, a revolution in mental health care was already in full swing there. The leader of this revolution was not Basaglia himself, but Tommasini. From 1965 onwards, Tommasini had begun to empty the asylum, and with some speed. His tactics were a mix of Basaglian ideas and the application of his own deeply practical social and cultural policies applied to mental health and other total institutions. If Basaglia was a theoretician and a practitian at the same time, Tommasini was interested above all in getting things done. He was *uninterested* in theory. Tommasini was attacking and undermining the asylum from the outside, using his power and resources to reduce the population inside the asylum. It was almost a military operation.

So Basaglia found himself in a situation where a strong, locally based personality, with very clear ideas about reform (which were similar but also different to his own ideas), had already started to empty the *manicomio*. What was left for him to do? And although Tommasini had managed to gain some political support for his policies, there was still considerable opposition in the town and within the party to what he was doing.

There may also have been personality clashes. Franco Rotelli called Tommasini and Basaglia a 'strange couple'. Basaglia was nominally in

---

54 Ongaro, *Vita e carriera di Mario Tommasini*, p. 14.
55 Ibid., pp. xiv-xv.

charge but Tommasini was ever present at meetings, including those inside the hospital itself (it is said he would go there five days a week, including Sundays). So, even though Basaglia had almost complete political support, he was by no means in total control. The PCI did not block a Basaglian revolution in Parma; they carried out their own revolution (without Basaglia, *and* with Basaglia). It might have been the case that Parma was not a big enough town for the both of them.

The two men certainly argued over a number of issues. As Tommasini later said, 'Basaglia became very intransigent, he wouldn't hold back, even in public debates', and 'I had some very serious clashes with Franco'.[56] One of the subjects that caused the most division was the fate of a new section of the asylum, which Basaglia argued should have been handed over to the university to create a kind of Centre for New Psychiatry, while Tommasini saw the area as perfect for those patients who were demanding a different kind of space within the hospital.

In hindsight, many accounts of Basaglia's time in Parma make a general point about PCI strategy with regard to mental health. Basaglian versions often dismiss the PCI or the Emilian model as ignoring the suffering going on in asylums, or as creating networks of mini-asylums and/or clientelistic networks. This version also has the added attraction of including the Jervis experiment in Reggio Emilia as a failure, or as a conservative alternative to Basaglian ideas and practice. But all this is a gross vulgarization of what happened, as well as a simplification of the position of the PCI (which was never monolithic, as Perugia showed). Finally, it tends to play down any achievements in terms of change in Parma, Perugia, Reggio and other places. History was more nuanced in the real world. It was never black and white.

Despite the fact that the two men were close friends (and would remain so), this dualism created a set of tensions. Despite full and unconditional political backing from Tommasini, Colorno was a difficult place for Basaglia to work. Change *was* taking place outside of the hospital, but the hospital itself was somewhat impermeable, even for its new director. It was exhausting. The Communist Party would take time to come round to a pro-Basaglian position, although things had begun to move by the end of the 1960s. Other offers began to seem very attractive.

---

56   Tommasini, 'Il mio rapporto con Basaglia', pp. 40–1.

Perhaps Basaglia could not face such a political battle again. He wanted to be in charge. Basaglia did take part in some set-piece moments, such as the taking down of bars on windows (which were captured by photographers for posterity), but these events were rare compared to Gorizia and to Trieste afterwards.

In 1971, Basaglia said this about his time in Parma:

> I worked for ten years in the psychiatric hospital in Gorizia, then they moved me to another hospital (Parma). When I arrived there I was greeted with another press campaign, in favour of and against me. The hospital where I worked was divided into two groups – those who were waiting for me to perform the miracle of Gorizia, and those who were waiting for something to happen so that they could say that I was wrong. Well, in six months nothing happened at all. The institutional reality remained as it was.

Thus, even while he was immersing himself in the ongoing debates in Colorno and Parma, and going back to Venice every weekend, Basaglia was plotting his next move. One of the young politicians who had become interested in the Gorizian experiment was Michele Zanetti, who was president of the Province of Trieste. Zanetti offered Basaglia carte blanche, without political interference (but *with* political support) and a hospital which had been unaffected by any kind of reform. He was also a much more reserved personality than Tommasini and would clearly play second fiddle to Basaglia. This time, Basaglia would hit the ground running. There would be no therapeutic community, no long and gradual battles to close wards, no general meetings. All of that had already been done in Gorizia. The aim in Trieste was to close the hospital itself, as quickly as possible, not make that institution more humane (and thus prolong its life).

There was to be no 'golden cage' in Trieste: the cage itself was being dismantled. In addition, times had changed: 1971 was not 1961. Basaglia now had a vast national and international movement behind him. He also had a ready-made équipe to work with, as well as alliances in other Italian cities. Young, talented and enthusiastic people began to turn up in droves, clutching battered copies of *L'istituzione negata*. A network of

Basaglian institutions was now in place. The Basaglian movement was powerful, and it would push towards what Basaglia himself had outlined in London in 1964: the destruction of the psychiatric hospital. In 1973 Basaglia would set up an umbrella organization in an attempt to co-ordinate the movement – Psichiatria Democratica.

The real story in Colorno was thus extremely complicated, and also had to do with the offer that came from Zanetti in Trieste. Trieste came with many advantages: total control and political support, an asylum untouched by change (and therefore excellent as an example to the others) and a location where the Basaglians could work a little out of the national spotlight. Basaglia himself would be in complete command.

It was perfect, and Basaglia said yes. Tommasini was offended for a time, but the pair remained lifelong and close friends. Ferruccio Giacanelli took over in Parma in February 1972, and Colorno became a symbol of change on a par with Trieste and Gorizia, thanks also to a well-known and extraordinary documentary made there later in the 1970s – *Matti da slegare*.[57] A history of the anti-asylum movement has to include Colorno and the work of Mario Tommasini.

The departure from Parma was controversial. Franca seemed against the move to Trieste, not least because she believed that it was important for Basaglians to succeed in areas that were dominated by the Communist Party. The outcome of Basaglia's time in Parma was intensely disappointing for Tommasini himself, who had tied himself to the Gorizia project from the mid-1960s onwards. Basaglia's brief appearance in Colorno (and his commuter status in the city) left Tommasini open to vicious attacks in the local press and from his political enemies (including those in his own party). Yet Basaglia defended Tommasini and the two men remained friends for the rest of their lives. The revolution in Colorno was completed by the PCI itself and another director (from Perugia).[58] But the attention of most of those who have studied the movement moved on to Trieste.

---

57   See the brilliant analysis in David Forgacs, *Italy's Margins*, pp. 243–50.

58   Giacanelli, 'L'ospedale psichiatrico di Colorno', pp. 570–83.

Two Tactics?

Two roads to deinstitutionalization now appeared to be available. The two methods were not exactly in contrast with each other, or contradictory, but they did appear to have different priorities. Slavich described them as 'antagonistic, or at the very least in competition with each other'.[59] One supposed tactic, which came straight from Gorizia, centred on the asylum itself and argued that the struggle against that particular total institution was the main priority for the movement. Another tactic, that adopted (for different reasons) in Perugia and Reggio Emilia, favoured the idea of the territory and the creation of alternative mental health services or other institutions that were closer to the people they were meant to serve.

The idea of two models emerged after 1969. On the one hand there was the territory and the creation of CIMs, something made possible by the 1968 Mariotti law. This territorial model was most successful in areas with a strong Communist Party presence: Perugia, Reggio Emilia, Parma. Some argue that this was also a model that emphasized political control and encouraged the spread of clientelism. The Basaglian model moved from Gorizia to Trieste and kept its focus on the asylum before moving out into the real world. So-called sectoral reformers steered a middle way between these two models.

In reality, the differences between these roads were not as significant as they appeared at the time. *None* of the people involved defended the old asylum system, and everyone believed that new, alternative institutions were needed. Differences were also linked to personality and political clashes, which exaggerated real contrasts at the level of practice and policy. For the supporters of the 'two models' idea, Basaglia's 'failure' in Colorno was proof of the pudding.

For Tommasini the asylum *was* central (it was almost an obsession for him), but the strength of opposition to change within that total institution meant that Tommasini decided to use the territory (the outside world) in order to close down the asylum. He attacked the asylum largely from the outside (the occupation in 1969 was another example of this tactic). Giacanelli (who took over in 1972) came directly from the

---

59   Slavich, *La scopa meravigliante*, p. 32.

Perugian revolution, which had quickly moved beyond the asylum to the territory, and so was the perfect man for this task.

Colorno and Trieste: At the Crossroads

Colorno saw the coming together of a new generation of radical and critical psychiatrists, sociologists and activists who would take the anti-asylum struggle to a new level. Many of those who would become protagonists of the Trieste experience in the 1970s passed though Colorno. Franco Rotelli was from Cassalmaggiore near Colorno and had worked in a criminal asylum in Castiglione delle Stiviere near Mantua). Peppe Dell'Acqua arrived from the south of Italy in the spring of 1971. Another key figure was Luciano Carrino, who had trained as a dentist and then worked in an asylum in France, and who introduced Dell'Acqua to Basaglia. Carrino had been in contact with Basaglia from the late 1960s onwards. The Colorno–Trieste axis also included Assunta Signorelli and Giovanni Gallio (who was from Simonetta, which is also close to Colorno).⁶⁰

Rotelli recalled the daily meetings inside the asylum:

> He would gather us together at eight in the morning in Colorno, in the midst of the fog. I remember how sleepy I was. But it was beautiful to have democracy for breakfast. It seemed to us, and it started to seem so to them as well, the mad, that . . . a day that started in such a way had some sort of meaning.⁶¹

He has since argued:

> That was a turning-point for psychiatric reform – a crossroads. I first arrived there in 1971, I met Basaglia and it was hard for me to under-stand what was happening in those strange theoretical encounters which seemed so inconclusive, and were often interrupted by the energetic Tommasini, who got the mad out of the asylum by using his

---

60   See for example the accounts of Rotelli and Dell'Acqua in Gallio, 'Basaglia a Colorno'.
61   Franco Rotelli, 'Quando c'erano i manicomi', in Gallio, 'Basaglia a Colorno', p. 10.

homemade territorial network, and ignored the furious attacks on him in the local press.[62]

Colorno thus led directly to Trieste. Basaglia was only director of the asylum there for some eleven months or so, and he was only physically in Colorno for six months on a regular basis. As we have seen, a number of Basaglians had been sent ahead from Trieste at the end of the 1960s to prepare the way for Basaglia himself, including two members of the original Gorizian equipe: Schittar and Slavich. They reported back to Basaglia on the problems they faced in Colorno on a regular basis: the bureaucracy, the power of a group of nurses inside the asylum, the fact that a plan for alternative care structures was already in place (inspired by Tommasini), the violent atmosphere within the asylum. Yet Basaglia's six months in Colorno were crucial in a number of ways. That period saw the core of the Basaglian leadership come into direct contact with the students from the 1968 movement, something that never took place in pre-1968 Gorizia (which had no university). Basaglia's university teaching in Parma also helped in this regard. By 1970, he was a celebrity, one of the stars of the movement, and his lectures were packed. Young people read *The Negated Institution* and Goffman, Laing and Cooper were almost obligatory, and some began to dedicate their lives to the fight against total institutions.

Colorno and Basaglia

According to Giovanna Gallio, Colorno was important for Basaglia in a series of ways: it showed him the possible uses of the Mariotti law, the limits of Gorizianism and the different role that could be played by meetings.[63] Colorno thus refined Basaglia's methodology, helping him understand the importance of political power, the need to use co-operatives and the advantages of simply getting the patients out of the hospital, into the real world, without years of preparation. All of these

---

62   Rotelli would also forge a strong friendship and working relationship with Tommasini; see Rossi, *Mario Tommasini*, pp. 242–56.

63   Gallio, 'Colorno, occasiona mancata?', p. 174.

ideas would come to fruition in Trieste. Colorno also helped Basaglia understand the Italian Communist Party, and how that organization could be won over for reformist ends. Tommasini had moved fast (despite local opposition). He gave patients responsibility over their own lives. He linked the fate of the asylum to that of the city, and he provided resources to facilitate change.

Tommasini's policies and the work of the équipe and the nurses inside the hospital managed to reduce the number of patients from a peak 991 in 1964, to 700 in 1970, to 558 in 1975, and to just 400 in 1978.[64] This was a huge drop, which also included numerous patients from other provincial institutions. These remaining patients were often those who were impossible to move on – the left-overs of the asylum system who would remain inside those walls until they died. As such, the asylum became a kind of glorified old people's home in its final years of life. If the aim was, first of all, to close the asylums down, Tommasini's methods seemed to be as successful as anywhere else in Italy.

Yet Tommasini is sometimes criticized for *not* having closed the asylum. Some accounts even claim that Colorno's asylum was 'undisturbed' by Tommasini's activities. But this is a ridiculous claim. There were very few places that were able to completely close their asylums before the 1990s. Moreover, Tommasini had set up a series of alternative work-based and therapeutic associations and spaces across the province, as well as making a serious attempt to see the whole network of total institutions as one big, connected problem.

A Basagliacentric account is unfair to Tommasini and to Basaglia himself. The anti-asylum movement in Italy was *polycentric*, involving a number of actors (psychiatrists, intellectuals, ordinary citizens, patients, journalists, academics, students), cities and institutions. Nobody had the right answer. Everyone made mistakes. Each area adopted its own road to reform, and success was measured in different ways. None of these roads were right or wrong. They were different, and they were all moving in the right direction.

---

64   Gallio's point that 'the push to deinstitutionalization slowed down greatly after 1971' is not backed up by the evidence we have available to us. Ibid., p. 185.

Memory and Afterlife: Colorno and Tommasini

'We have given more than 1,500 people back to the city – men, women, children.'

Mario Tommasini[65]

Colorno has a crucial importance in the memory of the anti-asylum movement. *Matti da slegare* affected people. They remembered it, it moved and inspired them, and they were struck by its extraordinary range of characters and personalities, including Tommasini. The film also circulated in France where it was praised by Félix Guattari among others.

Today, the building itself in Colorno contains no museum, and the extensive archive is almost hidden away in a cold room at the back of the complex. The ex-asylum was largely abandoned and rat-infested when I visited it in 2009. As a place, it still has some of the aura and architecture of a total institution, with its battened-down benches. These were a very familiar symbol of the old asylum system, and were the only architectural feature in the prison-like courtyards where patients spent much of their day wiling away the time. These benches and the people sitting on them were often captured by photographers in the late 1960s and early 1970s, and were also drawn by Hugo Pratt in the late 1960s – an image which was later used on posters and on the cover of *What Is Psychiatry?*

Today, as a *place*, Colorno is largely an example of forgetting. It now houses a cooks' school among other services, and the link with mental health care has been broken, apart from one surviving bar where ex-patients occasionally visit, and the memories of a dwindling group of locals. In 2008 the provincial government in Parma issued an official apology to 'all the people who were interned in Colorno's psychiatric hospital'. The press release also made reference to the 'civic miracle' which had been the Basaglia law of 1978.[66]

---

65   Venturini, *Il giardino dei gelsi*, p. 197.
66   'La Provincia chiede scusa agli internati in manicomio', *La Repubblica*, 13 May 2008.

NINETEEN

Reggio Emilia:
Out into the Territory, 1969–75

'The ill people who are outside are lying on the ground, or sitting on benches, closed like beasts inside their cage . . . You need a key to enter the ward and the first thing you see is the refectory – a place where more than 100 people live who, at certain times of the year, do not move an inch.'

Description of the San Lazzaro asylum, Reggio Emilia[1]

'The problem of psychiatry is linked to the political struggle for prevention.'

Giovanni Jervis[2]

Giovanni Jervis and Letizia Comba left Gorizia in June 1969.[3] Their destination was Reggio Emilia, one of Italy's reddest cities, where the Communist Party was an overpowering presence. The province of Reggio Emilia was divided into the historic town

---

1 Severino Delogu, 'Distruggere il S. Lazzaro', in *Reggio 15*, IV: 1 January 1969, pp. 13–14. *Reggio 15* was a radical local periodical.

2 Giovanni Jervis, 'Psichiatria e politica', *L'Unità*, 27 August 1974.

3 He was offered a role there in April 1969 by Lauro Gilli, who worked for the province. 'The administrators', he later wrote, 'were looking for someone who could organize psychiatric care services outside the hospital, through a network of clinics'. *Il buon rieducatore*, p. 27.

of Reggio itself, down in the Po Valley, and a mountainous area that was made up of a series of villages marked by high levels of poverty, emigration and depopulation. Reggio Emilia was extremely proud of the reformist institutions it had built in the post-war period. People said, for example, that the city had the best nurseries in the world. As new psychiatric ideas began to spread, this solid but radical reformist tradition was now to be applied to mental health services and mental illness itself.

The province was not lacking in psychiatric institutions. It had a huge, historic and (in psychiatric and Italian terms) 'modern' asylum – which was known as the Istituti Ospedalieri Neuropsichiatrici San Lazzaro. This massive asylum-system, however, was run in part by a religious charity (under overall state control) and not directly by the local authorities, who nonetheless paid for it. The management of San Lazzaro was extremely complicated and changed on numerous occasions through the 1940s and 1950s. The Province of Modena, whose patients also ended up in San Lazzaro, was also heavily involved. There would be a lengthy struggle over the control of mental health services and over attempts to limit the power of San Lazzaro. After a series of disputes and negotiations, rule changes in 1973 meant that the hospital board was made up of nine members – three of whom were nominated by the Province of Reggio and three by the Province of Modena.[4] Reggio's provincial services and the asylum were merged into one overall organization in 1980, the year the outer walls of the asylum were knocked down.

San Lazzaro's history was extraordinarily rich, as Christian De Vito has shown.[5] The institution also produced one of the most important academic-psychiatric periodicals in Italy – the *Rivista sperimentale di freniatria e medicina legale delle alienazioni mentali* (started in 1875). Reggio Emilia was a rarity in Italy – a city with two asylums. A criminal asylum set up in there in 1892 was the institution Giovanni Miklus was

---

4   See Simone Fari, 'Tra rinnovamento sociale ed efficienza economica. La gestione dell'assistenza psichiatrica nella Provincia di Modena dal dopoguerra alla legge 180' in Andrea Giuntini, ed., *Povere menti. La cura della malattia mentale nella provincia di Moderna fra ottocento e novecento*, Provincia di Modena: Tipografia TEM Modena, 2009, pp. 168–9.

5   Christian De Vito, *I tecnici ragazzini*, p. 71–3.

sent to in 1968 (and where he died).[6] The concentration of asylums in Emilia-Romagna was probably greater than in any other part of Italy. There were provincial asylums in Bologna and Ferrara, Imola had its own, gargantuan psychiatric hospital, and we have already discussed the one in Colorno.

San Lazzaro was a vast institution, in every sense. It cast a shadow, laid out in a vast tract of land just outside the city to the east, on the road to Modena. It was organized architecturally around a series of pavilions set in extensive parkland, close to the railway line. Each pavilion was dedicated to certain types of patients, as in many other Italian asylums at the time.

Gabriele Vezzani was a mental health service volunteer who became a young assessor for health services for the province between 1972 and 1975 (when he still had not finished his degree). This is Vezzani's analysis of the importance of San Lazzaro for the city:

> Psychiatry in Reggio meant San Lazzaro, the madhouse for the provinces of Reggio Emilia and Modena, which had been in place since the eighteenth century and which held large numbers of people and gave work to more than 2,000 people. It was a city within the city, the most important factory in Reggio.[7]

As with Colorno, Reggio's asylum was a large-scale institution with high costs and a magnet for services of all kinds. It was also an important source of clientelism and patronage, a place where political resources could be distributed and exchanged for votes or influence.

Vezzani has also given us this description of Giovanni Jervis in 1969:

> He was tall, shambling, awkward, with heavy glasses. He was quick to form a very good relationship with us. He was curious to get to know Reggio and to set up links, and I was tired and lacking in motivation

---

6   Presumably. There is no public information available on this.

7   Gabriele Vezzani, 'Leggevamo Gramsci e Marcuse', *Psicoterapia e Scienze Umane* XLIV: 3, 2010, p. 384.

thanks to the climate in the city, and I was confused about my future, annoyed by the formally democratic air in Reggio, which was, in reality, closed to new ideas and diffident towards 'outsiders'.[8]

Jervis and family set up home in Reggio, and the first provincial mental health centre was also founded in the city itself.

Jervis's mandate was at the same time complicated and straightforward. He would not have to reform or work within the asylum itself. The aim, instead, was to set up, develop and co-ordinate a string of mental health centres across the province using, in part, the powers allowed by the 1968 Mariotti law. The sphere of activity would be the territory, and not the total institution. Jervis had cut his teeth as a radical psychiatrist within the asylum in Gorizia. In Reggio, he would be operating in the cities, towns and villages of the entire province, outside of the hospital setting. There would be no therapeutic community, no internal battles over tying up patients or long debates over the opening of ward doors. None of this was under Jervis's control. He was free to explore alternative methods of care and to set up new institutions that, it was hoped, would penetrate deep into society and the family itself. Yet, the asylum's role was still important – if not central. San Lazzaro and its patients could not be ignored altogether. After 1969, Jervis was often criticized for discounting or even supporting the asylum system. This debate was over strategy, but it also took on a moral tone. Could change occur if the asylum remained in place?

The legacy and history of this period in Reggio Emilia has been caught up within a series of bitter personal conflicts and sectarian accounts that have obscured the real force of what happened in the late 1960s and 1970s. The analysis is often reduced to a personal dispute – as in 'Jervis against Basaglia'. Research on the psychiatric health reforms in Reggio Emilia in the 1960s and 1970s has suffered from this split between Jervis and Basaglia, and the closures and partisanship that have followed. The so-called personal battle between the two men has also been used as an excuse to simply ignore the Reggio experience.[9] Christian De Vito's

---

8   Ibid., p. 386.
9   As with Perugia, Reggio is often reduced to a footnote or excluded altogether.

recent study is by far the most detailed and far-ranging study that we have (although most of it remains unpublished).[10] The other problem (which applies to many other cities and towns) is that so many of the accounts we have come from the protagonists. A plurality of voices and texts have appeared, but few of them are from the outside.

The Jervis-Basaglia dichotomy makes little sense at all *now*, from our place in time, even if this supposed personal rivalry and its background have continued to occupy minds and print space ever since the mid-1970s. It is surely time to move beyond this reductive version of events, with the ritualistic and banal citing of selected quotes from certain texts.[11]

There were certainly divisions between the two wings of the movement at the time, and these conflicts were to hamper the progress of Psichiatria Democratica in the 1970s. A real basis for these bitter disputes, however, is difficult to detect from a historical point of view. *The work in Reggio Emilia was pushing in the same direction as that in Parma and later Trieste.* These experiences were part of the same movement, but, of course, there were bitter arguments over strategy and priorities (some of which were dictated by context).

The acrimonious debates at the time thus seem overblown to us now. To the historian, it appears that everyone was working in the same direction, and 'new psychiatrists' moved fairly easily between Reggio and other Basaglian places of change. Yet public pronouncements and debates often make it seem as if these experiences were on different sides of the barricades. Decentralized services were similar in Reggio, Parma, Trieste, Perugia and Arezzo, with important and interesting theoretical and practical distinctions. In addition, the aim of these models was identical: the closure of asylums and a new understanding of mental health. In short, the critical literature has made far too much of the differences between Reggio and elsewhere.

---

10   However, see Christian De Vito, 'Tecnici e intellettuali dei "saperi speciali" nei movimenti degli anni Settanta a Reggio Emilia', in Luca Baldissara, ed., *Tempi di conflitti, tempi di crisi. Contesti e pratiche, del conflitto sociale a Reggio Emilia nei "lunghi anni Settanta"*, Naples: L'ancora del Mediterraneo, 2008, pp. 387–426.

11   The two texts usually cited here are *Il buon rieducatore* and *La nave che affonda*.

The Territory and the Asylum in Reggio Emilia

'We wanted to see if it was possible to carry out psychiatric work in neighbourhoods, villages, hospitals, amongst the people, in the heart of the social fabric, and no longer at the asylum itself.'

Giovanni Jervis[12]

'For most of the 1970s, Jervis dedicated himself to a vast work of institutional construction. While the struggle against the violence of the asylum regime went on, he was able to experiment in the Province of Reggio Emilia with the first ordered and coherent networks of mental health centres.'

Stefano Mistura[13]

'Reggio Emilia, via Racchetta 5: Centre of Mental Hygiene of the Provincial Administration. This is the counter-attraction to San Lazzaro, the city's asylum. Those working in the centre (psychiatrists, doctors, nurses, social workers, psychologists, sociologists) are not all here. Their work takes place elsewhere, in the cities or in the villages of the Apennines, right in the heart of families themselves, in factories, in schools, in places where people meet. Here there are no beds or patients. Mental illness is taken on in a new way.'[14]

In order to understand what happened in Reggio from 1969 onwards, let us start with Jervis's own semi-autobiographical account, from *Il buon rieducatore* (1977). 'The experience of the Centres for Mental Hygiene in Reggio Emilia', he wrote, 'absorbed all my energies for a number of years'.[15] Jervis argued that the reality of mental illness he observed in Reggio led him to re-evaluate some of the ideas he had followed in Gorizia. 'I found', he added, 'that I had to quickly overcome some of

---

12   Jervis, *Il buon rieducatore*, p. 11.

13   Stefano Mistura, 'Giovanni Jervis, La forza di passioni condivise', *Il Manifesto*, 5 August 2009. Of course, Perugia had also started to set up centres around the same time.

14   Domenico Commisso, 'Un modo nuovo per affrontare e curare le malattie mentali', *L'Unità*, 31 January 1972.

15   Jervis, *Il buon rieducatore*, p. 28.

the ideological ghettoization which had been part of the Gorizian experience'.[16] In Reggio, Jervis was working in the 'ordinary, everyday' reality
of the world, in an area dominated by the Communist Party as well as
other institutions, which he listed: 'families, hospitals, doctors associations, the right-wing press who smeared us, the provincial administration,
our own organization'.[17] Psychiatry was out on the streets: 'The workplace
was to be found in houses, fields, bars, neighbourhoods.'[18] Some of this
was romanticized. These psychiatrists and volunteers often saw themselves as part of an idealized, Maoist, 'cultural revolution' – as
metaphorically shoeless. Jervis argues that this work was more difficult
than that within the asylum. It was more risky, more tiring, more open-
ended. It begged a number of questions, and not least this fundamental
one: 'How far could "alternative" psychiatry go, through working in
society itself?'[19]

In 1969–70 Jervis set up his own équipe with a number of activists,
some of whom had been in contact with Gorizia and Basaglia.[20] Many
of these young students and doctors were from the extra-parliamentary
left, but few were Communists (in the sense of party members). Hardly
any were from Reggio. These people were outsiders. The work looked to
penetrate into a rapidly changing peasant society, as well as that of the
local working class. De Vito argues that the activists who worked with
Jervis and others in the late 1960s and early 1970s were political militants
who were part of the movement.[21] Medical competence or qualifications
were not seen as important or even necessary. This type of approach was
similar to that in Trieste, Arezzo and elsewhere in the 1970s.

Jervis argues that the activities of the équipe (and later a group of

16   Ibid., p. 29.
17   Ibid.
18   Ibid.
19   Ibid.
20   This was the case, for example, with Stefano Mistura. According to Vezzani, Jervis chose
his collaborators very carefully, in particular the nursing staff: 'Jervis did not want professional
nurses. He chose, from the beginning, people from other realms of life – workers, artisans,
peasants – people who were politicized, but not too politicized. He didn't want to deal with
those who were "affected" with institutionalization.' Vezzani, 'Leggevamo Gramsci e Marcuse',
p. 388. This choice was probably influenced by the difficult relationship with the nurses (or
some of them) in Gorizia.
21   De Vito, *I tecnici ragazzini*.

équipes) made the whole idea of the negation of the role of the technician (the psychiatrist, in his case) unsustainable. This, of course, was part of the ideology that emerged from Gorizia, not least in *L'istituzione negata*. For Jervis, it was useless to pretend otherwise. His position was clear: he worked for the state. But his work and that of his colleagues could still expose 'margins of dissent and dysfunctionality in the system'.[22]

It became clear to Jervis that Reggio Emilia was a complicated and contradictory place, beyond its image as a red city. Social structures (such as schools) often turned out to be ultra-conservative, and the family played a key and suffocating role in society. He also came across discrimination against the handicapped and the mentally ill. Reggio Emilia was very left-wing, but attitudes towards 'others' (of all kinds) were not particularly tolerant. Jervis, however, was given strong political backing for a limited time, and his experimental work was tolerated and encouraged.

While Jervis was in charge of the CIM system (known as the *Servizio psichiatrico provinciale* or SPP), Reggio did not produce any literature on a par with *L'istituzione negata*. In the late 1960s and early 1970s, Jervis was marginalized and then effectively sacked by Einaudi, although he put a gloss on this when he wrote that 'as soon as I earned enough elsewhere I resigned as a consultant with Einaudi'.[23] Jervis (as author) moved to Feltrinelli (where Basaglia had already discussed the possible publication of *L'istituzione negata* with Enrico Fillipini). Jervis then published two significant texts with the Milanese publishing house, both of which were directly inspired by his time in Reggio: the *Manuale critico* (1975) and *Il buon rieducatore* (1977). These two volumes both appeared after Jervis had left Reggio (in 1975) to become a university lecturer in Rome.

The Reggio experience *was* influential but always (and increasingly) played second fiddle to the Basaglians, especially once Trieste was up and running. There was also a sense that people (activists, supporters, researchers) had to choose *between* Basaglia and Jervis. Things became quite tribal, and media attention followed Basaglia far more than it did Jervis. In addition, the work of Jervis and the SPP in Reggio was far less

---

22   Jervis, *Il buon rieducatore*, p. 30.
23   Ibid., p. 35.

media-friendly than that in Trieste, Arezzo or Gorizia. Individual work with patients in the family setting did not lend itself to the kind of reportage that exalted the liberation of the mad within asylums themselves. The work in Reggio was far more slippery, less visual, less spectacular. Perhaps it was all too dry to be taken seriously, too real, too interested in concrete results. It was difficult to capture or make interesting, the painstaking work which was carried out with families and in small remote towns.

Reggio produced few slogans. The *operatori* there simply got on with what they wanted to do. It was also more difficult to measure the success or otherwise of the Reggio experiment, which was working to achieve long-term results. In Trieste, it was clear what was happening, as the asylum itself was closed down from the inside. Reggio was more wide-ranging, less easy to photograph or film, more complicated to report on.

Reggio's mental health services after 1969 were interested in preventing mental illness completely (a highly ambitious aim). The idea was to stop people from ending up in the asylum (or returning there once they had left). De Vito wrote: 'In Reggio the aim was to build a filter in front of the asylum's doors, in order to "drain" it.'[24] The services co-ordinated by Jervis worked closely with those who had been released from the psychiatric hospital, their families and their local communities. The centres took on a series of individual cases, which were documented and discussed at length. Psychiatrists and others attempted to link up with the everyday lives of those they were treating. As Jervis wrote, the idea was that 'daily life, private life, emotional life – these are the places where capitalism exercises its power in the most effective ways'.[25]

The technicians thus went out to the people, working within their own living environments. They saw patients in their homes, got to know them (and where they lived, and their families), ate and drank with them. A relationship was formed. It was similar (if not identical) to the strategy adopted in Gorizia, but (crucially) it was all taking place outside of a total institution, in the real world.

We should not be fooled into believing that any of this was easy, or

---

24   De Vito, *I tecnici ragazzini*, p. 156.
25   Giovanni Jervis, *Manuale critico di psichiatria*, 10th ed., Milan: Feltrinelli, 1980 (1975), p. 15.

that these relationships were idyllic and unproblematic. Dogmatic points of view were common. *Everything* (a speech, a text, the whole approach) was highly politicized and often rhetorical. As Vezzani wrote,

> The ideological dimension was still very strong, there were often barriers which held back our work and could create tension with families and communities, and there was not always a sense that you needed to act with care and tact, or the acceptance that time was required for things to work.[26]

This work was intensely experimental. There were few models available. It was new and exciting but also extremely difficult and open-ended. As Yvonne Bonner, a psychologist who was also part of the group, put it: 'Working on the ground meant that we were far from the coercive nature and security of an institution and in a flexible situation which could move in any number of directions.'[27] Yet these *operatori* had the strength of a movement behind them, as well as other institutions and the (at times) local Communist Party. Bonner argued, 'We felt to be part of a movement, strengthened by our rejection of the past and by the freedom of action which opened up gaps in the system.'[28]

The SPP services were aiming to prevent, 'care for and socially rehabilitate the mentally ill through non-centralized structures, linked to society and which in this way tend to avoid the separation of the patient from their normal living environment, and thus avoid their institutionalization'.[29] Often, for example, families were reluctant to accept patients back from the asylum. This was a key problem for the SPP *operatori*, who spent time trying to convince families to take back their relatives, and offered support for the return of patients to the community. This strategy was backed by attempts to document mental illness and its

---

26 Vezzani, 'Leggevamo Gramsci e Marcuse', p. 389.

27 Giorgio Bartolomei and Ulrich Wienand, *Il mal di testa. Illusioni e realtà dei giovani psicologia in Italia,* Milan: Feltrinelli, 1979, p. 14 (Bonner's contribution can be found on pp. 139–51).

28 Bonner in ibid., p. 142.

29 Giovanni Jervis, ed., *L'Amministrazione Provinciale e l'assistenza psichiatrica esterna. Relazione sull'assistenza individuale erogata nei primi mesi di funzionamento del Centro di Igiene Mentale,* Reggio Emilia: n. p., 1970.

context. A series of sociological research projects were carried out. Jervis and his équipe were fond of inquests (a strategy much in vogue at the time, as was Mao's maxim 'If you don't carry out research, you have no right to speak'). Some of this was a form of ethno-psychiatry, looking, for example, at links between emigration and mental illness, or repetitive factory work and neuroses of various kinds.[30]

Operatori also worked in factories and other places of production. Part of their brief was to carry out research into the relationship of work, society, family and mental illness. The idea was – always – to put mental illness into context. They were attempting to understand what they saw as the multiple and complicated causes of mental illness.

Jervis's work outside of the asylum setting was often portrayed as a betrayal of Gorizian orthodoxy. But in Reggio Emilia there was little possibility of change on the inside of the psychiatric hospital (or at least not directly). Jervis had no choice but to concentrate on the territory, and he was aware of this when he accepted the post. His mission was clear, and he was given considerable resources with which to work. By 1972 there were nearly forty people working within the SPP system in Reggio. When Jervis started his work he had been one of a group of five.[31]

Reggio Emilia was similar in its aims and strategies to Perugia, with the important caveat that the asylum in the Emilian city was still operational in the 1960s and 1970s, and beyond. This does not mean, however, that the asylum in Reggio was unaffected or undisturbed by the work of Jervis and his team (as is often claimed).[32] In the late 1960s and early 1970s San Lazzaro was the focus of constant protests and pressure from the outside (and to some extent from the inside). The attention paid to the asylum in Reggio was also developed through a series of extraordinary public events that became a cause célèbre for the radical psychiatry movement in Italy – the so-called *calate* (descents). During the *calate*, groups of people turned up at the asylum from

---

30   See for example Giovanni Jervis, 'Condizione operaia e nevrosi', *Inchiesta* III: 10, April–June 1973, pp. 5–18.

31   Two doctors (Jervis and Adelmo Sichel), Letizia Comba, a social worker and a nurse.

32   This accusation is simply wrong, but is frequently made; for a critique of this critique see Giuseppe Micheli, *Il vento in faccia. Storie passate e sfide presenti di una psichiatria senza manicomio*, Milan: Francoangeli, 2013, p. 26.

villages and towns of the province and demanded they be allowed to inspect the institution. They wanted to visit their relatives and friends inside and see for themselves how these people were being looked after. This was a radical, public and full-frontal political attack on the asylum from the outside, and it has remained in the memory as a semi-mythical set of events ever since. Beyond the *calate*, there were numerous attempts to document how San Lazzaro worked, or to denounce the workings of the total institution. On one occasion, for example, a group of militants slipped into the asylum (via a back fence) and took photos, which they published in the periodical *Reggio 15*. This event led to police charges (as did the *calate*). Far from being forgotten or undisturbed, San Lazzaro was very much at the centre of the movement's strategy in Reggio (before and after the arrival of Jervis). *Reggio 15* continued to publish attacks on the asylum system (and San Lazzaro in particular) as well as other pieces linked to mental health and the services being set up by the province. A Gruppo di Studio sulle Istituzione Psichiatriche was also quite active before Jervis's arrival in Reggio. This group compared the asylum to a concentration camp (January 1969). De Vito wrote:

> As in other places in Italy, the distance between the *actual workings* and the *appearance* of that institution [San Lazzaro] was revealed through an intense work of 'counter-information' and investigation which Reggio Emilia found space on the pages of the journal *Reggio 15*.[33]

There were evident contradictions, however, in the role of the Communist Party and its attitude towards large-scale public institutions. On the one hand, the PCI was influenced by anti-institutional ideas and in favour of reform and decentralization (and participation). But on the other hand, the party naturally favoured big state organizations – both ideologically (as part of the socialist state in some way) and as transmission belts for the distribution of jobs and resources. These two attitudes lived together in Reggio, and they were often in conflict with each other.

---

33   Gruppo di Studio sulle Istituzione Psichiatriche, 'Manicomio come lager', *Reggio 15*, 4: 1, January 1969, pp. 15–16. See also Severino Delogu, 'Distruggere il S. Lazzaro', *Reggio 15*, 4; 1, pp. 13-14.

Jervis and his group were given solid backing, but they were also viewed with suspicion.

In the early 1970s two tendencies emerged from within the SPP in Reggio. Put very simply, those linked to Jervis took up a more conservative and realist set of positions, based around careful work with individual patients but also constant negotiation with the Communist Party, the unions and other institutions. The other group was led by a young psychiatrist called Giorgio Antonucci and adopted an anti-psychiatric stance. It was this position that inspired the *calate*. In the end, the clash between these two positions would lead to a crisis in the provincial psychiatric services in Reggio. The anti-psychiatrists were eventually defeated, but the memory of what they had achieved lived on in various accounts. Both positions adopted Marxist language to explain mental illness (often in a fairly crude way) and described the asylum system in ways similar to that used by the Basaglians.

The Calate

'When they came back they told terrible stories: of children who were tied up, of dirt, all kinds of violence. Had we fought in the Resistance for this? No. We hadn't fought for this! Those from San Lazzaro wanted us to believe what they said and it was necessary to use force to open some of the doors. In San Lazzaro, the only mentality which ran that place was that of marginality and segregation.'

Giorgio Antonucci[34]

'We went to see the patients in faraway hills on the crests of mountains, where some raised sheep. The mayors of these towns, some of whom were left-wing, but most of whom were Catholics, were aware of the question of helping those in the asylum return home.'

Gabriele Vezzani[35]

---

34   Giorgio Antonucci, *Il pregiudizio psichiatrico,* Eléuthera, 1999, eleuthera.it.

35   Vezzani, 'Leggevamo Gramsci e Marcuse', p. 389. Vezzani also wrote that 'Our objective was to make this situation known to the public, to document it', ibid., p. 384.

The Province of Reggio saw a direct and radical attack on the asylum from the outside. On a number of occasions, hundreds of people descended (usually from the mountain areas of the province) on San Lazzaro. They were angry and worried. They wanted to see their friends, family members and neighbours and check on the conditions in which they were living. Some of these people were psychiatrists, but most of them were ordinary citizens (from the most deprived parts of the province, and strong links were made between the poverty of these mountain areas and the relatively high numbers of their citizens in the asylum). These *calate* were inspired and organized by radical psychiatrists working for the SPP, most notably Antonucci, who had worked in Gorizia and had been in Cividale with Cotti. The PCI and Jervis were said to have helped with (or oversaw) the organization of the first *calate*. It is doubtful whether the *calate* changed anything in real terms (and they may have made things worse), but they were a spectacular moment of protest – and they terrified the authorities in charge of the asylum.

The first and most celebrated of the *calate* took place on 23 November 1970.[36] About forty people from the Comune di Ramiseto[37] descended on San Lazzaro in a hired coach. Ramiseto is a small mountain town some fifty-six kilometres from Reggio Emilia. In 1971, about 2,200 people lived in the whole area, in a series of scattered villages and neighbourhoods. The delegation included the mayor of Ramiseto and was preceded by a series of public meetings around issues linked to mental health organized by the local CIM. The 'descent' was an attempt to carry out 'direct control by the population in terms of the health and sanitary structures'.[38] On this first visit, the delegation took the director of the asylum by surprise, and they were allowed in. They were shaken by what they saw.

Worst of all, perhaps, was the children's ward. Here, small children were found tied to beds and high chairs. One of the participants, Piero Colacicchi, took a photo in secret. In it, a child is lying on a bed, tied up. It was a shocking state of affairs, indefensible in any civilized country. Even today, the photo is upsetting. The asylum had been unmasked,

---

36   See Collettivo di Reggio Emilia, 'Un'esperienza di intervento popolare nelle istituzioni', *Inchiesta* I: 2, 1971, pp. 61–5.

37   This version is a fiercely partisan, heroic and epic account of the *calate*.

38   Cited De Vito, *I tecnici ragazzini*, p. 94.

deep in the heart of Communist Reggio Emilia. Colacicchi later described this photo as 'dark and not well framed' but also 'important . . . I took it in the De Sanctis ward'.[39]

Other *calate* followed,[40] most of which were organized with the active participation of the psychiatrists and others in the new decentralized mental health centres. One of the demands made, for example, was that the asylum should be open to visitors without restrictions. There was also considerable protest over the costs of San Lazzaro. Some argued that it would have been cheaper to put each and every one of the patients in Reggio's best hotel. The asylum had some 1,300 patients and 1,000 employees. Years earlier, in 1965, provincial politicians had complained about the way that their role was simply that of being asked to pay for the asylum. In March 1971 there was a *calate* from Castelnovo ne' Monti, another mountain town where Antonucci ran the mental health centre. This descent involved some 150 people. A group of Ramiseto's citizens descended again in March. A locally elected people's committee in Ramiseto made this statement, which stands as a kind of manifesto for the Reggio movement:

> The committee, after having seen that the problem of psychiatry has precise class origins, linked to economic backwardness, social inequality, exploitation – and which need to be resolved through reforms, increased social justice and new health policies which are linked above all to prevention and to the participation of citizens and the contribution of public bodies[41]

San Lazzaro was described as 'a class-based instrument which has the precise task of punishing those citizens who do not have the strength to support the weight of injustice, backwardness and exploitation'.[42]

---

39   Quoted in Centro di Relazioni Umane, 'Le visite popolare al manicomio San Lazzaro di Reggio Emilia', centro-relazioni-umane.antipsichiatria-bologna.net. In 1953 a section for children 'of low intelligence' (aged between five and twelve) had been set up. It was closed in 1975.

40   26 November 1970 from Ramiseto, 11 December 1970 from Carpineti, 30 January 1971 from Montecchio.

41   Collettivo di Reggio Emilia, 'Un'esperienza di intervento popolare nelle istituzioni', p. 65.

42   Ibid.

The asylum director, Piero Benassi, who had taken over in 1964, soon lost patience with the *calate*. He called in the authorities. In March and April 1971, seventeen people were asked to nominate a lawyer, including the mayor of Castelnovo, the director of the CIM, students, administrators, doctors, nurses and social workers. The charge was from Article 340 of the Penal Code: 'disruption of a public service'. The authorities claimed that the leaders of the *calate* were provocative and had used violent, 'defamatory' language.

> They incited and harangued the poor and unprepared visitors against the hospital, criticizing openly the assistants and handing out advice and arrogant opinions about the technical behaviour of those looking after the patients . . . they were clearly acting in a denigratory and defamatory way towards the hospital.[43]

A trial was eventually held. The accused enjoyed the support of the mayor of Reggio and the provincial administration, but other parties and local conservatives went on the attack, accusing them of invading the asylum. Many of those who had taken part gave their own names to the authorities voluntarily, declaring that they were also (and all) collectively responsible for what had happened.[44]

Benassi was director of Reggio's psychiatric hospital for thirty years, and a prominent member of Italy's psychiatric hierarchy. He published numerous articles and a book about his experience in Reggio and the end of the entire asylum system. Looking back, Benassi had very little to say about Jervis and the SPP, and he ignored the *calate* completely. For Benassi, the 'total separation' between the province and the *manicomio* was 'damaging to the patients'. He also accused Jervis of an ideological approach to mental health care. Benassi's book (and its whole outlook) is the polar opposite of that of the radical psychiatrists. It is technical, packed with references, and highly institutional.[45] He described the case of Reggio Emilia in the 1970–78 period as a

---

43   De Vito, *I tecnici ragazzini.*
44   Ibid., p. 94.
45   Piero Benassi, *La fine dell'era manicomiale. Verso una nuova era psichiatrica*, Rimini: Guaraldi, 1993.

dichotomy . . . in which the psychiatric activity inside the walls of the hospital and that of the territorial services . . . were in complete ideo-logical opposition on a practical and operational level – both in general terms and when specific cases needed to be analysed.[46]

These 'two institutions' were 'independent of each other' (up to 1980) and 'represented two centres of activity with completely different ideo-logically opposed sources of power, and as such they damaged the therapeutic and rehabilitative plans for many patients'.[47]

What were the long-term effects of the *calate*? Like the occupation in Colorno in 1969, the end result may well have been counter-productive, reinforcing the power of the institution against change (and underlining a fear of the movement). Were the *calate* a triumph of form over content, an example of spectacle taking the place of serious work and the building of new institutions to deal with mental illness? San Lazzaro survived until the 1990s, and the *calate* did little to bring about its end. They remain as a heroic chapter in the struggle against the asylum system, a kind of Jacobin moment. In reality, it seems, what lasted over time were the centres, pro-cedures and practices created by the others.

The *calate* underlined the presence of two schools of thought within Reggio Emilia among the decentralized équipes built up by Jervis. It was Jervis who invited Antonucci to work with him in Reggio, but the alliance between the two men was short-lived. It was a time of intense debate – 'there were often furious discussions about the idea of mental illness'.[48]

In 1970 Antonucci was a key figure in the CIM in the mountain town of Castelnovo ne' Monti. According to his own account (which is more or less the only one we have), 'Our activity was aimed at avoiding the commitment of people to the asylum.' The approach to mental illness was multifaceted, taking in social issues, the family, the cultural context and politics. Antonucci argues that differences quickly emerged between

---

46   Ibid., p. 96 (see also p. 24). For Benassi the CIM set up in 1969–70 were in 'total disagreement' with the authorities running the asylum and were 'totally detached from the institutional activities of the hospital' (p. 15). Benassi describes the reforms carried out inside the asylum from the 1960s onwards on pp. 13–33. He only cites Jervis once by name, on p. 43.

47   Ibid., p. 15.

48   Antonucci, *Il pregiudizio psichiatrico*.

his own policies and those adopted by Jervis, who, he said, had a psychiatric mindset that 'distinguished between "the most serious cases" who were to be interned and those "less serious and less dangerous" who were to be helped at home'.[49] For Antonucci, his approach was very different:

> I thought of things in terms of the conflict between the individual and society, and of the right of the individual to be respected in terms of their freedom in a society which is aiming to become more open and more tolerant.

Antonucci was working with rigid principles; Jervis with reality, on a case-by-case basis. De Vito sees Antonucci's strategy as an extension of the asylum meetings held in Gorizia: 'With the famous "descents" to San Lazzaro they affirmed in a clear and explicit way the principle of popular control over the work of the technicians, which is still a key issue today.'[50] Antonucci's anti-psychiatric outlook was not simply ideological – it looked to mobilize support and protest.

The idea of the *calate*, in Antonucci's account, came from the people themselves. His conclusions were radical:

> We need to avoid people being institutionalized with political acts of prevention. People become desperate and are institutionalized because of factors which are easy to identify and are therefore avoidable. It is not enough to destroy a prison or an asylum – we need to stop the system violating the liberty of individuals and institutionalizing them. We need to struggle for a society which guarantees rights, for radical reform which helps the working class. In this way all the asylums like San Lazzaro will exhaust themselves on their own.

Jervis would have seen such a statement as essentially utopian. Both men were charismatic leaders, but Jervis would win the battle.

---

49   Antonucci's version of events has appeared in various publications over the years, and is widely available online in a series of versions (*Il pregiudizio psichiatrico*). Jervis's version can be found in *Il buon rieducatore*, p. 36.

50   De Vito, *I tecnici ragazzini*, p. 157.

The challenge to Jervis from within the SPP ended when Antonucci was sacked, after allegedly refusing to take part in a *concorso* (a public competition) in 1972. He went on to document the role played by Jervis (or his own version of that role) in numerous publications that have appeared since. Antonucci placed Jervis and the PCI in the same conservative camp, as proponents of psychiatric orthodoxy. This is a simplification. The PCI was not monolithic, and Jervis was never a slavish follower of the party line (nor was he ever a member of the Communist Party). The key questions remained the same: What was mental illness? Who had the right to diagnose and treat this illness? What was the precise role (if any) that was to be played by technicians and institutions? It appears that the Antonucci outlook was popular at the time and constituted a threat to Jervis's leadership. As Vezzani later wrote, Antonucci had 'an incredible following among the specialists in the field and the population as a whole'.[51]

The Crisis and the End of the 'Golden Age' in Reggio Emilia, 1972

'The Centre for Mental Hygiene was divided into two tendencies in terms of its work. The majority of doctors (including Jervis) and some nurses – in a contradictory way – did not deny that psychiatrists had a professional role to play but rejected the repressive aspects of that role and thus they separated the good parts (therapeutic work, neutral technical aspects) from the bad ones (the use of power). The other tendency which included most of the nurses and just a couple of doctors (including myself) tried to overcome the split between employees and non-employees, and between the technicals and the incompetent – aimed to destroy psychiatry as a separate technique through the involvement of the population as a whole.'

Giorgio Antonucci

In 1972, Giovanni Jervis's world appeared to be falling apart. He wrote, looking back: 'It was, at the same time, a political, personal and

---

51   Vezzani, 'Leggevamo Gramsci e Marcuse', p. 387.

professional crisis.'[52] On return from a study-tour to China in 1971 (Letizia Comba was also on the trip) he found the équipe system to be riven by serious divisions and disputes. His leadership was being challenged from below. Jervis was also faced by the breakdown of his marriage.[53] Finally, he saw how things were changing politically: 'It wasn't only '68 which was over, but also the dream of a cultural alternative.'[54]

This crisis was resolved in three ways: first with the defeat of the left/anti-psychiatric wing of the Reggio movement, second with the end of the Jervis-Comba relationship/partnership and finally with the writing of two texts for Feltrinelli: the *Manuale critico della psichiatria* (1975) and *Il buon rieducatore* (1977), which would become the new bibles for many radical psychiatrists from the mid-1970s onwards. The *Manuale critico*, in particular, was based on a series of lectures and seminars that Jervis gave in Reggio Emilia. It was a book he had been planning since the late 1960s and which had been proposed to Einaudi on more than one occasion. The chapters in *Il buon rieducatore* were also in part inspired by Jervis's time in Reggio, both in terms of the autobiographical essay which opens the book and the discussions of anti-psychiatry which are included in the collection.

Conclusion: Analysing Reggio Emilia

De Vito has argued that the Reggio experiments were innovative and interesting:

> The approach of the Reggio administration . . . aimed to move the question of mental illness from a purely psychiatric terrain to a socio-historical level, and tried to bring together a modern and

---

52 Jervis, *Il buon rieducatore*, p. 35. Jervis's comments here seem prescient.

53 Vezzani is one of the few commentators from the time who discusses on Comba and her position vis-à-vis Jervis: 'I became a friend of Gionni, I would go to his house where he lived with his wife at the time, the psychologist Letizia Comba, who had also worked in Gorizia and had the difficult task of being the wife of an intellectual of that type and – at the same time – trying to preserve her own identity.' 'Leggevamo Gramsci e Marcuse', p. 387 .

54 Jervis, *Il buon rieducatore*, p. 41.

specialized psychiatric hospital system with work on the ground which
was aimed at prevention and social integration.[55]

Did this strategy work? The number of patients held within San Lazzaro
did begin to decline. San Lazzaro contained nearly 1,900 internees in 1968
(though figures tend to vary). By 1971 this number had fallen to around
1,500.[56] On the surface, it appeared as if the Jervisian institutions were
having an effect.[57] Prevention was combined with the reintegration of
those who were released. This was the prototype of a community-based
care system. The revolving-doors experience of so many patients in the
asylum system was being broken at the source. But the numbers alone do
not tell the whole story, and reformist changes within San Lazzaro itself
were also part of the explanation for this fall in patient numbers. In the
1970s the political balance on the board running the hospital had changed,
as well as the mechanisms for running the asylum. The Communists were
now in charge, and this created a problem. It was no longer clear that the
SPP would be asked to work directly against the asylum system. The radical
phase of decentralization and community participation began to slow
down. Realism and politics took over. Jervis later argued that by 1976, the
situation in Reggio was 'normalized'.[58]

Politicians

As in Parma and Perugia, politicians in Reggio backed radical reform in
mental health care. The key figure in Reggio Emilia was Velia 'Mimma'
Vallini (1922–90), the first woman to become an assessor in the Province
of Reggio Emilia.[59] Vallini had taken part in the Resistance and was a

---

55   De Vito, *I tecnici ragazzini*, p. 79.

56   The numbers went from a peak of 2,025 in 1969 to 1,401 in 1974. Micheli cites figures
which saw a fall from 2,400 to 150 between 1969 and 1977 (*Il vento in faccia*, p. 26).

57   In some ways this pressure from the outside began to affect the asylum itself. See De
Vito, *I tecnici ragazzini*, p. 101.

58   This might be another example of Jervis's tendency to see things in a narcissistic way,
linked above all to his own presence and activities.

59   She was also the only woman to be elected to the Provincial Council for the whole decade
of the 1950s. See Claudia Finetti, 'Lavoro e maternità. Donne, sindacato e sviluppo dei servizi per

member of the Italian Communist Party.[60] She had also helped to create the celebrated nursery system in the area. For Vezzani, Vallini was 'a woman of action, not words, [who] believed that San Lazzaro could not be reformed and on this point created a strong alliance with Jervis in terms of ideas'.[61] Vallini had been interested in issues linked to mental health care from the 1950s onwards. She argued that mental illness had social origins and argued for participatory forms of health care. As she said in 1974: 'The management of health and assistance needs to be controlled by the people but they require the instruments in order to do this.'[62]

In 1973, Vallini gave a speech in which she said that the age of the asylum was over.[63] A year later, she underlined this point again in another speech: 'Together we need to look at all the problems linked to the management of the asylum, while the overall objective is that of moving beyond that whole institution.' Vallini backed Jervis's reforms and worked tirelessly to set up alternative and democratic systems which worked across the whole health system, and not just related to mental illness.

Legacy, Memory, History

What happened to all those who had participated in the glorious period of the SPP in Reggio Emilia? Some left the world of day-to-day psychiatry for the university system. Jervis took up an academic post in Rome in 1975, and Letizia Comba also went on to have an (unorthodox) academic career. Many others remained within the psychiatric system. Stefano Mistura was still inside the system in 2015. He wrote: 'For nearly all of us a season opened up which led to increased specialization and competence within services which were increasingly bureaucratic

l'infanzia a Reggio Emilia (1945–1971)', in Luca Baldissara et al., eds, *Un territorio e la grande storia del '900. Il conflitto, il sindacato e Reggio Emilia*, Roma: Ediesse, 2002, pp. 359–404.

60   Provincia di Reggio Emilia, *Velia Vallini. Una donna dei nostri tempi*, 2010; Anna Appari, *Velia Vallini. Istituzione e cultura dei servizi a Reggio Emilia (1951–1974)*, Provincia di Reggio Emilia, 1992.

61   Vezzani, 'Leggevamo Gramsci e Marcuse', p. 385.

62   Speech during the Provincial Council Meeting of 16 April.

63   Cited in De Vito, *I tecnici ragazzini*, p. 108.

and fragmentary.'[64] The radical years of the late 1960s and 1970s had come to an end (although it did not seem that way for many, at the time). For Jervis, 'That which has been for a few years a movement which has broken with the past has become reformist, interested in management and compromise.'[65]

For Mistura, the services he helped set up in Reggio Emilia in the 1970s were an inspiration to many others across Italy. They became a blueprint which was copied elsewhere:

> In particular . . . those departments of mental health which now include adult psychiatric services, as well as those for children and adolescents, alongside other health and social assistance agencies, as well as those for drug addicts and psychiatric care inside prisons.

His experience in Reggio Emilia taught Jervis a number of lessons, which he discussed in his books published in the 1970s and afterwards. Some of these lessons were in contrast with the experience and arguments made at the time of Gorizia and *L'istituzione negata*. Jervis's language became more realistic, more technical, more willing to accept the reality of mental illness, more pragmatic – reformist even. He wrote in 1975, 'You can't make a revolution with psychiatry.'[66] Jervis also became critical of the idea that a psychiatrist (or a doctor, or a judge) could 'negate their own role' in some way. This concept, he argued, was an illusion. The real world was different: 'Those who don't want to change jobs', he wrote, 'have to make compromises'.[67] Jervis began to see anti-psychiatry as part of the problem, not part of the solution. His *Manuale* was just that, a real, concrete guide to forms of mental illness. It was published just seven years after *L'istituzione negata*, but it was light years away from the message in that book. Illnesses and diagnosis were not 'in brackets' any more. They were out in the open.

---

64   Cited in De Vito, *I tecnici ragazzini*, p. 205.
65   1979, cited in ibid., p. 207.
66   Jervis, *Manuale critico*, p. 137.
67   Ibid.

TWENTY

Gorizia: The Second Équipe, 1969–72

After the departure of Lucio Schittar, Antonio Slavich, Giovanni Jervis, Letizia Comba and Franco Basaglia, a new, second équipe took shape under Agostino Pirella, the natural heir of Basaglia as director of the asylum, and Domenico Casagrande, the final Basaglian director in Gorizia. Young psychiatrists and activists flocked to the city to join the project there, to work as volunteers or simply just as visitors. Even without Basaglia in charge, Gorizia remained a key reference point for new psychiatry in Italy (and also to some extent abroad).

Many from this second wave were so impressed with what they saw in Gorizia that they decided to stay on. Vieri Marzi later spoke of the 'overwhelming' impact of seeing the Basaglian asylum at work. It was a vision that changed his life.[1] He was not alone. For Paolo Tranchina, 'It wasn't difficult to fall in love with Gorizia, to understand the novelty of its anti-institutional message, to participate daily in the situations, attitudes and answers which overturned established points of view.'[2] People quickly fell in love with Gorizia. After the often lonely struggle of a tiny vanguard group around Basaglia from 1961 to 1968, a movement was now on the march.

---

1   Marzi was in Gorizia from January 1969 to 1972. He moved to Pavullo six months before the resignation of the second équipe, and then to Arezzo to join Pirella.

2   Paolo Tranchina, 'I Fogli d'Informazione verso il quarantennale', latorreelarca.wordpress. com.

Very little has been written about the 1969–72 period in Gorizia. Studies have since tended to follow Basaglia's journey. *The Negated Institution* went through various editions and continued to sell throughout the 1970s, but it was not updated to take into account any changes in the hospital itself. The account remained fixed in time, while the asylum became something else. After the second edition in April 1968, the text remained the same. But without Basaglia, some of the spark left the city, and attention shifted elsewhere. Journalists and others still turned up and wrote pieces, but without the same enthusiasm as before, and Gorizians (however defined) spoke at conferences and seminars. Gorizia had become old news. At the same time the focus of Basaglia and others was moving on – to cities where they would be given free rein and full political support. Gorizia had reached an impasse. Politics in general was becoming more and more radical, as was political language. The whole idea of a therapeutic community seemed increasingly out of date, reformist, almost conservative. Connections were being made with extra-parliamentary groups and struggles in other countries. The idea, now, was to change the world, not just one psychiatric hospital. Revolution, not reform, was apparently on the agenda.

In Gorizia the second équipe became ever more frustrated by local politicians and local politics. Despite the best efforts of those within the hospital, the province refused to open a series of external mental health centres. The experiment desperately needed to move beyond the walls of the hospital and out into the province, or the 'territory' as it was often called. But the authorities were extremely reluctant to sanction this shift. The Gorizian experiment was at a dead end. The question was about *when* it would come to an end, not *if*.

For their part, the authorities in Gorizia had had enough. Clear evidence of this was an extraordinary, long article published in the local magazine, *Iniziativa Isontina*, in September 1972. The author of the article was Ermellino Peressin, a distinguished Democrazia Cristiana politician who had been appointed assessor of health for the province. The article was an extended critique of the theory and practice of the Basaglians in Gorizia, based in part on *L'istituzione negata* and other

Basaglian texts.[3] It set itself up as a counter-investigation into the hospital and its Basaglians, and the title was a parody of the subtitle of *L'istituzione negata*. But the most important aspect of this article was the way it blamed the Basaglian équipe for the Miklus murder and for numerous suicides and escapes that it claimed had taken place in the late 1960s and early 1970s. Peressin painted a picture of an asylum in a state of chaos, inhabited by Maoists (which he named). For Peressin, Miklus was a turning-point. The murder was not 'an isolated episode but took on the features of an explosion of an entire situation'.[4] The patients were confused and abandoned. It was time for this experimentation to come to an end, for the good of the patients themselves. This, by 1972, was the official position of the DC in Gorizia.

Despite the fact that he had left Gorizia, Basaglia remained a strong influence behind the scenes from 1969 to 1972. No key decisions were taken without consulting him. Other Gorizians also came back to the city for occasional meetings and discussions. In 1971 Pirella left to run the asylum in Arezzo, leaving behind only Casagrande from the original 1960s équipe. A Basaglian diaspora was now in place, right across Italy. A movement was taking control of a whole system. It was time to leave Gorizia behind. It had served its purpose.

The End, 1972

'We will continue to discuss the end of Gorizia for some time.'

Agostino Pirella[5]

'In ten years of work we have been able to show how . . . psychiatry can be an instrument of liberation and not of oppression, as it has been for too long.'

Press release (October 1972)[6]

---

3   Ermellino Peressin, 'Rapporto da un ospedale psichiatrico. Esperienze a Gorizia sull'istituzione negata', *Iniziativa Isontina* 14: 3, August–September 1972, p. 55,.

4   Ibid., p. 67.

5   Agostino Pirella, *Fogli d'Informazione* 4, January 1973, p. 36.

6   The texts of the three resignation letters from Gorizia (the two collective resignations and Basaglia's individual resignation from October and November 1972) can be found in various

On 20 October 1972, the équipe (both old and new) decided to force the issue. This was a decision that had been brewing for some time. On that day Domenico Casagrande called a press conference in his home in Gorizia. Local journalists later described his statement as 'sensational' and 'a bombshell': *the entire équipe had decided to quit.* The main reason for this shock decision, according to the équipe, was the lack of progress in terms of health centres in the province. One proposed centre had been in the planning stage since 1964, and rent had been paid on the premises for two years, but the authorities would not sanction its use for mental health care.[7] It lay empty and unused. These local issues were key, but the resignation was also political and ideological. Casagrande's statement underlined the contradictions in the management of a total institution. This was a Basaglian statement (in the spirit of Frantz Fanon), an anti-psychiatric call to arms: 'Our presence in the psychiatric hospital, as well as being useless, is damaging for those patients . . . for whom we continue to represent, as psychiatrists, the justification of their internment'.[8] Casagrande also claimed that the decision to resign had been taken 'in full agreement with those patients'.[9]

For Casagrande, then, the work of the Basaglian équipe *inside* the hospital was over. A whole period of change, which began in 1961, had come to an end. And Casagrande went even further: *asylums themselves were no longer required.* The hospital itself was obsolete. Of the asylum's patients, 130 were described as better and ready to leave, and had been issued with certificates to prove it, while another sixty-eight were to be re-classified as guests. Only fifty-two people were to remain within the asylum as non-guests. This statement (which was limited in its real effects, because the power to release patients back to society forever was ultimately in the hands of the judiciary, not the doctors) caused almost as much comment locally as the resignation of the Basaglian équipe, and

---

places. They were later republished in *Crimini di pace. Ricerche sugli intellettuali e sui tecnici come addetti all'oppressione*, Milan: Baldini Castoldi Dalai, 2009 (Einaudi, 1975), pp. 33–41. This section also includes a letter from Basaglia to the president of the Gorizian Province.

7   Two nurses later confirmed that they had been ready to leave for the Cormons centre before the province apparently changed its mind.

8   Domenico Casagrande, 'Dichiarazione di dimissioni', *Fogli d'informazione* 2, November 1972, p. 42.

9   *L'Unità*, 20 October 1972.

was taken very seriously at a local level. What it meant, in theory, was the end of the psychiatric hospital as an institution. But the équipe knew that there was little or no chance of a bloc of patients being released in this way. The Basaglians were pushing the envelope, and perhaps they did not expect their offer to resign to be accepted so quickly by the provincial administration.[10] A stand-off followed which lasted a full month, by which time the provincial authorities were obliged to either accept or reject the resignations.

The 130 certificates that claimed the patients had been 'cured' were handed over to Bruno Pascoli, the same prosecutor who had charged Basaglia and Slavich with manslaughter in 1968 and had brought the case to trial in 1972 against Slavich. Nobody really expected the 130 patients to actually be released. These certificates and press announcements were a political gesture, aimed at forcing the politicians to act. But this tactic appeared to misfire. Another interpretation might be that the movement (and in particular Basaglia himself) had decided that Gorizia had gone far enough, and to make as much capital as possible out of their departure.

After all, by late 1972, spaces for change were opening up all over Italy. Gorizia required a great deal of time and energy but very little further progress was being made there. The city had not embraced the Basaglian experiment, especially in the wake of Miklus. Administrators across the country were queuing up to employ Basaglians. It was time to move on. The movement didn't need Gorizia any more. Moreover, the whole judicial process post-Miklus in the city had left a bitter taste in the mouths of those who had been accused, interrogated and put on trial (not just Slavich and Basaglia personally, but the whole équipe). The split between the city and the Basaglian reformers had never been healed. A decision had to be made. The choice was to move forward with Basaglian institutions, or return to the old ways used in the past. This decision was now in the hands of the provincial government in Gorizia.

An extensive and lengthy debate followed in the press and in the Provincial Council chamber. Gorizia was still a symbol for many activists across Italy, and the unprecedented mass resignation was national news.

---

10   'Tutti a casa: medici e guariti allo "psichiatrico" di Gorizia', *Il Piccolo*, 21 October 1972.

Provincial politicians claimed publicly that they wanted to continue working with a Basaglian hospital, but behind the scenes (and somewhat unexpectedly) it was clear that the key forces within the provincial admin- istration had decided to close the entire Gorizian experiment down and 'normalize' the hospital. They had grown tired at what they saw as the in-fighting and politicization of the Gorizian équipe. Other psychiatrists were sounded out (largely in Padua) and a new team was quickly put in place.

The neo-fascist MSI, as ever, went on the attack, criticizing what it called the 'situation of increased chaos which affects our psychiatric hospital'. MSI politicians were proud to underline their long-term opposition to the asylum experiments: 'We have always been against the introduction of new methods in the psychiatric hospital, ever since 1961.' By the end of November 1972, the Basaglians would all be gone. They would only return to the Gorizian asylum as visitors.

Post-Basaglia

On 20 November 1972 the new director, Giuseppe Carucci, took over the reins of the asylum from Casagrande. The official handover was at eight thirty that morning. Carucci was a thirty-two-year-old psychiatrist from Padua. He claimed that he had 'accepted the job in Gorizia as long as we don't go back to the past', but he also stated, importantly, that 'I am not a politician, here we don't do politics'. One of the most common accusations against the Basaglian équipe in Gorizia was the excessively political vision of their role (and that the hospital had become a den of subversives). On the same day, Basaglia resigned from the commission set up to appoint a new director, with a highly critical open letter to the president of the province.[11] He thus gave up any idea of influencing the

---

11   'Lettera al presidente della amministrazione provinciale di gorizia', Trieste, 20 November 1972, *Fogli d'Informazione* 3, 1972, pp. 5–6. (from Basaglia). It is often said that Basaglia had wanted a reformist psychiatrist called Edoardo Balduzzi to take over in Gorizia. Balduzzi confirms this in his book, *L'albero della cuccagna. 1964–1978. Gli anni della psichi- atria italiana*, Edizioni Stella, Nicolodi Editore, 2006, p. 47. See also Jervis, *Il buon rieducatore*, p. 25.

future of Gorizia. All bridges had been burned. After eleven years, the Basaglian management of Gorizia's asylum was over.

A second, much-celebrated and oft-quoted statement was then issued by the Basaglians.[12] This was a different document to the first Casagrande letter and was signed this time by the full original équipe, as well as Franca Ongaro *and* those resigning from the new équipe (only one of the doctors present in 1972 did not resign).[13] This was a statement with one eye on posterity: a bold, romantic and revolutionary declaration. The testimony related to the *entire* Gorizian experience, and not just to the political situation in 1972. The big guns had come out to make a final proclamation. It was a beautiful, polemical and almost poetic last stand, and it was also reminiscent of one of Basaglia's favourite texts, Fanon's own resignation letter cited in *L'istituzione negata*. The letter was addressed to the patients and nurses who would remain in the hospital, but its message was for the whole movement.

'Dear Friends', it began, 'after eleven years of work today we are leaving the hospital and you can imagine how we feel, as you must be feeling the same way'. The resignation letter combined the languages of community with those of struggle. Patients now had power, the Basaglians argued, but they were still imprisoned within the institution. The choice to leave was a painful one: 'As we leave you, we are calm but also upset.' But the letter also expressed confidence in the survival of what Gorizia had created: 'We know what we have achieved with you and nobody can destroy that.'[14] On this point, the équipe would be proved wrong in the years to come.

In Gorizia, a political crisis followed the acceptance of Casagrande's collective resignation, which revealed just how difficult the Basaglian legacy had become. The Socialists left the provincial coalition in protest on 24 November, issuing a strong statement in support of the outgoing équipe. They claimed that their aim was to

---

12   'Lettera di congedo dall'ospedale', *Fogli d'Informazione* 3, December 1972, pp. 7–9.

13   Domenico Casagrande, Piero Croci, Nicoletta Goldschmidt, Bruno Norcio, Vincenzo Pastore, Renato Piccione, Paolo Serra, Ernesto Venturini, Franco Basaglia, Franca Basaglia Ongaro, Giovanni Jervis, Letizia Jervis Comba, Vieri Marzi, Agostino Pirella, Lucio Schittar and Antonio Slavich.

14   'Lettera di congedo', pp. 7–9.

mobilize the party alongside the progressive forces in the city – both political and in terms of the trade unions – in order to reverse this restoration of the past which is being enacted here and restart with the work of innovation which is being brutally crushed [as well as] to watch over things so that the 130 cured patients are effectively restored to their families and to society.[15]

Yet this protest was short-lived, and the 130 patients were not released. Soon afterwards, in January 1973, the Socialists returned to the coalition. It seems that the political forces in Gorizia (apart from the Communist Party) had agreed that enough was enough. It was time to pull the plug on the Gorizian experiment.

In November 1972, then, all the Basaglian doctors (the second équipe) departed, leaving behind the structures of the therapeutic community and patients who had all become used to living within an open Basaglian hospital, as well as a number of nurses who identified strongly with Basaglia's ideas. Some of the medical team went to Arezzo or followed Basaglia to Trieste, at least at first, although others fanned out across Italy as part of a wide and ever-growing Basaglian diaspora.[16]

Giving up so much power seems a strange decision, in retrospect. The province would probably not have sacked the entire Basaglian équipe on their own initiative (despite the fact that tensions had been high for some time). Many within the movement as a whole were perplexed about the decision to leave Gorizia. It was a drastic choice, to abandon the patients and an institution that had been created through eleven years of hard work and struggle. Many felt guilty about what had happened. The movement as a whole struggled to grasp why this decision was being made. But there was no turning back. The Basaglian revolution would move on to other cities: Trieste, Arezzo, Ferrara, Colorno. Gorizia, meanwhile, slowly returned to being just another asylum, with a very famous past.

---

15   *Fogli d'Informazione* 3, December 1972, inside cover text.

16   Goldschmidt went to Arezzo; Pastore to Trieste and then later to Livorno and other places. Casagrande and Venturini went straight to Trieste. Vieri Marzi was already working in Pavullo in the Province of Modena at the time of the resignation. Bruno Norcio was in Trieste from 1974 onwards.

The New Équipe: Restoration and Forgetting

'The provincial administration succeeded in one of the most incredible acts ever seen: they overturned an entire health-based and
scientific apparatus in order to empty it of meaning, to cancel out
all the therapeutic and rehabilitative instruments constructed over
the years. Assurances were given over the safeguarding of certain
principles – but they were working at the same time in order to
suffocate them . . . and mercenary doctors took the place of those
who had dedicated themselves with great force to the success of a
non-repressive psychiatric system.'

Agostino Pirella[17]

The doctors and others (whom Pirella would dub 'medical mercenaries')
who replaced the Basaglian équipe arrived at the hospital on the morning
of 20 November. The historic handover was tense but polite and formal.
Nine years later, one of the doctors involved wrote an account of what
had happened on that momentous day. She painted a picture of the
asylum at the time that was far removed from that described by the
Basaglians.[18]

Vittoria Cristoferi Realdon told her story from an autobiographical
point of view, in a book which has hardly even been cited (let alone read)
by those studying Gorizia. Realdon was clearly not an anti-Basaglian, at
least on paper. She had read *The Negated Institution*, and her husband
had worked as a volunteer in the Gorizian asylum. She had also taken
part in a 1968 counter-course in medicine in Padua and had seen Basaglia
speak there to 'a room full of young people'.[19] This was not the biography
of a 'reactionary' doctor.

Back in 1972 Realdon was young, inexperienced and worried. Gorizia
the city seemed, at first, to be a forbidding place, cold and distant. In a
meeting with the new équipe, local politicians painted a picture of the

---

17   *Il Territorio* 10, 1984, p. 38.
18   'L'esperienza. Nove anni a Gorizia (1972–1981)' in A. Realdon, V. Cristoferi Realdon,
R. De Stefano, B. Spazzapan, *Oltre l'antipsichiatria. Dopo nove anni a Gorizia, riflessioni critiche
da un ex ospedale psichiatrico*, Padua: Piccin Editore, 1981, pp. 1–34.
19   Ibid., p. 5.

hospital as politicized and in a state of chaos. Realdon claimed that she was anxious not to turn the clock back on the Basaglian experiment, a point that was also made publicly by Carucci. On that first day at work, Realdon was taken on a tour of the hospital, a visit that turned into a long and emotional goodbye for the female doctor who served as her guide. One of the patients pleaded with the new appointee: 'Oh, don't lock us away again, don't build up the fences and bars as it was before!'[20]

The next day the new équipe attended their first general assembly. Realdon remembered 'an enormous room full of people, smoke, coughing, confused voices, shouting'.[21] Her overall conclusion was that this reformed hospital had become a trap (a conclusion similar to that of many in the Basaglian équipe, although *L'istituzione negata* was never cited but only mentioned in her piece). She argued that one of the reasons that it was difficult to reduce the numbers in the hospital was the central role played by the patients inside the asylum itself. Outside, they were nobody; inside they were part of a Basaglian therapeutic community. It was as if the perfection of the Basaglia system was preventing patients from taking responsibility for their lives. Like the Basaglians, Realdon felt that Gorizia had become a 'golden cage'.

Realdon also painted a picture of a deeply divided institution, where an internal war was going on (and had been for some time) between Basaglians and anti-Basaglians. Giovanni Jervis had written in the 1970s about the splits within the équipe after 1968 (and Basaglia confirmed, indirectly, these very same problems[22]): 'After May 1968, in Gorizia as elsewhere, the divisions became dramatic and irreversible, and the "Gorizian group" was idealized by its supporters as politically coherent (which it never was)'.[23] Jervis later argued that Basaglia wanted to close down Gorizia in 1968, and that this position was opposed by Pirella among others. But Jervis's explanation for this position was personal,

---

20   Ibid., p. 11.

21   Ibid., p. 13.

22   'Gorizia is what it is and I don't think I can ever return there for reasons that you are well aware of: the whole thing has become so problematic that it seems to me that my presence could simply make things worse'. Letter to Bollati, 31 January 1969, Einaudi Archive, Basaglia Folder, 34.

23   Jervis, *Il buon rieducatore*, p. 22.

not political.[24] Ever since 1972, these differing versions concerning the end of Gorizia have gone into battle in various texts. As we have seen, however, there were good political and strategic justifications for what happened in 1972, from the point of view of the movement. There is no evidence that Basaglia's personal ambitions played any role in all this.

Giuseppe Carucci's time as director of the asylum in Gorizia was very brief. He was given a three-month contract, which was not renewed, and he duly resigned in February 1973.[25] The next director was Professor Domenico Zamparo, who also came from Padua. Locally, it was clear that the Basaglian period was over, forever.

> The appointment of Zamparo, three months after Carlucci, was seen as part of the desire of the provincial administration to close down in a definitive way any kind of innovatory aspects of care there. In Gorizia they are saying that this is a 'restoration' of the past.[26]

Internally, within the hospital and in the wider city, there was a long struggle (by a minority) to defend the reforms and changes that had transformed the asylum. In early 1972 a local organization was set up to fight against what had been dubbed 'the restoration' of old methods and rules. This organization (the COSP, Circolo Operatori Sociali e Psichiatrici), which later became the local branch of Psichiatria Democratica, was active for a number of years and brought together nurses, patients and other local citizens.

Nor did the movement as a whole forget Gorizia, at least in the years immediately following the mass resignation. In 1974, Psichiatria Democratica decided to hold its first big gathering in the city. The event was a huge success, with thousands of participants.[27] Speakers at the

---

24   'Basaglia was not very happy with the idea that there could be a "Gorizia without Basaglia"', ibid., p. 26.

25   'Finiti i tempi degli "esperimenti" all'ospedale psichiatrico di Gorizia', *La Stampa*, 19 February 1973.

26   Ibid.

27   See the proceedings collected in *La pratica della follia. Atti del 1 Convegno Nazionale di Psichiatria Democratica. Gorizia. 22–23 Giugno, 1974*, Critica delle istituzione, Centro internazionale studi e ricerche, Venezia, 1974. The congress was organized by the COSP in Gorizia.

congress argued that 'Gorizia belongs to the movement and documented what they saw as the 'slow return to the past' inside the asylum.

> The provincial administration has appointed doctors who are willing to reject that which the previous doctors have declared – with their presence and their work. These doctors have had to recreate the mad-house to justify their existence . . . the hospital in Gorizia has become a madhouse.

A local Communist Party representative said that 'in twenty months the assemblies have been stopped; in twenty months there have been five directors of the hospital, as if it was a garage or something'.[28]

Real power inside the hospital, that held by the doctors, was no longer in Basaglian hands. Over time, Gorizia quickly lost its centrality. Nobody wrote about it any more, apart from a few journalists who paid brief visits, usually in order to document its 'return to the past'. Attention shifted elsewhere. Numerous asylums were undergoing radical change all over Italy, and mental health centres were being set up across the country. Gorizia became interesting for its history alone. *The Negated Institution* remained the bible of the movement, but its link to the real situation inside Gorizia was more and more tenuous. In other places in Italy, however, Gorizianism was very much alive and kicking.

---

28   Ibid, pp. 19, 22, 26.

TWENTY-ONE

Arezzo: The Gorizian Diaspora

'The hospital is yours.'

Agostino Pirella to the patients in the Arezzo asylum[1]

'It must be abolished, but how?'

Paolo Bonizzoni[2]

After 1968, Gorizia's diaspora spread its tentacles across Italy, finding space to act where innovative local politicians were willing to take risks to deal with their asylums. One of these places was Arezzo, a wealthy, medium-sized Tuscan town. Arezzo was still known for its production of jewellery and links to the gold trade, and had seen a period of medieval splendour. It also had a big provincial asylum, not far from the city centre but on the 'wrong side' of the railway tracks, beyond the main station. In the 1970s Arezzo became a key part of the 'psycho-tour' undertaken by many young psychiatrists and volunteers at that time.

The Communist assessor for the province, Bruno Benigni, had begun to court Agostino Pirella in the late 1960s. He promised Pirella full

---

1 Gianni Micheli, ed., *Utopia e realtà. Una memoria collettiva. Ricordi e testimonianze della memoria orale dell'ospedale neuropsichiatrico di Arezzo*, Florence: Edifir-Edizioni, 2009, p. 43.

2 *Fogli di Informazione* 7, May–June, 1973.

political backing, in marked contrast to the hostility the Basaglians had experienced in Gorizia. Benigni has argued that the push to transform the hospital was a moral, universal struggle, which united left and right, Catholics and Communists. He claimed that Pirella and many politicians and administrators were working to free the patients, but at the same time for the liberation of those working in the asylum, as well as administrators and politicians – a liberation from their prejudices and the stigmas they attached to others. Another Communist called Mario Bellucci, the president of the province from 1964 to 1975 (who had first been elected to the town council in 1946) also supported the push for reform. Many of these politicians also had real jobs, in the outside world – Benigni and Italo Monacchini in Arezzo were also teachers. These people were not all career politicians who saw institutional issues through the distorted prism of clientelism and/or as ways of simply gaining or maintaining consensus.

Benigni was tireless in his pursuit of change, often in the face of local opposition. He built a strong personal and political alliance with Pirella and with other members of the new and extended équipe. The key aim of everyone involved was the 'the liberation of the patients'.[3] Like other administrators before him, Benigni's first visit to the hospital was a vision of hell. The worst wards – at the back of the hospital – were 'a disaster, a human disaster'. He witnessed the shocking sight of 'people in the midst of shit, naked, shouting . . . the circles of hell'.[4] Benigni's role was crucial before, during and after the final closure of the asylum. He went on to become a key figure in national Communist Party policy, and thus an important force behind the push towards the 1978 law.

But Benigni was not alone. Italo Galastri was elected to the Provincial Council in 1970. He was a member of the Socialist Party and was appointed as *assessore alla cultura* and president of the health commission. His first experience of the asylum was very similar to that of Benigni. 'I had never seen anything like it – naked patients, lying down in the middle of the corridors, on top of ugly granite tiles, and everywhere there was a terrible smell of urine and faeces'.[5] Like other politicians and

3   Micheli, *Utopia e realtà*, p. 53.
4   Ibid., p. 62.
5   Ibid., p. 163.

psychiatrists before him, in Perugia, Parma and Gorizia, Galastri's reaction was clear: this state of affairs could not be allowed to continue.

> We could not accept this . . . the reality of the madhouse, in the centre of a 'red' city in 'red' Tuscany. It didn't fit with our plans to run the city and the province in a new way and the fact that we had declared ourselves to be on the side of the weak.[6]

Debates were launched in the council chamber and political alliances were formed. The result of all this was that contacts were made with Gorizia and Basaglia and a meeting was arranged with a key Gorizian – Agostino Pirella – in Venice, on the Lido. As an austere Communist, Benigni was worried about the cost of the restaurant where the three men had lunch, but a pact was made. Pirella would come to Arezzo as director, and he would send a group of like-minded doctors ahead to prepare the ground.[7]

None of this was easy. Pirella's appointment itself was controversial. There were concerns in the city about the arrival of a radical Gorizian. By this time, Basaglia and the Gorizia experience were well known. The asylum and its future was a hot issue: 'Every day in the provincial offices we discussed psychiatry, from morning to evening.'[8] Mental health reform became a reference point for reforming politicians, and passions ran high. 'As administrators we were there all the time – there were constant discussions, debates, meetings with health workers and patients, politicians and administrators.'[9]

The Communist Party (locally and nationally) was never unequivocal in its support for Pirella and the asylum reforms. In order to underline this point, Benigni later compared Arezzo and Perugia:

> It was easier in Perugia because the Communist Party was in agreement. In Arezzo the party was divided . . . I remember the jokes which

---

6   Ibid., p. 163.
7   The two young doctors who preceded Pirella were Gianpaolo Pesce and Gian Paolo Guelfi.
8   Micheli, *Utopia e realtà*, p. 166.
9   Ibid., p. 169.

did the rounds at the Casa del Popolo di Arezzo, . . . and Pirella who was often looked upon with suspicion. In Perugia the experience of change in terms of psychiatry was always seen as part of the community.

As in Gorizia, each individual life story was seen as important, and every person was taken seriously.

> In terms of every single act of a patient . . . anything . . . we tried to understand what meaning it had for them, for their individual history, for the family, for the history of the institution, and the history of their relationship with the health system. And then there was society as a whole – it was truly a place where the particular supported a universal vision.[10]

The worst wards were where change began, including one called the *fondaccio*. These were the places that had so shocked Benigni and Galastri.

Pirella finally arrived to take up his post as director of the asylum in Arezzo in the summer of 1971. Before long, it had become one of the centres of the anti-asylum movement and was a hive of activity, attracting militants, students, volunteers, intellectuals, TV producers, film-makers and others from across Italy and the world at large.

Arezzo's psychiatric hospital had been built in 1904, and as in Gorizia, the asylum there was set up as a pavilion system in extensive gardens. It had a grand, gated entrance and a long road up to the main, director's 'palace'. Behind, in open countryside, were a series of other pavilions and buildings. In 1966, the asylum reached a maximum intake of 720 patients. As in most total institutions, the layout of the asylum complex marked that of the 'career' of its inmates. By 1978, patient numbers had been reduced by more than half to just 346 (*before* the Basaglia law was passed).

When Pirella got to Arezzo, in July 1971, he found himself to be in charge of an ordinary asylum. It was a pre-Gorizian total institution, with space rigidly divided by gender and diagnosis and separated by

---

10   Ibid., p. 363.

elaborate systems of walls, fences, doors and corridors. The hospital, however, also had a tradition of mild reformist polices and a humanist approach to the patients. Pirella later described it as a 'place of death'[11] in comparison with Gorizia, which had been so alive and marked by activity and debates. In Arezzo, some of the wards were known as 'tombs'. It felt like a prison, or a cemetery. As in other asylums, cigarettes were a form of internal currency.

Pirella took his time. He had learnt many lessons from Gorizia, not least the need to avoid open conflict with the nursing staff. He passed a 'terrible summer'[12] working out how Arezzo's total institution functioned.[13] The first steps were obvious ones – an end to the tying up of patients and a halt to adding more people to the worst wards and to pointless transfers between wards. Gorizia, Perugia and Parma had made things easier and hastened change. This was clearly a second phase of the struggle. The movement now had a history. As Maria Grazia Giannichedda later said, 'We had already taken on board the lesson of Gorizia.'[14]

Pirella began to transform the inside of the hospital with the support of a broad alliance of politicians and administrators, and at the same time services were moved out into the territory and new centres set up across the province. It was not just a matter of reducing the numbers of inmates. Patients, doctors *and* nurses all began to leave the asylum. Many ex-patients were moved into housing or integrated back into their families. At the same time, doctors and nurses set up the provincial services, as had happened in Reggio Emilia and Perugia. A dynamic équipe made up of ex-Gorizians and others worked tirelessly to implement reform.[15] Communist Party nurses, as in other places (such as Gorizia) played a key, vanguard role, and as in Parma and Perugia, plans for an entirely new hospital were put on hold (and never taken forward).

As in other cities, this whole process was accompanied by bitter debate and the constant fear of incidents (especially given the memory of Miklus

---

11   'Un luogo di oppressione e di morte', ibid., p. 14.

12   Ibid., p. 14.

13   Agostino Pirella, 'L'esperienza di Arezzo' in Micheli, *Utopia e realtà*, pp. 13–22.

14   Micheli, *Utopia e realtà*, p. 184.

15   Paolo Serra and Nicoletta Goldschmidt came straight from Gorizia to Arezzo in 1972. Vieri Marzi moved to Arezzo after working in Pavullo in the Province of Modena. Paolo Tranchina had also worked in Gorizia.

in Gorizia). The local press, and in particular *La Nazione*, ran a strong campaign against the presence of what they saw as radical ideologues within the hospital in Arezzo. There was a form of moral panic: 'For months in Arezzo the fear of armed "mad people" who were ready to kill and rape was ever present.'[16]

Pirella inspired his own cult of the personality in Arezzo – and he created a strong, loyal and enthusiastic équipe around his leadership. But there were important differences between Pirella and Basaglia. Pirella was extremely attentive to detail, and methodical in the way that he implemented change. He was much less interested in high theory than Basaglia, and much less political on a *national* scale, although he was certainly interested in politics. Pirella was politically astute *locally* – he was 'a man of the left'.[17] He spent a great deal of time mediating between the hospital, politicians and administrators.

Paolo Tranchina worked closely with Pirella in Arezzo, and later remembered him in this way:

> In Arezzo the door to his office was always open. He was always ready to discuss things. But he was very clear that everyone had their own responsibilities. Sometimes he would come to a ward where things were going badly and very quickly he was able to put things right. Other times he would say, 'Go and talk to the nurses to work out what is going on.'

Arezzo developed into a mixture of the experiences of Gorizia, Perugia, Reggio Emilia and Trieste. It combined active work in the outside world (the territory) with radical and rapid reform within the asylum itself. The Tuscan city was also important as one of the centres for Psichiatria Democratica. The first national congress of the Psichiatria Democratica was held in the city in September 1976, following a key meeting in 1972, and numerous other meetings followed in the 1970s. *Fogli d'informazione*, the key publication of Psichiatria Democratica and of the Basaglian movement, was put together in Arezzo for a time.

For a while, Basaglia was very much in control of Pirella's destiny. He

---

16   Aldo Barnà, cited in *Fogli d'informazione* 17, 1974, p. 439.
17   Micheli, *Utopia e realtà*, p. 242.

may have suggested the move to Arezzo and was, as we have seen, on the three-man commission that appointed Pirella to the post of asylum director. This selection process was controversial (as were many such competitions over the years) and led to political debate. However, once Pirella started work in Arezzo, he was his own man and was not afraid to work in ways that differentiated his work from that of the équipe in Trieste.

The arrival of Pirella and the work with Benigni and the other political allies produced a revolution in the Arezzo asylum system. De Vito wrote:

> From a place at the edges of Italian psychiatric care, Arezzo became a centre which attracted young health workers of all kinds who were interested in anti-institutional issues. It became one of the key laboratories for an alliance between the anti-asylum movement and the Communist Party.

What happened in Arezzo was not merely technical. The idea was to 'totally reshape relationships and understand problems in a global way'.[18] It was an ambitious project.

Arezzo and Trieste: Two Capitals

As the two capitals of the Basaglian movement, exchange between Arezzo and Trieste remained strong throughout the 1970s. The majority of the ex-Gorizians chose between Trieste and Arezzo. Giannichedda highlighted the strong and constant ties between the two cities: 'We were from the same family . . . Trieste and Arezzo were brother and sister, cousins.'[19] She remembers numerous train journeys between the two places (not an easy journey; even now it takes at least five hours). But Giannichedda also emphasized the differences between the two cities and their strategies for change.

> Every time that we discuss the Italian situation, it seems to me that on the one hand we need to underline the existence of a movement,

---

18 Aldo D'Arco in ibid., p. 364.
19 Micheli, *Utopia e realtà*, p. 183.

a vast movement, which was marked by internal variations of many different kinds, and many situations which were clearly different from each other.[20]

The Sala dei Grandi and the General Meetings

'It was the room of science, academic, bombastic, where the patients were absolutely not allowed to go, ever. It was the place of science with a capital S . . . It was a room of taboos, the untouchable room, the place where people with no power or little power could not go – those disgraceful people . . . whose lives were unworthy of being lived at all, who were destined to be forgotten, and in that room there was a kind of Copernican revolution.'

Luigi Attenasio[21]

The mural is still there, in all its glory. It is now part of the university library of the city, with students working under the shadow of the huge image behind them. The image is a kind of roll call of the giants of Italian psychology and psychiatry. It depicts a series of grand men, some in white coats, some in suits, some in cloaks. This was where the patients in Arezzo were given a public voice, and the use of that particular space was important to the success and public visibility of those meetings.

Paolo Tranchina wrote about the mechanics of these encounters:

Our politics and our work was based around daily life – daily struggles, critical reflections, the systematic use of and control over anti-institutional practices. The group – this intellectual collective met some thirty times a week and carried out therapeutic meetings at a series of levels – with individuals, families, groups, inside and outside of the hospital, in schools, neighbourhoods, banks, factories permeated with all these practices – this was the secret of our strength . . . even

---

20   Ibid., p. 183.

21   Ibid., p. 43. See for the *assemblea* in Arezzo the extracts from the meetings, chosen by Attenasio, Gisella Filippi, Luciano Della Mea, *Parola di matti* and the three RAI TV documentaries produced by *Cronaca*.

when we were alone, in some distant mountain town, or a situation which seemed hopeless.[22]

It was, according to Vincenzo Ceccarelli, an 'extraordinary collective experience'.[23]

Luigi Attenasio's life was changed, he later claimed, by the first congress of the Psichiatria Democratica held in Gorizia in 1974. He was twenty-five years old and had just graduated. He moved to Arezzo in that very same year. Attenasio recalled the huge numbers of meetings in Arezzo, some thirty-five or so every week. Another participant remembered that 'Our day was marked by meetings.'[24]

Big general meetings were held in Arezzo on a regular basis. These happenings were spectacular and became part of the folklore of the 1970s, and not just in Arezzo. In Trieste, Basaglia ditched general meetings, but in Arezzo they were a key part of Pirella's strategy. The events themselves were a mixture of exhilarating and boring, anarchic and hierarchical. Big claims were made for their significance: 'The patients showed an incredible ability to analyse situations and discuss issues.'[25] Other meetings were also held regularly following the Gorizia model. The president of the *assemblea* sat behind the big table in front of the images of famous psychiatrists, while a mobile microphone with a long wire was passed around the hall. These meetings were open to the outside world – volunteers, factory workers, family members, journalists and filmmakers were among the audience at different times. On occasion, meetings were filmed.

This is how Pirella himself described the general assemblies:

In the autumn the general assembly began, in the room close to the bar, and then in the Sala dei Grandi, a meeting space with big chairs, a table for speakers and paintings of great scientists on the back wall. Over 500 meetings were to follow, and these were crucial in terms of

---

22   *Resoconto convegno Arezzo: Memoria e attualità*, 7 April 2009.

23   Micheli, *Utopia e realtà*, p. 5.

24   Cesare Bondioli in ibid., p. 88.

25   Agostino Pirella, *Il problema psichiatrico*, Centro di Documentazione Pistoia, 1999, p. 96.

helping patients rediscover their own subjectivity. They were given
back the power to speak, to accuse, to criticize and to be listened to
– and these were people who, for years and years, had been given no
alternative to their own decline and chronic forms of delirium.[26]

Chairs were elected by the assembly, while other patients took minutes.
The medical staff sat among the public. Some nurses tended to stand at
the back. As Pirella noted, all the hierarchies of the total institution had
been overturned (at least on the surface).

The regular ninety-minute meetings lasted for eleven years and were
held on Mondays and Fridays. Minutes were kept and preserved, and a
book was published with selections from the meetings.[27] These meetings
were, according to Attenasio, 'the instrument which overturned meanings
and power-structures'.[28] The event or institution of the assembly itself
was also described as a 'parliament'. Each general meeting was followed
by a further feedback meeting, also open to all. The meetings attracted
up to a hundred people at a time. For Tranchina, 'It was a moment of
collective processing, it was the guarantee that this transformation was
democratic.'[29]

These meetings inside the asylums were different to many of the more
politicized meetings that dominated the life of activists in the late 1960s
and 1970s – they were rarely theoretical or directly political, and they
discussed real problems, mundanities, day-to-day issues and problems.
It was this combination of practice and theory that made them so radical
and, apparently, so effective. It was not talking for the sake of talking:
'They weren't generic discussions.'[30]

There was also another kind of overturning going on here. In the total
institution, the individual was reduced to a thing, a body, a number. The

26   Amministrazione provinciale di Arezzo, ed., *I tetti rossi. Dal manicomio alla società*,
Milan: Mazzotta, 1978, p. 89.

27   For a taste of these meetings see the section in the documentary *L'uomo ritorna.
Rapporto sull'esperienza psichiatrica di Arezzo*, Giampaolo Guelfi, Franca Rinaldelli, Giacomo
Cittadini, Amministrazione provinciale, Arezzo, 1972. See also *Voci* (which uses the interviews
collected as the basis of the Micheli volume and oral history project), Stefano Dei, 2009.

28   Micheli, *Utopia e realtà*, p. 41.

29   Ibid., p. 363.

30   Ibid., p. 244.

overturned institution put the individual and their history at the centre of things. Benigni argued that the meetings helped the patients play an active part in the transformation of the hospital. Before Pirella's arrival, 'Their day was reduced to begging for cigarettes and smoking them, small things which became a daily ritual . . . they were passive and accepted their concentration camp–like conditions.'[31]

These claims were possibly exaggerated or perhaps self-congratulatory. Some even called the meetings 'revolutionary'. In addition, real structural changes were implemented from above, not from below. Was the real value of these meetings more symbolic than real? Was it true that the hospital was no longer run by the doctors, as in some claims ('it looked like the hospital was no longer controlled by the doctors, but it was for everyone, and above all for the patients')?[32] Or was this just a feeling? Meetings performed a variety of functions; they had 'a cultural value, a social value, but also a value in terms of the critique of dominant psychiatric science'.[33] They were also a 'collective epistemological process',[34] giving a sense of identity to the patients – important from the point of view of subjectivities. They *felt* very important, at the time. The patients were given a platform; it *appeared* as if they had power. As to their long-term influence, this is still to be assessed. It is almost as if the scepticism of *L'istituzione negata* had been replaced by a rhetorical approach to the power of these meetings.

Leaders and Followers

Various patient leaders, as in Gorizia, played a key role in these meetings. A central figure was a man called Pasquale Spadi (who was often known as 'il maestro' or 'il maestro Spadi'), who came from a small town in the hills above Arezzo (Stia). He usually had a book under his arm and was often president of the assembly. He had a fine grasp of language and expressed himself forcefully, holding the audience in the palm of his

---

31   Ibid., p. 53.
32   Attenasio, in ibid., p. 41.
33   Pirella in Micheli, *Utopia e realtà*, p. 21.
34   Micheli, *Utopia e realtà*, p. 16.

hand. Spadi argued that 'every meeting should end with the release of a patient'.[35]

As in Gorizia, a patient 'elite' tended to dominate the meetings, in part because of the layout of the room itself, with its raised table and the need to use a microphone. But these were not orderly or regimented events. Sometimes, they appeared to be almost anarchic: 'someone sat down, someone stood up, there was shouting, people interrupted others', it was 'passionate, from the heart, angry'.[36] Most patients did not actually contribute to discussion, but Pirella argued that even those patients who did not speak 'recognized the assembly as an instrument of emancipation'.[37]

The debates in these meetings were at another level to those in Gorizia. The Basaglians were winning. There was no need to go over some of the old arguments. Arezzo's assemblies were permeable. Striking workers came. Administrators were asked to explain themselves. Journalists and film-makers reported on what was happening.

Spadi's story became linked to that of the end of the asylum itself. Released in 1976, he was clearly experiencing problems in the outside world when a TV crew tried to interview him in that year (he refused to speak to them). By 1982, however, when the documentary crew returned again, he was filmed teaching young trainee nurses and others about psychiatric care. Spadi's story seemed to symbolize that of all patients. He became a key part of the story to be told, and he turned up again in the recent *Voci* documentary, which used oral history interviews gathered in order to tell the story of the movement for change in Arezzo.[38] The self-styled radical television programme *Cronaca* visited Arezzo three times in the 1970s and 1980s, documenting the changes to individuals in some detail and showing past film they had shot in the main piazza in the city.[39]

---

35   Attenasio in ibid., p. 42.

36   Gianni Michele, *Utopia e realtà*, p. 335.

37   Ibid., p. 16.

38   *Voci. Il superamento dell'ospedale psichiatrico nell'esperienza aretina. Frammenti di storia*, Stefano Dei, 2009.

39   *Cronaca*, 1974; *Dietro l'alibi della follia*, 1976 (RAI); *Il fantasma del manicomio*, 1982. See also *L'uomo ritorna*, Gian Paolo Guelfi, 1972.

Breaking Up the Asylum

As in Gorizia, walls and fences were knocked down, and bars removed. This destruction took place in ritual fashion, over a long period of time, and was often carried out by the patients themselves. 'Happiness can be defined as breaking down the walls of the madhouse with a hammer. I had blisters on my hands, but it was intensely satisfying.'[40]

A restaurant was opened. Popular parties were held in the hospital grounds. The asylum became a centre for political agitation in the city, with debates and cultural events of all kinds. All of this was familiar. It had been done before. But the differences with Gorizia were also extremely important. Benigni's support meant that there was a strong and decisive 'move towards the territory' – as had already happened in Perugia and elsewhere. In addition, this political support meant that the outside and the inside of the asylum worked together. There was never a sense of a perfect but isolated therapeutic community. Right from the beginning, it was clear that the patients were to be moved out into the real world, and that alternative structures were required.

Story of a Fence

Yet, just as fences and walls were coming down, so others were being constructed. As a sign of change, a school was opened within a building in the asylum grounds (in the part of the asylum which had so shocked Italo Galastri and Benigni).[41] However, some of the people working in the school were worried about the patients and wanted to prevent inter-action with the students. Pirella's reforms had not removed stigmas linked to the mentally ill. In some cases fear had been reinforced or fanned by the more visible presence of patients and ex-patients in the city. As a result of these fears, a two-metre high fence was built to 'protect' teachers and children on their way in and out of the school. There were long debates over this fence/wall.

Then, in the early 1980s, a group of school students marched to the

---

40   Bruno Astrologhi in Micheli, *Utopia e realtà*, p. 33.
41   Galastri in Micheli, *Utopia e realtà*, p. 169.

hospital and pulled down the fence. They carried a golden painted chimera, the mythical creature that was one of the symbols of Arezzo itself. This event was filmed for the RAI participatory documentary series *Cronaca* and transmitted in 1981 as part of a programme called 'Il fantasma del manicomio' (The ghost of the asylum).[42] When news of this event filtered through to Italo Galastri, he went down to the hospital to see what was happening for himself. He claims that he even took part in the removal of the barrier. 'It was a great moment, a kind of party took place, and from that moment on everyone was free to come and go as they pleased.'[43] Massimo Gherardi later remembered that 'the people took the fence down'.[44] No incidents followed. The wall had been superfluous. It was not rebuilt.

Into the Territory

As patients were moved out, and no new patients were accepted, there were often clashes with local residents. But decentralized mental health centres and housing structures were quickly created in the city of Arezzo and in the provincial areas of the Arno valley. The hospital in Arezzo was effectively closed by the mid-1970s. The reintegration of the remaining patients was as much a social problem as a mental health issue. In 1974 an external mental health centre was opened in Arezzo (with six nurses and one doctor) and others followed across the province. As in Reggio, patients were treated outside of the asylum. Debates were constant. There was general agreement over final objectives – the end of the asylum system – but conflict over the way to reach that point, and over ideology, theory and politics. None of this was easy. But things moved fast.

As the asylum began to wind down, only the most difficult cases were left behind. The psychiatric hospital became a place that was officially still open, but which, by the middle of the 1970s, 'appears to belong

---

42 'Il fantasma del manicomio (Arezzo 1981)', from *Cronaca,* posted by RAI Cultura, 24 February 2010, youtube.com/watch?v=8h5LWPVKlOY.

43 Micheli, *Utopia e realtà*, p. 169.

44 Ibid., p. 177.

definitively to the past'.[45] No new patients were accepted into any asy-lums in Tuscany after 1981.[46] There were, however, some bitter local battles over the relocation of patients. In some cases, local opposition succeeded in preventing accommodation or centres from being opened. Life was not easy for ex-patients in the outside world, as the TV docu-mentary series *Cronaca* showed in harrowing detail. Yet this was an organic, political project – which moved far beyond the walls of the asylum. Pirella said that 'our work provides for the possibility of a common struggle between citizens, specialists and workers to eliminate the causes of mental illness'.[47] Christian De Vito wrote:

> In Arezzo the Basaglian principle of 'keeping the contradictions open' was translated into a kind of 'organized disorganization'. The model there was not to provide a specialist or organizational model for others, but create a kind of cultural hegemony, a laboratory for the construction from below of improved health for the people begin-ning with the sense of keeping the specialists and the political aspects of this work together. The assemblies in the Sala dei Grandi of the asylum worked in parallel with the debates in Sala dei Grandi of the Provincial Council. Patients were dismissed from the psychiatric hospital at the same time as territorial and decentralized services were set up, but also those linked to society and health services in general, something which prefigured the birth of the national health service and involved council administrations from various parts of the region.[48]

As in Colorno, Perugia, Reggio Emilia and elsewhere, the Arezzo experience also took a global approach to issues linked to institutions, marginality and education. The asylum was merely part of an entire

---

45   Ibid., p. 79.

46   Ota De Leonardis, *Dopo il manicomio. L'esperienza psichiatrica di Arezzo*, Quaderni di documentazione del CNR (Consiglio Nazionale delle Ricerche), no. 7, Rome: Il Pensiero Scientifico, 1981.

47   'Una domanda ad Agostino Pirella sull'esperienza di Arezzo' (1975), in Amministrazione provinciale di Arezzo, ed., *I tetti rossi*, p. 267.

48   Christian De Vito, *I luoghi della psichiatria*, Florence: Edizioni Polistampa, 2010, p. 34.

system that needed reform – from special classes for 'backward' kids to old people's homes and handicapped centres.

Narrating Arezzo

The events in Arezzo have been brought to us, once again, mainly by those directly involved in the movement. Arezzo produced a large number of texts of different kinds, as had Gorizia and as would Trieste: novels, histories, oral histories, TV documentaries, photographic accounts and so on. The city's reforms were well documented in *Fogli d'informazione*, and later in publications sponsored by the administration. It was also the subject of a long essay by the activist, publisher, writer and journalist Luciano Della Mea, and three RAI documentaries (where the inmates helped with the films and the scripts) which nonetheless (despite being shown in Venice) had nothing like the impact of Zavoli's 1969 documentary. For the general public, a certain 'asylum fatigue' seemed to have set in.

Memory of a Movement: Memory of a Total Institution

Arezzo has been tireless in promoting the memory of the asylum and the anti-asylum movement for change in the city, perhaps more so than in any other place beyond Trieste. Much of this has been co-ordinated by the local Centro Franco Basaglia (set up in the early twenty-first century by the province). In 2009 Pirella was given honorary citizenship of Arezzo, and at the same time Italy's first monument to the victims of the asylum was inaugurated in the ex-hospital grounds. An extensive series of filmed oral history interviews have been collected together (this project is ongoing and has led to a documentary) and a number of conferences organized. The asylum site contains the aforementioned monument as well as signposts and guides to the past history of the buildings that now host part of the university.

Arezzo was also one of the places where researchers looked in detail at the end of the asylum system, and documented what happened to patients once they had left the total institution.[49] With the closure of the asylum, the buildings began to crumble until, in the 1980s, they were restored and reopened as part of the university. Although, as in Rome, Venice and elsewhere, the original building exteriors were maintained, many of the internal features were changed. Local activists and those who had been associated with Pirella tried to ensure that the asylum, and the way it was closed, would not be forgotten.

Their strategy involved a series of panels on the site as well as a unique monument 'To those who died in the asylum', which was opened in a special ceremony. In some ways, this monument took a traditional approach to the problem of asylum memory, looking above all at the aspects of pain and suffering linked to these places. Its form was also traditional, in marble, with a small child holding out her hand, similar to many Catholic monuments. It was linked to a celebrated photo of the Arezzo asylum that was used time and again in publications and posters. This monument represents the first attempt, in the world, to officially commemorate those who perished inside these total institutions. Although the number of patients had officially become residual by the end of the 1970s, the asylum in Arezzo was only officially closed at the beginning of the 1990s – on 29 June 1990, to be precise.

---

49   CNR, Paolo Crepet, Loris Prosperi, *Ipotesi di pericolosità. Ricerca sulla coazione nell'esperienza di superamento del manicomio di Arezzo*, Rome: Il Pensiero Scientifico, 1982.

TWENTY-TWO

Trieste: The End of the Asylum, 1971–79

'It is extremely difficult to destroy an institution.'

Franco Basaglia[1]

'From Monday 24 January [1977] the San Giovanni of Trieste psychiatric hospital . . . no longer exists.'

Franco Basaglia[2]

'Trieste was the first city in the world to close down its asylum.'

Valeria Babini[3]

Numbers of patients (without guest status) in the San Giovanni Psychiatric Hospital, Trieste:

    1971: 1,182
    1972: 1,058
    1973: 930
    1974: 625

---

1   Ernesto Venturini, *Il giardino dei gelsi. Dieci anni di antispsichiatria italiana*, Turin: Einaudi, 1979, p. 217.

2   'Intervista a Franco Basaglia sulla chiusura dell'ospedale psichiatrico di Trieste (1977)', *Panorama*, 1 February 1977, in Luigi Onnis e Giuditta Lo Russo, *La ragione degli altri. La psichiatria alternativa in Italia e nel mondo: storia, teoria e pratica*, Rome: Savelli, 1979, p. 277.

3   Valeria Babini, *Liberi tutti. Manicomi e psichiatri in Italia. Una storia del novecento*, Bologna: Il Mulino, 2009, p. 280.

1975: 470
1976: 253
1977: 132
1978: 87

In January 1977, Franco Basaglia held a press conference in Trieste. The news was a simple announcement. The city's vast asylum was to be closed by the end of the year. It did not quite happen that quickly, but the hospital stopped accepting patients in 1980, and soon there were so few patients inside the complex that even to call that institution a hospital was clearly incorrect. After just six years as director, Basaglia had achieved what many had thought to be impossible. The institution was not merely 'negated'; it had been obliterated. Today, the site of the ex-hospital is a quiet, peaceful place – with a school, university departments, a theatre, a bar and a magnificent park. A bus line runs through the park.

This peace is another legacy of the Basaglian movement, which reached its peak and achieved its moment of greatest fame in Trieste during the 1970s and afterwards. As Peppe Dell'Acqua wrote, the area has been

> given back to the city . . . That segregated place, closed by gates and walls, was opened up in order to release people. And today it is still open to welcome people, groups and institutions who give life back to that place which was born in order to destroy it.[4]

San Giovanni can claim to be the first asylum in the world to be closed for political and moral reasons – because those who ran it believed it to be an abominable place, a concentration camp. The events in Trieste also led directly to a national law – the 180 – the 'Basaglia law' that called for the closure of *all* Italian asylums.

This chapter tells the story of this revolution, and its legacy.

---

4 Peppe Dell'Acqua, *Fuori come va? Famiglie e persone con schizofrenia. Manuale per un uso ottimistico delle cure e dei servizi*, Feltrinelli: Milan, 2013, p. 293.

Phases of Closure

Basaglia moved fast. Between 1971 and 1974 the asylum went through many of the changes that had taken almost double that time in Gorizia. Patients were given back their basic human rights, wards were opened, cruel treatments were phased out. The rigid spatial gender divisions in the asylum ended (leading to a series of moral panics over intimacy between patients). Some of the steps taken were new ones. The hospital was quickly divided into sectors (corresponding to different areas of the city and province) in preparation for its closure. In practice, the Basaglians borrowed from other experiences and ideas – including those of sectoral reformers and the policies employed by territorial reformers such as those in Perugia and Reggio Emilia. Co-operatives were also set up in various sectors. This was another new tactic that allowed patients to move straight into the world of work. Co-operatives would be widely used across Italy to reintegrate mental health patients back into society in the 1970s, 1980s and 1990s.

This period also saw the formation of a vast and multilayered équipe (or a set of équipes) as well as the more spectacular aspects of a creative strategy, such as street theatre and the celebrated Marco Cavallo art-event-happening. Finally, regular meetings were held each day at 5 pm. This ritual became a kind of 'small parliament'.[5] These were not general meetings across the whole hospital, but smaller encounters that were concerned with policy and strategy. There were also regular ward meetings to which everyone was invited, sometimes on a daily basis.

The second phase led directly towards politics with a capital *P*, and the 180 Law. The celebrated press conference announcing the closure of the asylum took place in 1977, in the lead-up to the law being passed in 1978. Basaglia's 1977 announcement took some of his own collaborators by surprise, as Peppe Dell'Acqua recalls in his book about the movement in Trieste in the 1970s, 'Non ho l'arma che uccide il leone' (I haven't got a weapon to kill a lion).[6] Some were worried that simply declaring the

---

5   Giovanna Gallio, Maria Grazia Giannichedda, Ota de Leonardis, Diana Mauri, *La libertà è terapeutica. L'esperienza psichiatrica di Trieste*, Milan: Feltrinelli, 1983, p. 260.

6   'In the evening Franco Rotelli called me . . . we asked ourselves about how our work would change . . . there were still more than 500 patients in San Giovanni including fifty or so

asylum closed would provoke resistance and create a climate of fear around the new mental health centres which were opening up. This period was accompanied by political events linked to the praxis of 1968, and the expansion out to permanent territorial centres in various areas and inside the city's hospital. Closure was not quite as immediate as was promised, but it was pretty rapid. In any case, Basaglia was pushing the envelope, as ever. He was forcing the others to catch up with him.

During the 1970s the psychiatric hospital grounds in Trieste were transformed into an experimental space, hosting art and theatrical projects, exhibitions, plays, conferences, concerts, numerous debates and meetings and international congresses. Militants, students, intellectuals and practitioners flocked to Trieste. It was a time of extraordinary ferment. All of this was conducted with the political support of the governing majority in the province, led by Michele Zanetti, a Christian Democrat. Most of the considerable flak and criticism linked to all this was taken by Zanetti, leaving Basaglia and his collaborators relatively free from the constant interference that they had experienced (in different ways) in Gorizia and Parma. Basaglia later referred to this support as 'the political support of the majority on the Provincial council'.[7] Zanetti's administration came to an end (after seven years and two elections) in January 1977. A (minority) left-wing administration took power in February 1977 and continued the work carried out by Zanetti, Basaglia and others.

Institutions were replaced with other, alternative structures. This process was given different labels: deinstitutionalism, anti-institutionalism – but the word 'negation' was used more sparingly than in the past. Trieste was nonetheless one of the places where 1968 was put into practice. The slogans which popped up all over the hospital were those of the movement: 'Freedom is therapeutic', 'The truth is revolutionary'.

Community housing was set up while wards were unlocked and closed, at first *inside* the hospital complex itself. Wards became

---

patients who were interned under the "forced" regime . . . I realized that I was not the only person to express some perplexity about what had happened'. Dell'Acqua, *Fuori come va?*, pp. 226–7; see also pp. 225–30.

7 Venturini, *Il giardino dei gelsi*, p. 211. For Zanetti's version of events see Parmegiani and Zanetti, *Basaglia. Una biografia*, and Zanetti, 'La provincia di Trieste e la riforma' in *L'ospedale psichiatrico di San Giovanni. Storia e cambiamento 1908/2008*, Milan: Electa, 2008, pp. 70–3.

community flats. The spaces of the asylum were subverted and reused. The Trieste experience mobilized thousands of people. Links were forged with the city and strengthened with student activists all over Italy and internationally. Volunteers began to arrive hoping to work at the site, including students and others from abroad, from local schools and universities, as well as psychiatrists and other medical experts influenced by Basaglian thinking and practice. As one visitor at the time said, 'Everybody went to Trieste.' For Crossley, 'Trieste exerted a "magnetic pull" for radical psychiatrists and animated them.'[8]

From the beginning, Basaglia set up democratic structures (first seen in Gorizia) where everything was discussed at length, in long daily meetings with patients, nurses, psychiatrists and family members. This practice alone revolutionized the way the asylum had previously been run. The total, hierarchical and closed institution was thus opened up internally as well as in terms of its relationship with the city.

Many patients were released quickly back into society, or were moved to a special form of guest status thanks to local reforms (which were challenged by the judiciary). Some were divided by where they came from, not by their 'dangerous' character or through diagnoses that Basaglia and his équipe saw as outdated or useless. This tactic was borrowed from sectoral reformers, although the Basaglians continued to label sectoral reform as the opposite of what they were trying to do.

The methods employed by those working with or alongside the psychiatrists in Trieste were often those of the wider movement, and included occupations and strikes. In February 1978, for example, an abandoned building called the *Casa del marinaio* was occupied in order to make the case for its reuse as a mental health centre.[9] On this occasion, the movement outflanked Basaglia to the left. He opposed the occupation on the grounds that it was a tactical mistake. Basaglia had little truck with gesture politics or events he could not control. He wanted real change.

As in Gorizia and elsewhere, the so-called deinstitutionalization of

---

8   Nick Crossley, *Contesting Psychiatry: Social Movements in Mental Health*, London: Routledge, 2006, pp. 3872, 3920. See also the whole of Chapter 8.

9   After thirteen days the police cleared the building. Basaglia distanced himself from this occupation at the time. See Peppe Dell'Acqua, *Non ho l'arma che uccide il leone. Trent'anni dopo torna la vera storia dei protagonisti del cambiamento nella Trieste di Basaglia e nel manicomio di San Giovanni*, Viterbo: Stampa Alternativa, 2008, pp. 252–65.

Trieste's asylum in the 1970s was a constant struggle: against the local judiciary (as Basaglia said later, 'there was a direct attack upon us from the judiciary'[10]) against public opinion, against the local press (which was extremely hostile to Basaglia and his team) and in the face of organized political opposition (the neo-fascist party was strong in Trieste). There were constant internal political debates, which would become more and more intense as the 1970s wore on. Trieste also had its own, widely publicized incident in 1972 (in fact, there was a whole series of incidents, but only one attained national news status). These incidents will also be discussed in this chapter.

However, as with Gorizia, Parma and elsewhere, there are problems with studying the Basaglian experience in Trieste in the 1970s. The experience of Trieste has been much more cited than studied, and much more *celebrated* than understood. The key elements of the Trieste myth have become yet another standard story – repeated time and time again in almost exactly the same way. The hugely successful TV 'fiction' based on Basaglia's life did much to cement these mythical qualities. Generally, this standard story moves from Basaglia's arrival through to Marco Cavallo and on to the 1977 press conference, taking in a concert by Ornette Coleman, plays by Dario Fo and the stormy *Réseau* (a short-lived international radical psychiatry organization) debates on the way. The sources here are generally circular (the protagonists have created their own narratives), and critical or even alternative voices are rarely heard or even cited. There is no point at all in simply repeating this standard story. It is already out there, in numerous versions – text, film, journalistic. For a historian, the only possible route is to take a critical approach to both the sources available and to the past itself.

The Asylum: San Giovanni

The asylum complex was made up of forty buildings built over a huge site between 1902 and 1908, under the Austro-Hungarian Empire, including over twenty patient pavilions, a church, a theatre and other service and administrative buildings. San Giovanni was officially opened

---

10   Venturini, *Il giardino dei gelsi*, p. 214.

on 1 November 1908, and the city of Trieste (and its asylum) became part of Italy in 1918. During World War Two, a number of Jews were deported by the Nazi occupiers from the asylum to death camps (or to Trieste's own concentration camp).

Trieste's complicated and divided history as a city was closely linked to questions of mental health. Those working in this sector noted the high numbers of exiles in the hospital in the post-war period. Over 250,000 people of Italian origin had left their homes in Istria and else-where in the 1940s and 1950s following the establishment of communism in Yugoslavia. This exodus led to large refugee-exile populations in Trieste, many of whom were housed in cramped temporary accommo-dation for some time, before large housing estates were built for them on the edge of the city. The stresses and strains of this forced migration and change in living conditions, not surprisingly, led to cases of mental breakdown.[11] Doctors and others working in the asylum drew direct connections between the social and political context of post-war Trieste and those who ended up in the psychiatric hospital.[12]

In general, however, the history of Trieste's asylum was unexceptional, and similar to that of many other psychiatric hospitals across the peninsula.

Trieste never produced a written text to rival *The Negated Institution*, which remained the bible for the anti-institutional movement throughout the 1970s, alongside the more theoretical texts produced by the Basaglias in the early part of that decade. It also never produced a television pro-gramme with the impact of *I giardini di Abele*, nor a set of photographs that worked in the same way as those in *Morire di classe*.

Times had changed. Nobody expected the asylum to last for long. There was no point in documenting the total institution or even

---

11   For the history and memory of the *esodo* see John Foot, 'Memories of an Exodus: Istria, Fiume, Dalmatia, Trieste, Italy, 1943–2010' in Daniela Baratieri, Mark Edele and Giuseppe Finaldi, eds, *Totaliarian Dictatorship. New Histories,* London: Routledge, 2013, pp. 232–50, and for divided memories in Trieste see John Foot, *Fratture d'italia. Da Caporetto al G8 di Genova. La memoria divisa del paese,* Milan: Rizzoli, pp. 119–60.

12   Giovanna Gallio, 'Sugli assetti politico-professionali dell'assistenza' in Gallio et al., *La libertà è terapeutica,* pp. 76–9, and see also 'La storia esemplare di Giovanni Doz' in Dell'Acqua, *Non ho l'arma,* pp. 18–22.

denouncing it. That battle had been won. Photographers and film-makers were interested, now, in capturing images of a movement and an institution undergoing rapid change – shots from a revolution, in short. Trieste quickly became Italy's prime example of a concrete utopia, a place 'people visit . . . in order to learn how to practise differently, how to perceive, think and act in different ways'.[13] It was a place of pilgrimage, where new ways of doing things and new theories were explained, demonstrated and put into practice.

Basaglia made complete use of the 1968 reforms and Zanetti's full support. Ex-patients were provided with cash benefits and housing. Other patients were 'volunteers' who had never been under the previous 'forced recovery' regime. Some of these were private patients. Basaglia and Zanetti filled the hospital with doctors, volunteers, psychologists, sociologists, militants, artists and musicians, and emptied it of patients. An incredible 122 people were taken on to work in the asylum under the Basaglia regime. In Gorizia, there had only been six doctors. Paradoxically, as the numbers of patients diminished, the number of Basaglian *operatori* increased massively. By the end, there were more *operatori* than patients. It became a kind of university or training-ground for new psychiatric practice.

Basaglia was the undoubted leader of this whole experience. He was also more of a one-man band than he had been in the past. Although Franca Ongaro was often around in Trieste, she was based in Venice throughout this time. Her role in Gorizia had been much more central than during the 1970s. The couple still worked together on a series of books and projects, but Basaglia also collaborated with others. His writing became more obscure as time went on, and less incisive. In Gorizia, the Basaglia family had been an integral part of the experience. In Trieste, the undoubted protagonist and leader was Franco Basaglia. The family played a supporting role.

Basaglia commuted back and forth between the two cities and lived in various places in Trieste – most often in a flat inside the hospital grounds itself. It was a heady and intense time. Basaglia had recharged his batteries after the difficult end to the Gorizia experiment and the problems in Parma.

---

13   Nick Crossley, 'Working Utopias and Social Movements', *Sociology* 33: 4, 1999, p. 817.

He was also working on a number of fronts and at a number of levels –
inside the hospital, in the territory, in the political arena (in Rome). As in
Gorizia, big risks were taken by the doctors involved on a daily basis. A
number of well-publicized incidents took place in Trieste in the 1970s.
However, unlike Gorizia in 1968, these incidents did not threaten to bring
the whole process of change to a halt.

The Second Incident: Giordano Savarin, June 1973

'The crazy murderer'

Il Piccolo on Giordano Savarin[14]

'We had been in Trieste for just three months. A young patient,
who had spent various periods in the asylum over a period of years,
was dismissed . . . in December 1971, and killed his father and
mother. This was the Savarin Case. It had a shocking effect on
public opinion. The first open doors, the first dismissals, the first
meetings were obscured by furious debates, accusations, trials and
ferocious attacks which wanted to label our work as utopian and
above all dangerous.'

Peppe Dell'Acqua[15]

Giordano Savarin was forty-three years old and had been committed to
the San Giovanni asylum on at least three occasions since 1970. He had
been released experimentally from the asylum in February 1972 and
went back to the family home. The Savarins lived in a small suburb of
Trieste – Aquilina – very close to the border with Yugoslavia. The Savarin
family were poor: Giordano and his parents slept in the same bedroom
in their farmhouse dwelling. Giordano Savarin (or his illiterate mother
– this was a point of contention at the trial) was given a long list of
medication that he was supposed to take.

On the day of the murders, it seems that Savarin argued with his
mother (Caterina Stupancich) over the use of a cutting machine and

---

14   'Padre e madre massacrati da un folle a coltellate', *Il Piccolo*, 11 June 1972.
15   Dell'Acqua, *Non ho l'arma*, p. 130.

about money. Savarin then killed his mother with a 'rudimentary' knife in the kitchen. When his father, Giovanni Savarin, heard the screams, he was also stabbed to death on the outside stairs. *Il Piccolo* published a horrific photo on its front page, showing the bloodstained staircase on the outside of the house. Savarin was readmitted to San Giovanni that evening.

Savarin was judged (in 1973), like Miklus before him, to be 'of unsound mind at the time of the incident and socially dangerous' and sent (like Miklus) to the criminal asylum in Reggio Emilia for a minimum of ten years. He was diagnosed as a paranoid schizophrenic. None of the works dedicated to the Savarin case make any mention of what happened to him after that. He disappears completely from the story, which then centres on Basaglia.

Events then followed in Trieste that were highly reminiscent of Gorizia in 1968, although this time, Basaglia knew what to expect and was confident that he could win. The local press ran a strong campaign against what was happening inside (and outside) of the asylum, and Basaglia was duly charged with manslaughter, although the rationale behind the charge was somewhat tenuous. Savarin's mother was illiterate, and therefore the prosecutor argued that she would not have been able to administer the cocktail of drugs prescribed to help him, and that it was therefore irresponsible of Basaglia to release Savarin to his mother's care.

Meanwhile, there was something of a moral panic in the city, and the neo-fascist Italian Social Movement went on the attack.[16] The neo-fascists were very strong in Trieste, and the party won nearly 15 per cent of the local vote in 1958, 13 per cent in 1962, 10 per cent in 1966 and 12.5 per cent in 1972, which were figures well above the national average. The local neo-fascist deputy Renzo de' Vidovich was particularly active in Parliament itself, asking questions about the Savarin case which were hostile to Basaglia. It was said in the press that Savarin had threatened neighbours and others, although none of this seems to have had much impact on the legal process. Another (much less well-known) doctor was also charged and eventually convicted in association with the Savarin case. His name was Edoardo De Michelini, and he worked in one of the first decentralized mental health clinics in the city, the closest to where

---

16 'Angoscia dopo l'atroce delitto', *Il Piccolo*, 12 June 1972.

the murders took place, in Muggia on the other side of the bay from
Trieste.[17] Michelini was accused of failing to keep an adequate check on
the condition of Savarin in the outside world.

In March 1975 (nearly three years after the murders) it was decided
that Basaglia and De Michelini would both stand trial in Trieste.[18] The
trial finally began on 24 November 1975, and it was national news.[19]
But it only lasted two days, with Basaglia cleared and De Michelini given
a sixteen-month suspended sentence. In 1977 an appeal was held (for
both men – in Italy the prosecution can also appeal) and Basaglia and
De Michelini were both cleared. The drawn-out legal process finally
came to an end in the high court in April 1978, with the confirmation
of these decisions.

Later, Basaglia looked back on what had happened with Savarin. He
argued that the judges in the city had decided to 'attack us immediately',
while in Gorizia they had waited ten years before acting.[20] For Basaglia,
the fact that the Trieste movement had begun to unmask systems of
power and re-evaluate stigmas attached to mental health patients represented a threat to institutions in general.[21] He saw these charges as a
case of a reactionary institution defending itself from reform and change.
There were also constant attempts by magistrates to make the work of
Basaglia and his team more difficult in other ways, such as the limits
placed on guest status for patients. Further investigations followed into
the use of the contraceptive pill by patients in the hospital or in mental
health centres, as well as into such important issues as the cost of sheets.
The whole Trieste experience was marked by constant struggles with the
judiciary in the city, but none of this had much effect on the progress of
the movement. The magistrates were fighting a losing battle.

---

17   This was a small *Centro per igiene mentale* (CIM), set up under the provisions of the
1968 reforms. A fully-fledged *Centro per la salute mentale* (CSM) was opened in 1975 in Muggia.

18   'Basaglia a giudizio per omicidio colposo', *La Stampa*, 9 March 1975.

19   'Il professor Franco Basaglia difende l'ospedale aperta', *La Stampa*, 25 November 1975.

20   Venturini, *Il giardino dei gelsi*, p. 214.

21   Ibid.

The Third Incident: Maria Letizia Michelazzi, 1977

Maria Letizia Michelazzi of Trani turned up in San Giovanni on 27 June 1977. She was twenty-seven years old and needed help (she had tried to commit suicide on a number of occasions). She explained that a lobotomy had been performed on her in Switzerland after a psychiatric crisis. The two doctors on duty decided not to admit her to the hospital and Michelazzi left. They appeared not to believe her lobotomy story. Two days later, she drowned her four-year-old son, Paolo, in the bath at her home. She then went to the police station and gave herself up. As with Miklus and Savarin, Michelazzi was sent to a criminal asylum (this time in Tuscany).[22] She committed suicide there in 1982.

Both doctors, Vincenzo Pastore and Lorenzo Toresini, were charged with manslaughter. The investigation continued for more than a year. Then, an anonymous letter arrived which claimed that Michelazzi had threatened to kill her own son during the original meeting with the doctors. This seemed to tip the balance for the prosecution. The first trial was held in 1980 and both doctors were cleared. In 1982 there was an appeal, and the result was the same. Given the horrific nature of the case, this murder led to extensive debate in the city. It was studied in detail by one of the doctors involved (Toresini), who later published a book with an in-depth analysis of the murder and its aftermath.[23]

Basaglia in Trieste: History and Memory

Michele Zanetti was a young and bespectacled Christian Democrat politician. He was also a high-flyer and was just thirty when he became president of the smallest provincial government in Italy, that of Trieste, in 1970. Zanetti was in charge of a centre-left administration with a thin majority, which did not include the Communist Party, but the Socialists, Republicans and Social-Democrats as well as the DC.

Like Mario Tommasini, Ilvano Rasimelli, Bruno Benigni and others

---

22 In 1994 Paolo's father also committed suicide.

23 Lorenzo Toresini, ed., *La testa tagliata. Figlicidio e leucotomia. Un processo storico a due psichiatri riformatori*, Merano: Verlag Edizioni, 2001.

before him, Zanetti was appalled by what he saw in the asylum under his control, and like those other administrators he was very interested in what had happened in Gorizia in the 1960s. A dinner was arranged with Franco Basaglia in Venice, and Zanetti offered Basaglia complete autonomy (and support) if he were to take over the Trieste asylum. Basaglia accepted and became director there in 1971 following a competition. After the hiatus following the Miklus incident, the revolution in Italian mental health care was about to start again in earnest. This time, things would be very different. At the same time, Agostino Pirella took over in Arezzo, and Antonio Slavich had decided to go to Ferrara. Giovanni Jervis and Letizia Comba were already established in Reggio Emilia, and Lucio Schittar was in Pordenone. Domenico Casagrande, meanwhile, would go on to take over (and eventually close down) both psychiatric hospitals in Venice. The former members of the Gorizian équipe were now in charge of asylums across Italy. This was another sign of the way the tide was turning their way.

Trieste was not Gorizia, and 1971 was not 1961. A vast movement was in full flow across the world, and what became known as anti-psychiatry was a key part of its driving ideology. Once in charge in Trieste, Basaglia and his team moved with great speed. The plan was simple: to *close down the hospital*, from above, and quickly. Everything seemed possible. The Gorizian utopia was to become a concrete reality in Trieste. It was as if things were stuck on fast forward.

The contradictions inherent in the Basaglia project – a group of people in charge of an institution they did not believe had a right to exist, and that many of them saw as akin to a Nazi concentration camp – was to be resolved. This time, the doctors would not leave the institution intact. The resolution of the contradiction would take place in another way in Trieste, with the end of the institution itself. The institution was not to be negated; it would be eliminated, forever.

As the 1970s wore on, and right into the 1980s and 1990s, Trieste became a beacon for change. It was the symbol of what could be done, of radicalism in general, of a social, cultural and medical revolution. Much more than Gorizia, Trieste became a concrete utopia, a place where transformation could be touched, experienced, seen with your own eyes. Basaglia presided over all this with the experience of Gorizia and Parma behind him.

He wasn't interested in creating another 'golden cage', or a Maxwell Jones–
like therapeutic community. All of that was superfluous, a waste of time.
The key work would be outside of the asylum, in the city of Trieste and
across the province. It was time not just to break down the walls, but to
construct something entirely new, an alternative to the psychiatric hospital
itself. Time would not be lost in internal conflicts with hostile doctors,
nurses or administrators. Things were moving firmly in the direction the
Basaglians wanted. They had, literally, taken over the asylum.

The general assemblies used in Gorizia (and continued in Arezzo) were
abandoned and replaced with daily open staff meetings that were used to
decide on strategy.[24] Much more than in Gorizia, the strategy employed
in Trieste reached out way beyond the walls of the asylum. The whole array
of the movement was employed in order to galvanize public opinion and
as part of a sophisticated media strategy, in alliance with artists, theatre
directors, actors, musicians, film-makers and others. Trieste became a
magnet for the left across Europe and beyond. For example, a number of
activists from the anti-psychiatric SPK (Socialist Patients Collective) movement in Heidelberg, which had been closed down by the authorities,
turned up to work in Trieste. Some are still there today.[25]

Trieste became the heart of a national movement. The Basaglians felt
powerful, that anything was possible. On one occasion, a number of
patients were taken on holiday in order to facilitate the closure of wards.
As Basaglia said in an interview at the end of the 1970s, 'We began to
see that it was possible, with tenacity, to get all the patients out of the
madhouse, one by one.'[26]

This revolution did not end with the closure of the asylum. In many
ways, as Franco Rotelli and others have argued, this closure was just the
beginning. Basaglian methods were to be applied to health care across
the board. Rotelli (who had worked with Basaglia in Parma and was his
successor in Trieste) eventually became head of the entire health service
in the city, and psychiatrists working with Basaglian methods remained

---

24   Although it appears that there were weekly general meetings in 1972. Giovanna Gallio,
'La distruzione dell'ospedale psichiatrico. Una cronologia: 1971–1981' in *L'ospedale psichiatrico
di San Giovanni*, p. 54.

25   For an account of the SPK see *SPK. Turn Illness into a Weapon for Agitation* by the
Socialist Patients' Collective at the University of Heidelberg (Heidelberg: KRRIM, 1993).

26   Venturini, *Il giardino dei gelsi*, p. 212.

in charge of the system right up to the early twenty-first century. In recent years, however, the whole radical system in the city has come under pressure. There is a strong sense that the revolutionary period has come to an end, and that those who remain have found it difficult to defend what was constructed in the past. Trieste became a model for world health care reform, recognized by the World Health Organization as such. Teams from the city were (and are) sent in to trouble spots to sort out asylums that needed changing, or closing.

Trieste was very different to Gorizia, and to Colorno. Basaglia was given total political support and the team was already preformed, backed by a mass of activists and volunteers. The phenomenon that was 1968 had happened, and was ongoing. Moreover, although there was political opposition in the city, there was no sense of an *alternative* project. Trieste was a big and multi-ethnic city, with a university, international connections and a working-class movement. This was no backwater. There was certainly considerable opposition to the Basaglians in the city, but the overall project – the closure of the asylum – was seen as inevitable.

Trieste was where Basaglia had his greatest impact (between 1971 and 1979 directly, but before and after those dates in terms of his ideas) and where his legacy is the greatest. The city, and in particular its asylum, became the centre, the capital, of the Basaglia project. After the frustrations of his experiences in Gorizia and Colorno, Basaglia worked quickly. The gates and many of the walls came down almost immediately, often in symbolic demolitions carried out by patients and others.

With respect to Gorizia and Colorno, the decision-making structures were streamlined. The asylum was made more humane, but only as part of a strategy for its elimination. General meetings, as noted, were abolished. They were part of the past. This is not to say that there were not meetings in Trieste – far from it. But these meetings were strategic: they took decisions, and quickly. They were not seen (at least by Basaglia) as important in themselves. This choice was controversial within the movement, which was still very much attached to the idea of the general meeting. In Arezzo and elsewhere, general meetings were a key part of the anti-asylum outlook, but not in Trieste.

Part of the first and second équipes from Gorizia came with Basaglia to Trieste in 1971, but most of the key members of the original Gorizian movement spread out across Italy. This was now an enlarged national équipe, covering a number of cities and different types of asylums. The national organization set up by Basaglia and others – Psichiatria Democratica – worked in a haphazard fashion but was fairly effective for a time, despite bitter and occasionally farcical internal struggles. There was general agreement on the overall strategy (even when the debates themselves were constant and personal divisions hampered progress), and contact between different movements and cities was frequent, as were exchanges of ideas and personnel. This national organization did its best to co-ordinate strategy and spread the word.

But each experience also had its own history and created its own specific legacy. This was a polycentric movement. After the closing down of the Gorizian experiment in 1972, many Gorizians came straight to Trieste, at least for a short period, most notably Casagrande (1973–78) and Ernesto Venturini. Michele Risso and Gianfranco Minguzzi were a constant presence. A further part of the Trieste équipe followed Basaglia directly from Colorno, including Franco Rotelli, Luciano Carrino, Peppe Dell'Acqua and Giovanna Gallio.

A key aspect of the strategy in Trieste lay in the connections made with the city (an issue which had been a key sticking point in Gorizia). In Trieste the walls between the city and the asylum were broken down symbolically and physically. Patients and technicians took their struggle out into the city, and the city was invited into the asylum. In many cases, this took the form of provocation, in a typically Basaglian fashion. Things were pushed to the limit, to expose the contradictions in the system. Great risks were taken.

Besides the numerous patients who were soon released from the asylum, either temporarily or permanently, hundreds more were rapidly given guest status (as a result of special measures passed by the Trieste provincial administration in 1973 which went further than the provisions allowed under the 1968 reforms), which meant that they were free to leave. In this sense, Guattari described the work of Basaglia as 'a war of liberation'.[27] Co-operatives were encouraged to work with patients and ex-patients in order to reintegrate them into society. Basaglia believed

---

27   Gary Genosko, ed., *The Guattari Reader*, Oxford: Blackwell, 1996, p. 42.

strongly in the therapeutic and liberatory aspects of work. Patients created and ran a bar on the hospital grounds, known as Il Posto delle Fragole. Others set up a theatre company. Concerts and political meetings were held in the grounds of the asylum. Other initiatives borrowed from situationist and even surrealist thought.

Artists played a key role in the communication and media strategies employed by Basaglia, who encouraged groups of artists to work with patients within the hospital, including his cousin Vittorio. Another artist – Ugo Guarino – created extraordinary and powerful sculptures out of the (by now largely unused) architectural furniture of the total institution – beds, bars, strait jackets. *I testimoni* was one of his most powerful works.[28] Guarino also used innovative forms of graphic design to create propaganda for the struggle – cartoon strips, murals, posters and logos.

Numerous concerts and political meetings were held in the grounds of the asylum. In September 1975, a group of patients was taken up in a specially arranged flight around Venice, something that had been denied to them in the past (none had ever been in a plane before). This event was filmed and became part of the folklore of the 1970s.[29] It was also used to criticize Basaglia and portray him as an amateurish practitioner interested in short-term stunts.

Marco Cavallo: *The Horse, the Project, the Myth*

In Trieste, as in Arezzo, Parma, Perugia and Ferrara, the closing down of the asylum was 'carried on in a very public fashion'.[30] It was, in some ways, a series of 'happenings'. Most famously of all, in a celebrated act of symbolic liberation, a large blue papier mâché horse (known as Marco Cavallo), constructed in an art workshop within an ex-ward, was wheeled through town by patients, artists and activists. This moment developed

---

28   See Ugo Guarino, *Zitti e buoni. Tecniche di controllo*, Milan: Feltrinelli, 1979, ecn.org, and the photos of Guarino's work at porto.trieste.it. See also the magazine *847* (a title taken from the number of patients inside the hospital at that particular time).

29   *Il volo* (Silvano Agosti, 1975). See also the photographs in Claudio Ernè, *Basaglia a Trieste*, at cinemaepsicoanalisi.com

30   Michael Donnelly, *The Politics of Mental Health in Italy*, London: Tavistock, 1992, p. 67.

into a key memory of change relating to the Basaglian movements and of the 1968 movements *tout court*, and was filmed for posterity in grainy Super 8, as well as shot by a number of photographers.[31]

The origins of the Marco Cavallo happening took place during the 1972 Christmas holidays, when a series of meetings was held in Venice involving Franco Basaglia, Giuliano Scabia, Vittorio Basaglia and others. According to Scabia, Basaglia's invitation was very open: 'Come and do what you want!' Scabia kept a diary of what happened next (parts of which were reconstructed afterwards for a publication based on Marco Cavallo). Scabia had been born in 1935 in Venice. He was an experimental theatre practitioner and writer, interested in street and political theatre. Later, Giulio Bollati convinced him to produce a whole book dedicated to his experiences in Trieste. The story of this blue papier mâché horse became such a powerful memory of the whole Basaglian experience that it is difficult to read an account of Trieste in the 1970s that does not mention Marco Cavallo.

Scabia, Vittorio Basaglia and a small group of collaborators and friends were given free run of the hospital grounds. Everything was very spontaneous and open, in keeping with the spirit of the times. Students, sociologists, artists, doctors and patients were all involved. The whole experiment was referred to as a laboratory. The group moved around the spaces inside the vast grounds of the hospital, asking for contributions and ideas. People dropped in and out. Most of the artistic work was carried out in an ex-ward (Reparto P). A little platform was set up and people were encouraged to tell their own stories. Slowly, more and more people (and especially patients) started to come along and contribute. White paper was put up on the walls, and an old wooden cart was wheeled in. The story of the horse – which became Marco Cavallo – was originally told by a patient. The horse had a real connection to the hospital and its history:

His name was not plucked from thin air. Marco had been the name of the horse who used to cart away the hospital's dirty linen – the only one, as some of the older patients quipped, who managed to get out of the hospital.[32]

---

31   For the Marco Cavallo event and its history see Giuliano Scabia, *Marco Cavallo. Un'esperienza di animazione in un ospedale psichiatrico*, Turin: Einaudi, 1976.

32   Donnelly, *The Politics of Mental Health in Italy*, p. 67.

The theatre laboratory that would 'make' Marco Cavallo worked through January and February 1973. A daily newsletter was produced and big puppets were made, with massive heads. Some people even wanted to paint a portrait of Basaglia himself. But some of those in the hospital were not happy with what was going on. They wanted to privilege the idea of struggle, not celebrate what had already been achieved.

According to the story often told about this event (and portrayed in the TV film about Basaglia), the horse was too big to fit through the doors of the ward, so it was decided that this barrier needed to be knocked down in order to 'release' the work of art. This was a classic Basaglian moment, in line with practice from Gorizia onwards. A famous photo of Basaglia shows him trying to break through the metal grates that had imprisoned the horse statue. However, in the end, one final metal door resisted all efforts to destroy it, and the horse was moved sideways through the gap (as Scabia confirms in his account).[33] At the time, characteristically perhaps, a huge debate took place over the *meaning* of the horse's exit and above all its political significance. Peppe dell'Acqua, a key participant and later chronicler of the Basaglian experience in Trieste, tells of a discussion that raged on until four in the morning. There were even threats of a physical confrontation.[34]

In the end, an agreement was reached: 'the horse will leave'; and a leaflet was drawn up to accompany the event. This document was a classic Basaglia combination of philosophical thought and media strategy ('Marco Cavallo is a symbol of the ongoing liberation process for all those who suffer in the life of the asylum'), alongside specific political and economic demands (about hours and working conditions). The leaflet was signed by the nurses, doctors and artists from the psychiatric hospital of Trieste, 25 March 1973 (but not, interestingly, by the patients).

The Marco Cavallo leaflet was also instructive in terms of its radical language. Its demands were very concrete – working hours, housing for patients, resources to support the closure of the hospital. And these demands were backed up not by rhetoric, but by explicit links to strikes and other struggles. However, in the ways that the memory and the

---

33   Scabia, *Marco Cavallo*, p. 188. See also Dell'acqua, *Non ho l'arma*, p. 152.

34   Dell'Acqua, *Non ho l'arma*, pp. 154–6 (and for the whole Marco Cavallo event and history of the horse, pp. 147–65).

Marco Cavallo narrative have been transmitted through time *since* 1973, this radical, social edge has been removed from the whole story.

The Marco Cavallo event is often recounted as a joyous, purely symbolic moment. There were, as we have seen, a number of happenings which accompanied the movement, but what really mattered was a series of practical measures designed to create alternative institutions – in terms of form *and* content – to the asylum. These included housing, subsidies, co-operatives, mental health day centres and an emergency centre inside the city's hospital. This network of support institutions and structures replaced the asylum. At no point were patients simply pushed back towards their families or abandoned in the outside world (at least in Trieste). But each city had its own particular experience and its own stories to tell.

The symbolism did not end with the wall, its destruction or the horse's exit/liberation. Basaglian philosophy centred on the elimination of barriers between the 'ill' and the 'normal', and those between doctors and patients (an idea common to many critical psychiatrists at the time). So, by taking the 'mad' *out* into the world of the 'normal' (the horse had been invited to a local street festival in the city), this philosophy was being put into practice. Basaglia argued,

> The opening up of the hospital and freedom of communication can only work if the *external* world participates as one part of the relationship – freedom of communication will remain an artifice if we are unable to open up and keep a dialogue going between the *internal* and *external* worlds . . . It is necessary at this stage that the external world recognizes the psychiatric hospital as its own, and that a connection is made between an institution which is helping to rehabilitate people and a society which desires rehabilitation . . . Once the exclusionary nature of the traditional psychiatric institutions has been made clear towards the experimentation with new therapeutic dimensions, it is the external world which will determine the degree to which this new communication will be accepted.[35]

---

35 Franco Basaglia and Franca Ongaro, Introduction to *Morire di classe*, Turin: Einaudi, 1969, p. 6; also (without the italics) in Franco Basaglia, *Scritti. II. 1968–1980,* ed. Franca Ongaro Basaglia, Turin: Einaudi, 1982, p. 78.

This was a relatively new strategy which had emerged from the synthesis of the experiences of Gorizia, Reggio Emilia, Perugia and Parma, and from the 1970s in general. The city itself was being appropriated by the movement, and the 'long march through the institutions' was reaching out into society itself. In Gorizia, the city had been absent from the whole experience, apart from it in a negative sense. To cite Basaglia again:

> In Trieste patients have returned to life in different ways, and without those instruments which seemed indispensable in Gorizia – ward meetings, general assemblies and so on. There were still meetings in Trieste, but, symbolically and in reality, they were held with a city in crisis.

Scabia, the radical theatre practitioner who was a key figure in this whole project, said (perhaps somewhat optimistically): 'This is an important moment. Marco Cavallo is about to leave. And the whole madhouse will leave with him.' Thus the exit of Marco Cavallo brought together the philosophy and practice of the Basaglian movement. The 'mad' and the 'normal' were thrown together. It was also a moment of pure theatre, a provocation, a situationist act – a creative use of various forms of media. In itself, however, it changed absolutely nothing. Basaglia recognized some of these points in an interview given at the end of the 1970s. 'Probably', he said, 'we have done much which could be seen as propaganda . . . and which have given our critics on the left a lot of ammunition . . . we have used all the means at our disposal.' 'Trieste was', he concluded, 'in reality, a kind of "Tachai" [a model village used as an example by Mao and the Maoists]'.[36]

A final touch was provided by another form of concrete utopia, as patients were encouraged to write down their dreams and hopes, and these scraps of paper were then integrated into the bright blue papier mâché form of Marco Cavallo. As the horse was wheeled through the gate, down the hill and into the city itself, he was carrying with him the

---

36   This referenced supposed model agricultural communes, which took on mythical qualities in the West in connection with Mao's China. Venturini, *Il giardino dei gelsi*, p. 212. Jervis, for example, was withering in his criticism of initiatives such as 'the plane' and Marco Cavallo in Luigi Onnis and Giuditta Lo Russo, eds, *Dove va la psichiatria? Pareri a confronto su salute mentale e manicomi in Italia dopo la nuova legge*, Milan: Feltrinelli, 1980, pp. 92, 94.

dreams of those who were still unable to leave. So the exit of Marco into the town was symbolic at a number of levels. It showed that the patients themselves were also on the verge of being released, and that some of their dreams could be fulfilled, but only in alliance with the 'normal' population.[37]

David Forgacs takes up the story of what happened next:

> Four hundred patients from two mental hospitals accompanied the blue horse through the streets of Trieste . . . The symbolism could be interpreted as that of the Trojan horse in reverse: wheeled from inside a walled compound to the outside, not to invade and capture a city but to free captives.[38]

The elaborate construction of the horse had also been an attempt at a form of therapy. The complicated story of Marco Cavallo, then, from beginning to end, was part of a wider process of change – moving between personal, institutional and political levels. The horse statue was not actually made by the patients, but 'the patients built it, without ever touching the horse itself . . . producing something which was more durable, more indefinite'.[39] Marco Cavallo's trip was not to be his last: 'It was exhibited in schools, fairs and marketplaces, and it travelled outside Italy as well.'[40] The horse continues to appear across Italy, and a permanent copy was made by Vittorio Basaglia after his cousin Franco's early death in 1980.

By the 1970s, the '1968' movement was powerful and in full swing. Politics was everywhere, and a whole generation had been politicized. As a result, debates within the Trieste movement embraced a whole range of political positions, some of which were undoubtedly extreme. Basaglia had little patience with excessively ideological discussions, even if he himself had helped to provoke them with his writings. He was interested

---

37　See Donnelly, *The Politics of Mental Health in Italy*, p. 67.

38　David Forgacs, *Italy's Margins*, p. 221.

39　Dell'Acqua, *Non ho l'arma*, p. 152.

40　'The Utopia of Reality: Franco Basaglia and the Practice of Democratic Psychiatry' in Scheper-Hughes and Lovell, eds, *Psychiatry Inside Out*, p. 30. This use of Marco Cavallo continues to this day; see for example the video on Marco Cavallo at teatrovalleoccupato.it.

in bringing theory and practice together. But by 1973 every issue was the subject of lengthy debate and long communiqués. The movement took itself very seriously indeed.

After Basaglia: Memory and Forgetting in the Trieste Ex-Asylum

There are still walls around the edge of the ex-hospital, but the gate has gone. Anyone can drive or walk in and out of the grounds. Even today, the site has explicit links with the Basaglian-inspired revolution that took place there. Two Marco Cavallo horses stand in the grounds. One is a proper statue in bronze. It has no textual information to accompany it. The shape alone is enough to remind visitors (but not all of them) of the power and importance, symbolically, of the Marco Cavallo event in 1973. But this is a somewhat static monument, a traditional representation of a revolutionary moment, the near-fossilization of a dynamic experience. It could also be seen, alternatively, as a reminder of the distance that separates the Trieste of today from that of 1973.

In order, perhaps to counteract the sensation of the bronze Marco Cavallo, further down the hill there was a striking blue version of the horse (in 2008), standing on its wheels outside the new museum (which is now closed). This horse sends out a different message to the other statue: *the revolution goes on*, in line with the theory and practice of Franco Basaglia. This version of the horse has been placed in different parts of the ex-hospital over the years, including, strikingly, at the entrance itself. It also, occasionally, goes on tour.

On the thirtieth anniversary of the 1978 Basaglia law, a theatre production was staged in Trieste by a company that rehearses in spaces that were once part of the asylum itself. Many of the actors in the company were patients at one point, or have had dealings with mental health care services. This production centred on the experience of Marco Cavallo, and used a copy of the horse to tell the story of change that had its core in Trieste. Moreover, this production was at the same time a form of therapy, and had its origins in the use of theatre and art by Basaglia for those with mental health problems.

In 2008, a packed crowd filed into the Slovenian Theatre in Trieste for a production which was part of this anniversary. This play was the centrepiece of a series of celebrations and debates, and its title was significant – *Long Live Basaglia*. Although nostalgic, the play was Basaglian in terms of its method, including a sequence where the actors and actresses wore false moustaches and all claimed to be the head of mental health services in the city at the time: Peppe Dell'Acqua. The cries, 'I am Peppe Dell'Acqua' and '*No, I* am Peppe Dell'Acqua' were a clear attempt to debunk versions of the past and present, which often verged on hagiography. When Peppe Dell'Acqua got up on-stage and joined in the fun, with his own 'No, I am Peppe Dell'Acqua', the boundaries between the real and the fictional, and the hierarchies of care and power, had been broken down, at least in this brief instance.

The play was about memory (of asylums, of the movement, of Marco Cavallo – who appeared on-stage) but it was also a study of change, as the actors played themselves and described the ways in which they had been transformed by institutional and political change. Moreover, the links to Basaglian memory and to Basaglian places were many. This company was a living example of Basaglian ideas, a memory of itself, and a force for change, all at the same time, looking backwards and forwards simultaneously.[41]

Trieste started to make its archive public, and a museum was set up inside the grounds of the former hospital in 2008–09. This project utilized a multimedia archive and drew on the memories of those people linked to the Basaglia project who still work and/or live in the city. The archive was organized through interactive tables, set up by the art group Studio Azzurro, which specializes in multimedia exhibitions and museum layout. Even the form of this museum was Basaglian, with its emphasis on interaction, choice, and participation. Each interactive table allowed access, through touch screens, to a series of photographs that were linked to the memory of three distinct but related stages of asylum and mental health care history. First, there was the history of the total institution, then the story of change (the negated institution) and finally the ongoing story of Basaglian institutions today.

41   Giuliano Scabia ed., *La luce di dentro. Viva Franco Basaglia. Da Marco Cavallo all'Accademia di Follia*, Corazzino: Titivillus Mostre Editoria, 2010.

These tables allowed participants (visitors, schoolchildren) to make their own albums from the photos they chose, and to take these images away with them at the end of the visit. All this was housed in a significant place, close to the offices where Basaglia worked and to flats created on-site for ex-patients to live in which had begun to break down the logic of the repressive institution. Five ex-patients still lived on the site at the time, creating a real bond between the work of the past and that of the future. Finally, there was a conscious attempt to demystify Basaglia himself. Around the walls of the small museum stood various statues (created ad hoc for the exhibition) of previous directors of the asylum. These included a bust of Franco Basaglia that was, however, covered with a sheet in order to create a disconnection between his institutional role and that of his predecessors, and also to debunk the Basaglia myth. In some ways, then, this is 'a museum for something that couldn't be put into a museum'.[42] Nonetheless, in the photos themselves and in many of the documents available there, this myth *was* reinforced time and time again. The image of Basaglia as a saint, prophet and martyr is ever present in much of the literature relating to Basaglia, as well as the cultural production (documentaries, TV films, books, photographs) that has appeared since his death.

A key feature of the ex-asylum site in Trieste was continuity with Basaglia theory and practice. The area still hosts a number of activities linked to mental health care – co-operatives where ex- and current patients work, a theatre company, administrative offices for those running mental health care services in the city and province. A radio station called Radio Fragola, run on co-operative lines, produces programmes on-site dedicated in part to mental health issues, as well as providing training for broadcasters.[43] Many of these programmes are transmitted across radio networks constructed out of a series of free and radical stations set up in the 1970s and still in operation today. Basaglian principles reach out from this core into the network of services across the city and province, creating a link between past and present, and between theory and practice.

---

42   Stefano Graziani, 'A story told backwards. At some point I noticed that Basaglia always wore a tie' in Garcìa, *From Basaglia to Brazil*, p. 23.

43   This radio station has recently run into financial difficulty, however.

Emergency mental health cases are dealt with in an unlocked centre inside Trieste's main city hospital. Here the layout of the centre is closer to a hotel than a hospital ward. It feels in no way like being in a hospital. This sensation is confirmed by the details inside – the furniture, the layout, the very terminology of the place. In addition, the doctors working there wear normal clothes (there are no white coats to be seen). This emergency drop-in centre thus applies Basaglian principles to mental health care, attempting to deal with issues that arise as much from a social or cultural point of view as from a medical one. Nobody is meant to stay for long in these places. There is a conscious attempt here to avoid any sense of reinstitutionalization (from the point of view of doctors and nurses, and from that of the patients).

Trieste today has four day-centres dealing with mental health.[44] These were originally set up at various points in the Basaglian period after a long political struggle. Patients and others can drop in when they please, see psychiatrists and pick up prescriptions but also simply hang out with others and receive basic care as well as food and shelter. Operators working in these centres are acutely aware of the dangers of creating mini-asylums, an accusation often levelled against the Basaglians that they are still working within the logic of psychiatric care and therefore part of the system which had created asylums.[45] Attempts have been made to create an architectural and social context that prevents asylum-like practices reappearing, but these can backfire, leaving the system open to a charge of utopian thinking. For example, in one day-care centre I was told that a balcony created for the patients upstairs had to be kept locked up after suicide attempts.

Moreover, the feeling here, on the front-line, was that drugs were often used to keep things quiet, and that the revolutionary drive of the Basaglia period was on the wane given pressure on resources. Memory and forgetting thus also appear in the very shape of these institutions, their everyday practice, and the personnel who work within them as well as their patients.

---

44 Originally there were more centres (seven was the peak), but some have closed due to population decline and other factors.

45 This critique of Basaglia, fashionable on the far-left in the 1970s, has faded from view in recent years.

There is a constant struggle, in Trieste, between the application of Basaglian principles and the harsh realities of everyday life, without the vast movement of 1968 and its political support. This is not to say that those working in Trieste's health-care system are not able to move with the times. The previous orthodoxy about the housing of patients with mental health issues was linked to *collective* housing, where group therapy (be it explicit or social – created spontaneously through the very act of living together) is being replaced by an increased emphasis on individual housing structures. In this area, as in so many others, the Trieste model is leading the world. The Trieste experience contradicts the lapidary judgement of Roy Porter in his *Madness. A Brief History* that 'chaos ensued' after the 1978 law in Italy.[46]

On the site of the ex-asylum itself, other examples of continuity with the past included the survival of some of the revolutionary graffitti from the 1970s, such as the phrase 'The truth is revolutionary' scrawled on one of the walls. However, over the years, whether by design or simply because of ignorance, many of these have now been painted over.[47] Here we have a clear case of forgetting, or wilful erasure.

A final example from Trieste relates to the patient-run bar and restaurant known as Il Posto delle Fragole (the Italian translation of Ingmar Bergman's 1957 film, *Wild Strawberries*). A Basaglian site par excellence, this place encapsulated a series of features symbolizing changes in the 1960s and 1970s. First there is the name itself: utopian and creative. Second, there is a sense that patients were being given control over their own lives, through work that existed within the same area that had enforced their repression. They were given a voice, the right to speak, they could order and serve a coffee, and they could earn money. Finally, the bar was a place of constant discussion and debate, drenched in cigarette smoke, mirroring the endless meetings that marked the Basaglian period (and in some ways the entire 1970s). The bar of the time was captured by a series of photographs that documented the Basaglia revolution, and are now available in books and archives. Today, the bar survives, although it bears little relation to the place of the past apart from three crucial ways – its name, its physical site and the fact that it

---

46   Roy Porter, *Madness. A Brief History*, p. 210.
47   'Guarino, via i murales dell'era basagliana', ilpiccolo.gelocal.it.

is still run by ex- or current patients through a co-operative, which also employs recovering addicts and others.

Today, mental health services in Trieste are seen as amongst the best in the world. For years, throughout the 1980s and 1990s, budding psychiatrists visited from across the world. A trip to Trieste was a key stage on the way to understanding how things could change in a post-asylum world. Italy was a model and acknowledged as such by the World Health Organization.

Trieste did not rest on its laurels. It also became a centre which was able to provide expertise on closing asylums elsewhere. Groups of *operatori* and doctors from the city's services are still frequently called upon to deal with outdated mental health institutions in other countries. This continuity was seen most dramatically in the case of Leros, an island in Greece that was exposed as a dumping ground, with appalling conditions for around 3,000 patients at the end of the 1980s. A team from Trieste was sent to Leros to reform and close down that total institution, something that was traumatic for the people involved in the operation, as their minds went back to the scenes they had witnessed in Italian asylums in the past. The Leros scandal was highlighted in Trieste's short-lived museum, providing further evidence of a clear link between Basaglia practices in the past and those of the present day.[48]

When Basaglia became director in Trieste in 1971, there were 1,182 patients in the hospital, 90 per cent of whom were non-voluntary and still held under the provisions laid out in the 1904 law, while the remaining voluntary patients came under the 1968 reform. By the beginning of 1977, only 51 patients inside San Giovanni were being held as forced inmates (although there were still many others with guest (433) or volunteer (81) status. In August 1980, nine years after Basaglia's arrival, Trieste's asylum closed for good.[49]

---

48   Leros was not closed down completely, and recent reports imply that there are still 400 patients there and that the hospital has serious problems with resources (and even food). Patrick Cockburn, 'Starved of Funds, Now Starved of Food. Pain Bites at Greek Hospital', 14 June 2012, independent.co.uk.

49   See for another account from the inside Giuseppe Dell'Acqua, 'Gli anni di Basaglia' in Mario Colucci, ed., *Follia e paradosso. Seminari sul pensiero di Franco Basaglia*, Trieste: Edizioni E., 1995, pp. 151–5.

Trieste's hospital was not just closed down, with speed; its whole raison d'être was undermined, built as it was on separation, exclusion and silence. The period of closure was noisy and joyful, and impossible to ignore. From a total institution, built on its own rigid set of rules, violence and the idea of a closed world, the Trieste asylum was transformed into an open, creative place, where freedom and debate were more common than in the outside world, a model for change. It had become an anti-asylum. It is now something else, an *ex*-asylum.

The Meaning of Trieste Today: Nostaglia, Struggle and the Future

'It is possible to create a credible, efficient alternative to the psychiatric hospital [but] . . . it did not happen with Scabia and it did not happen with Marco Cavallo.'

Franco Rotelli[50]

'Ideologies are freedom while they are in development, oppression once they are formed.'

Franco Basaglia[51]

'Trieste had an importance which went way beyond the line we took at the time, in Gorizia.'

Franco Basaglia[52]

The memory of what happened in the 1970s, 1980s and 1990s in Trieste and San Giovanni is neither uncontroversial, nor uncontested. Within Trieste, the prevailing view is that there is a general pride and acceptance of the city's role as the capital of the anti-asylum movement. Yet this consensus is often based on a watered-down and simplified version of the end of the asylum system. Nonetheless, there is little doubt that there is some form of agreement, today, around *that* watered-down memory,

---

50   Dora Garcia, 'An Interview with Franco Rotelli and a Footnote by Antonio Artaud, Trieste, May 2010', in Garcia, *From Basaglia to Brazil*, p. 139.

51   Cited in Graziani, 'A story told backwards', p. 25.

52   Venturini, *Il giardino dei gelsi*, p. 212.

and this in a city where memories have been so bitterly divided in the twentieth century.[53] At the same time, the site itself has been slowly emptied of active memory relating to the Basaglian period. The museum set up there is now closed (forever, it seems) and the Basaglians who were in charge of health and mental health services have almost all retired. Their places have been taken by a second and a third generation of Basaglians, but the services built up since the 1970s have come under intense pressure in recent years, leading to a series of disputes and protests. Often, the movement has ended up simply defending what was constructed in the past.

There is also a problem of sources and the whole approach to an understanding of the past. The history of Trieste and Franco Basaglia's role there has been told largely by the protagonists of that experience. The key texts here are the popular books by Peppe Dell'Acqua (first published in 1980), more academic studies by Giovanna Gallio and Maria Grazia Giannichedda as well as classic texts by Franco Basaglia and Franca Ongaro, the work of Giuliano Scabia, and Marco Turco's TV fiction as well as various writings by Rotelli. Very few outsiders have studied the Trieste experience, and when they have, they have largely used these sources to do so.

It is perhaps not surprising, then, that studies of Trieste tend to be circular. Basaglians did not just control mental health services in Trieste (which they themselves built from scratch), but they eventually took charge of the entire health system in the city. This was a power base of some magnitude, and it helped the movement to construct a past, physically and mentally, and to control how that past was narrated and studied.

However, there is debate about how to relate to that past *among* the ex-Basaglians who work (or used to work) within health services in the city. On the one hand there are those who criticize what they see as a nostalgic revival of the 1970s, and the concentration on spectacular moments like Marco Cavallo. The most powerful exponent of this strand of opinion/memory is Franco Rotelli, heir to Basaglia in Trieste and formerly a key player in health service management and administration

---

53   See John Foot, *Italy's Divided Memory*, 2010, pp. 50–2, and *Fratture d'Italia*, pp. 119–60.

in the city. He is currently (as of 2015) an elected regional councillor in Trieste. Rotelli is tired of talk of Marco Cavallo. For him, the true Basaglian revolution came *after* the closure of the asylum, not before. Rotelli states that 'we did not demonstrate: we simply did', and argues that it is the 'active services [in the city] that have turned the old logic of psychiatry upside down'.[54] The Trieste experience, he argues, has shown that 'it is possible to create a credible, efficient alternative to the psychiatric hospital'.[55] Rotelli believes that the concentration on and constant repetition of the Marco Cavallo version of events, far from exalting the changes in Trieste in terms of mental health care, has begun to actively obscure what has happened since the asylum closed. Thirty years of work is being ignored. The Marco Cavallo memory has become an empty, diversionary, trivial and celebratory way of seeing the past, as well as the present.

A second strand of memory in Trieste comes close to what has been called 'possessive memory'. I have argued elsewhere that 1968 'also pro- duced a "possessive memory"', where those studying the past were above all those who had taken part in that past'.[56] To cite Barbara Armani, there has been 'a "possessive" use of memory by the generation which had access to the public sphere, and elaborated the "facts" while also setting out, at the same time, their own "self-representation"' – and the creation of a "mythology of 1968"'.[57] When applied to the Basaglian past, it is easy for possessive forms of memory to ostracize any critics of that past, and to indulge in celebratory rhetoric. Critical voices are often excluded.

The 1968 movement has had a difficult relationship with memory, and its own past. As Graziani writes,

> The subversion of power that took place in the Trieste asylum started off with the destruction of an archive that categorized the patients: the violent ones, the dirty ones, the suicidal ones, the quiet ones, the men, the women; the significance of this decision made it

54   Garcia, 'An Interview with Franco Rotelli', pp. 144–5.

55   Ibid., p. 139.

56   Foot, *Fratture d'Italia*, p. 372. See also Peter Braunstein, 'Possessive Memory and the Sixties Generation', *Culturefront*, Summer 1997, pp. 66–9.

57   Barbara Armani, 'Italia anni settanta. Movimenti, violenza politica e lotta armata tra memoria e rappresentazione storiografica', *Storica* 32, 2005, pp. 43–5.

impossible to create a systematic archive of the revolution as it was taking place.[58]

Part of the work of the Basaglians was to free patients from their medicalized past, from the tyranny of the clinical records that had followed them around for so long.

The movement in Trieste has, however, attempted to build a lasting memory of itself. As we have seen, an extensive archive of various kinds of material was used to open an innovative museum in the former hospital site. This overall project was known as 'Beyond the Gardens' and utilized a rich multimedia archive. Yet, this project (which reached out to schools, scholars and visitors) was quickly closed down as funds ran out. Visitors to San Giovanni today are given little guidance as to what happened there in the 1970s.

Conclusion: Narrating Trieste

Trieste's Psychiatric Hospital 'can stop working and therefore be closed down.'

Provincial Administration of Trieste (21 April 1980)

It is not easy to write about this movement, with its myths, splits, silences and possessive memories. A further danger is the simple regurgitation of well-worn versions from the past. There was also something about the movement itself that created problems in terms of memory. As Giovanna Gallio has written,

Given the multiplicity of groups and actors involved, and the complexity of practices, the writing of a 'historical memory' appears something which only multiple authors could carry out. But the fact that this memory has not yet been written up is not merely due to the fact that there are many memories available.[59]

---

58   Graziani, 'A story told backwards', p. 26.
59   Giovanna Gallio, 'Fasi della de-istituzionalizzazione' in Gallio et al., *La libertà è tera-peutica*, pp. 18–19.

For Franco Rotelli, Trieste was 'a patient and collective adventure, deeply practical and for this reason almost impracticable, impatient and obsessive, specific and global . . . something which it is difficult to narrate'.[60] A version of that past does exist – but it is largely celebratory. Rotelli has always argued for an acceptance of the complexity of the issues at stake in the attempts to reform institutions and forms of mental health care. The prevailing, public versions of the Trieste–Basaglia story tend, however, to simplify the past.

---

60   'Prefazione' in Gallio et al., *La libertà è terapeutica*, p. 11.

TWENTY-THREE

The 180 Law: History, Myth and Reality

'The vast mental hospitals are gone, a truly staggering achievement.'

Tom Burns[1]

'It was a victory . . . a transitional law, passed in order to avoid a referendum and for this reason not free from compromise. We should avoid a sense of euphoria.'

Franco Basaglia[2]

'On 13 May the law did not decide that there was no more mental illness in Italy, but it did decide that in Italy the response to mental distress should no longer be that of internment and segregation. But this does not mean that it is enough simply to send people home with their anxieties and their problems.'

Franca Ongaro Basaglia[3]

---

1   Tom Burns, *Our Necessary Shadow. The Nature and Meaning of Psychiatry*, London: Allen Lane, 2013, p. 182.

2   Cited in Pietro Greco, 'Cominciò come uno scandalo, e divenne una riforma', *L'Unità*, 12 May 2003. The original interview was in Franco Gilberto, 'Che dice Basaglia', *La Stampa*, 12 May 1978.

3   'Storia di una donna che esce dal manicomio', *La Stampa*, 19 September 1978.

A Race against Time

Time was short, very short. The campaign against the 1904 law governing psychiatric hospitals and care, led by the Radical Party, had already gathered some 700,000 signatures. Before long, there would be a referendum and the Italian public would have the chance to vote to eliminate that law altogether, leaving Italy's psychiatric hospitals in a possible legislative vacuum. But there was no guarantee that a majority of Italians would vote against the previous law. As on other occasions during the Italian republic, the possibility of a referendum concentrated the minds of politicians who otherwise might have prevaricated for years to come. Quickly, the major parties came to an agreement. It was a time of national crisis and of solidarity governments.

As a result of this race against time, the key debates and discussions around the 180 Law took place not in the parliamentary chamber itself, but in the back rooms where the two health committees sat (for the lower and upper house). Basaglia was involved in the whole process, but he was not the only voice that was heard. Moderate psychiatrists and professional organizations also had their say, and the key players were the political parties. In the end, the law was a compromise, dictated by circumstances. Only in retrospect has it been seen as revolutionary, or even as, in Norberto Bobbio's much-repeated words, 'the only real reform' in Italian history.

Unpacking the Myths: The Six-Month Law

There are a number of myths and stories told about the 180 Law, and much of the discussion of the reform is based on false premises. Let us try to outline exactly what happened. First, the 180 (as a separate piece of legislation) never came to the parliamentary chamber. It was passed in commission. Deputies were never given a chance to discuss or vote on the measure (except as part, later on, of the wider health reform law – the 883). Many accounts, however, state that Parliament voted through the law. It did, but only in a technical sense.

Secondly, Law 180 had a very dull name, and much of the text was not specific to mental health at all, or to asylums. It was called 'Accertamenti e trattamenti sanitari volontari e obbligatori' (Voluntary and obligatory health treatment and checks).[4] This could also be seen as a radical break with the past in itself, as it eliminated (as least linguistically) the difference between mental health and other health issues. Nonetheless, a large part of the discussion around the law was not about psychiatric care at all, but rather around the possibility of using forced treatment for *all* health patients, *including* those with mental health issues.

This was a partial reform, voted for and discussed in Parliament only by those few deputies and senators who sat on the health commissions in the lower and the upper house (but with input from many others). Moreover, the context in which these discussions took place meant that hardly anyone, at the time, took much notice of what had happened. The world's eyes *were* on Rome in May 1978, but not because of impending mental health reform. The leading Christian Democrat politician Aldo Moro had been kidnapped by the Red Brigades in the centre of the capital on 16 April. Five of Moro's bodyguards had been murdered. The capital was in lockdown and Italy was in a state of shock. The fallout from that event would last for years. It was therefore a time of crisis for the Italian state, so much so that very few people noted the passing of what would become known (later on) as 'the Basaglia law'. On 9 May, after fifty-five days in captivity, Aldo Moro's body was found in a car boot in the centre of Rome. Debates over those fifty-five days are still going on today.

In addition, it was one thing to pass a law, and quite another to put it into practice. On its own, the 180 meant very little. Many asylums in Italy had been more or less untouched by the reform movement. Vast resources and strong political will would be needed to actually close down these asylums. There were numerous attempts to reverse the Basaglia law after 1978, even before it was implemented. Franca Ongaro, in particular, dedicated the rest of her life to a defence of the 180/883 laws, and to a tireless campaign to see the law put into practice, something that only became a reality in the late 1990s, after years of struggle *and* resistance. The 180/883 was on the statute books, but decades would pass before the last asylums

---

4   13 May 1978. The law was published in the *Gazzetta Ufficiale* on 16 May 1978, no. 133.

would close their gates, forever. Yet the 180 also marked a turning-point. No new asylums were to be built (and this has remained the case). Mental health patients became just that – *patients* – with rights and responsibilities. Their treatment would not be imposed upon them – it was voluntary – apart from in exceptional circumstances.

This was a law that reflected some of the concerns of those places that had moved things forward since the early 1960s – Trieste, Perugia, Arezzo, Reggio Emilia. However, it was not a particularly radical measure in itself. Much of the content, the fine print, so to speak – the speed of change, the nature of the services themselves, the extent to which forced treatment would or would not be used – was left up to individual regional administrations, doctors and bureaucrats. The stage was set for a wide disparity in the speed and nature of the reform and of services themselves over the 1980s, 1990s and 2000s. Italy would never have a single, national model of mental health care.

Parts of Italy would become a model for many practitioners across the world (and some already were in the 1960s and 1970s). But the country would also continue to host some of the worst and most backward examples of mental health care in Europe. A two-track system was developed. Islands of excellence existed in parallel with places where little or nothing had changed. The future, the present and the past were all visible inside Italy's mental health system. Meanwhile, debates over the 180/883 laws and their consequences would rage on for years, dividing psychiatrists, families, activists, politicians and patients. The 'Basaglia law' label/name was not only used in a positive way. It was also employed to *blame* the Basaglian movement for a whole series of problems and issues, many of which had nothing to do with the movement at all.

Law 180 is also *no longer a law*, as it was integrated into wider health service reforms at the end of 1978. The 180 lasted about eight months as a separate entity. It was already part of history by the end of 1978. In December 1978 the 180 was merged into general health reform legislation. Despite this fact, most commentators continue to analyse the original text of the law and talk about the law as if it exists as a separate entity. Often, the text of the 180 Law is reprinted in books about Basaglia and mental health reform: a law which is not operative.

The 'Orsini Law'

The reality was much less romantic than the version that has developed into a myth. The 180 Law was passed thanks to the hard work of a number of moderate politicians – including, for example, the now-notorious one-time Christian Democrat politician Paolo Cirino Pomicino and the Republican Susanna Agnelli. Its real name should have been the 'Orsini Law', after the proposer of the bill Bruno Orsini, a psychiatrist and a Christian Democrat deputy, who presented the measure and pushed it through.[5] Orsini guided the 180 through the commission stage (which was its *only* stage). He had first been elected to the lower house of Parliament in 1976 and remained there until 1992, when he became a senator. Orsini was a member of the AMOPI (the Association of Italian psychiatric doctors and organizations), which was far more moderate in its outlook than Psichiatria Democratica. The AMOPI was to have a major input into the 180 and 883 laws.[6]

Context

Debates over far-reaching reform in the psychiatric care sector had been going on for some time before 1978, mainly as part of the tortuous path towards setting up an Italian national health service.[7] Finally, in December 1977, an integrated health service law was presented to Parliament for discussion – including a number of measures relating directly to asylums and mental health care. However, it was clear that this would all take considerable time to be approved. Each article was hotly debated, and the left in particular were worried about measures allowing for forced health care. Basaglia and Psichiatria Democratica

---

5   Michel Legrand claims that Orsini had been the director of the asylum in Quarto. *La psychiatrie alternative italienne*, p. 308. Orsini had visited Gorizia, according to Antonio Slavich, *All'ombra dei ciliegi giapponesi*, unpublished manuscript, p. 2.

6   Some have argued that the text of the law was more of a reflection of the position of the AMOPI's position at the time than that of the PD. See Davide Lasagno, *Oltre l'Istituzione. Crisi e riforma dell'assistenza psichiatrica a Torino e in Italia*, Milan: Ledizioni, 2012, p. 152.

7   See ibid., pp. 146–55.

appeared to be in radical opposition to the way the reform was going at a whole series of levels.[8] Basaglia, for example, was clearly against the setting up of mental health units inside hospitals. As he argued in April 1978, this measure would 'create "small asylums" inside normal hospitals, which are already inefficient'.[9]

Minds were then focused, as we have seen, on events outside of Parliament, which had nothing directly to do with Basaglia or his movement. The Radical Party (which only had four parliamentarians at the time) had collected 700,000 signatures for a campaign to abrogate the 1904 law (as well as for numerous other referendums). The signatures had been ratified and the referendum was declared admissible. If replacement legislation was not passed by 11 May then the referendum would take place.

On the surface, this might have seemed like a good thing for the reformers. A referendum would have led to a national debate about the 1904 law and the state of psychiatric hospitals in Italy. It would have given the Basaglians a platform on which to express their views to the Italian public. It was also possible that Italians would vote to strike off the 1904 law from the statue books altogether, which would have been a victory for Basaglia and the radical psychiatry movement.

But the risks were also very high. The ruling political class was worried that voters might choose to leave asylums without any legal structure at all. This was an unpalatable situation that could not be countenanced. The second danger was a potential disaster for the movement itself. Italians might well vote to *keep* the 1904 law in place (or *against* its abolition). This could have put back the entire struggle for years and made reform extremely difficult to achieve. Basaglia himself was aware of this risk.[10] In the end, these twin threats led to an alliance among the

---

8   Franco Basaglia and Agostino Pirella, *Comunicato*, n.d., in Archivio ALMM, cited in Lasagno, *Oltre la istituzione*, p. 149. Lasagno has argued that Orsini's posthumous version of the facts is mistaken in its claim that the main psychiatric parts of the health law had already achieved parliamentary approval in January 1978. Ibid., p. 150.

9   This point, and others, were made to the parliamentary groups involved in debating the law. See 'Psichiatria democratica: "Questa legge del governo va modificato"', *L'Unità*, 14 April 1978.

10   'Basaglia contro il referendum', *Il Giorno*, 19 December 1977,

movement, the more moderate psychiatrist associations and politicians in Rome. Everyone agreed that a law was needed, and quickly. In this context, they (finally) got down to work.

The twin dangers provoked by the impending referendum forced the political parties to act fast. Normal procedures were by-passed. The solution was ingenious. First, the psychiatric parts of the wider health reform law would be separated out from the rest (and this was a regressive feature introduced by the referendum campaign – it once again made mental health into something different from other kinds of health care, at least for legislative purposes). This section would then be passed as a separate law. Once the referendum danger had been averted, there could be further discussion (about everything), and the psychiatric reform could be collapsed back into the overall law.

There was not time for Parliament as a whole to vote on these reforms, so an emergency procedure was adopted, which allowed for the health commissions in the lower and upper house to pass a law – as long as the party leaders agreed, along with the presidents of both wings of parliament. This rarely used procedure, and the combined efforts of the major parties, saw the 180 Law discussed and passed in just twenty days.[11] The text of the law was also influenced, it seems, by the points made by a distinguished and well-known opponent of radical reforms, the writer and psychiatrist Mario Tobino.[12]

Twenty Days

Bruno Orsini, writing twenty years later, was proud of what had happened:

---

11   Bruno Orsini, 'Vent'anni dopo', psychiatryonline.it.

12   It seems that a member of the commission wrote to Tobino to assure him that one of the articles in the law (allowing for the recovery in psychiatric hospitals of those who had already been patients there) had been changed thanks to an article he wrote in *La Nazione*, cited in Primo De Vecchis, 'Nota storica. Tobino, Basaglia e la legge 180. Storia d'una polemica' in Mario Tobino, *Gli ultimi giorni di Magliano*, ed. Primo De Vecchis and Monica Marchi, Milan: Mondadori, 2009, p. 12, n. 32. The commission member who wrote to Tobino was Maria Eletta Martini (DC), who was from Lucca.

It was a small miracle: the passing of a law, which was of huge technical, social and political importance, less than three weeks after its presentation to Parliament. It was signed on 13 May by the Head of State [Giovanni] Leone, by the Justice Minister [Francesco] Bonifacio and by the Health Minister [Tina] Anselmi, the text, published in the *Gazzetta Ufficiale* no. 133 of 16 May 1978, became a law of the state and was operative the next day.[13]

In 1977, Orsini had underlined the moderate nature of the reforms. 'We are not proposing the victory of anti-psychiatry; we want psychiatry to become civilized and we are thinking of this law as an important step towards this objective.' Orsini continued:

> In the final phase (1976–78) there were high level negotiations, which included well-known and less well-known people, from scientific societies and trade unions [the Society of Psychiatrists and the aforementioned AMOPI and Psichiatria Democratica], intellectuals, political parties, and some parliamentarians who displayed great intellectual honesty and a clear sense of morality. Nobody, and certainly not Basaglia, saw everything they wanted included in the final text.

The language of the debates in the health committees was a long way from the reality of discussions in Trieste and elsewhere. It was largely bureaucratic, political, technical, with some notable exceptions.

Moreover, much of the discussion about the law, at the time, did not centre on asylums or their future. The key question dealt with in the commission was forced treatment (and not just for mental health patients). *When* was it possible to *impose* treatment, and for what kinds of people? What guarantees would be put in place for the patients who were subjected to such treatment? These proposals had already attracted criticism from Basaglia and Psichiatria Democratica in 1977, and one deputy had compared them to a form of medical arrest.

Yet, the fiercest critic of the whole committee process, and its content, was the leader of the Radical Party – Marco Pannella. Speaking in the committee, Pannella was withering about what was happening. 'You are

---

13   For Bruno Orsini's version of events see Orsini, 'Vent'anni dopo'.

acting to avoid acting. You have created a farce, yet again. A farce which is lacking in fantasy and rigour.'

It was not surprising that Panella was furious. A law was being passed – *in extremis*, without a full parliamentary debate and in record time – in order to avoid *his* referendum. All the efforts and political push from the Radical Party to hold a referendum on the issue of the 1904 law were being usurped by the politicians in Rome. And Pannella was also very critical of the law itself. In a long intervention to the commission he took the law apart, point by point. How would these measures be put into practice? he asked. Who would pay for all this? What did it all mean? It was all too vague. He even cited Basaglia himself, *against* forced treatment.

Pannella was right in most of the points he made, but he was also unrealistic and utopian. No reform of this time could have got through Parliament without the agreement of the Communists and the Christian Democrats.[14] Any reform would be a compromise between these forces, with pressure and input from those on the outside. Sometimes, politics is the art of the possible. In 1978 the 180 was what was possible.

For all of its problems, vagaries and lack of concrete detail about how things were going to be achieved on the outside, in the real world, the 180 Law was important, and even historic. Very simply, the 180 Law made people inside asylums into Italians, for the first time. Their rights were now guaranteed in line with the constitution. They were equal before the law, and in the future, mental health patients would always remain so (in most cases). As David Forgacs has argued, the law 'made central the patient's human and civil rights'.[15] Treatment of mental health patients was not to take place in specially built asylums, but in normal hospitals or decentralized centres. Babini wrote, 'Once every reference to the patient's dangerousness or to "public scandal" had been removed, the psychiatric patient became an "ill" citizen like any other, and this was another example of the law's secular and modernizing nature'.[16]

---

14   For the position of the Communist Party at the time of these debates, see Sergio Scarpa, 'Facciamo il punto sulla legge per la psichiatria', *L'Unità*, 27 April 1978, and Vanda Milano (responding directly to the criticisms of Pirella, Basaglia and others), 'Psichiatria e riforma: perché non si può parlare di "fermo sanitario"', *L'Unità*, 22 December 1977.

15   David Forgacs, *Italy's Margins*, p. 256.

16   Valeria Babini, 'Curare la mente. Dall'universo manicomiale al "paese di Basaglia"',

Pannella was also angry about the way things were being done, and the separation of the part of the reform affected by a possible referendum.

> The separation of this part of the law from the overall reform of the health system shows how once again you are building castles in the sand, with the aim not of creating a good law but of acting out a farce.

However, Pannella's polemical intervention was out of line with all the rest of the speeches and comments in both committees. In general the tone of the debates was low-key, and everyone was aware time was short and they had to work together. It was a period of reform – perhaps the most important in Italy's history – as the push from the 1968 movements (and the referendum campaigns) finally made its way into parliament itself. On 2 May Italy's first abortion law was also approved (another law so famous that it is usually known by its number – the Law 194).

The debate on the commission in both the lower and upper house was of a high level. Many of those on the commission were psychiatrists or medical doctors. They knew what they were talking about, and they were also aware of the historic nature of the reforms they were discussing. Given the time available, the debate was carried through with a strong spirit of collaboration. Many bit their tongues in order not to waste time. Corners were cut. In any case, it was clear that aspects of the law were to be modified later, when the health reform itself was discussed in its entirety, and this was in fact what happened. As Agostino Pirella later pointed out, many of the features of the 180 were watered down in the global health reform (the Law 883).[17]

The members of the commission were often very clear about their dislike for the asylum system. However, they also underlined their opposition to anti-psychiatric or more radical positions with regard to mental

---

in Claudio Pogliano and Francesco Cassata, eds, *Scienze e cultura dell'Italia unita*, Turin: Einaudi, 2011, p. 650.

17   Agostino Pirella, 'Poteri e leggi psichiatriche in Italia (1968–1978)', in Francesca Cassata and Massimo Moraglio, eds, *Manicomio, Società e Politica*, Pisa: Biblioteca Franco Serantini, 2005, pp. 126–9.

health care. Dario Cravero (a surgeon) who was on the Senate commission, argued that the old ways of doing things were no longer acceptable: 'We must overcome our old rigidities, closures, prejudices.' But, he added, at the same time 'we need to try and avoid errors linked to pseudo-modern or falsely democratic positions which seem to suggest that collective political action is the only therapy that works'.[18]

Meanwhile, Giovanni Giudice from the Senate commission, who had been elected as a left independent, recalled the horror of the asylum he had visited twenty years earlier, as a young graduate doctor:

It was the most horrible spectacle I have ever seen in my life – people abandoned in squalid courtyards surrounded by high walls, covered in dirt and flies, with those who still had the strength calling out for their freedom – asking for help to escape from that place without hope.[19]

Giudice's traumatic first visit to an asylum reminds us of other similar experiences which have marked out this book – the first visits of Basaglia himself, Mario Tommasini, Ilvano Rasimelli and Bruno Benigni.

Basaglia changed his position in 1977–79. After a period of radical opposition to the measures being discussed, and especially the medicalization of mental health care and forced treatment, Basaglia later took credit (on behalf of the movement) for the passing of a law that included both of these measures. 'As democratic psychiatrists, we spurred on this law. We are in a minority, but, as Gramsci once said, we are a hegemonic minority'.[20] In February 1978, however, Basaglia had complained that the law was 'undemocratic', described the obligatory treatment sections of the law as a form of 'criminalization' and attacked other parts of the proposed law.[21]

---

18   12a Commissione (Igiene e sanità) [Senate], 18° Resoconto Stenografico seduta di 10 Maggio 1978, Presidenza del Presidente Ossicini, Dario Cravero (relatore). See also for documentation and debates the transcriptions of the 28 April 1978 and 2 May 1978 sessions at legislature.camera.it.

19   Giovanni Giudice, independent left, Senate commission, 10 May 1978.

20   Cited in Saverio Luzzi, *Società e sanità nell'Italia repubblicana*, Rome: Donzelli, 2004, p. 336.

21   Francesco Bullo, 'Il medico poliziotto', *La Stampa*, 9 February 1978.

Basaglia was well aware of the limitations of the legislation. His movement had indeed stimulated the passing of the law, but they hadn't been able to write the law in their own terms. It *was* a victory (the result of 'years of struggle . . . by specialists'[22]) but there was much more to be done. After all, Trieste, Arezzo and Perugia had seen their asylums practically closed down before the law was even passed. The struggle would continue, and if it did not, things could easily revert to how they had been in the past. In fact, the struggle might become even more difficult without the spectre and the scandal of asylums to fight against. By 1978, old-style psychiatric hospitals had become unsustainable even for the far right.

Apart from Panella's outrage, there were very few voices of dissent. Even the criticisms from the Italian Social Movement committee members were mild in comparison to those, for example, from neo-fascists in Gorizia in the 1960s. The parliamentary chamber itself would certainly have been more critical (from both left and right) but it was not given the chance to vote at all.

According to the measures included in the 180 Law, people with mental health problems would be looked after in decentralized services, or, with more serious cases, in special units set up inside general hospitals. These could only have a maximum of fifteen beds (this was to prevent, in theory, the institution of little asylums that Basaglia had warned about). Crucial to the reform was the idea of the voluntary nature of treatment. The law allowed for forced treatment in certain cases, but provided strong guarantees in terms of human rights.

In itself, the 180 Law changed very little. There was no money provided for its actuation, and the timetable laid out in the comprehensive health reforms late in 1978 was hopelessly unrealistic. Moreover, the medicalized solution to emergency cases through the creation of special mental health units inside hospitals was a backward step for some of the more radical and ongoing experiments at that time – Perugia, Arezzo, Trieste. Perugia, for example, had to re-medicalize its services which were, at that point, entirely run outside the hospital system.

---

22   Franco Basaglia, *Scritti. II. 1968–1980*, ed. Franca Ongaro Basaglia, Turin: Einaudi, 1982, p. 479.

What the law did was set down some firm principles. Mental health patients were acknowledged as people – and given (back) their rights (to vote, to control their own care, to live in the outside world). Also, it was made clear that asylums were on the way out. No new patients could be admitted to them (although this part of the law was not always adhered to, and special extensions were added for some years). More importantly, in the long run, was the fact that *no* new psychiatric hospitals could be built (this turned out to be the case).

The 180 Law was fragile – a moveable feast. In December, as it was absorbed into the general health reforms, some of the features in the original law were toned down. For example, as we have seen, in the 180 the number of beds in the emergency hospital units was limited to fifteen, but the 883 Law set no limit at all. Bed numbers would be decided by individual regional health plans. The danger of small asylums was back on the agenda.[23]

Whose Law?

The term 'Basaglia law' – which has become part of the Italian language – is in many ways historical error. As Orsini and others have pointed out, the 180 Law was the outcome of discussions and alliances between political parties (above all the Christian Democrats and the Italian Communist Party) and numerous professional bodies. But without the push from below – without Perugia, Gorizia, Colorno, Reggio Emilia, Trieste, Arezzo and other experiences – it would probably never have been passed in the form it was.

The 180 and 883 laws were the *end* of one long story (the primary fight *against* the asylum system and its injustices) and the *beginning* of another (the battle for new kinds of services and systems). But the struggle against total institutions would go on for another twenty years *despite* the law – in order to put into practice what had been passed by Parliament. One of the key leaders of this post-1978 movement would be Franca Ongaro.

Franco Basaglia lived long enough to witness the passing of the 1978

---

23   For a discussion of this change see Pirella, 'Poteri e leggi psichiatriche in Italia', p. 126–7.

law (and to express his scepticism about it), but he did not see it realized. While the law in 1978 was viewed by many in the movement as a backward step, a 'little reform', a compromise, it soon became clear that this was a law that would need to be defended against attack for years to come. It was the best Italy could come up with.

The roots of the reform were multilayered – they were political, technical and cultural. As Ferruccio Giacanelli wrote, it was 'a law which followed a long polycentric process, made up of different and often asynchronous experiences that had one thing in common: the desire to overcome . . . the asylum'.[24] Giacanelli recalls feverish and worried discussions among groups of psychiatrists from different wings of the movement in Rome in May 1978. There was also a wide-ranging debate *among* radical psychiatrists about the reform itself, with a series of different positions being taken up.[25]

Within these debates, Basaglia took a pragmatic position. He understood the limits of what had happened, but he also saw the possibilities. In 1979 he decided to leave Trieste for Rome, where he would take over the regional mental health service sector for the whole of Lazio, a vast area covering some 5 million people. It was time to move on from the asylum itself. As he said at the time:

> I will go to Rome, to take on a different kind of task to that of Gorizia or Trieste. We now need to apply a law of the state . . . a complex reform. All specialists need to do what they can so that this law is applied in the best way possible.[26]

Unfortunately, a fatal brain tumour would deprive him (and Italy) of the opportunity to put this reform into practice. Others would have to do this work in his place. Basaglia himself would not live to see 'his' law implemented.

---

24   Ferruccio Giacanelli, 'Memorie ancora utili', *Fogli d'informazione* 5–6, 1 June 2008, psychiatryonline.it.

25   See, for example, 'Psichiatria democratica è in crisi?', *L'Unità*, 10 January 1978.

26   'Basaglia. Importante è applicare la legge', *L'Unità*, 21 August 1979. See also 'Psichiatria. Buona la legge, difficile la sua applicazione', *L'Unità*, 24 June 1978.

'In any case the construction of new psychiatric hospitals is forbidden, as is the use of those in existence as specialist psychiatric wings for general hospitals or psychiatric or neurological or neuropsychiatric divisions.'

Law 180 (1978)

It surprised nobody that the closing down of the asylum system was much easier said than done. There was still considerable resistance from within the system to change – from administrators, psychiatrists, nurses and also some patients. Resources were needed to find housing and work for thousands of ex-patients, and jobs were at stake. The movement itself was on the wane, as the 1980s brought a general retreat from political commitment and activism. Many patients were reluctant to leave and families were, understandably, unwilling to take on the burden of looking after their relatives again, often after many years. Some patients had no desire to leave. Most asylums took over twenty years to finally shut down, and change varied greatly from region to region. This was a long struggle, and it was led by Franca Ongaro, who took over the mantle of defending and implementing the 180 Law after her husband's death in 1980. This was therefore also 'the Ongaro law'. Once again, it was Franco *and* Franca who moved things forward.

In Italy, structural and systemic reforms of this kind have been extremely difficult to achieve. And once they have been passed, these 'historic' laws have tended to remain on the statute books – and become unchanging laws that are defended, usually by the left against the right. This also means, however, that these laws have often failed to keep up with the times. This is true, for example, of both the divorce and abortion laws (1974, 1978) – which were radical when passed, but look far less radical in today's world, and this is also the case with the health service reforms of the late 1970s.

In the period following the 180 Law, Basaglia and others were frequently accused of 'abandoning patients' and 'overloading families with the burden of mental health care'. These points have been raised time and time again, and continue to this day.[27] Mario Tobino, the writer

---

27   See, for example, Franco Stefanoni, *Manicomio Italia. Inchiesta su follia e psichiatria*, Rome: Riuniti, 1998.

and psychiatrist who worked in Lucca's asylum, was a particularly notable (and vocal) opponent of the law. In 1979 he wrote in a letter to a friend that

> this 180 Law has some good principles behind it, but as often happens in Italy there will be many problems ahead. Patients need to be looked after and loved. Politicians will ruin everything, as usual. As usual we will be isolated, and fashionable ideas will win out. Goodbye, patients, dear companions of my life.[28]

Tobino blamed numerous suicides on the 180 Law. He also saw mental illness as hereditary and genetic, and not linked to society.

For Tobino the mentally ill had simply been abandoned to their fate. He wrote that 'there is no alternative to the madhouse'. This debate exploded again after Basaglia's death, in 1982, when Tobino published *Gli ultimi giorni di Magliano* (The last days of Magliano).[29] Another prominent (and violent) critic of the law was the Communist Antonello Tombadori. There were also many critics from within the movement, such as Basaglia's old foe Giovanni Jervis.[30]

While he was alive, Basaglia took on his critics: 'The destruction of the madhouse does not imply that patients will be abandoned, but it creates the conditions under which they can be looked after in a better way in terms of their real problems.'[31] He also replied to Tobino:

> Where were those obscene and evil women, those interesting female personalities described by Tobino? In the reality of the madhouse it was not a case of having pity or understanding for the suffering of the patients, but of working hard to break down those walls, day by day.[32]

---

28   De Vecchis, 'Nota storica', p. 13, n. 35 (3 July 1979).

29   See 'Tobino contro Basaglia. Si riaccende la polemica sulla follia', *La Stampa, Tuttolibri*, 9 January 1982.

30   For Jervis's critique of the law, see Luigi Onnis and Giuditta Lo Russo, eds, *Dove va la psichiatria? Pareri a confronto su salute mentale e manicomi in Italia dopo la nuova legge*, Milan: Feltrinelli, 1980, pp. 90–6, and Corbellini and Jervis, *La razionalità negata*, pp. 136–70.

31   'Conversazione: A proposito della nuova legge 180' in Basaglia, *Scritti. II*, pp. 473–85.

32   Franco Basaglia, *Paese Sera*, 4 May 1978.

The 180/883 laws were a turning-point for Italian psychiatry, and marked the beginning of the end of the asylum system. Basaglia and the movement for reform had come a long way since that first, vomit-inducing day in 1961 in Gorizia. They had managed to force Italy's notoriously conservative political class into action – with a little help from Marco Pannella and the Radical Party. It was a victory – and it was much more than a 'little reform'. No new patients (in theory) would ever disappear behind the walls of an Italian asylum again. The shapeless mass of bodies that had inhabited those corridors and rooms for so long had become people, with rights, responsibilities and duties. A hundred thousand 'slaves' would no longer be treated as second-class citizens. Whatever happened after 1978, *that* battle had been won. But there was still a long way to go. As Basaglia himself said in 1977: 'The plan assumes that there is already a democratic health reform in place, a democratic culture. But in reality the people are what they are, the doctors are what they are, as are the hospitals.'[33] Agostino Pirella also defended the law but recognized that there had been a counter-revolution.

> Powerful forces have reorganized themselves, after going through a crisis thanks to the reform and the practices of the democratic and participatory psychiatric movement. A new generation of magistrates has rediscovered the old stereotypes about mental illness – supported by young, self-confident and cynical psychiatrists. Patients are afraid – literally – to speak out, to comment, because their destiny can be decided by the 'respectful' nature of their behaviour. Physical restraint (the tying up of people to beds for long periods) is interpreted as a 'health measure' or in some way 'therapeutic'. Psychiatric power has moved back to the centre of the stage, and it has no intention of leaving.[34]

The last word should be left to Basaglia himself. In 1971 he attended a student meeting in Padua, the place where he had studied for years. The student movement was at its peak. A huge crowd turned out. This

---

33   Cited in Gianluigi Ambrosini, 'Giudice e medico, a chi la responsabilità?', *La Stampa*, 27 December 1977.

34   Pirella, 'Poteri e leggi psichiatriche in Italia', p. 128.

was how he started his first lecture to the students, and his words contain
a warning that all those working in this area should heed:

> I had thought that there would be a few people here with whom I
> could discuss and argue about your struggles within the student move-
> ment and our battles within psychiatric hospitals. But I find myself,
> instead, in a room where I am . . . surrounded by a lot of people who
> want me to tell them about all kinds of things. Perhaps this is the result
> of the publicity which has surrounded me. I have become famous
> because I 'opened up' a psychiatric hospital and the press described
> me as the 'man who freed the mad' . . . then I had even more luck . . .
> I was charged with a crime. The institution reacted. And I have become
> a star for the bourgeois world – with lots of invitations from students,
> Social-Democrats, Communists, everyone . . . because everyone wants
> to know what to do, what can be done . . . and this is another way of
> destroying an experience. I think that today, I have become an insti-
> tution . . . and I think that the people here today want to know things
> from me, and discuss specific issues, but they are asking me for some-
> thing that I cannot deliver.[35]

---

35   Seminario. Istituzioni psichiatriche. Liviano. Sala dei giganti, 'Franco Basaglia,
Antipsichiatria' (22 April 1971, ed. Collettivo della Facoltà Umanistiche), Basaglia Archive.

TWENTY-FOUR

Conclusion

Gorizia and Italian History

'The hospital was run by the doctors. It isn't any more and it will never be so again.'

> Opening sentence from the huge (3 x 2 metre) poster
> put up in December 1975 by Antonio Slavich on the open
> door of the asylum in Ferrara, after he became director there[1]

Gorizia was the beginning of a story that would develop and intensify in the 1970s. The Italian movement spread across Italy. Gorizians and their followers took control of mental health services in Ferrara, Arezzo, Reggio Emilia, Parma, Trieste, Pordenone, Naples, Venice, Genoa, Imola and many other cities. In Perugia politicians and psychiatrists worked together to close down the asylum there and replace it with dynamic, decentralized mental health centres. A national organization was formed – Psichiatria Democratica – which attempted to bring together activists and technicians. In the end, all the hospitals (apart from the criminal asylums)

---

1 Antonio Slavich, *La scopa meravigliante. Preparativi per la legge 180 a Ferrara e dintorni 1971–1978*, Rome: Riuniti, 2003, p. 176.

were closed down, although the legacy of the movement remains controversial and divisive.

It was an extraordinary time, a period of revolutionary language accompanied by real reform. If, as Balduzzi has argued, 'a psychiatric hospital is
the barometer of society', then Italy in the 1960s and 1970s was moving
in a new direction.[2] Psychiatrists, patients, nurses, volunteers and others
experimented with 'new "ways of working"'.[3] Young people dedicated
their lives to their patients. Hierarchies were broken down and subverted.
Asylums became centres of change and hope, at least for a time.

Much of this had its origins in Gorizia. The place that Franco Basaglia
saw in 1961, that 'place which was like a concentration camp',[4] was
similar to the horrific descriptions left by Ugo Cerletti in 1949, where
'when I opened the door I was forced back by a confused wave of shouts,
screams and guffaws' and where each and every patient had been stripped
of their identity and dignity, as well as their possessions: 'They have
nothing, not a chair, not a piece of furniture, not a single object of their
own.'[5] These cries, thanks to Basaglia and others, could no longer be
ignored. Basaglia refused to accept this state of affairs, and with the help
of many others, and in alliance with other experiences elsewhere, he
refused to be a part of that system.

Gorizia was not the only place where change took place, but it was the
most important and in many ways the most interesting of the experiments
in reform. This new history has attempted to look back at that experience,
with all its faults, gaps, dreams and dark sides. Today, the asylum in Gorizia
stands empty, apart from a few administrative offices and scattered health
services. The patients and many of the doctors are long gone. The names
of Basaglia, Antonio Slavich, Agostino Pirella, Giovanni Jervis, Domenico
Casagrande, Letizia Comba, Franca Ongaro, Lucio Schittar, 'Furio', 'Carla',
and others now belong to the past, a past this book has analysed and

---

2   Cited in Angelo Del Boca, *Manicomi come lager*, Turin: Edizioni dell'albero, 1966,
p. 13.

3   Ferruccio Giacanelli, 'Edelweiss Cotti negli anni di crisi della psichiatria istituzionale'
in Libero Bestighi et al., eds, *Specialista in relazioni umane. L'esperienza professionale di Edelweiss
Cotti*, Bologna: Pendragon, 2001, p. 15.

4   Alberto Manacorda and Vincenzo Montella, *La nuova psichiatria in Italia. Esperienze
e prospettive*, Milan: Feltrinelli, 1977, p. 48.

5   Ugo Cerletti, 'La fossa dei serpenti', *Il Ponte* 5: 11, 1949, pp. 1373, 1376.

worked over. 'In Italy', as Franco Ongaro wrote in 1982, soon after the death of her husband, 'there were people who refused to accept the fact that there in a hospital the patients could be destroyed, annihilated, crushed . . . and those people started to do something'.[6] Gorizia was where this work began. That empty building is a testimony to how far that work went, but it is not the whole story, which is still to be told.

The Story of a Movement

'The history of the "new psychiatry" in Italy has never been written.'
Giovanni Jervis[7]

'A stereotypical and restricted view of the years of anti-institutional struggle have led to problems in terms of the communication of a past which still has a lot to say to us.'
Matteo Fiorani[8]

The story told in this book began in Gorizia in the early 1960s and then moved onto a whole series of other places – Perugia, Parma, Reggio Emilia, Arezzo, Trieste. Unfortunately, I have had to leave much of the story out altogether. Space has not allowed me to discuss the extraordinary features of the movement in Ferrara, Imola, Materdomini and Naples, Volterra, Florence, Pavia, Pordenone, Turin, Rome, Genoa and elsewhere. I hope to be able to tell these other stories one day.

Along the way, we have seen how a small group of radical psychiatrists refused to accept the state of affairs they had come across inside asylums across Italy. In their push to change things these psychiatrists were aided by a number of nurses, numerous volunteers and above all (in some places) by a new class of administrators and politicians. This post-war political class wedded itself to the desire for a new kind of psychiatry

---

6   Franca Ongaro Basglia, *Manicomio perché?*, Milan: Emme Edizioni, 1982, p. 25.

7   In Luigi Onnis and Giuditta Lo Russo, eds, *Dove va la psichiatria? Pareri a confronto su salute mentale e manicomi in Italia dopo la nuova legge*, Milan: Feltrinelli, 1980, p. 75.

8   Matteo Fiorani, 'La storia della psichiatria italiana negli ultimi vent'anni', in *Bibliografia di storia della psichiatria italiana, 1991–2010*, Florence: Firenze University Press, 2010, p. 32.

and for the transformation (and eventual closure) of the old asylum system. They were not driven by greed or the desire for power. Humanistic principles and a moral imperative (these places were simply *not acceptable*) pushed them to press for reform. If Basaglia, Jervis, Pirella, Ongaro, Schittar, Slavich, Comba, Casagrande, Manuali, Scotti, Brutti, Tesi, Giacanelli and others are the psychiatric heroes and heroines of this story, they would have achieved little without the support of Rasimelli, Zanetti, Tommasini, Benigni and many others.

This was a collective 'no'. And this 'no' changed the world. It was unacceptable to treat human beings in the way they were being treated – without rights, without autonomy, without the possibility of using knives and forks, without their own hair, without any control over their own treatment, without freedom. It was wrong to electrocute these people, cut out bits of their brains, or tie them up for years on end. This movement was a struggle for liberation, for democracy and for equality. Those 100,000 inmates of mental asylums had disappeared from history. As Carlo Brutti and Francesco Scotti have written,

> The conditions of patients inside psychiatric hospitals became the symbol of the protest movement: the fact that they were abandoned, marginalized, repressed, was taken up as symptomatic of more general forms of oppression which could be seen, in a more subtle and underhand way, in all kinds of social institutions.[9]

Those 100,000 people needed to re-emerge – to be given back their own identities and dignity. That generation of politicians and psychiatrists was a post-war, anti-fascist generation, and there was something profoundly anti-fascist about the anti-asylum movement. It was a movement about human rights. The inmates inside the asylums were *people*.

The other protagonists of this book, therefore, are the patients themselves. They were also part of the movement, although they have rarely been seen as such. People like Carla Nardini – who had been in Auschwitz – or Mario Furlan (who later committed suicide) – or 'il

---

9　Carlo Brutti and Francesco Scotti, *Psichiatria e democrazia. Metodi e obiettivi di una politica psichiatrica alternative,* Bari: De Donato, 1976, p. 36.

maestro' Spadi in Arezzo. These people had their lives changed by the revolution in psychiatric care, but they also retook control of their own lives. Without them, the movement would never have even begun to have an effect. They formed the other, unexpected, leadership of the movement.

This movement had its beginnings in Gorizia, but its scope and reach went far beyond the story of Franco Basaglia and Franca Ongaro. As Ferruccio Giacanelli argued, 'The metamorphosis of Italian psychiatry was the result of a polycentric movement.' The Basaglians were crucial – central – to the movement for change. But Perugia came first and went further than Gorizia or Trieste, and other areas introduced innovations and change. By reducing the history of psychiatric reform to the life story of Franco Basaglia, we are doing the history of the movement a great disservice. To cite Brutti and Scotti again, 'the risk today . . . [is] that the past is presented in an epic way, where individuals become heroes'.

Every city, every asylum carried forward its own version of change: 'There is no model for anti-institutional psychiatry; the experience of Trieste was different to that of Perugia, Turin or Naples, and each experience had its own specificities and traditions.'[10] Tullio Seppilli underlined this point: 'The anti-institutional movement in Italy was a font of ideas and experimentation . . . it is interesting to see it as a varied, complex and controversial movement, not something linked to a few iconic personalities or places.'

Along the way, great risks were taken. Some people were brutally murdered, others committed suicide. Families had to deal with sons, daughters, mothers and fathers who had serious problems, and who had been shut away behind closed doors for years. The burden placed upon people was often unacceptable (both those who were released, and those who had to deal with the released). The outside world was a difficult place in so many ways. It was easy for ex-patients to fall through the cracks in society. Once the asylum system had been done away with, the real work began. As David Forgacs has written, 'The story of psychiatric reform in Italy did not end with the

---

10   Patrizia Guarnieri, 'Per una storia della psichiatria anti-instituzionale. L'esperienza del rinnovamento psichiatrico in Umbria, 1965–1995', *Annali di neurologia e psichiatria e annali ospedale psichiatrico di Perugia* 92: 2, April–June 1998, p. 8.

passing of Law 180 in May 1978. On the contrary, the most difficult phase of the movement for reform began when the law came into force.'[11]

Undoubtedly the movement was also marked by numerous excesses of ideology, exaggerations and the use of inflammatory and dangerous language, simplifications and dogmatisms, sectarianism and bitter disputes over what seems, today, to be very little indeed. These excesses were often taken up by the followers of the movement, whose sloganeering and empty phrase-making did little to help those with mental health problems in the real world. Basaglia himself was aware that mistakes had been made. As he said at the end of the 1970s:

> I think we made a serious error . . . when we thought that we needed to criticize the asylum in order that the real face of illness could emerge and for this reason we said that we needed to put the diagnosis in brackets.[12]

Often, the language used by the movement provided the movement's enemies with ready ammunition. Maoist slogans and language were common. The envelope was frequently pushed too far. Too often, a problematic link between social class and mental illness was drawn or simply stated – as if it was an obvious fact. In the heady and violent times of the 1970s, 'traitors' were easily identified and dismissed, and the movement was marked by conflicts, jealousies, personal division and hyperbole. Only in retrospect can we pick through the embers of what happened and try and bring some order. It was a time of excess. The revolution appeared to be around the corner. It was not.

The final key component of the movement were the fellow travellers – intellectuals, writers, publishers, film-makers, journalists, photographers and artists who gave up their time and their talents in order to press for change. These people were central to the success of the movement, as they provided a connection between the high theorizing of the leaders and the masses. This was true of publishers and editors (above all Giulio Bollati and Giulio Einaudi, but also many editors at Feltrinelli),

---

11   David Forgacs, *Italy's Margins*, p. 255.
12   Ernesto Venturini, *Il giardino dei gelsi*, p. 222.

TV and film producers and directors (Sergio Zavoli, Silvano Agosti, Marco Bellocchio, Gianni Serra), artists and theatre directors (Ugo Guarino, Vittorio Basaglia, Giuliano Scabia), photographers (Gianni Berengo Gardin, Claudio Ernè, Carla Cerati, Uliano Lucas and others). When more than 10 million people saw patients from Gorizia's psychiatric hospital speaking to Sergio Zavoli on the TV screens inside their own homes in January 1969, the movement was given a push which it would never have had by any other means.

Today, Italy's former asylums perform a variety of functions. Some are empty and abandoned. Others are 'museums of the mind'. Many still have links to health and mental health services. Some are schools, some are universities, some have become housing. Most are now beautiful parks, at least in part. The 'great internment' described by Foucault gave way, in the 1970s, to a 'great liberation'. Society absorbed most of the 100,000 inmates who had been kept inside the places. This process was forced on the system from a movement that acted from inside the institutions themselves, in a way that was unique in the Western world. Italy's asylums were closed down by the people who worked inside them. In doing so, these people abolished their own jobs – forever. Nobody, today, is employed in the posts that were held by Basaglia, Giacanelli, Pirella and Casagrande in the 1960s and 1970s – as directors of psychiatric hospitals. *Nobody, today, is the director of a psychiatric hospital in Italy.* The movement acted against its own self-interest – in a way that was the opposite of clientelism, patronage and nepotism. It was a negation of itself.

Much of what was called for in the heady days of the movement never came to pass. The interest in radical psychiatry began to fade, and the backlash began in earnest. The movement ended up on the defensive – clinging onto the gains of the 1960s and 1970s. As one protagonist wrote in 1969:

We were looking for an alternative to psychiatry, we wanted to explore the possibilities and limits of a new way of doing things. In our society, however, a real alternative to psychiatry can only be partly realized – in a specific context and for a certain time period. Afterwards, especially if our work was effective, it became 'dangerous' – and then the forces of repression intervened to stop everything in its tracks, or to reintegrate and neutralize things within the system. All of this was inevitable and we knew that this was the case, but we have all learnt a great deal during this long march.[13]

---

13   Giovanni Jervis, 'L'esperienza di Reggio Emilia' in *La ragione degli altri*, p. 259.

Index